Monstrous Nature and Representations
of Environmental Harms

Avi Brisman and Nigel South

MONSTROUS NATURE AND REPRESENTATIONS OF ENVIRONMENTAL HARMS

A Green Cultural Criminological Perspective

TEMPLE UNIVERSITY PRESS
Philadelphia • *Rome* • *Tokyo*

TEMPLE UNIVERSITY PRESS
Philadelphia, Pennsylvania 19122
tupress.temple.edu

Library of Congress Cataloging-in-Publication Data

Names: Brisman, Avi, author. | South, Nigel, author.
Title: Monstrous nature and representations of environmental harms : a
  green cultural criminological perspective / Avi Brisman and Nigel South.
Description: Philadelphia : Temple University Press, 2025. | Includes
  bibliographical references and index. | Summary: "This book looks at
  representations of nature in popular art and media, including fiction,
  to trace its construction in Western culture as justly vengeful. By
  depicting nature as monstrous, abject, or apocalyptic, these works lead
  popular audiences to imagine nature opposed to human harm and exacting
  justice in response"— Provided by publisher.
Identifiers: LCCN 2025003086 (print) | LCCN 2025003087 (ebook) | ISBN
  9781439923009 (cloth) | ISBN 9781439923016 (paperback) | ISBN
  9781439923023 (pdf)
Subjects: LCSH: Ecocriticism. | Offenses against the environment—Social
  aspects. | Nature in popular culture. | Monsters in popular culture. |
  Apocalypse in popular culture. | Human ecology in literature. | Human
  ecology in motion pictures.
Classification: LCC PN98.E36 B73 2025 (print) | LCC PN98.E36 (ebook) |
  DDC 809.9336—dc23/eng/20250311
LC record available at https://lccn.loc.gov/2025003086
LC ebook record available at https://lccn.loc.gov/2025003087

The manufacturer's authorized representative in the EU for product safety is
Temple University Rome, Via di San Sebastianello, 16, 00187 Rome RM, Italy
(https://rome.temple.edu/).
tempress@temple.edu

9 8 7 6 5 4 3 2 1

In memory of Vincenzo Ruggiero, 1950–2024

Contents

Photo gallery follows page 72

Preface

Developing the Script on Representations of Environmental Harm

reen criminology is concerned with crimes and harms affecting human and nonhuman life, ecosystems, and the planet as a whole. It considers the causes, consequences, and pervasiveness of environmental crimes and harms, as well as responses to and prevention of acts and omissions prohibited by law. It is also attuned to environmental disruptions that are legal and take place either with the knowing consent of society or by virtue of the exercise of denial or strategic ignorance. *Cultural criminology*, in turn, explores the convergence of cultural and criminal processes in contemporary social life, and it seeks to comprehend how crime and crime control are constructed, enforced, represented, and resisted.

Green cultural criminology strives to bring together *green criminology* and *cultural criminology*, and to identify points of overlap. *Green cultural criminology, inter alia*, attempts to highlight means by which green criminology might adopt a cultural criminological lens: (1) by assigning greater consideration to the way(s) in which environmental crimes, harms, and disasters are constructed and represented by news media (e.g., online, print) and social media and in popular cultural forms (e.g., art, books, films); (2) by dedicating increased attention to patterns of consumption, constructed consumerism, commodification of nature, and related market processes; and (3) by devoting heightened concern to the contestation of space, transgression, and resistance in order to analyze the ways in which environmental harms are opposed in/on the streets and in day-to-day life.

Monstrous Nature and Representations of Environmental Harms: A Green Cultural Criminological Perspective serves as a sequel to our book *Green Cultural Criminology: Constructions of Environmental Harm, Consumerism, and Resistance to Ecocide* (Brisman and South 2014). Instead of engaging in a "script rewrite" (Hayward 2016) for *green cultural criminology*, our goal with this book is to advance the *green cultural criminological* script by developing further the first of the three approaches or "agenda items" (while noting their areas of imbrication). So, here, we identify and discuss three *dominant* and *interrelated*—primarily Western—depictions of the relationship between humans and the environment: (1) nature as *monstrous* or fear-inducing (nature and horror or "ecohorror"); (2) nature and the Earth (or parts of it) as *abject* (the abjection of the Earth); and (3) the entanglement of nature and the *apocalypse*, wherein nature is contributing to the end of the world, with an end point sometimes conceptualized as one without humans (by some with misanthropic ecophilosophies). Such *"analysis* is *not undertaken* simply for *its own sake,"* to quote Giuliani (2021: 15, emphasis in original). Rather, we argue that such representations have material consequences, and we make the case for challenging them so that we neither perpetuate them nor retreat into cynicism and defeatism about the future of our planet.

Monstrous Nature and Representations
of Environmental Harms

1

Introduction

*Exposing and Challenging Environmental Messages
in Popular Cultural Forms*

According to Welsh, Fleming, and Dowler (2011: 458), "Cultural criminology . . . views films and other media sources as cultural products that provide insight into . . . shared meanings about crime, justice, and punishment (Berets 1996; Ferrell 1999)." More recently, Sothcott (2016: 434) has clarified that cultural criminology is "less concerned with establishing scientific certainties than with establishing the variable cultural meanings that are applied to notions of criminal transgression." Our own extension of these propositions—*green cultural criminology*—takes a similar view. Simply put, this is the suggestion that various forms of media and/in culture can provide insights into shared and contested meanings about environmental crime, harm, and justice.[1] As outlined in previous work (see, e.g., Brisman 2014, 2015, 2017a, 2017b, 2017c, 2018, 2019a; 2019b, 2020; Brisman and South 2012, 2013a, 2014, 2015, 2017a, 2017b, 2017c, 2018; Brisman, McClanahan, and South 2014; McClanahan, Brisman, and South 2017), there is much one can learn from the environmental themes in popular cultural forms, and part of a green cultural criminological endeavor is to expose and reveal those environmental messages (which may be more or less explicit) and to evaluate and critique them. This undertaking entails, *inter alia*: (1) asking what these popular cultural forms have done or might do differently; (2) identifying flawed (environmental) reasoning and representation(s) in such popular cultural forms; and (3) interrogating the impact that such popular cultural forms might have on audiences (whether listening, viewing, or engaging in immersive experiences).

We return to these questions later, following an exploration of a recently expanding universe, the genesis and development of which have been greeted with fan devotion and box office success as well as the concerns and dismissals of movie industry professionals and auteurs (Brody 2019).

From World-Building Mythologies to Apocalyptic Sagas

In October 2019, the award-winning American filmmaker Martin Scorsese offered an opinion on the difference between "franchise films" and "cinema," asserting that superhero movies (specifically, those in the Marvel Cinematic Universe, or MCU) did not qualify as art. "I don't see them," Scorsese stated. "I tried, you know?" he said. "But that's not cinema. Honestly, the closest I can think of them, as well-made as they are, with actors doing the best they can under the circumstances, is theme parks" (quoted in De Semlyen 2019; Fernández 2019; Langmann 2019; Lawrence and Archer 2019; Sharf 2019; Shoard 2019). As Scorsese explained, MCU "isn't the cinema of human beings trying to convey emotional, psychological experiences to another human being."

Unsurprisingly, some did not take kindly to Scorsese's comments, and so, a month later, he attempted to explain his position. "Many franchise films are made by people of considerable talent and artistry," Scorsese (2019) acknowledged in an op-ed for *The New York Times*. "You can see it on the screen." But, he continued, "the fact that the films themselves don't interest me is a matter of personal taste and temperament." For Scorsese, "cinema" entails "revelation—aesthetic, emotional and spiritual revelation," as well as "mystery or genuine emotional danger." Distinguishing "audiovisual entertainment" from "cinema," Scorsese asserted that with the former, "nothing is at risk. The pictures are made to satisfy a specific set of demands, and they are designed as variations on a finite number of themes." They are "market-researched, audience-tested, vetted, modified, re-vetted and remodified until they're ready for consumption."

Scorsese is not the only—or the first—to question the artistic value of superhero movies (see, e.g., Bruney 2019; "Esquire Editors" 2019; Langmann 2022; Lawrence and Archer 2019; O'Connor 2018; Sharf 2019).[2] Our guess is that the debate will continue. What interests us is not whether superhero movies, in general, and MCU, in particular, constitute *art* and, by the same token, whether they are *revelatory* (in the sense of disclosing, exposing, or uncovering something hitherto unknown). That might make for a titillating discussion, especially in light of Phillips's (2021: 77) observation that MCU is "a decidedly global brand, but one still deeply ensconced in American ideology." Rather, what animates us is the matter of whether such movies might be *revealing* insofar as they show or make something known and perhaps forgotten *more known*. And to this, we would say that they are.

To be sure, we are not movie critics (or actors, directors, or producers). Although we sometimes author film reviews (see, e.g., Brisman 2009, 2010, 2012a, 2012c, 2024), we do so through a criminological or sociological lens. Much the way that Ruggiero (2003: 1) states that his work, *Crime in Literature: Sociology of Deviance and Fiction*, "is not a book of literary criticism, but a book written by a sociologist who reads classic fiction sociologically," we readily admit that our book, *Monstrous Nature and Representations of Environmental Harms: A Green Cultural Criminological Perspective*, is not an attempt at literary or film criticism. We are humanities-inspired social scientists interested in how environmental conflicts, crimes, harms, and disasters are constructed and represented by the news media and in popular cultural forms.[3] In this endeavor, we do not differentiate between so-called "high art" and "low art" (or between "highbrow," "middlebrow," and "lowbrow").[4] By the same token, and consistent with Saunders (2012), we do not restrict ourselves to a single medium (e.g., visual [films] versus textual [books]). As Saunders (2012: 100n11) contends, "It is important to recognise the increasingly ephemeral borders between media platforms in the current digital age, where all media are connected by the Internet and are susceptible to republication (or rebroadcasting) in cyberspace, a place where they can be consumed, altered, and reinterpreted." Accordingly, our concern is not with a particular medium but with *the messages* of these popular cultural forms—what they depict, what they say/might say, what they do not convey—and the *impact* they have or might have. We care little for categories—what and who distinguishes types or styles. Indeed, because we are cognizant of the fact that popular culture is, by definition, "that which appeals to and is well liked by a mass audience" (Foy 2010a: 2)—and because we are sensitive to arguments that "pop culture . . . is a commercialized opiate . . . that popular culture and entertainment *pacify* and *insulate* the . . . public from the real obligations and challenges of democratic citizenship" (Foy 2010a: 4, emphasis added)—we do not silo "high" and "low" (art or -brow), visual or textual. When it comes to trying to understand the mediated and cultural constructions and representations of environmental conflicts, crimes, harms, and disasters, we find such grouping shortsighted and stilted.

We began the precursor to this book, *Green Cultural Criminology: Constructions of Environmental Harm, Consumerism, and Resistance to Ecocide* (Brisman and South 2014), with a discussion of *Monsters, Inc.*, the 2001 comedy film produced by Pixar Animation Studios for Walt Disney Pictures. Our point was that *Monsters, Inc.* functions as an allegory of a self-interested species (with monsters representing humans) whose power (or energy) source is disappearing. We then lamented that *Monsters University* (2013)—a prequel to *Monsters, Inc.* produced by Walt Disney Pictures and Pixar Animation Studios (and released by Walt Disney Studios Motion Pictures)—makes no mention of the impending energy crisis or prospects of alternative energy sources and that instead, the message/solution is that if we reminisce about our past, an "earlier Edenic existence, [then] our present realities will disappear" (Brisman and South 2014: 2).

It seems fitting that we begin the present book, *Monstrous Nature and Representations of Environmental Harms: A Green Cultural Criminological Perspective*, in a similar fashion, contemplating several other Walt Disney films.[5] To return to our contention that MCU movies can be illuminating and instructive (or hold the potential to do so), let us consider two pairs of MCU films—first the worldbuilding of *Black Panther* (2018) and *Black Panther: Wakanda Forever* (2022) (hereinafter *Wakanda Forever*), and then, the saga-like tales of *Avengers: Infinity War* (2018) (hereinafter *Infinity War*) and *Avengers: Endgame* (2019) (hereinafter *Endgame*).

Black Panther and *Wakanda Forever*

In February 2018, MCU's highly anticipated Afrofuturistic *Black Panther*, the eighteenth film in the MCU, was released in theaters around the world.[6] (In the United States, February marks Black History Month, and thus the release date was intentional.) Produced by Marvel Studios and distributed by Walt Disney Studios Motion Pictures, *Black Panther*, in its first weekend, earned $242 million in the United States and $427 million worldwide, which shattered box-office records (Desta 2018)[7] and, perhaps more important, garnered praise for its positive portrayal of the African continent (Associated Press 2018a; see also Bowden 2018; Lane 2018; Phillips 2021; Sow and Sy 2018; see generally Richardson 2023; Ugwu 2018; Wallace 2018)—a welcome development in light of then-President Donald J. Trump's reference to African nations as "shithole countries" a month earlier (see, e.g., Davis, Stolberg, and Kaplan 2018; Vitali, Hunt, and Thorp 2018; see also Bouie 2024; Haberman and Gold 2024; see generally Ugwu 2018). In this light, *Black Panther*—the first MCU film to be headlined by a Black protagonist (Chadwick Boseman, since deceased), to star a majority-Black cast, and to be filmed by a Black director (Ryan Coogler) (see Ugwu 2018; see generally Lane 2018; Wallace 2018)—could be seen as an instance of speaking truth to power. But the film is also, in the eyes of Mariama Sow and Amadous Sy

(2018) of the Brookings Institution, the Washington, D.C.–based nonprofit public policy organization, instructive for its ideas about natural resource management.

In the beginning of *Black Panther*, which was adapted from the Marvel Comics comic book of the same name, we learn that millions of years ago, a gigantic meteorite made of "vibranium," the strongest substance in the universe, landed in East Africa in the area that would later become the (entirely fictional) country of Wakanda. The Wakandans used vibranium to develop technology more advanced than any other country in the world, but as Wakanda thrived, the nations surrounding it fell into turmoil and disarray. Seeing these horrors—and seeking to keep the(ir) vibranium safe— Wakanda disguised itself, pretending it was a "primitive backwater" (Ugwu 2018)—a non-industrialized country with a dense population, high levels of poverty, and poor infrastructure (what would once have been called a "Third World" country and is now referred to as a "least developed country" or "less economically developed country" [for a discussion of this terminology, see Chapter 3]). The film centers on Prince T'Challa (played by Boseman), who returns home to his isolationist, technologically-advanced Wakanda to serve as its new king. T'Challa faces challenges from factions within his own country as well as external threats (see Wallace 2018).

As Sow and Sy (2018) put forth, "Despite its fictional nature, Wakanda shares key similarities with many African countries [and] African policy- makers and their partners can draw lessons about good resource governance and economic integration from the movie." Sow and Sy (2018) explain that Wakanda uses vibranium to enhance technology (including to hide from the rest of the world) and to create economic development for its people, thereby generating significant benefits that are shared widely in Wakandan society. While Wakanda follows an autarkic economic model, guarding its vibranium and refusing to trade its natural resource with the rest of the world, Sow and Sy (2018) highlight that resource-rich African countries tend to rely heavily on their exports, noting that in 2015, for example, "mineral exports made up *more than 90 percent* of exports in Equatorial Guinea, Nigeria, and Angola," and that "the high dependence on oil exports in certain African countries has led to misaligned exchange rates, the decline of non-resource sectors, political authoritarianism, conflict, and economic inequality" (emphasis added). Lest one think that the "resource curse" (or "paradox of plenty") is an inevitable fate for every resource-rich country and that avoiding it is possible only on the silver screen,[8] Sow and Sy (2018) point to Botswana (diamonds) and Norway (oil), which have invested their revenues in sovereign wealth funds (the Pula Fund—in the case of the former—and the Government Pension Fund Global (*Statens pensjonfond utland*, known as the "Oil Fund" or *Oljefondet*)—in the case of the latter).[9] Diamonds and oil may not have the same properties as the fictional metal vibranium and thus cannot, in themselves, be used to advance technology, Sow and Sy (2018) acknowledge, but the revenues they generate can be reinvested in technology, manufacturing, and other sectors.

In many respects, then, *Black Panther* can be understood as a film about how a country *might* use its resources. The film's antagonist, N'Jadaka/Erik "Killmonger" Stevens (played by Michael B. Jordan), disapproves of Wakanda's isolationism and contends that the country's vibranium, as Sow and Sy (2018) succinctly put it, "should be used to liberate the large numbers of people of African descent living in impecunious and oppressive conditions worldwide." Killmonger finds it "despicable that Wakanda, the most powerful nation in the world, refuses to use its vast resources to help Black people elsewhere" (Wang and Zhang 2023: 185). In the words of St. Félix (2018), Killmonger is "hell-bent on arming all the [B]lack people in the world." As Phillips (2022) describes, "Killmonger, who grew up in Oakland, California, without a father and with all the disadvantages that come with being a Black man in America, wants to use Wakandan technology to empower Black people all over the world. His plan is violent, but it's not that far from the Black Power movement's extreme factions in the 1960s."[10] Thus, when Killmonger defeats T'Challa in ritual combat and gains access to the throne, one of his first acts is to try to distribute Wakandan weapons (see Phillips 2021: 93; see also Wang and Zhang 2023: 185): "Where I'm from . . . when Black folks started revolutions, they never had the firepower . . . or the resources to fight their oppressors. We got spies embedded in every nation on Earth," Killmonger states. "Already in place. I know how colonizers think. So we're gonna use their own strategy against 'em. We're gonna send vibranium weapons out to our War Dogs. They'll arm oppressed people all over the world . . . so they can finally rise up and kill those in power. And their children. And anyone else who takes their side. It's time they know the truth about us!" (see IMDb 2018).

Killmonger's position shares some similarities with that of Nakia (Lupita Nyong'o), T'Challa's love interest. Like Killmonger, Nakia believes that Wakanda should use its resources to help other nations and to share their technological knowledge. She urges T'Challa to do so—a path "more realistic and less destructive" than Killmonger's (Sow and Sy 2018).

In contrast to T'Challa's support for isolationist policies, Killmonger's call for worldwide violence,[11] and Nakia's advocacy for foreign aid and knowledge-sharing, Sow and Sy (2018) offer the perspective of a hypothetical Wakandan economist: "Wakanda's massive investment in technology gives the fictional country a clear competitive advantage, which, in turn, makes the potential benefits of international trade quite high," they submit. "Its monopoly on vibranium gives Wakanda another one," they continue. "The high quality of its governance suggests that Wakanda would also be able to manage the expected revenues from trade for current and future generations of Wakandans. Moreover, if vibranium can play the role the steam engine played during the Industrial Revolution of the 19th century, Wakanda would be the catalyst for a surge in global trade; sending goods using those technologically advanced flying engines would drastically lower costs and facilitate the movement of goods." Unlike the Industrial Revolution, however, to which many anthropogenic environmental and climate change impacts can be traced, a "vibranium revolution" would seem to be a green one, apparently producing no pollution as a result of extraction or use (Hirschmann 2023).[12]

Contra Lane (2018: 62), who wonders "what weight of political responsibility can, or should, be laid upon anything that is accompanied by buttered popcorn," and contra Carnes and Goren (2023: 5), who adopt a middle-ground approach, treating movies (and popular culture, as a whole) as both a "product" and a "driver" of "any society's politics," Sow and Sy (2018) suggest that *Black Panther* "can pave the way for an increased number of movies painting Africa in a positive light"—a sanguinity we share—and which is why we noted both its box office earnings and the praise it had received for its affirmative portrayal of the African continent.[13] Sow and Sy (2018) conclude by asserting that "fictional Wakanda provides an image of . . . prosperity and technological advancement [that] awaits properly managed resource-rich countries." *Black Panther* ends with T'Challa revealing to the world its highly advanced technology, good resource governance, and strong and successful economic integration (see Phillips 2022); Sow and Sy (2018) end their article by expressing the hope that "subsequent technological proliferation and increase in global trade will . . . be featured in the Black Panther sequel."

If only.

As noted earlier, in environmental terms—and not only by that benchmark—*Monsters University* was a disappointing follow-up to *Monsters, Inc.*, avoiding any allusion to a looming energy crisis or to the potential for alternative energy sources, and preferring instead to engage in a prelapsarian reverie. *Wakanda Forever* is not quite as unsatisfying.[14] For example, we concur with Marshall (2022) that the film is "a powerful meditation on grief and power" (see also Ugwu 2022; Wellbeck, quoted in DeLuca 2022), and that it successfully "celebrates the reclamation of an African identity through references to creation myths and diasporic storytelling traditions where ancestral wisdom is passed down through generations." Our criticism rests with some of the ways in which the theme of colonialism appears in the film and the shortcomings of its environmental message.

At the beginning of *Wakanda Forever*, we see the United Nations pressuring Wakanda to live up to its promise to share its vibranium with the world, with some foreign entities attempting to steal it by force. As Timothy Wellbeck, an Assistant Professor of Instruction in the Department of Africology and African American Studies at Temple University and the director of the Center for Anti-Racism, contends, this "mirrors the imperial and colonial efforts to mine Africa of its resources, disregard the wishes of the people, and cut up the continent" (quoted in DeLuca 2022). True, but Wellbeck's point could have been made more explicitly in the film, with examples and references to actual historical patterns and practices. The film need not have dwelled much on the past or shifted from superhero movie to documentary. But "entertainment" and "education" are not mutually exclusive, and situating Wakanda's challenges in the history of Western colonialism would have served as a reminder to (White) audiences in the Global North that the major conflicts of the twentieth century were prompted, at least in part, by access to and control over natural resources—and that we can trace the origins of many instances of contemporary exploitation of natural resources to such efforts to exert domination and control.[15] Such contextualization might also have helped to underscore just how difficult it was for resource-rich countries (in Africa, in Asia) to try to avoid Western colonial destruction, just how unusual Wakanda is in avoiding (such) colonization (by turning inwards and developing without foreign intervention), and why Wakanda represents "the Afrofuturist imagination of what Africa could be" (Wellbeck, quoted in DeLuca 2022)—why it reflects "the dreams of a Black African utopia" (Marshall 2022).[16]

Early in *Wakanda Forever*, we are introduced to the vibranium-rich, Mesoamerican-inspired underwater kingdom of Talokan—"a hidden Atlantis-style underwater civilization of Indigenous peoples" (Phillips 2022)—and thus we learn that Wakanda is not the only place with vibranium deposits and that the Wakandans are not the only people to hide from the world and refuse to participate in global affairs.[17] The Talokanil are blue-skinned, water-breathing superhumans, led by Namor (Tenoch Huerta), "a direct victim of colonization who has witnessed the enslavement of his people" (Phillips 2022). When Americans discover vibranium in the ocean, the entire Talokan civilization comes under threat. Namor proposes an alliance between Talokan and Wakanda against the rest of the world, but he also threatens to destroy Wakanda if it refuses. The Wakandans and Talokanil go to war with each other, and one gets the sense (or, at least, viewers *should* get the impression) that the White Western world hopes that the two peoples will destroy each other, which would better ensure access to their vibranium resources.

Indeed, as Phillips (2022) observes, "On one level, the conflicts in these movies [*Black Panther* and *Wakanda Forever*] are insular: communities of color are set against one another, which is so much more real than an evil robot or a big purple dude snapping half the universe away"—a reference to Thanos and "the Blip" in *Infinity War* and *Endgame*, discussed later. But, as Phillips (2022) continues, "in 'Wakanda Forever,' although the big battle is between Wakanda and Talokan, the actual villains are the countries searching for vibranium in their bids for power. . . . In these films, the true villain is a history of white oppression and power, but the enemy—whether another person of color or a Black person elsewhere in the diaspora—is on the same team."[18] Ultimately, in *Wakanda Forever*, Wakanda and Talokan reach a peaceful agreement, although Namor does so with the intention that this new cooperation will enable the Talokan to eventually conquer the surface world, thereby echoing the goals and ideology of Killmonger in *Black Panther*.[19]

Wellbeck (in DeLuca 2022) regards the pact between Wakanda and Talokan as an indication that "they are stronger together than they are apart"—a position echoed by Guerrero (2022)—although the understanding developed between the two nations seems more like a "cold peace" than an expression of "united we stand, divided we fall." Wellbeck also adds, "Of course, the messaging here is that regardless of how people may manifest their cultures and societies, they ultimately want the same thing: agency, autonomy, the ability to love and the ability to rear their children" (quoted in DeLuca 2022). That *might be* the lesson. But if the goal was to communicate something greater, then it seems as if the film missed the opportunity to envision the kind of global trade and benefits of good natural resource governance that Sow and Sy (2018) described and hoped would feature in the sequel. Wellbeck speculates that should there be a "third *Black Panther* movie [it] will revisit these themes of rebuilding identity, embracing community and communal customs, and the power of aligning with other people" (quoted in DeLuca 2022). That *might be* what transpires, but here are some other possibilities:

1. Why cannot a third *Black Panther* film explore the ways in which vibranium is extracted without environmental degradation or how it might be used to reduce fossil fuel consumption or how vibranium might reverse some of the effects of climate change or how it might close the climate gap?
2. Why do we feel as if the third *Black Panther* movie will double down on the belief that differences over access to and possession

of natural resources always trigger conflict? As we alluded to earlier, while environmental factors are usually not the sole cause of conflict, the exploitation of natural resources and associated environmental stresses can contribute to and catalyze conflict (see, e.g., Andersen 2019; United Nations Peacekeeping n.d.). That said— and as we have written elsewhere—"linkages between conflict and the environment are varied and not all negative . . . some factors, such as contested resource wealth, that in some circumstances, may precipitate or support or subsidise conflict, may, in other circumstances, provide *a route out of,* or *insulation from,* conflict . . . valuable resources can help jump-start development, secure sustainable growth, raise living standards, and increase economic equality" (Brisman, South, and White 2015: 1–2, emphasis in original).[20] Essentially, conflict over natural resource possession is not inevitable, but environmental degradation and destruction almost always occur as a result of war, social conflict(s), and assertions of colonialist power (see Brisman, South, and White 2015: 10–15). Could a third *Black Panther* film acknowledge as much?

3. Why could not *Wakanda Forever*—or why cannot the third *Black Panther* movie—emphasize that, to quote Todd, "with a broken planet, we will have no gay rights, no feminism, no respect for trans people, no attempt at fairness and justice for people of colour" (2019: 70)?

In sum, for all of the accolades that *Wakanda Forever* deserves for its engagement with the themes of grief, resilience, and ritual, and its representation of Africa, Black female power, and Indigenous people (see generally Richardson 2023), its references to the environmental legacies of colonialism and its suggestions of the relationships between environmental resources and conflict are a bit anemic. It is not that Scorsese (2019) is right—that "*nothing* is at risk"—but that *more could have been at risk* (or that more risks could have been taken). Looking ahead to a possible third *Black Panther* film, we wonder whether it (too) will be "made to satisfy a specific set of demands" (Scorsese 2019)—designed as distilled variations of the themes in the first two films. This is not to imply that *Black Panther* and *Wakanda Forever*—or that a third *Black Panther* movie (would)—function only as "audiovisual entertainment" and fail to "convey emotional, psychological experiences" (Scorscese 2019). Rather, we assert that *Black Panther* and *Wakanda Forever* have green cultural criminological value for their environmental messaging, but that they could have done more.[21]

Infinity War and *Endgame*

After Scorsese made his provocative claims, Francis Ford Coppola, the film director, producer, and screenwriter, weighed in, stating:

> When Martin Scorsese says that the Marvel pictures are not cinema, he's right because we expect to learn something from cinema, we expect to gain something, some enlightenment, some knowledge, some inspiration. . . . I don't know that anyone gets anything out of seeing the same movie over and over again. (quoted in Bruney 2019)

As we attempted to illustrate in our discussion of *Black Panther* and *Wakanda Forever*, while there is *something* one can learn from these movies, both films—especially the latter (the sequel)—could have been more illuminating and edifying with respect to colonialism, resource governance, resource use, and conflict. There is, as we have argued elsewhere (Brisman and South 2014: 2), value in contemplating and exploring the meaning, significance, and representation—as well as the "*non*-representation"—of media constructions and depictions of environmental issues (emphasis in original). Whereas our green cultural criminological critique of *Black Panther* and *Wakanda Forever* centers on their ambiguous and fragmentary messages about the challenge and difficulties—and benefits—of good resource management, the negative impact of colonialism on the environment, and the complex relationship of environment and conflict, our trouble with *Infinity War* and *Endgame* pertains to a slightly different set of ecological concerns (albeit ones that are, unfortunately, also ambiguous and incomplete in their presentation—and troubling as a result).[22]

In *Infinity War*, Thanos (played by Josh Brolin), the movie's main villain, subscribes to Malthusianism—the theory that food production/supply increases at an arithmetic or linear rate, while population rises exponentially.[23] Based on this growth model, overpopulation is inevitable: when population growth exceeds agricultural production, living standards are reduced, bringing about famine, war, and societal collapse (see Anti-Creep Climate Initiative 2022; Johnston 2021; see also Andrews 2019a; Wilson 2019). In the movie, Thanos recounts that on his planet (Titan), population growth, combined with dwindling resources, led to suffering, loss of life, and global catastrophe (see Chamary 2018; Plante 2018; Taylor 2018; Townsend 2018; Wang and Zhang 2023). To ward off such disaster on a universal scale, Thanos gathers all of the "Infinity Stones" (each with its own name: space, mind, reality, power, soul, and time), which he places in the "Infinity Gauntlet," created by Eitri (Peter Dinklage), king of an ancient race of skilled dwarves. As Miller (2015) explains, the Infinity Stones are "six rocks of inexplicable power that combine to create exponentially more inexplicable power."[24] Wearing the Infinity Gauntlet and wielding all six Infinity Stones, Thanos snaps his fingers, exterminating half of all life in the universe, chosen indiscriminately—an event known as "the Blip." Thanos then destroys the Infinity Stones to prevent his work from being undone and "retires" to the "Garden" (also known as "Planet 0259-S" and "Titan II")—a greenfield planet—and starts a farm (see Townsend 2018).

Thanos's stated reason for such universal mass genocide is to bring about balance in the universe—killing half of its population at random so that the survivors may thrive (see Brody 2018; Hirschmann 2023: 166, 173–79; Phillips 2021: 99; Wang and Zhang 2023: 186–88)—a "grand plan" that evokes Jonathan Swift's Juvenalian satire, "A Modest Proposal," published in 1792 (see Townsend 2018).[25] Proselytizing Thanos's "eliminationist" beliefs (to borrow from Wilson 2019), Ebony Maw, Thanos's adopted child (voice and motion-captured by Tom Vaughan-Lawlor), proclaims:

> Hear me and rejoice. You have had the privilege of being saved by the great Thanos. You may think this is suffering, no. It is salvation. The universal scale tips toward the balance because of your sacrifice. Smile. For even in death, you have become children of Thanos.

Thanos's desires for stabilizing universal overpopulation are further revealed in this exchange with another of his adopted children, Gamora (portrayed by Zoe Saldaña):

GAMORA: I was a child when you took me.
THANOS: I saved you.
GAMORA: No. We were happy on my home planet.
THANOS: You were going to bed hungry, scrounging for scraps. Your planet was on the brink of collapse. I'm the one who stopped that. You know what's happened since then? The children born have known nothing but full bellies and clear skies. It's a paradise.
GAMORA: Because you murdered half the planet.
THANOS: A small price to pay for salvation.
GAMORA: You're insane.
THANOS: Little one, it's a simple calculus. This universe is finite, its resources, finite. If life is left unchecked, life will cease to exist. It needs correcting.

GAMORA: You don't know that!

THANOS: I'm the only one who knows that. At least, I'm the only one with the will to act on it.[26]

In comparison to some antiheroes who want to rule the galaxy (see Tassi 2018) or, say, to the supervillain Steppenwolf in the DC Extended Universe (DCEU) media franchise, who wants to destroy everything (see Plante 2018), Thanos's goal (at least in *Infinity War*) is not, as Fullerton (2019) notes, to obliterate the world: "he just wants to balance it, wipe out exactly 50 per cent to reduce the strain on resources."[27] Alexander Menrisky, an Assistant Professor in the Department of English at the University of Connecticut, claims that "Thanos's motivation in the films . . . to wipe out half the universe's population to conserve resources for the other half . . . is a neatly distilled ecofascist story" (quoted in Hancock 2022). Ecofascism usually involves xenophobic and racist ideas, blaming environmental degradation and demise on *specific populations*, and this has been reflected in recent statements from a worrying variety of sources.

For example, Mackay (2020) reports on the text of a statement believed to have been compiled by the gunman who killed twenty-two people from the Latino community in El Paso, Texas, on August 3, 2019. The "El Paso manifesto," as Mackay (2020) refers to it, was called "An Inconvenient Truth"—ironically copying the title of the 2006 documentary on the threats of climate change presented by former U.S. Vice President Al Gore—and suggests that "the people of America are 'too stubborn' to change their lifestyles 'so the next logical step is to decrease the number of people in America using its resources. If we can get rid of enough people, then our way of life can become more sustainable.'"[28] In March 2021, Mark Brnovich, a member of the Republican Party and Arizona's attorney general at the time, who had "misrepresented climate science" in previous comments, "cited environmental protection when he sued the Biden administration for loosening immigration laws" and argued that "migrants would use up resources, cause emissions and pollute the environment if they weren't kept out by a wall with Mexico" (Walsh 2022). Finally, Craig Lewis, executive director of the anti-immigration organization "Negative Population Growth," has promoted a similar argument related to global warming and CO_2 emissions, claiming that "if the goal is to reduce emissions, it stands to reason that the number of emitters must be part of any calculations considered" (quoted in Milman 2021). This kind of call for "living space" for those designated as deserving of their "homeland" sounds remarkably like the Nazi settler-colonialist concept of *Lebensraum* (Mackay 2020; Walsh 2022).

According to Anson (2020: 69), "ecofascism is a political philosophy that deploys ecological themes to justify the necessity of totalitarian violence for survival. It depends on stories of past, present, or predicted apocalyptic environmental events—a once idyllic and pure but now threatened nature [or universe, according to Thanos in *Infinity War*] demands population control . . . and the elimination of certain groups."[29] For Menrisky (in Hancock 2022), "ecofascism is any environmentalism that advocates or accepts violence and does so in a way that reinforces systems of inequality or targets certain people while leaving others untouched."[30] Later, in the same piece (Hancock 2022), Menrisky adds,

> Other familiar ecofascist ideas include misanthropic statements that the world would be better without humans, which not only leaves open the possibility that it might be ethically permissible for mass numbers of humans to die (a popular suggestion early on during the COVID-19 pandemic) but also opens the door for eugenic arguments among explicit ecofascists about which humans deserve to live and which do not. Given that it is typically able-bodied, white, Anglo-Saxon, cisgendered heterosexual men who explicitly declare themselves ecofascists, the answer is often unsurprising.

Essentially, (contemporary) ecofascists would not necessarily endorse Thanos's 50–50, "heads you live, tails you lose" approach[31] because, as Menrisky (in Hancock 2022) clarifies, when ecofascists assert that "humans . . . are a disease on the planet," they "mean[] to exempt themselves." But this does not end our inquiry. Rather, we can now: (1) ask what these popular cultural forms might have done or do differently, as we suggested earlier with *Black Panther* (2018) and *Wakanda Forever* (2022); (2) identify flawed (environmental) reasoning and representation(s) in such popular cultural forms, as we also did with *Black Panther* (2018) and *Wakanda Forever* (2022); and (3) interrogate the impact that such popular cultural forms might have on audiences and viewers. We flesh out these three types of inquiries here.

With respect to the first, *Infinity War* and *Endgame*, in which the Avengers essentially reverse "the Blip," evoke ecofascist themes, as we have already noted. But consider two possibilities of how the franchise could have engaged with these themes in more fruitful ways:

a. Imagine versions of the films in which beings/lifeforms/peoples/ species appeal to Thanos to snap his fingers but wipe out only *some specified groups* and not others—i.e., not indiscriminately.[32] In these scenarios, Thanos desires to wipe out half of all life at random, the Avengers want to stop him (for fairly simplistic reasons: he is "evil"; they are "good"), various others want to thwart "the Blip" because their "societies . . . are functioning perfectly well and wouldn't ben-efit at all from their population being halved" (Tassi 2018), and still other beings/lifeforms/peoples/species support "the snap" to wipe out "invasive species" (however defined) but not "native species" (how-ever defined). Would that not have produced a more absorbing plot and a more sophisticated take on ecofascism? To be clear, we certainly do not support mass murder as a solution to environmental problems and we definitely agree with Andrews (2019b) that "killing people to save the planet is not an effective strategy,"[33] as well as with Osaka (2020a) that "you can't save a world by destroying it" (meaning, one cannot save a universe by destroying half of all life). But we do contend that the story could have exposed Thanos's genocidal ide-ation and could have underscored how "ecofascist myths fuel white supremacy, ultra-nationalism, patriarchy, ableism, [and] authori-tarianism" (Anti-Creep Climate Initiative 2022; see also Anson 2022)[34]—and that doing so might have helped make Thanos a less sympathetic character—a point to which we will return. Aside from the exchange between Thanos and Gamora quoted earlier, nothing in *Infinity War* or, worse, in *Endgame*, concedes that Thanos's ideology is based on faulty logic and challenges him on this.[35]

b. If Thanos can snap his fingers and wipe out half of life, could he not have snapped his fingers and, say, *increased* global resources or, better yet, increased *access to* global resources? Given that hunger is more a problem of *distribution* than *overpopulation* (see, e.g., Anti-Creep Climate Initiative 2022; Tassi 2018; see generally Crossette 1999; DeGregori 1982; Taylor 2018; cf. Foy 2010b), could Thanos have snapped his fingers and addressed the former? It is hard to imagine that stones powerful enough to wipe out life could not also *create the conditions for* better life. Indeed, as Tassi (2018) maintains, "If [Thanos's] goal is to make society sustainable, can't he use the power of the Infinity Gauntlet to make that happen in a less horrific way? Can't he snap his fingers and instead of murdering trillions, produce food and water, cure disease, and create new utopian plan-ets for people to live on to avoid overcrowding?[36] If the point is that the gauntlet makes him God with all six stones, can't he be the benevolent overlord he's supposedly trying to be rather than just . . . murdering people?"[37]

With respect to the second, Thanos is probably overly confident in his understanding of astronomy and astrophysics; moreover, his reasoning is faulty and his arithmetic/mathematics suspect:

a. While there is general agreement that the universe is expanding (see, e.g., Greshko 2019, 2021), there is some debate as to whether the universe is "finite" or "infinite" (see, e.g., Gillani 2021). Thanos, however, is convinced that the universe is, in fact, finite *and* that *its resources* are finite, which are not one and the same. Moreover, Thanos assumes that *all planets* are like Titan and Earth—with finite resources. This seems slightly more plausible, but what if there were planets that had developed the replicating technology one encounters in *Star Trek*? As Saadia (2016: 69) explains in *Trekonomics*, "The name says it all: the replicator is a machine that replicates stuff. Almost any stuff. You ask it for stuff, and the stuff you just asked for instantly materializes before your eyes on the device's softly lit plate." "There are some limits and safeguards to what a replicator will make," Saadia (2016: 69) continues. "For instance, Starfleet regulations put a software lock on the replication of weapons aboard a ship. Also, replicators do not have the ability to make living tissues or organisms because of the exponentially higher complexity of life compared to inanimate objects. Thus, replicators can produce nutritious meals and savory beverages, but not Kumamoto oysters on the half shell." But what is key for our purposes is that with the replicator, "imbalances in supply and demand have largely become moot" (Saadia 2016: 70). In response to Thanos's assertion that "if life is left unchecked, life will cease to exist," Gamora could have appealed to Thanos to create replicator technology as a means of bringing about a "post-scarcity economy" (North 2015). But as Hirschmann (2023: 173) points out, Thanos "seeks to use his phenomenal power not to create some new resource or technology—such as more vibranium or some other self-renewing material—but to eliminate half the population of all planets in the universe."

b. Thanos holds fast to the idea that more beings/lifeforms/peoples/species means more (environmental) problems and that drastic population decline is necessary in order to save the universe. As Johnston (2021) correctly observes, while "Thanos may want to solve overpopulation[,] . . . no matter how many people he eliminates, Malthus' theory will always remain true. Population, even halved, will still grow exponentially, and food production (even with a head start) will eventually prove insufficient to support the rapidly expanding amount of lifeforms dependent on it." Thus, Thanos—whom Townsend (2018) refers to as the "ultimate Malthusian"—would need to snap his fingers whenever population growth outpaces food production. Bradshaw and Brook (2014), who used scenario-based matrix modeling to project the global human population in 2100, found that even a catastrophic mass mortality event of two billion deaths over a hypothetical five-year period in the mid-twenty-first century would still result in a global human population of 8.5 billion by 2100—leaving Townsend (2018) to quip, "Population control doesn't control population for long."[38] Tassi (2018) concurs: "This [Thanos's plan] is a temporary fix. Eventually, the remaining 50% will build themselves back up again to be close to 100% of the population before." "Do you just . . . keep doing this over and over then? When do you decide when it's time?" he asks. Tassi (2018) argues that no society could function if "every so often 50% of everyone is killed by [Thanos's] finger snaps." (Of course, Thanos renders this impossible when he admits to destroying the stones.) Johnston's (2021) and Tassi's (2018) arguments resonate with that of the Anti-Creep Climate Initiative (2022), which maintains that "if you destroy half of all life, that includes the resources we all need to live. That kind of defeats the purpose, right?[39] Plus [and this is Johnston's point], population would rebound within 1–2 generations and then we'd be back where we started." Thanos would either have needed to preserve the Infinity Stones in order to repeat "the Blip" or set up a situation akin to that in the dystopian *Logan's Run* (1976), directed by Michael Anderson, where everyone undergoes the rite of "Carrousel" when they reach the age of thirty—killed under the guise of being "renewed."

c. At the end of *Infinity War*, we witness cars colliding with each other as half of life in the universe disintegrates with Thanos's snap of his fingers. If someone dies in an accident (or if someone suffers injuries and then dies), is that person part of the 50 percent that were supposed to die? What about the surgeon who dies mid-operation, resulting in the death of his/her/their patient? How does "the Blip" account for (the) ensuing deaths or what Tassi (2018) calls the "collateral damage"? In other words, halving the population of the universe at once would actually mean killing *more than* half. It does not appear that Thanos—or MCU—thought this through.

The third line of inquiry—considering the impact that such popular cultural forms might have on audiences and viewers—is perhaps the most important. Here, the question is not so much what MCU could have changed to make for a more explicit and elaborate engagement with ecofascism or a more intellectually stimulating set of movies (ones without the deficiencies in Thanos's philosophy and in the calculus of "the Blip"—or, at least, ones that challenge the weaknesses in Thanos's ideology), but that so many viewers of *Infinity War* and *Endgame* responded *favorably* to Thanos's position. As Menrisky (in Hancock 2022) laments, "Despite the fact that Marvel casts Thanos as the villain, the franchise did not address his environmental concerns, which were very real. As a result, after *Infinity War* came out, numerous people online agreed with Thanos and his ideas." This might be because, as Fullerton (2019) points out, "Directors Joe and Anthony Russo have been open about the fact that Infinity War is structured to have Thanos as *its main protagonist* (he certainly has more screen time than any other character)" (emphasis added). As a result, Thanos is the most developed character (at least in *Infinity War*) and the most sophisticated, arguably making him sympathetic in the minds of viewers, who are left feeling that he "means well."[40] This aspect of *Infinity War* leads Taylor (2018) to observe that "in an odd way, the movie endorses [Thanos's] population control concept"—what Taylor refers to as "demi-genocide"—which Thanos and the MCU present "as a drastic solution, to be sure, but one that actually works."

Scary stuff.

Bowden (2018) remarks that "films reflect the tastes and values of the period in which they are made." Welsh, Fleming, and Dowler (2011: 458) take this point a step further, maintaining that "crime films not only reflect current attitudes and tensions in society, but also 'shape the ways we think about these issues'" (quoting Rafter 2006: 3). This resonates with Carnes and Goren (2023: 4), who posit that "the MCU is influenced by the politics of its day. . . . Popular culture artifacts (like the MCU) are often inspired by real-world events, consumed by people with less fully formed political opinions, and effective at generating powerful emotional responses that truly impact audiences." As green cultural criminologists, we argue that a broader swathe of films not only *reflect* current attitudes and tensions in society regarding the environment and environmental harms but can *reaffirm* or *influence* the ways in which we think about environmental issues.[41] *Infinity War* was released in the United States on April 27, 2018;[42] in an article published on May 1, 2018, some *four days later*, Plante (2018) reported that more than twenty thousand people "in the real world" (although who knows where their minds are or in what universe they are living!) agreed with Thanos "enough to subscribe to a subreddit called /r/thanosdidnothingwrong." (As of early May 2024, the forum had 641,000 members.[43]) Given that MCU has not, to the best of our knowledge, commented on this development, we might conclude that the franchise is either oblivious to Thanos's Malthusianism (which seems hard to believe) or indifferent to the way that Thanos's perspective might stoke the flames of ecofascism, which seems more plausible (although no less perverse) in light of comic book writer Alan Moore's pronouncement that such movies are "very much white supremacist dreams of the master race" (quoted in "Esquire Editors" 2019; see also Langmann 2022).[44]

To unmask some of the fallacies in Thanos's argument—and to contest some of the ways in which the MCU might echo and affect prevailing societal notions about the causes of environmental harm(s)—Menrisky has teamed up with a group of educators from universities around the United States (April Anson, Cassie M. Galentine, Shane Hall, and Bruno Seraphin) to form the Anti-Creep Climate Initiative and create a "web zine"—*Against the Ecofascist Creep: Debunking Ecofascist Myths*—that uses the storyline from *Infinity War* and *Endgame* to "explore [Thanos's] assumptions and present[] other ways of dealing with environmental challenges than advocating violence." As the Anti-Creep Climate Initiative (2022) states at the outset of its zine,

> Thanos saw a world experiencing rapid climate change, staggering social inequality, and violence. His plan was to gather the Infinity Stones and cull half of life to help those people that remain. Though Thanos was a powerful supervillain, he wasn't original. His plan repeated long-held ideas that extreme violence is necessary to save the environment.
> It isn't.

The comic then breaks down six "everyday ecofascist myths": "overpopulation is an environmental crisis," "humans are naturally, tragically, selfish," "humans are a virus," "city people are the problem," "strong borders protect our scarce resources," and "environmental and social collapse are desirable."[45]

In many respects, Menrisky and his colleagues, with their Anti-Creep Climate Initiative, encapsulate/embody/exemplify the green cultural criminological project—one that seeks not just to tabulate the *content* of popular cultural forms but also to explore *the impact* that such popular cultural forms (whether social scientifically/scientifically/logically sound) might have—and to *interrogate them*.

In the final section of this introductory chapter, we take a step back to present a description of the ways in which we think popular cultural forms can operate, which we use as a foundation for our explorations in this book.

Mirrors, Windows, and . . . Sliding Glass Doors? Prisms?

Rudine Sims Bishop (1990), the educator who has been referred to as the "mother of multicultural literature" (Chenowith 2019), once wrote:

> Books are sometimes *windows*, offering views of worlds that may be real or imagined, familiar or strange. These windows are also *sliding glass doors*, and readers have only to walk through in imagination to become part of whatever world has been created or recreated by the author. When lighting conditions are just right, however, a window can also be a *mirror*. Literature transforms human experience and reflects it back to us, and in that reflection we can see our own lives and experiences as part of the larger human experience. (quoted in Harris 2007: 153, emphasis added)

Sims Bishop's words have become, as Harris (2007: 153) has put it, "a succinct metaphor for some of the primary purposes of sharing multicultural literature with children,"[46] especially given that nonwhite children in the United States have often learned to read from books that omit them, barely mention them, or misrepresent or caricaturize them.[47]

Using similar figures of speech, albeit in a different context—that of news media—Jewkes and Linnemann, in *Media and Crime in the U.S.* (2018: 66), propose that

> despite often being described as a "window on the world" or a mirror reflecting "real life," the media might be more accurately thought of, borrowing Ferrell, Hayward, and Young's (2015) imagery, as a carnivalesque "Hall of Mirrors," bending and distorting the viewer's perception of the world.[48]

Interestingly, in the original version of that book, under the title of *Media and Crime* (authored by Jewkes, first published in 2004, with a second edition in 2010 and a third in 2015), the phrasing is slightly different:

> Despite often being described as a "window on the world" or a mirror reflecting "real life," the media might be more accurately thought of as a prism, subtly bending and distorting the view of the world it projects. (Jewkes 2015: 45; for a discussion, see Rothe and Kauzlarich 2022)

Windows (or windows on the world)? Mirrors (or carnivalesque halls of mirrors)? Sliding glass doors? Prisms?

Elsewhere, we have posited that "media images and representations are the *windows* through which most people see the planet they live on, and this also applies to their knowledge of their more immediate environments, nationally and locally" (Brisman and South 2023: 529, emphasis added). While we stand by this description, as we have also written elsewhere—and as we explore further in this book—*all* of these metaphors (windows, mirrors, sliding glass doors, prisms) are helpful because our cultural, literary, and visual worlds are saturated with "images" of nature and the natural, both positively and negatively presented—as sources of life and sustenance (as well as awe, epiphany, inspiration, and revelation) but also of danger and fear (Brisman and South 2022, citing Brisman and Rau 2009; South 2017). These are common features of most, if not all, cultures, but they may be portrayed in different ways—in different places and at different times—to different degrees. In this book, we are most interested in a certain type (or types) of *distorted* or *refracted* images. To be sure, these are not the only ways to categorize and explore representations of humans' connections to and relationships with the environment, nature, and nonhuman animal life. Moreover, our examples in each chapter are *illustrative*, not *exhaustive*. Our goal is threefold:

First, we seek to illuminate three specific—and, we would contend, prevalent, if not *dominant*—(primarily, but by no means exclusively, Western) depictions of the relationship between humans and the environment, as seen in terms of:

- Nature as *monstrous* or fear-inducing (nature and horror or "ecohorror")
- Nature and the Earth (or parts of it) as *abject* (the abjection of the Earth)
- Nature and the *apocalypse*, wherein nature is contributing to the end-of-the-world, with an end-point sometimes conceptualized as one without humans (by some with misanthropic ecophilosophies)[49]

In their introduction to their volume, *Fear and Nature: Ecohorror Studies in the Anthropocene*, Tidwell and Soles (2021b: 3) assert that "ecohorror may be the dominant mode in which we talk to ourselves about the global climate crisis and the real-life ecological horrors of our current Anthropocenic moment." In contrast, we suggest and try to demonstrate that ecohorror is *one of* a number of dominant modes (or tropes or themes) in which the environment and nature are represented.

Second, we argue that these depictions are *interrelated*—that the view of nature as monstrous (and our monstrous treatment of nature) can contribute to the belief that nature and the Earth (or parts of it) are *abject*—and thus the desire to abject Earth (or parts of it). This, in turn, can facilitate notions of environmental apocalypse as inevitable. It is, of course, more complicated than that: as we attempt to articulate, abjection leads to (further) "othering"—of nature, of other people—which, in turn, can generate or accelerate the conditions for societal and environmental collapse or produce and catalyze the circumstances that make it harder to avoid cataclysmic events ("the apocalypse"). This is not the only sequence or ordering, however, and as we describe at the end of the third chapter, how one views the succession or progression depends on how one conceives of the abjection of the Earth (or parts of it) and how one conceptualizes "apocalypse."

Third, we assert that despite these grim depictions, it is incumbent upon us (criminologists, sociologists, researchers, scholars, students—and residents of this planet) to remember and recognize our agency. As Foy (2010a: 7) reminds us, "We are [not] forced to imitate the messages or portrayals within popular culture, nor does popular culture serve entirely as a social mirror." In other words, we are not passive recipients of mediated culture; we can, to quote Welsh and colleagues (2011), "negotiate and develop" our social reality/the social reality that is reflected.

Essentially, our ambition for this book is not just to *chronicle* human-environment (or human-nature) representations in popular cultural forms or to *identify* and *highlight* frequent themes. Rather, our aspiration is for a book that functions as an "intervention" in the way McGregor (2022: 1) conceives of it: as "an act of interposing or interfering in an affair"—in our case, a certain social reality—"so as to affect its course or consequences." Although neither one of us is a particularly violent individual, we might extend our earlier series of rhetorical questions in the following way: "Windows (or windows on the world)? Mirrors (or carnivalesque halls of mirrors)? Sliding glass doors? Prisms? Maybe they need to be smashed? Or perhaps broken and reconfigured, as we have attempted to do in our reading of *Black Panther* and *Wakanda Forever* and *Infinity War* . . . ?"

Depictions or themes—of nature as *monstrous* or fear-inducing (nature and horror or "ecohorror"); of nature and the Earth (or parts of it) as *abject* (and our abjection of the Earth); and of nature and the *apocalypse* (or nature as contributing to the end of the world—or "the end of the world as we know it")—serve as the subjects of the first three substantive chapters of this book. We turn now to an overview of those chapters.

Outline of Chapters

In his foreword to Caroline Joan S. Picart and John Edgar Browning's edited volume *Speaking of Monsters: A Teratological Anthology*, Skal (2012: xii) tells us that "the term [*monster*] descends from the Latin noun *monstrum* (divine portent) by way of the French verb *monere* (to warn)" (see also Cohen [1996: 4], who notes that "the *monstrum* is etymologically 'that which reveals,' 'that which warns'"). Later in the same volume, Long (2012: 201), quoting Augustine of Hippo (1063), explains, "The word 'monster,' we are told, clearly comes from 'to demonstrate' [*monstrare*], because monsters are signs by which something is demonstrated. 'Sign' [*ostentum*] comes from 'to show' [*ostendere*]; 'portent' from 'to portend', that is 'to show in advance' [*praeostendere*]; and 'prodigy' from 'to speak of what is far away' [*porro dicere*], that is, to foretell the future." Whatever the etymology of the word *monster* may be, it is clear that they, monsters, possess metaphorical value. For Skal (2012: xii), "monsters are slippery, ever-adaptive metaphors, but above all, they are natural teachers and teaching tools. Monsters *demonstrate* things" (emphasis in original). Likewise, Cohen (1996: 4) contends that "the monster is born only at this metaphoric crossroads, as an embodiment of a certain cultural moment—of a time, a feeling, and a place" (for a discussion, see Picart and Cohen 2012). For her part, Long (2012: 205) emphasizes that "the monster is the site where meaning is made." Others have certainly made similar assertions (see, e.g., Giuliani 2021; North 2014; see also Carroll 2021; Christie 2020). Of course, the point of teachings and demonstrations is *to learn* from them, possibly *to improve* the "moment" or change the future. As Gilmore (2003: 12) suggests, "For most Western observers the monster is a metaphor for all that must be repudiated by the human spirit," and it follows, as Robbins (2014: 51) puts it, that "the monster appears so that we may learn from it and make necessary changes in our lives and social systems."

Chapter 2, "Monstrous Nature and the Roots and Growth of Ecohorror," certainly does not attempt to catalogue all monster metaphors. Rather, employing the existing tropes of "monstrous nature" (see, e.g., Murray and Heumann 2016; Tidwell 2014; see also Alaimo 2001: 279; Parker 2016: 326) and "ecohorror" (see, e.g., Foy 2010b; Merchant 2012; Rust and Soles 2014; Tidwell 2014, 2018; Tidwell and Soles 2021a, 2021b; Ulaby 2008), our goal is to bring together green cultural criminology and Gothic criminology, connecting Gothic imaginings of the power and vengeance of nature—specifically, nature wronged by humans—from the late eighteenth to the twenty-first century. How we go about defining what is "monstrous" and naming our monsters has been the subject of prior criminological concern (see, e.g.,

Linnemann 2016: 217),[50] and this chapter builds on South (2017) in situating "monstrosity" in a spectrum—one that recognizes that some depictions of environmental harms and problems offer images or tales of "reassurance," others of "return to safety" or "temporary reprieve," and still others (which we argue tend to dominate) of "monstrosity."

In *A Critical Psychology of the Postcolonial: The Mind of Apartheid*, Hook (2012: 46) explores the "dehumanizing, denigrating, abjecting features of racism." Drawing on both Kristeva (1982) and Butler (1993), Hook introduces the notion of "abjection as an 'operation of repulsion,'" which, he reminds us, is "a form of both recoil and response, repugnance and reflex" (2012: 48, 69). Abjection is always, then "activity, *action* as much as it is revulsion" (2012: 69, emphasis in original). In Chapter 3, "The Abjection of the Earth," we borrow from Hook to present the idea of the Earth as "abject"—as that which we wish to abandon or reject because of its monstrosity—a "status" (or, better, a "condition" or "state") originating in our perceptions and enhanced by our actions (see Chapter 2). Whereas Hook's (2012) focus is on *the subject* who *experiences abjection*, our contention is that we have made the Earth monstrous and horrid and now wish to cast it off (or, at least, parts of it)—or to turn away or hide from it—because of its horridness and "monstrous nature." Thus, our interest centers not on "those *who are made to be abject*" but on depictions and manifestations of the Earth (or parts of it) *as abject* and on *the abjectors*—who seek protection from "monstrous nature" and "abject Earth" (recognizing, of course, that the "action" of abjection entails the "practice [of] social forms of exclusion" [Hook 2012: 74, emphasis in original; see also Arya and Chare 2016: 2]). As Arya and Chare (2016: 2) explain, for Kristeva (1982), "in a Judeo-Christian context, religion . . . assumed the rule of guarding against the abject," but that "the rise of secularism in modernity . . . led art to take over this function." We suggest that instead of religion or art protecting (us) against the abject, the period of late capitalism is characterized by "bunkerization," "seasteading" (permanent dwellings at sea outside territory claimed by nation-states), "fortressing" (creating "fortresses," private islands such as Indian Creek in South Florida, and "air domes" or "walled compounds" [Brisman, South, and Walters 2018a, 2018b, 2020]), as well as efforts at space colonization (see Lam et al. 2025). The important difference, however, is that *we* are the ones creating the abjection. *We* are responsible for that which is characterized as abject.

Following the discussion of monstrosity and abjection, Chapter 4, "Apocalyptic Imaginaries," looks at ecocidal tendencies and select depictions thereof in film and literature. Since the beginning of time (or, at least, humans' development of the concept of time), we have been imagining and anticipating the end of the world—from fire and brimstone to nuclear holocaust to environmental disaster. This chapter explores contemporary visions of the demise of planet Earth and its ability to support its biotic and abiotic components—specifically, the cinematic (e.g., *Pandorum*, *Waterworld*) and literary (e.g., *Down to a Sunless Sea*, *Player One*, *World Made by Hand*) depictions and meanings of different end-time scenarios of environmental catastrophe. We consider the significance of such depictions of apocalyptic environmental harms as well as criticisms thereof (including conservative pundits' use of the term *apocalyptic environmentalism* to refer to environmentalists' harrowing portrayals of the Earth's future resulting from continued fossil fuel consumption and natural resource depletion). Rather than assess the plausibility of such end-of-the-world predictions, this chapter considers what we might learn from these dark (green) visions and contemplates what is missing from them. This chapter concludes by suggesting why such an examination is fruitful for those interested in cross-disciplinary environmental and sustainability research.

Monstrous Nature and Representations of Environmental Harms: A Green Cultural Criminological Perspective closes with Chapter 5, "Conclusion: Goodbye, Earth (?)(!)," in which we describe and discuss a number of books that share the words "Goodbye Earth." We examine the various visions presented in the books and the assorted solutions (or propositions), if any—in the hopes that we never actually have to say, "Goodbye, Earth."

2

Monstrous Nature and the Roots
and Growth of Ecohorror

According to Plumwood, in contrast to cultures "which stress what connects us to nature as genuinely human virtues" and "which emphasize continuity and not dissimilarity" (1991: 10), in Western thinking, "the human is set apart from nature as radically other" (1999: 98), claiming superiority and dominance over nature but ever threatened by nature's transgressions and traversing of borders and boundaries (Arya 2014). Hence, humans create "laws and restrictions . . . to protect the boundaries by using a variety of different means and sanctions, while recognizing that abjection remains a continual threat that may overpower the system" (Arya 2014: 41). "Protection" can, ironically, also mean "pollution" in order to signal appropriation of nature and create boundaries and warnings, such as when "a factory empties its effluents into a nearby river, diffuses them in the atmosphere, or transports them to a remote swamp; *of course nobody sees that this means appropriation of the place.* Who doesn't understand that no one can drink the water, breathe the air, or get close to such an area? These spaces are better protected than by walls, locks, or bolts" (Serres 2010: 43, emphasis in original). Hence degradation and abjection (which we discuss in the next chapter) can be *used* by humans to deliberately set nature apart.

In other instances, though, abjection occurs in cases of uncontrolled and invasive sources of contamination and impurity, disease, and death. Indeed, one of the lessons of the COVID-19 pandemic is that the virus (severe acute respiratory syndrome coronavirus 2 or "SARS-CoV-2") that causes the disease was an unintended consequence of "our polarization with the natural world" (Friedman 2020b; for a discussion, see Lam et al. 2023). As Dr. Johan Rockström, chief scientist at the American nonprofit environmental organization Conservation International, explains, "When you simultaneously hunt for wildlife and push development into natural ecosystems—destroying natural habitats—the natural balance of species collapses due to loss of top predators and other iconic species, leading to an abundance of more generalized species adapted to live in human dominated habitats. These are rats, bats and some primates—which together host 75 percent of all known viruses to date, and who can survive and multiply in destroyed human dominated habitats" (quoted in Friedman 2020b; see also Friedman 2020a). The science underpinning these conclusions regarding hosts and vectors of viruses is sound; it also reminds us of the power of less scientific but widely believed historical diagnoses of the causes of plagues that have left culturally significant legacies. In Bram Stoker's novel, *Dracula* ([1897] 1920), rats and bats feature as portents of disease and infection, while Renfield, Count Dracula's mesmerized servant, repels and fascinates with his taste for flies and spiders. Spiders are, of course, a well-known source of a phobia; as Gloyne (1950) suggests, they provoke a reaction of disgust among many people because this is an expression of a "disease avoidance" response. Davey (1994: 22) explains that "During the Middle Ages, spiders were . . . perceived as harbingers of the Great Plagues that swept across Europe from the tenth century onwards," perhaps partly because some spiders may bite and produce an irritated skin reaction and also because they tended to be found in areas of properties also occupied by the black rat, which carried the fleas that were the real carriers of the plague. As Davey (1994) notes, from such beginnings, through children's stories, as well as horror and science fiction media, modern arachnophobia has grown.[1]

Societies have a long history of mixing science and superstition in attempts to understand the bountiful and the baleful offerings of nature. We are concerned, here, with Western cultural expressions of our ambivalence, anxiety, and fear regarding nature and so-called "wildlife"[2] which, we argue, has led to the abjection of the Earth (see, e.g., Kristeva 1982; Watson 2015), which we discuss in greater detail in Chapter 3.

Humanity has had a sundry relationship with nature, the environment, and other species. There has, however, been little green criminological exploration (or green cultural criminological exploration, for that matter) of this ambivalence and the duality of *fear of* nature. To take such exploration forward, we consider two voids in green (cultural) criminology—the state of "ecophobia" and the duality of "awe" and the "sublime."

First, the condition or state now labeled (unsurprisingly) *ecophobia*: Estok (2009: 204, 208, 216) defines this as "contempt for the natural world"—"an irrational and groundless hatred of the natural world . . . rooted in and dependent on anthropocentric arrogance and speciesism."[3] Whether groundless or not, such attitudes and anxieties reflect what Linnemann (2022: 61) observes as a trend among "Hollywood tastemakers," who seem "quick to bet on the end of the world. From plagues and pandemics to comets, meteors, zombies, and alien invasions."[4] Crosby (2014: 514) is more specific, arguing that "as global climate change, pollution, and habitat destruction" have been transforming "a comfortable earth" into one that is "increasingly hostile and strange," it appears that "horror is becoming the environmental norm" in representations found in "apocalyptic TV shows and movies" (for a discussion, see Parker 2016: 216–17).[5] This does not mean that such a "norm" is transformative of behaviors or politics regarding preservation and valuing of nature, but that the theme of environmental catastrophe and horror has come to be an entertainment staple. Indeed, that it has been so for some decades now has arguably become a source of reassurance and a well of stories justifying denial of any dire consequences of environmental crisis. As Ulaby (2008) reports, "movies with environmental themes are nothing new. Back in the '70s—another era defined by an oil crisis and discussions of alternative energy—movie audiences entertained themselves with disaster movies (*Earthquake*) and creature features (*Prophecy, Frogs*)." "What makes today's eco-horrors different," Ulaby (2008) continues, "is that the entire *planet* is seen as vengeful and malevolent towards its human inhabitants" (emphasis in original; for a discussion, see Tyburski 2013: 147). As we attempt to demonstrate in this chapter and harking back to our point in Chapter 1, such "ecohorror" may both reflect and exacerbate Estok's (2009) notion of "ecophobia."

Second, there is a close relationship between *awe* of nature, which is expressed in terms of appreciation and romantic delight (Pepper 1996), and the experience of the *sublime* with respect to nature, which enfolds both fascination and a sense of terror (Deibler 2015). Elsewhere in this book (Chapter 3), we draw upon ideas of abjection as it emerges from the "monstrous." In this chapter, we connect Gothic imaginings of the power and vengeance of nature—specifically, nature wronged by humans—from the late eighteenth to the twenty-first century.

Before doing so, however, a word about how this chapter operates in relationship to Robin L. Murray and Joseph K. Heumann's *Monstrous Nature: Environment and Horror on the Big Screen* (2016) is in order. Murray and Heumann organize their book in relationship to what they contend are four recurring themes in films that construct nature as a monster: (1) *monstrous anthropomorphism* (which focus on documentary[6] and feature films[7] that construct monsters as insects or benefactors because they resemble humanity so closely); (2) *human ecology and nature as monster* (which highlight cinematic depictions of the interdependent relationship between human and nonhuman nature)[8]; (3) *evolution and monstrous nature* (which explore filmic stories that paint a gloomy image of humanity's future)[9]; and (4) *gendered landscapes and monstrous bodies* (which employ an ecofeminist lens to examine gendered bodies in relationship to nonhuman nature).[10] Like us, Murray and Heumann (2016: xi, xviii) are interested in cinematic depictions of the "monstrous result[s] of humanity's destruction of the environment," where "the real monsters are the humans." There are, however, at least a couple of differences.

First, they focus on films (both documentary and feature films) (see Tidwell and Soles 2021: 8). While we acknowledge the green cultural criminological value of examining documentary films (see, e.g., Brisman and South 2014: 36–38, 40–41), here, we restrict our filmic scope to feature films, although we also expand our gaze to include literature. Second, Murray and Heumann devote their entire book to a particular cinematic vision of "monstrous nature" and engage with "ecohorror" (although the authors contemplate a wider array of films beyond just horror); we dedicate just one chapter to a broader cultural notion of "monstrous nature" (which we intertwine with "ecohorror" and Gothic imagery), situating representations of "monstrous nature" and "ecohorror" in relationship to "abjection" and "apocalypse." Thus, in some respects, our endeavor is narrower (because we allot fewer pages to "monstrous nature" and reflect on fewer examples), but in other regards, it is more expansive (in terms of our literary references and effort to position "monstrous nature" in conversation with other constructions and depictions of humans' interactions with nature and the environment). Ultimately, we view our chapter (and book) as participating in a dialogue with and complementing Murray and Heumann's work—upon which we draw later—rather than competing with it.

The Ambiguity of Nature in Gothic Literature and Film

The Gothic, Sothcott (2016: 434) writes, "is and always has emphasised *ambiguity*" (emphasis in original)[11]; it feeds on fear of the world turned upside down—the "carnivalistic" in the Bakhtinian sense. As Bakhtin (1984: 122) proposes, "Because carnivalistic life is drawn out of its *usual* rut, it is to some extent 'life turned inside out,' 'the reverse side of the world' (*'monde à l'envers'*)"—where, as Hall (2016: 244) puts it, "All ordinary laws, prohibitions and proscription are suspended." The familiar becomes unfamiliar—or out of control or wild—and thus when monsters appear in Gothic media (in literature and, later, in film), they present as images that both fascinate and repel (see, e.g., Skott et al. 2021: 390; Sothcott 2016: 435, 438, 442; Valier 2002: 331; see generally Arya and Chare 2016: 7, 11; Bishop 2009: 20; Clasen 2017: 42; Kniss 2021: 68; Levina and Bui 2013: 4).[12] As Skal (2012: xiii) states, "While carnival monsters certainly serve the cathartic function of reinforcing one's own shaky sense of physical normalcy, and general good-standing membership in the tribe, they are also anxiety avatars for an age in which the familiar structures of society and identity are inexorably morph-ing."[13] If monsters are, then, products of the anxieties of their time, so, for Fiddler (2013: 297), quoting Williams (1995: 89), "not only may Gothic conventions fit easily into historical fictions . . . they may equally express anxiety about *socio-political* upheavals" (emphasis added). Indeed, Sothcott (2016: 435) points to the Gothic imagination's "continual popularity since the eighteenth century" as resting upon "a capacity to address . . . prevailing concerns and anxieties." While "the cause of such anxieties might change over time, generating new themes and motifs," he continues, "the Gothic will always speak to feelings of uncertainty, insecurity and doubt" (Sothcott 2016: 435).[14] Correspondingly, for Rafter and Ystehede (2010: 265, 271), the "Gothic sensibility" can be seen as emerging from the "Romantic reaction to Enlightenment rationalism," whereby the Romantics, who favored freedom, expression, and exploration, "look[ed] to nature for inspiration, . . . reach[ing] for a sense of the sublime, the shudder of horror, and other powerful feel-ings."[15] Of all the landscapes untamed by rationalism and likely to provoke fear, yet also seen as symbolic of freedom and the ideal environment for exploration, the idea of wilderness stands out.

William Cronon (1995) has challenged and interrogated the notion of "wilderness" in "The Trouble with Wilderness: Or, Getting Back to the Wrong Nature," and it is worthwhile charting his genealogy.[16] Cronon begins by explaining that his intention is to "rethink wilderness" (1995: 69). While acknowledging that this will seem like a "heretical claim to many environmentalists" because "the idea of wilderness has for decades been a fundamental tenet—indeed, a passion—of the environmental movement, especially in the United States," he points out that it is important to revisit and (re-)examine the "peculiar history" of "wilderness" (1995: 69).

"Far from being the one place on earth that stands apart from humanity," Cronon explains, "it [wilderness] is quite profoundly a *human creation*—indeed, the creation of . . . very particular human cultures at very particu-lar moments in human history. It is not a pristine sanctuary where the last remnant of an untouched, endangered, but still transcendent nature can for at least a little while longer be encountered without the contaminating taint of civilization. Instead, it is a *product* of that civilization and could hardly be contaminated by the very stuff of which it is made" (1995: 69, emphasis added).[17] As Goyes and South (2019: 92) observe, this "construction of natural spectacle and packaging of wilderness as a national treasure" was very much a *product* occurring "alongside the removal of the original settlers and owners" and, hence, requiring a "rewriting of history" and ushering in the commercialization of such spaces.

As Cronon continues, if one were to look back 250 years in American and European history, one does not "find nearly so many people wandering around remote corners of the planet looking for what today we would call 'the wilderness experience'" (1995: 70). Indeed, "as late as the eighteenth century, the most common usage of the word 'wilderness' in the English language referred to landscapes that generally carried *adjectives far different from the ones they attract today*" (1995: 70, emphasis added). "To be in a wilderness," Cronon maintains, "was to be 'deserted,' 'savage,' 'desolate,' 'barren'—in short, a 'waste,' the word's nearest synonym. Its connotations were anything but positive, and the emotion one was most likely to feel in its presence was 'bewilderment'—or terror" (1995: 70; for a similar description, see Kniss 2021: 72–73).

Today, "wilderness" has a certain exotic or romantic feel. Or it often does to environmentalists and nature-lovers, as Cronon himself states: (some) people try to spend their holidays or vacations in "wilderness" or hope to retire to backpack/camp/hike in "wilderness" (see, e.g., Creamer 2022; Hutchinson 2022; see generally James 2015: 128). Years ago, Cronon contends, the sentiment was just the opposite: "When Adam and Eve were driven from that garden [Eden], the world they entered was a wilderness that only their labor and pain could redeem. Wilderness, in short, was a place to which one came only against one's will, and always in fear and trembling" (1995: 71).[18] Cronon proceeds to explain that by the second half of the nineteenth century, the tides of fashion and curiosity had started to change: "the terrible awe that Wordsworth and Thoreau regarded as the appropriately pious stance to adopt in the presence of their mountaintop God was giving way to a much more comfortable, almost sentimental demeanor" (1995: 75).[19] While this period was accompanied by the belief that "the wasteland that had once seemed worthless had for some people come to seem almost beyond price" (Cronon 1995: 71)—that "America's wild places were oases in a fast-spreading desert of civilization" (James 2015: 122)—the evolution of such thinking was by no means without questions and interruptions.

Indeed, this is not a clearly linear or consistent history. The early use of the "Gothic" label was applied to that which was dismissed for not conforming to the Classical style—for being associated with a conflation of the barbaric, medieval, superstitious, and irrationally wild (Lenhardt 2020). By the end of the nineteenth century, as Rafter and Ystehede (2010: 265) note, the Gothic was hybridizing, as "themes and figures from contemporary sciences" were added to "repertoires of the ghoulish and perverse" in a powerful but unstable combination. In this respect, the perfect shock to certainty and the status quo was provided by Darwin's evolutionary theories and the rupturing of conventional and religious assumptions about human origins and identity—a jolt that shook up and echoed through literature and the visual imagination. Numerous images and themes followed and flourished in Gothic and modern literature and, subsequently, film (see Murray and Heumann 2016: xiii), and Rafter and Ystehede (2010: 272) list among these the works of Mary Shelley and Edgar Allan Poe, who "stressed horror, the strange and exotic, sexual vulnerabilities and abnormalities, the ubiquity of the supernatural, monomanias, and the dark taints of corruption" as the signs of perverse and perverted nature.

Importantly, while Darwin was aiming to provide *scientific* certainty about the relationship of "humans to nature," for the creative imagination, this clarification simply presented complexity, which needed further exploration. In his review of Richter's (2011) *Literature after Darwin*, Abberley (2011) notes how varieties of cultural theory that draw on French poststructuralism and psychoanalysis (e.g., Kristeva, Lacan) can be employed to

> examine texts' complex negotiations of human and animal identity post-Darwin. This makes for some thought-provoking insights into tropes like the "missing link" between man and beasts in fin de siècle fiction. H. G. Wells and Stanley Waterloo's imaginings of the Paleolithic past bolster the privileged position of humans by bestializing their Neanderthal cousins. . . . Occupying the borderland between humans and animals, they act as buffers, partially repairing the boundaries which Darwin had toppled.

The Gothic entices and excites because it presents challenges to classification and civilized behavior. The monstrous Frankenstein creature or Dracula—as well as other classic figures of horror in both literature and later in film (Twitchell 1985; see also Sothcott 2016: 431–32, 437n3 and 437n4 and accompanying text)[20]—function as characters with some distinctly human emotions and feelings that are, nevertheless, unknowable and uncanny because we fixate on their differences (Fiddler 2013; see also Kāmîr 2012; Khapaeva 2020; see generally Berreby 2011).[21] This may, in turn, "block our attempts to classify, categorize and hence control them" (Twitchell 1985: 24).[22] These "in-between" creatures or characters, to use Pihlström's phrasing (2020: 35, 36, 37, 44), "blur[] . . . the familiar human form and what is alien, frightening, and inhuman in nature" (Kniss 2021: 68),[23] and occupy spaces and zones of the twilight, the liminal, the interstitial. These are places where we deposit our dead and unwanted waste—the "underground spaces" (Hwang 2013: 7) and "subterranean cities" (Pike 2005) beneath us, that are sources of anxieties, "myths, fantasies and psychic messes" (Hwang 2013: 7). Some of this is replayed in the subsequent genres of sci-fi and horror, where the venous system of the city hosts mutations in the sewers (Lambie 2011; see generally Kweku 2017) or devouring plants bite back in revenge (see Keetley 2016: 19–21; see generally Giuliani 2021: 3; Parker 2016: 216, 222), as in the 2008 Canadian Christmas horror-comedy short film, *Treevenge* (see Piepenburg 2015), and the 2008 natural horror film or "vine-horror-film," *The Ruins* (Scherer 2016: 45).[24] Keetley (2021: 24–25) identifies "the moment[s] when nature *refuses* to stay in the background . . . when nature refuses its place within the human mapping of the world" (emphasis in original) as a "tentacular ecohorror," where "nonhuman nature . . . reaches out to grab and entangle the human" (see also Tidwell and Soles 2021: 10).[25] Whatever the nomenclature, we see a similar, recurring refrain. As the film scholar Kendall R. Phillips (quoted in Ulaby 2008) contends, one key theme in various ecohorror films is that "somehow, the planet has grown tired of us. We've overstayed our welcome"—although, as we note later, "'revenge of nature' narratives"—"works of literature and film in which human characters are attacked by natural forces—typically animals and plants" (Rust and Soles 2014: 509, 510; see also Tidwell and Soles 2021: 2)—represent but one form of ecohorror. In the next chapter, we return to this theme and some of the potential problems with the "revenge of nature" narratives—often conveyed or portrayed as nature "biting back" or "stomping and smashing" and often accompanied explicitly or implicitly with the provocative claim that humans are akin to a "virus" or "cancer" on planet Earth. Our point, for now at least, is that with all horrors, real human follies and anxieties lie beneath these phenomena, as public health is endangered, the environment is damaged, and toxicity accumulates.

Monstrous Distortions of Human Nature: From Lombroso's Primitives to the Werewolf Complex

Over the course of the eighteenth and nineteenth centuries, the interpretation and representation of murder, sin, and unnatural and morbid behaviors were transformed from explanations and lessons (pamphlets and sermons) rooted in the centrality of church and community to narratives of a post-lapsarian culture reflecting Gothic fascinations and constructions of criminal transgression (Halttunen 1998). As Rafter and Ystehede (2010: 272) point out, the secular, Gothic discourse about the mystery and horror of the crime of homicide replaced the notion of the killer as human sinner and instead "deplored the utter otherness of the murderer. . . . The Gothic and the arch-criminal converged."[26] Through the romanticism of the Gothic, serial killers have found their way into popular culture as "monsters," although in many cases, their monstrousness is all the more terrifying because they are capable of retaining an outward presentation of ordinariness and likeability (see, e.g., Green 2011).[27] This may reflect two contrasting tendencies in criminology which have been described as a *criminology of the self,* characterizing offenders as rational and ordinary—"just like us"—and a *criminology of the other* (or a "criminology of the alien other"), defining the offender as a threatening stranger—someone very much *not like us* (Garland 1996: 446, 461; see also Valier 2002: 330).[28] The "other" may be visibly and evidently "not normal" (Long 2012)—of monstrous body, mind, or both—but even more frighteningly, the "other" may be able to hide his/her/its/their "true nature" from any visual scrutiny. With this realization, the door (creakingly) opens to numerous fantasies and fears of horror, possession, zombification, alien invasion, and serial killers.[29] The "stranger within" is a phenomenon familiar from moments when changes in behavior seem uncharacteristic, or personal secrets emerge that change the balance of relationships, or more frighteningly, the safe becomes unsafe. This is the subject of other kinds of analysis concerned with the late modern or postmodern fascination with violence and the Gothic in mainstream culture.

Skott and colleagues (2021: 387) contend that "the Gothic . . . permeates our contemporary cultural imagination, prevalent in numerous forms of media, ranging from literary works to graphic novels, theater, and video games (Picart and Greek 2007; Spooner 2007)."[30] This is not a particularly new observation, for it is not a particularly new phenomenon. Almost twenty-five years before, Edmundson (1997: xii) declared that "American culture at large has become suffused with Gothic assumptions, with Gothic characters and plots." Similarly, in his book, *The Werewolf Complex* (1998), the French cultural sociologist Denis Duclos examined American popular culture in this light, searching for an answer to the question of why the United States has the highest number of multiple murderers. Duclos (1998) did not attribute the cause of violence and murder to Lombroso's primitive urges but to cultural influences on the shaping of human nature. In this interpretation, American society can be imagined as a werewolf—human most of the time but hiding a savage within that breaks out with regularity—reflecting a swing between an appetite for destruction and a need for order (see also Grønstad 2008). As Picart and Greek (2007) argue, the new serial killer has replaced monsters of previous centuries and new myths and fears emerge yet can also provide continuity with the vampires, werewolves, and cannibals of the past. Like Dr. Jekyll and Mr. Hyde, these creatures may be outwardly "normal," average, and respectable but conceal a monster hidden within (see Sothcott 2016: 432).[31]

The significance of these different perceptions of human nature in relation to nonhuman nature and the natural world is that from the late nineteenth century onward, the mix of the Gothic and the scientific "forced a rethinking of traditional ideas about humans' bodies and their relationships with other forms of life" (Rafter and Ystehede 2010: 273), and there followed a "narrative within which any combination of morphic traits, any transfiguration of bodily form, was possible; species integrity was undone" (Rafter and Ystehede 2010: 273). As Ricard (2019: 131–32) notes, while the term "trans-corporeality" is a "recent invention," recognition of the "inevitable imbrication of the human and the non-human" is traceable to scientific and related developments of the Victorian period. The popularization of Darwin's (1859) theory of natural selection drew attention to the adaptive relationship between organisms and their environment, with implications of significance for "classical taxa, already buckling under the combined weight of new and unaccountable species," and with the resulting "vacuum of understanding" providing "an opportune moment for issuing challenges to previously unquestionable classificatory systems" (Ricard 2019: 132).

Subsequently, from Darwin to DNA, phrenology to psychoanalysis, the search for the key to unlocking the mysteries of "human nature" and the "natural" has driven major fields of science but also influenced creative interpretation and representation. For example, the search for elixirs, flowers, fountains, magical stones, and trees with properties that cure illness, heal injuries, and prolong and enhance human life is a centuries-spanning story (from the writings of Herodotus in Ancient Greece [425 BCE] to the 2021 Walt Disney film *Jungle Cruise*, as a recent example)[32] of human imagination, exploration, and experimentation with "elements" of nature such as water, blood, and earth.[33] If this seems folly to some, to others the miracle of long life or the dead rising was scriptural truth; to the Gothic imagination, it was the seed of Frankenstein and Dracula; to Indigenous cultivators of plants and later botanists, the abilities of some apparently dead plants to come back to life was proof of the possibility of resurrection. This phenomenon is still a puzzle for plant science; as Ryan (2016: 116) notes, the "exact mechanism" by which so-called "resurrection plants" reverse their "metabolic arrest" remains unknown, but these plants are able to "display the uncanny aptitude to return from the brink of ordinarily death-dealing conditions." This is another mystery and trick of nature of the kind that the Gothic and ecohorror genres mimic. As we suggested in Chapter 1—and as Bould (2021: 27) reminds us—"the first thing you should always ask of a monster is: what does it represent?"[34] With this in mind, the vampire, for example, represents an "impossible condition of 'living death,'" reversing conventional "definitions of identity and difference," "perverting the religious idea of resurrection," and capable of hiding its true form and nature (Butler 2010: 45).[35] It is to nature's talent for trickery and misrepresentation that we next turn.

Misleading, Unruly, and Threatening Nature

Fear of the impure, of transfiguration, and of the lack of integrity of species—i.e., a feeling that nature cannot be trusted—can also be traced to Victorian roots with implications that would ripple through literature and the visual—and of course influence perceptions of, and responses to, deviants, criminals, and the "other." Abberley (quoted in Gillespie 2014), for example, explores the concept of natural mimicry and its impact on Victorian thinking and ways of seeing the world:

> Natural mimicry is basically when organisms pretend to be things they are not.[36] For example, insects which are camouflaged by their resemblance to leaves, or butterflies which resemble the patterns and colours of other, inedible species in order to ward off predators. Naturalists like Alfred Russel Wallace and Henry Walter Bates were the first to argue that deceptions like these evolved through natural selection; that nature was constantly producing tricks and imitations. This idea was disturbing for two reasons. First, it disturbed religious models of a world created by a moral, truth-loving God. Second, it complicated scientific observation and objectivity, since mimicry involved imagining the mental processes of different animals as they interpreted each other's appearances in the wild.

Abberley (again quoted in Gillespie 2014) suggests that when Victorian science and the arts had to adopt new ways of seeing and representing nature to include ideas about mimicry and deception, they also had to contemplate questions about whether these phenomena were "primitive and bestial" or whether they held "the key to human evolution and even civilization." The key question became one of making sense of a "disorganised natural world in a constant state of flux" (Ricard 2019: 132). This provoked the frightening idea of evolution as something beyond control and hence gave rise to literary, visual, and scientific preoccupations with how to manipulate, direct, or resist it.

The diversity of nature, not just mimicry but "sexual polymorphisms and animals and plants with human characteristics," created "identity anxieties" (Rafter and Ystehede 2010: 274), as did "doublings," such as the Criminal Woman and the Normal Woman, Dr. Jekyll and Mr. Hyde, and the idea that "one identity might transmogrify into its opposite" or that, as Lombroso proposed, "children, far from being innocents, start life as little savages" (Rafter and Ystehede 2010: 274). The wild urges and forces of nature are within us all, and hence neither nature nor other humans can be trusted entirely.

While "being devoured is a primordial fear" (Foltyn 2020: xi), nature does not usually present a daily threat to human existence.[37] As Best (2018) explains, "Most species are considered social problems only when and where they become pests (Jerolmack 2008). Species in the wild—in their native habitat—are generally *not* deemed problematic until they interfere with people's activities. Thus, there are few claims about the dangers posed by large predators . . . so long as they remain in the wilderness" (emphasis added; see also note 2). Indeed, despite the fact that "animals have . . . long played a significant role in horror," underpinning fears based on disorientation in unfamiliar spaces and an accompanying dread of facing uncontrolled animals, both of these anxieties reflect "larger fears of death or the loss of self and humanity that frequently recur in horror" (Tidwell and Soles 2021: 7). Yet, notwithstanding that "many twenty-first-century ecohorror narratives involve animal attacks" (Tidwell and Soles 2021: 2), as Levin (2018: 140) notes, "Of all human deaths each year [in the United States], [nonhuman] animals cause only about 0.008 percent." In fact, an article in *The New York Times* in August 2023, reporting on a shark bite at Rockaway Beach (on the Rockaway Peninsula at the southern edge of the New York City borough of Queens on Long Island, New York) went to great lengths to stress that shark bites in that area are unusual, noting that there had been only twenty *unprovoked* shark attacks in New York State since 1837 and that the biting on August 7, 2023, was the first confirmed shark attack in New York City since the 1950s (Fadulu 2023).[38]

An article from a couple of months earlier might suggest a different story, however. The headline on May 25, 2023, in *USA Today*, the American middle-market daily newspaper, read "Shark Bites Off Leg of 22-Year-Old US

Woman Snorkeling Off Blue Haven Resort in Turks and Caicos" (Thornton 2023). Despite the title of the piece, one soon learns that "the total number of shark attacks around the world is 'extremely low' when considering how many people swim or do activities in the ocean"—that *worldwide* in 2022, there were fifty-seven unprovoked shark bites and thirty-two provoked shark bites (Thornton 2023).[39]

In contrast, Cooper (2023: 5) notes that "at least 120 people are killed every year in deer-vehicle collisions" (see also Martyn 2023), which, he explains, is "far more people than are killed by shark attacks or mountain lions." Nevertheless, "sharks . . . are a popular choice" in ecohorror (Tidwell 2018: 115), and Steven Spielberg's *Jaws* (1975) is often considered *the* "iconic" "'revenge of nature' narrative" (Rust and Soles 2014: 509). Levin (2022: 32) attributes the "fear and panic that [accompanies] shark sightings" to popular culture, stating that "over the past few decades, Hollywood has primed us to think of sharks as cold, emotionless killing machines that prey mercilessly on humans (see: *The Reef, The Shallows, The Meg*, and of course *Jaws, Jaws 2, Jaws 3* . . . the film in which a shark—*which has no vocal cords*—roars, and the inexplicable *Sharknado* franchise, among others)" (emphasis added).

Essentially, a global anxiety about one variety of marine species was generated by a single film portrayal, its plot, and its highly effective music score. As Francis (2012: 59) reminds us, at this time (the mid-1970s), "very little was known about sharks" and the media exploited a new source of public safety anxiety: "The media hype of sharks and shark incidents gave rise to an explosion of shark hunters, shark game fishing, shark tournaments, shark artefact sales and commercial fishing. The result was a plunge in shark populations worldwide"—and an increase in ecohorror films involving sharks.[40] Nevertheless, Levin (2022: 32) reports, one's "chances of being maimed or killed by [a shark] are staggeringly small . . . more human casualties are caused each year by lightning, vending machines, cleaning supplies, window blinds, and Grand Canyon selfies."[41] In fact, Munroe (2022) muses, one does not have to "spend long browsing police blotters" to corroborate that attacks by another marine species—orcas (killer whales), discussed in Chapter 3—are more rare "than documented cases of swimmers being attacked and bitten by *other humans*" (emphasis in original).

Importantly, when nature does present a threat to human existence, the experience can be *revelatory*. In her gripping and stirring story that recounts her near-fatal encounter with a saltwater crocodile, Plumwood (1999: 78, 88, 79) writes that when the crocodile attacked her canoe, "for the first time, it came to me fully that I was prey," followed by the thought, "*This can't be happening to me. I'm a human being, not meat, I don't deserve this fate!*," and only later that "the course and intensity of terminal thought patterns in near-death experiences can tell us much about our frameworks of subjectivity" (emphasis in original; for a discussion, see Hall 2016: 249).[42]

Somewhat similarly, the author Maxim Loskutoff (2018: SR4) recalls hiking along Grinnell Lake on the east side of Glacier National Park in Montana and realizing he and his partner were being stalked by a female grizzly bear—and that the bear wanted to eat them:

> It was a strange epiphany. To be human today is to deny our animal nature, though it's always there, as the earth remains round beneath our feet even when it feels flat. I had always been an animal, and would always be one, but it wasn't until I was prey, my own fur standing on end and certain base-level decisions being made in milliseconds (in a part of my mind that often takes 10 minutes to choose toothpaste in the grocery store), that the meat-and-bone reality settled over me. I was smaller and slower than the bear. My claws were no match for hers. And almost every part of me was edible.

Plumwood's and Loskutoff's experiences notwithstanding, unless one lives and/or works in nature, such as the park ranger encountered by Lostkutoff and his partner while being chased by the bear, it (nature) does not regularly imperil our lives (although this is changing with the increasing frequency of "natural disasters" brought about by human action and inaction; see, e.g., Chester 2020; Faust and Kauzlarich 2008: 99; Foy 2010b 184n11 [citing Achanbach 2008]; Green 2005; Green and Ward 2004; Lundberg 2023; Matczak and Bergh 2023 [citing Mena et al. 2022]; Murray and Heumann 2016: xi, 41).[43]

It seems, however, that such (perceived) threats have long been a theme of tales about the vulnerability of humans to environmental forces, as in flood stories (Spar 2009) and the importance of hunger in folktales (Willsey 2014), as well as in novels from the late Victorian period onward which, as Kneitz (2015: 48) puts it, were "situated within a toxic discourse . . . arising around the issues of sanitary reform" or expressing prescient forms of eco-consciousness (Kennedy 2017).

Mayer (2011: 79–80), for example, explores the "relationship between the human exploitation of nature" and social injustices that was of interest to William Morris in his lectures and essays; in one of which, he "envisioned a world liberated from human dominance," contributing to what Mayer calls the "ecological gothic" and predating ideas of posthumanism. Morris was not alone in probing the darker side of nature; his contemporaries included

Richard Jefferies, whose *After London* (1885) is a "grim portrayal of a future England taken over by the unchecked forces of a wild nature," where the "great watercourses" of the country have been "changed or destroyed by plant growth" and "nature takes its revenge," reducing humans to a "feudal state of existence, divided by conflicts and mired in ignorance and superstition." Today, as Monbiot (2014) notes, television programs boost ratings by demonizing wildlife and present narratives of towns "under siege by hungry predators."[44] These stories both challenge and stimulate the goal of eliminating risk and making the world safe, as well as rendering nature predictable and tame. Monbiot (2014) offers the Western Australian shark cull as an example of an exercise that "appears to be unscientific and counterproductive, a grand act of vandalism that endangers the top predators—already greatly depleted—which sustain the ecosystem of the seas . . . motivated by a desire with which many people can connect: to ensure that nothing untoward ever happens to anyone"—but also "informed by our desire . . . to believe that any remaining hazards presented by the natural world are far more dangerous than they really are." As we have noted already, in Monbiot (2014), a "huge entertainment industry—books, films, games—trades in this manufactured fear. It sells."

Ecohorror

Thus far in this chapter, we have made reference to "ecohorror" but have not yet proffered a definition of the concept or term, nor have we sketched its contours. We do so here.

In her essay for the *Posthuman Glossary*, Tidwell (2018: 115) proposes that if, in general, the horror genre is, at heart, about "fear" and concerned with "what frightens us" and perhaps, even in some sense "exorcising or taming that fear," then "ecohorror" can be defined as "the genre that deals with our fears about the environment." Ulaby (2008) treats "ecohorror" as synonymous with "environmental fright flick." Focusing on ecohorror in cinema, Merchant (2012) declares: "Eco-horror has been around forever, and the premise propelling the genre couldn't be simpler or more primal: man tampers with nature—or worse, *ruins* nature—and nature kicks man's ass" (emphasis in original; see also Keetley 2021: 36n1; Parker 2016: 217). Keetley (2021: 36n1) and Parker (2016: 217) echo Ulaby (2008), but draw on Foy's (2010b: 167, 182) more elaborate description of "ecohorror" films. Here, "fright flicks" are movies in which

> nature turns against humankind due to environmental degradation, pollution, encroachment, nuclear disaster, or a host of other reasons.

As a genre, eco-horror attempts to raise mass consciousness about the very real threats that will face humanity if we are not more environmentally cautious. . . . In the absence of . . . a revolutionary shift in consciousness, eco-horror films serve as a reminder of the nightmarish future that awaits. (Foy 2010b: 167)

Tidwell (2018: 115) acknowledges that ecohorror "grows out of and includes narratives that have been referred to, variously, as *nature horror, creature features*, and *'nature strikes back'* narratives, in which the central narrative is frequently one of some element of the natural world attacking humanity" (emphasis added), but she is careful to emphasize that ecohorror cannot be reduced to just "nature strikes back" narratives. Instead, she points to Rust and Soles (2014), who in their introduction to a cluster of articles on ecohorror published in *ISLE: Interdisciplinary Studies in Literature and Environment*, embrace a more capacious notion of "ecohorror." Noting that "as a literary and cinematic form, ecohorror has thus far been narrowly defined in popular discourse as those instances in texts when nature strikes back against humans as punishment for disruption," Rust and Soles call for "a more expansive definition of ecohorror" that "includes analyses of texts in which humans do horrific things to the natural world, or in which horrific texts and tropes are used to promote ecological awareness, represent ecological crises, or blur human/non-human distinctions more broadly" (2014: 509, 509–10; for a discussion, see Tidwell 2018: 115–16; 2021: 42, 47; Tidwell and Soles 2021: 3). Such ecohorror, they continue, "assumes that environmental disruption is haunting humanity's relationship to the non-human world" (Rust and Soles 2014: 116).[45] This is important, Tidwell (2018: 116) elucidates, because it signifies that ecohorror is not just "a distinct subgenre of horror but . . . an *effect* that may surface within other horror narratives as well" (emphasis added)—and, we might add, in narratives and representations that do not identify (or are not labeled) as "horror."

Drawing on Tidwell (2018) and Rust and Soles (2014), Tidwell and Soles (2021) develop further the ecohorror (sub)genre (although, as we have just mentioned and as we note again later, ecohorror is not solely a *genre*). In "Introduction: Ecohorror in the Anthropocene," the first chapter in their edited volume *Fear and Nature: Ecohorror Studies in the Anthropocene*, they identify "four full-length critical works on ecohorror about creatures and animals" (2018: 8), and it is helpful to examine their discussion of these works.

William Schoell's *Creature Features: Nature Turned Nasty in the Movies* (2008), Tidwell and Soles claim, "provides a clear (if somewhat limited) overview of creature-feature movies" (2021: 8). According to Tidwell and Soles

(2021: 8), Schoell's *Creature Features* is "more descriptive than critical, and his scope is somewhat limited by his focus on 'behemoths (discovered in time-lost worlds or ancient societies and somehow unleashed upon modern civilization) or normal-sized animals such as birds and bears that behave in strange ways'" (quoting Schoell 2008: 1), as well as by Schoell's "unwillingness to include monster movies that he judges as boring or sadistic."

Lee Gambin's *Massacred by Mother Nature: Exploring the Natural Horror Film* (2012), Tidwell and Soles (2021: 8) assert, "sees the revenge-of-nature narrative as central" and thus concentrates "solely on animal horror films," to the exclusion of other types of ecohorror.

Murray and Heumann's *Monstrous Nature: Environment and Horror on the Big Screen* has been discussed already; as Tidwell and Soles (2021: 8) explain, it "focuses solely on film . . . [and] advances the critical conversation about ecohorror and considers a broader range of films (not just animal horror and creature features)." For Tidwell and Soles (2021: 8), Murray and Heumann do not restrict their inquiry to one genre or subgenre, electing instead to include documentary and nonhorror drama films, to "'address a monstrous nature that evolved either deliberately or by accident and [which] incites fear in humanity as both character and audience'" (quoting Murray and Heumann 2016: xiv)—a description with which we agree.

Finally, Dominic Lennard's *Brute Force: Animal Horror Movies* (2019), like Schoell's *Creature Features* and Gambin's *Massacred by Mother Nature*, centers on animal horror and film but does so "in the context of evolutionary psychology" (Tidwell and Soles 2021: 9).

To this list, Tidwell and Soles (2021: 9) add a mention of Maurice Yacowar's chapter, "The Bug in the Rug: Notes on the Disaster Genre" in Barry Keith Grant's *Film Genre III* (2003), which analyzes the "natural attack film" as a subgenre of the disaster film ("the most common disaster film," according to Yacowar 2003: 277) and which subdivides the "natural attack film" into three categories: *attacks by animals* (normal, giant, or otherwise) on a human community; *attacks by the elements* (e.g., earthquakes); and *attacks by atomic mutants*. Tidwell and Soles (2021: 9) then distinguish their own perspective:

> Where Schoell, Gambin, and Lennard focus narrowly on animal horror, we provide a more expansive view of ecohorror; where Murray and Heumann discuss monstrous nature across genres, we maintain a focus on horror (on its own and in conjunction with other genres) and consider not just nature as monstrous but also nature as sympathetic or

as victim; where Yacowar sees these narratives as a subset of the disaster film, we cultivate an approach to ecohorror that emphasizes the *horror* over the disaster and seeks out narratives of more subtle natural horror. Finally, where all these critics attend specifically to film, we put film in conversation with other media, including television, novels, manga, short fiction, and poetry. (emphasis in original)

Tidwell and Soles also note two edited collections that have explored subsets of the ecohorror genre—Katarina Gregersdotter, Johan Höglund, and Nicklas Hållén's *Animal Horror Cinema: Genre, History, and Criticism* (2015) and Dawn Keetley and Angela Tenga's *Plant Horror: Approaches to the Monstrous Vegetal in Fiction and Film* (2016) (from which we draw in this chapter)—in addition to a number of other collections that have contained chapters or sections devoted to ecohorror. Their overall goal in providing such a literature review (and part of the reason that we set aside space to summarize it) is not just to articulate how their work *Fear and Nature: Ecohorror Studies in the Anthropocene* explores "how productive ecohorror as a cross-generic and cross-media mode can be for seeing broad trends and developments in the ways our culture uses media to scare itself with ecological terrors"—by which they mean *Western* culture (we think)—but to stress their desire to illuminate how "ecohorror is not defined only by fear *of* nature but also encompasses fear *for* nature" (2021: 10, 14, emphasis in original). In other words, they submit, "ecohorror is not simply a venue for ecophobia"—and such fears (fear *of* nature and fear *for* nature) can lead us to "multiple outcomes, some prompted by fear for ourselves and some prompted by hope for a different future" (Tidwell and Soles 2021: 14). "Fear for ourselves" connotes a certain anthropocentrism, Tidwell and Soles seem to suggest—a fear of the loss of the status quo—a way of living in which humans value themselves over nonhuman animal life; "hope for a different future" evokes one based on principles of biocentrism or ecocentrism. Because "ecohorror highlights the strangeness and horror of living in the Anthropocene and of engaging in less-than-positive ways with the nonhuman world," Tidwell and Soles (2021b: 14) argue, it "has the potential to reinforce our fears and estrange us from the nonhuman world." The challenge, then, is to use ecohorror not as a means for accentuating and exacerbating extant, prevalent, and persisting feelings of cynicism and defeatism but as a *mode* for promoting and exploring other "'forms of living'" (Tidwell and Soles 2021: 14, quoting Hediger 2018: 157)—other relationships between humans, nonhuman animals, nature, and the environment.

Later in this book, we will return to these concerns about cynicism, defeatism, and self-fulfilling prophecies—as well as to the prospects of/for ecohorror and other dominant modes/tropes/themes to envision different ways of living (and to the role of scholars and students in this regard). For our present purposes, we propose that not all "monstrous nature" is ecohorror because "monstrous nature" appears in other genres, such as in the documentaries analyzed by Murray and Heumann (2016). Does all "ecohorror," then, depict nature as "monstrous"? Not necessarily. In the poetic worlds of Algernon Charles Swinburne, for example, nature is not so much "monstrous" as bleak and barren; Stevenson (2021: 92) points to erosion as "part of what makes the sea's power horrifying and glorious." "A Forsaken Garden" and "By the North Sea," two of Swinburne's seaside poems, serve as "emblems of this horror," Stevenson (2021: 92–93) contends, depicting a "disanthropic ethos"[46]—not a "monstrous nature." Nature *is* quite clearly monstrous in *Treevenge* and *The Ruins*, but it is hard to argue the same in *The Happening* (2008).

What seems clear is that "monstrous nature" and "ecohorror" overlap. For now, the important point is that "ecohorror," like "monstrous nature," "reaches across media (literature, film, etc.) and works with concepts" (Rust and Soles 2014: 510)—as we do in this chapter, with those such as "Gothic" and "ecophobia." What is also significant is that "ecohorror" is not a recent development. Keetley (2021: 23) claims that the "revenge of nature" narrative—"the most common form of ecohorror"—has existed since at least the 1950s.[47] Rust and Soles date the term *ecohorror* to "at least the mid-1990s," but acknowledge that the phenomenon has a longer history. This is also Murphy's (2013: 181) contention. She suggests that American ecohorror has a long record rooted in the ecophobia of "white settlers who set out to create a 'new world' in the midst of a vast, unfamiliar, and often physically treacherous landscape." The reaction was what Crosby (2014: 515) calls a "deadly, compensatory ecophilia" based on the proposition that "if the colonists were going to love their new home, they would do so only by making it like them, and they embarked upon a self-conscious program to transform the 'wilderness' into a 'garden'" (for a discussion, see Kniss 2021; Rust and Soles 2014). This is the stamp of modern rationality on the ancient and wild, which can, as history shows, slide into the human-made monstrous worlds of genocides and ecocides. As Bauman (1989: 92) argued in his analysis of the Holocaust, "Modern culture is a garden culture. It defines itself as a perfect arrangement for human conditions. *It constructs its own identity out of distrust of nature. In fact it defines itself and nature, through its endemic distrust of spontaneity and its longing for a better and necessarily artificial, order*" (emphasis added). Of course, the terrible irony that Bauman reveals is how the aim of tempering or eradicating certain wild and distrusted specimens and forces of nature, constructed and feared as sources of weakness or disease, can result in unspeakable terror and evil more real and devastating than any imagined or ideologically conceived threat. Bauman's analogy helps us to glimpse the impulse of order and control that has tried to reinterpret both nature and humanity in an ordered, hierarchical, understandable way. As noted earlier, however, nature responds or, as some would say, it "fights back."

Nature and the oppressed can engage in "reverse colonization," or at least that is a fear underpinning the anxieties of conquerors of lands and builders of empires. Mayer (2011: 85 [quoting Arata 1990: 623]) describes this "terrifying reversal" as one in which "the colonizer finds himself in the position of the colonized" (which, one could argue, is what unfolds in *The Ruins*, in which carnivorous vines devour American and German tourists visiting an ancient Mayan ruin in Mexico). The cause of such change may be alien forces (terrestrial or other) or, as in the novel *After London,* may be a result of "monstrous forces" that "do not come from abroad but emerge, quite literally, from native soil" (Mayer 2011: 85). Discussing ecohorror in Australian genre cinema, Simpson (2010) is also interested in the resilience and resistance of animals and plants threatened by extinction, and hence in how certain films can be exploitative yet also signal important ecological and social issues. Using an "eco-postcolonial framework," Simpson (2010: 44–45) argues that "in their attitudes to foreigners, tourists and/or trespassers as 'prey,' these films extend postcolonial anxieties over settler Australian notions of belonging" and challenge "the notion of human mastery over nature." Simpson (2010: 45) also discusses the "new nature": "a cultural shift whereby animals have an uncanny knack of adapting and hybridizing in order to survive and sometimes even thrive. As such, they (the films and the animals) force us to acknowledge more culturally plural forms of being." Similarly, there are ways in which there has been a cultural pluralization of ways of *perceiving* nature; as Clark (2014: 64) puts it, in "our globalized culture . . . myths once limited to a single national reality can now enrich the understanding of our broader multicultural society." According to Clark (2014: 64), "The old notion of the power of nature as sacred, which commonly appears in third world and native American films, is now entering mainstream films in the US, such as *Star Wars* (1977–2015), *Lord of the Rings* (2001–3), *Avatar* (2009), *Shrek* (2001–2010), *Gravity* (2013), *Mama* (2013), and *Maleficent* (2014)."

The violation of nature as something (or *someone*) that is sacred is then represented in various ways. In response to the rape of nature (e.g., Collard and Contrucci 1989; Daly 1978) and the trauma of that which has been stolen, expunged, or overwritten, nature fights back against the colonizers and takes over (Mayer 2011) or else makes its wounded presence felt by appearing as spectral atmospheres and landscapes, even if only "imagined and felt as absent" but nonetheless haunting the present as polluted, barren, treacherous, and unsafe (Frosh 2013: 54; see also Fiddler 2019).

Nature, Hauntings, and the Gothic in Latin American and Caribbean Literature

Early in her monograph *Monsters, Catastrophes and the Anthropocene: A Postcolonial Critique*, Giuliani (2021: 8) makes clear that "at the core of [her] work is the epistemological assumption that all knowledge production is situated, as it reflects not only the socio-historical, geographical and cultural context in which it is produced but also and more importantly the social 'location' of the producer"—an epistemology that she describes as "grounded in a 'politics of location' (Rich 1987; Haraway 1988)." Thus, in contemplating nature, hauntings, and the Gothic in literature outside of our "social 'location,'" we do so cautiously and tentatively, as we have elsewhere (see Brisman and South 2020, 2022)—in the hopes of inviting and learning from similar inquiries pursued by those with greater expertise.

"For many," writes Byron (2012: 370), "there is a concern that identifying and reading" Latin American and Caribbean texts as Gothic is "a kind of colonial imposition" and the roots of "the Gothic" are, indeed, of course, part of an external and imported European tradition. Yet perhaps critics overprivilege the European Gothic. Common to all of these traditions is a revitalization of universal cultural tales and experiences rooted in the rise and fall of the sun and moon, reborn every day and night (Hertz 1960), the decomposition of animal and plant bodies that feed and fertilize other organisms, and the reanimation of the dead, which features in epics of the imagination as far back as the Sumerian epic poem of Gilgamesh, dating from approximately 2700–2500 BCE (Nugent et al. 2018). It should not be surprising, then, that Gothic moods and motifs merge easily with the "fantastic" in Latin American art and literature. Ordiz and Casanova-Vizcaíno (2018: 1) make this point by drawing on the work of the Argentine writer Maria Negroni (2009: 9), who suggests that "what has thus far been defined as fantastic literature in Latin America is, in fact, Gothic literature"—which Negroni describes as "nocturnal and feverish" and of an "unruly and chaotic nature." On this basis, according to Negroni (2009: 9), it is possible to "read" various Latin American writers and poets as "Gothic authors whose *oeuvre* reshapes Latin

American fantastic fiction and creates a new form that defies the 'prisons of reason and of common sense.'"

The idea of haunted nature or landscapes (Heholt and Downing 2016) can, as Lloyd (2018: 3) suggests, help to illuminate the complexity of "interaction between the landscape and the human." This can require appreciation of engagements between the two that range from the mundane to the "supernatural" or "super natural" (Morton 2010: 45). In Latin American Gothic film, literature, and media, ghosts, monsters, and the undead appear in various guises and with various purposes (Casanova-Vizcaíno and Ordiz 2018), but prominent among these are roles as representatives of fantasy, legends, and nightmares that aim to fascinate and repel. Indeed, they are products of anxieties—of attempts to impose control over uncontrollable forces (death, human resistance, nature)—but they may also often represent political critique. This is not unique to the Latin American Gothic and throughout this literature, stories that involve "the Gothic"—ghosts and magical realism—give voices to the silenced and can provide reflection and judgment on past and present (Armitt 2014). As Buell and colleagues argue (2011: 418), "By themselves, creative"—or, we might add, *critical*—"depictions of environmental harm are unlikely to free societies from lifestyles that depend on radically transforming ecosystems. But reflecting on works of imagination may prompt intensified concern about the consequences of such choices and possible alternatives to them." This can be accomplished in many forms of literary, oral, and visual storytelling, as well as in the kind of critical approaches that could be applied to the exploration of various troubled landscapes, such as "landscape studies, affect theory, psycho-geography, eco-criticism, history, memory studies, literary studies, film studies, folklore, trauma studies, and postcolonial theory," and connections to environmental injustice (Heholt 2016: 2).

Abjection and the Fragile State
of Human/Nonhuman Relations

In their discussion of "Gothic Nature," Parker and Poland (2019: 1) remark that in "the cultural imagination, Nature has always engendered fear, wonder, and fascination." Gothic writers engage with "our imagined fears of the nonhuman world: Nature is consistently constructed in our stories as Other, excessive, unpredictable, disruptive, chaotic, enticing, supernaturally powerful, and, perhaps most disturbingly, *alive*. It importantly threatens our very definitions of 'humanness'" (Parker and Poland 2019: 1, emphasis in original). At the same time, other "sinister and unsettling" forces and events are shaping our lives and planet, "from climate crisis and collapsing permafrost to mass extinction and microplastics inhabiting our bodies, Gothic depictions of Nature seem to have slipped, uninvited, into reality while we were busy making other plans." Monstrous illustrations of nature reflect humanity's monstrous *treatment* of nature, which has led nonhuman species to the brink of extinction and continues to wreak ecocidal destruction on our atmosphere, forests, landscapes, oceans, and seas—and the planet as a whole (Higgins et al. 2013; South 2010; Whyte 2020; see generally Tidwell 2021: 46). This ecocide is, in part, a product of modern scientific rationalism and market neo-liberalism, and a perpetuation of what Horkheimer and Adorno (2002: 193, cited in Deckard 2013) identified as one outcome of the Enlightenment—"a duality between externalized nature and internal human nature" that has served to "rationalize human domination of the material world" but that has also threatened "an eventual revolt of nature." There may be many reasons for this. Lostufkoff (2018: SR4) quotes the anthropologist Clifford Geertz's famous aphorism, "Man is an animal suspended in webs of significance that he himself has spun," and then reflects on how on "most days, [he] remain[s] fully entangled in this web, cursing at [his] smartphone while rolling across the earth in 4,000 pounds of steel." For Watson (2015: 275), the "human social order" has separated "itself from its fellow animals through a . . . process of abjection, denying subject status to nonhumans. To abject is to '*separate, reject, abject,*' to eject, . . . to throw," a topic we discuss further in Chapter 3.

3

The Abjection of the Earth

The opening of *Alien Resurrection* (1997), the fourth installment of the *Alien* franchise, begins with a voiceover by Ellen Louise Ripley (often known simply as "Ripley" and played by Sigourney Weaver): "My mommy always said there were no monsters. No real ones. But there are"—and, as Ripley discovers, monsters do exist. She meets the fictional endoparasitoid extraterrestrial species for the first time in *Alien* (1979) and encounters them again in *Aliens* (1986), *Alien³* (1992) and finally, sort of, in *Alien Resurrection* (1997)—some two hundred years after her death in the third movie.

In the previous chapter, we noted Keetley's (2021: 25) notion of "tentacular ecohorror," which is "structured first by an encounter with a recalcitrantly alien form of life and second by a character's becoming enmeshed with that life" (for a discussion, see Tidwell 2021: 59). In fact, this is pretty much exactly what happens to Ripley: in *Alien Resurrection*, "United Systems Military" elects to clone her for the purpose of retrieving the alien queen embryo that erupts from her chest in *Alien³*. The alien queen subsequently gives birth to a creature possessing both human and alien traits; the creature rejects the alien queen and embraces the cloned Ripley as its mother. Ripley learns not only that monsters are "real," but that they are our own creation[1]—a point we attempted to illustrate in the previous chapter and to which we return in Chapter 5.

Linnemann (2022: 16) contends that "monsters by definition are abject; their unnatural bodies and behaviors transgress and thus reveal and reaffirm the categorical boundaries of the natural order." As we shall explain, that which is abject (such as menstrual blood or excrement) is *rejected* or cast off.

In order to create an identity, Kristeva (1982: 32) submits, we must abject the maternal—the "object" (indeed, the *first* "object") that/who has created us (see, e.g., Arya and Chare 2016: 1; Watson 2015). In *Alien Resurrection*, the newborn kills the alien queen (its mother), but in an interesting twist on Kristevian psychoanalytics, Ripley (whom the newborn considers to be her mother) kills the newborn. At the end of *Alien Resurrection*, when the survivors (including the cloned version of Ripley) enter Earth's atmosphere and realize that they will be landing on the planet, Johner (played by Ron Perlman) quips, "Earth, man. What a shithole"—a declaration of *the planet* as abject.

It seems appropriate to begin this chapter by talking about aliens because, as we described in the previous chapter, "the view of humans as *outside of* and *alien to* nature seems to be especially strongly a Western one" (Plumwood 1991: 10, emphasis added). Indeed—and as we attempted to articulate in that chapter—in contrast, say, to the perspective of Australian aborigines (see Plumwood 1999), the "strong human/nature dualism" in Western thought (Plumwood 1991: 10) has contributed to the notion and treatment of nature as "monstrous."[2] In this dualism, which has been stressed in the rationalist tradition, "what is characteristically and authentically human is defined against or in opposition to what is taken to be natural, nature, or the physical or biological realm" (Plumwood 1991: 10). The preservation and continuation of such "sharp dichotomy and polarization," Plumwood (1991: 10) explains, "is achieved by the rejection of what links humans to the animal." She continues:

> What is taken to be authentically and characteristically human, defining of the human, as well as the ideal for which humans should strive is *not* to be found in what is shared with the natural and animal (e.g., the body, sexuality, reproduction, emotionality, the senses, agency) but in what is thought to separate and distinguish them—especially reason and its offshoots. Hence humanity is defined not as part of nature . . . but as separate from and in opposition to it. Thus the relation of humans to nature is treated as . . . oppositional. (Plumwood 1991: 10–11, emphasis in original)

Watson (2015: 275) puts it in more barbed terms: "The human social order . . . separates itself from its fellow animals through a . . . process of abjection." In this chapter, we focus not on the abjection of nonhuman life but on the idea of the Earth, as a whole (or parts of it), as abject. We begin with an overview of the concept of abjection and representations thereof before turning to how some are responding to this abjection.

Conceptions of Abjection

As noted in Chapter 1 and at the end of the previous chapter, abjection refers to something that is rejected. Before proceeding further—and just as we considered the etymology of *monster* in Chapter 1—we find it helpful to note the derivation and meaning of the word *abjection*. Arya and Chare (2016: 1), in their introduction to their edited volume, *Abject Visions: Powers of Horror in Art and Visual Culture*, offer the following:

> "Abjection" is a word with a long history in the English language. . . . Its use is traced back to the fifteenth century. At that time, some-one who had been brought low, rendered despondent or dejected for whatever reason, was referred to as abject. The term assumed its more familiar meaning of being degraded or despicable in the sixteenth century. Its etymological roots are to be found in the Latin word *abicere* meaning to cast away or rebuff.

Hook (2012: 68) echoes this origin story: "The literal meaning of abjection (in Latin *ab-jicere*) is to cast off, to repulse."[3] When one speaks of "the abject," Hook (2012: 68) explains, "one refers to the contemptible, the repugnant, the wretched, that which is unwanted, unclean, viewed as contaminating." (This is how we intend to use the term.) As Hook (2012: 68) expounds further, "*Abjection*, then, as a verb should be understood as an operation: the powerful visceral reaction toward a given object that is then denigrated, reviled." (To this we ask, "Is this how we view nature? The environment? The Earth?" We consider that shortly, but as we attempt to put forth, it surely has seemed that way—or, at least, it certainly appears that we [or some of us] see the Earth [or parts of it] as vile.) Hook (2012: 68) maintains that "the *abject*, . . . as a noun, should be understood as the apparent source of such reactions; abhorrent, sickening, it elicits fear, moral repugnance, and is known by the physical responses, the palpable anxieties, it elicits. To be *abjected* . . . is the condition of *being made abject*" (emphasis in original)—which is what we argue is happening to the planet: the Earth is "being made abject." As Hook (2012: 68) continues—and this, we feel, is perhaps most integral to our contention later—"abjection, as both process and condition, occurs in unison with, and as means of recapitulating the existing social order."

Quoting Herbst (1999: 16), Hook (2012: 69) writes:

> The process of abject*ing* [an operation] . . . is an active one in which one party rejects, banishes, degrades or in some way denigrates another

party; the state of *being* abject [a condition] . . . is what follows an act of abjection: it is a disposition, a place of exclusion. . . . Without exception, the party that does the abjecting is the one in a position of power . . . while the one degraded is robbed of power and the right to societal inclusion. (emphasis in original; insertions by Hook)

Hook's (2012) reliance on Herbst (1999) for the purpose of differentiating "processes" from "states" and "conditions" is useful, but his subsequent attempt at disciplinary distinctions is less so: Hook claims that "the interchange between psychoanalytic and anthropological notions . . . is instructive." Hook (2012: 69) then leans on Butler (1990: 169), who, in turn, draws on Kristeva (1982), to argue that "the abject" is "that which has been expelled from the body, discharged as excrement, literally rendered 'Other.'" Turning next to Douglas's ([1966] 2002) *Purity and Danger: An Analysis of Concepts of Pollution and Taboo*, Hook (2012: 69) asserts that for Douglas, "the irrationality of such compulsive exclusions is enacted at the societal and symbolic level, in the form of ritualized practices, rites of cleansing and avoidance, which, importantly, are never merely practical—adequately explained away, that is, by reasons of hygiene or health—and that bring to bear the full force of social taboo." Hook (2012: 69) suggests the following:

> It is the political dimension of such a response that Butler (1993) insists upon when she refers to abjection as an "operation of repulsion". A form of both recoil and response, repugnance and reflection, abjection, it should be remembered, is always activity, *action* as much as it is revulsion. Self-protection, or escape, is immanent in the subject who experiences the "border-anxiety" of abjection; there is immediate recourse to offensive action, indeed, to violent forms of response—even if primarily symbolic or psychological—that will keep the source of abjection at bay.[4]

It appears as if Hook is trying to distinguish a psychoanalytic conception of abjection (that of Kristeva) from an anthropological one (that of Douglas) to then tease out a political reading (via Butler).[5] This seems rather circuitous. In twentieth-century thought, abjection is often associated with either the psychoanalytical (or semiotic-psychoanalytical) account of Kristeva (1982) in *Powers of Horror: An Essay on Abjection* or the more socio-political orientation of Bataille ([1934] 1993) in "Abjection and Miserable Forms." Of the two, the Kristevian notion of abjection tends to have received more attention (see, e.g., Arya and Chare 2016: 1), although Bataille's essay predates Kristeva's.[6]

Given that Hook titles the second chapter of his book "Abjection as a *Political* Factor: Racism and the 'Extra-Discursive'" (our emphasis), it seems odd that he makes no reference to Bataille. Perhaps Hook relies on Kristeva because her writing on abjection is better known? Maybe Hook leans on Kristeva because his concern, as noted earlier, is really with racism, apartheid, and post-apartheid South Africa, which he examines through the lens of post-colonial thinkers such as Steve Biko and Frantz Fanon in order to promulgate a critical psychoanalytic postcolonial theory of racism?[7] Whatever the case may be, we find profit in both approaches.

Writing during Hitler's rise to power in the 1930s in Europe, Bataille ([1934] 1993: 9) focuses on the subversion by sovereign rulers (the "oppressors") of the freedoms of "the wretched population" ("the oppressed"). For Bataille ([1934] 1993: 9), "the imperative forces do not exercise their coercive action directly on the oppressed: they content themselves with excluding them by prohibiting any contact" with "the Other."[8] As Bataille ([1934] 1993: 9) contends, "The basic element of subversion, th[is] wretched population, exploited for production and cut off from life by [the aforementioned] prohibition on contact[,] is represented from outside with disgust [at] the dregs of the people, populace and *gutter*" (emphasis added). Bataille ([1934] 1993: 10) submits that "the deep rip which opposes the various aspects of existence is further revealed in the ambiguity of the word *miserable*" (emphasis in original), and the word, *miserable*, which used to evoke *pity*, "has now become a synonym for abject: it has stopped hypocritically soliciting pity for cynically demanding aversion."[9] "This last word," Bataille ([1934] 1993: 10) maintains,

> expresses an anger shattered by disgust and reduced to mute horror: it implies an attitude ruled by feelings of distress or excessive grandeur whose sadness is associated with wider human value. It thus appears situated at the confluence of the multiple contradictory impulses required by the aimless existence of human refuse.

This is significant, Bataille ([1934] 1993: 10) continues, because

> in the collective expression, *the misérables*, the conscience of affliction already veers from its purely negative direction and begins to pose itself *as a threat* [our emphasis]. All the same, in principle, no positive attitude nor any active leaning justifies the exclusion which ejects the victims of misery outside the oral community. In other words, misery does not engage the will and disgusts . . . both those who experience

it and those who avoid it: it is lived exclusively as impotence and does not leave any possibility of affirmation whatsoever.

What this means, Hennefeld and Sammond (2020: 3) explain, is that "for Bataille, it simply does not matter if the individual ego has the will to cast out certain gross or reviled matter"; rather, "abjection is imposed on the social body by the sovereign imperative, regardless of one's developmental bodily discipline."[10] Essentially, for Bataille ([1934] 1993), as well as for Lotringer (2020),

> abjection is not simply constitutive of culture through the individual, but also derives from and contributes to larger operations of sovereign subjectivation and social immiseration. For any oppressive ruling class to understand itself as justly sovereign, it must find its abject Other among the masses of the oppressed, and thereby demarcate the filth and decay from which it is inherently different (yet to which it is necessarily related), through means that are seemingly benign but manifestly cruel. (Hennefeld and Sammond 2020: 20)

This idea of the "oppressive ruling class . . . understand[ing] itself" through the *objectification* and *abjectification* of the masses of the "wretched population" foreshadows—and brings us back to—Fanon. As Varghese (2020: 5) explains, for Fanon ([1952] 2008: 104), "the 'lived experience' of someone constituted as 'black' is always mediated by a 'white' other . . . there is no black essence because the 'Negro experience is not a whole, for there is not merely *one* Negro, there are *Negroes*'" (emphasis in original). This "dialectical relationship" has been manifest throughout history: between Black and White, between colonizer and colonized, and, as Varghese (2020) argues, between Palestinian and Jew. Whereas for Fanon ([1952] 2008: 7), "not only must the black man be black; he must be black *in relation to* the white man" (emphasis added), for Varghese (2020: 7), "not only must the Palestinian be 'Palestinian,' he or she must be 'Palestinian' in relation to the Israeli Jew."

Essentially, for Bataille and his intellectual lineage, the emphasis is on "the politics of the social," rather than "the psychic training of the ego"— on "the sovereign imperative that excludes wretched social masses . . . in constant threat of collapse," not "the self-disciplining subject who reviles gross bodies" (Hennefeld and Sammond 2020: 2). In comparison, Kristeva's "semiotic-psychoanalytic account of the abject—that unbearable excess that the ego will always scramble to reject—primarily concerns issues of subject formation, particularly the negotiation of boundaries between the child and its mother" (Hennefeld and Sammond 2020: 2).[11] The body, then—that is, the *individual body*, rather than *bodies* (in the plural) or *people* or the *body politic*—is of central importance to Kristeva's notion of abjection (see Hook 2012: 60; Watson 2015: 270)—"dead bodies; spoiled food; or bodily fluids are all abject" (Fredriksson 2019: 263). As Kristeva writes, "Food loathing is perhaps the most elementary and most archaic form of abjection" (1982: 2), and a few pages later, "the corpse . . . is the utmost of abjection. It is death infecting life. Abject. It is something rejected from which one does not part, from which one does not protect oneself as from an object. Imaginary uncanniness and real threat, it beckons to us and ends up engulfing us" (1982: 4; for a discussion, see Hall 2016: 245).[12] But, as Kristeva (1982: 4) explains,

> It is thus not lack of cleanliness or health that causes abjection but what disturbs identity, system, order. What does not respect borders, positions, rules. The in-between, the ambiguous, the composite. The traitor, the liar, the criminal with a good conscience, the shameless rapist, the killer who claims he is a savior. . . . Any crime, because it draws attention to the fragility of the law, is abject, but premeditated crime, cunning murder, hypocritical revenge are even more so because they heighten the display of such fragility.[13]

Our goal here is not to delve deeply into Bataille's and Kristeva's work, nor to offer an intellectual history of abjection. Nor, too, do we wish to make broad claims about which perspective(s) on abjection are more/most salient. Rather, just as abjection has been used constructively to explore and explain practices of power, subjugation, and resistance in Britain (Tyler 2013) and the West Bank (Varghese), as well as to understand narratives surrounding gender-based violence in Sweden (Skott et al. 2021),[14] we concur with Hennefeld and Sammond (2020: 27) that abjection can function as a productive heuristic. To this end—and drawing on the theoretical orientations of both Bataille and Kristeva summarized earlier—we are interested in what we refer to as a kind of "double abjection." By this, we mean—and wish to interrogate—the way(s) in which the "super-rich" or "ultra-wealthy stakeholders" (Rushkoff 2022a) or "UHNWIs" ("ultra-high-net-worth individuals")[15]—both degrade the Earth with their carbon-intensive lifestyles (see Solnit 2023), earning them the moniker of "the polluter elite" (Watts 2023), and then abject what has been abjected—that is, reject the parts of the Earth that are impure (and, with it, those who reside there).[16]

Representations of the Earth as Abject

Giuliani (2021: 9) submits that "since early Modernity, ideas of *monsters* and *catastrophes* as external beings and events have been reinforced by the assumption that Europe and the West are isolated, under attack and faced with a threat coming from what is perceived to be an *incommensurable* and *ontologically dangerous* outside" (emphasis in original). Giuliani's goal here, and throughout her book, is to document and then challenge mainstream descriptions and depictions of migration as an "invasion"—indeed, a "*monstrous invasion*" (2021: 16, 29, emphasis in original). To this end, she points to how "migrant landings on Europe's southern shores are often represented as *alien* invasions requiring military force (as in the case of the Hungarian-Serbian, Turkish-Greek and Croatian-Bosnian Herzegovinian borders)" (emphasis in original), and how "this same iconography is allegorically rendered in . . . films, [with] the figures of the hungry, angry and bloodthirsty terrorist alien" (2021: 14).[17]

For Fredriksson (2019: 264), "the abject frightens because it disrespects borders and thus threatens individual, collective or national identity. . . . the abject is ejected in a process of boundary maintenance meant to protect identity"—and resources![18] Indeed, as Tyler (2013: 9) insists, migrants and other "figurative scapegoats" that she refers to as "national abjects" are "imagined to be a parasitical drain and threat to scarce national resources." To return to Giuliani's point about iconography and allegory (although Panofsky [1972] might refer to this as *iconological interpretation* rather than *iconographical analysis*), the aliens who attack Earth in *Battle: Los Angeles* (2011)[19] could be read as "leech-like bodies" (Tyler 2013: 27) that "rob the state of its vital resources" (Varghese 2020: 3) or vampiric migrants (to revisit our analysis in Chapter 2). A closer, more careful, more *critical* reading, however, would consider the following excerpt from the film:

MAN 1: Chief, do we have any idea why this is happening?
MAN 2: Well, it's clear there has been no attempt at any kind of communication.
MAN 2: No demands, nothing like that.
MAN 2: So, obviously, they are here for our resources.
MAN 2: When you invade a place for resources, you wipe out the Indigenous population.
MAN 2: Those are the rules of any colonisation.
MAN 2: And right now, we are being colonised.[20]

What is revealing about this exchange is that through a more critical lens, we can understand how it reflects Western expansion/global capitalist history. The aliens are not the "national abjects" of which Tyler (or Giuliani or Varghese [2020: 3, 4, 7, 10, 16]) speaks but the Western/Global Northern *us*. *We* are the ones who have invaded (other countries/nations/places) for resources, wiped out Indigenous populations, and colonized their lands. Indeed, as science writer Marc Kaufman, author of *First Contact: Scientific Breakthroughs in the Hunt for Life Beyond Earth* (2011), reminds us, "the history of powerful beings is that when they find others who perhaps aren't as powerful, they come and exterminate them," such as "when Europeans came to North America and elsewhere" (quoted in Davies 2011; for a discussion, see Brisman 2015: 301). Perhaps, then, this might explain why there are fewer representations of aliens invading Earth *for its natural resources* than for other reasons? Exceptions do exist: *Battlefield Earth* (2000)—based on the 1982 science fiction novel by L. Ron Hubbard, the founder of Scientology—set in the year 3000 C.E., in which the "Psychlos," an alien race, rule the Earth, stripping the planet of its gold (see Brisman 2015); *Independence Day* (1996), where the aliens invade planet after planet, consuming its (unspecified) natural resources before moving on (although the assumption is that Earth is one of many planets to encounter such a fate); "To Serve Man" (1962), the twenty-fourth episode of the third season of the television series *The Twilight Zone* (eighty-ninth episode overall), where the Kanamits, a giant species of aliens, land on Earth, ostensibly to offer their advanced technology to halt energy and food shortages and prevent human-made disasters and international conflict but who, in the end, are revealed to be interested in humans solely as a source of food.[21] Such instances or depictions aside, often, the aliens' goal is to *conquer*.[22] Essentially, in many science fiction representations, Earth is not portrayed as *desirable* for other (alien) species; rather, it is represented as *abject*—for *some of* us, that is, and caused *by* us.

Consider *Elysium* (2013), written, produced, and directed by Neill Blomkamp, in which "the divide between rich and poor has been actualized in space—literally" (Biello 2013). *Elysium* is set in the year 2154, when the Earth has become a destitute, dry, dusty, desertified, and polluted "environmental disaster" (Murray and Heumann 2016: 174)—a "Third World slum," as Smith (2013: 39) puts it, albeit without any consideration that the designation, "Third World," is now considered confusing, insulting, and outdated (see, e.g., Silver 2015, 2021; see also Kloß 2017; Patrick and Huggins 2023; compare Muni 1979, Wolf-Phillips 1987, and Litonjua 2014 with Tomlinson 2003: 308 and Haug et al. 2021: 1937n12). "The wealthy," as Smith (2013: 39) continues, "have long since departed, inhabiting an exclusive paradise called Elysium"—a "space station . . . of vaguely Mediterranean villas and rich (mostly) white people," in Bould's (2021: 57) words. Whereas on the "overpopulated and environmentally trashed Earth" (Biello 2013), the poor must contend with crime, starvation, violence, disease, and a lack of adequate medical care (Biello 2013; Giuliani 2021: 173, 182; Mirrlees and Pedersen 2016: 309; Smith 2013: 39), on Elysium—"an exclusive, luxurious and securitized gated community in space for the propertied rich" (Mirrlees and Pedersen 2016: 309)—the wealthy enjoy "advanced medical technology" which can "heal[] any ailment, from a hangnail to terminal cancer, in seconds" (Smith 2013: 39). As Mirrlees and Pedersen (2016: 310) describe, "on Elysium, the minority rich live healthy, happy and extended lives. They each own a private Med-Bay, an automated total health care machine that in addition to curing any disease and injury, can reverse the aging process and give their users reconstructed bodies and faces." Essentially, for the working class in "*favela*-ised Los Angeles" (Bould 2021: 57), the "garbage-strewn, poverty-stricken Earth" (Hiscock 2013) is "a neo-liberal dystopia of immiseration" (Mirrlees and Pedersen 2016: 310). For the "propertied elite" or "owning class" or "ruling class," Elysium is "a neo-liberal utopia of leisure, abundance and customer service" (Mirrlees and Pedersen 2016: 305, 309, 310)—"a lavish neighborhood in outer space" (Metz 2013) replete with "forests, green lawns, golf courses, and oversized homes" (Murray and Heumann 2016: 174).

The plot centers on Max Da Costa (Matt Damon), a parolee toiling on Earth for the Armadyne Corporation, "who must assemble the [very] security droids that the ruling class Elysians use to monitor and coerce him and other earthlings inside and outside the workplace" (Mirrlees and Pedersen 2016: 310). When Max is given the choice between entering a droid assembly chamber to fix a malfunction and keep production flowing (and Elysian shareholders happy) or risk losing his job, he (reluctantly) picks the former but is accidentally exposed to radiation. Told that he has received a lethal dose and has five days to live, Max realizes that the only way he will survive is if he can reach Elysium and make use of its Med-Bays. Unfortunately for Max, Giuliani (2021: 173) explains, "Earth's inhabitants are not allowed to enter Elysium. They are considered illegal immigrants and are routinely shot by the officers headed by Defense Secretary [Jessica] Delacourt (Jodie Foster) when their small spaceships approach the border"—something that, Giuliani (2021: 173) reminds us, "happens on many other borders around the world."

Max encounters Spider (Wagner Moura), a hacker who runs covert flights to Elysium for a price. Because Max cannot pay Spider, the two strike a deal: if Max can steal vital information, Spider will provide him with a ride to

Elysium. To assist Max in his quest (and because of his declining health due to the irradiation), Spider equips Max with an exoskeleton suit that increases his strength and stamina. For some commentators, it is this feature that makes the film compelling, with Murray and Heumann (2016: 175) noting that "despite the film's failure to address environmental racism and justice issues on Earth, *Elysium* provides an optimistic view of technology and . . . demonstrates how humans (especially men) may benefit from merging with technology."[23] Mirrlees and Pedersen (2016: 314) adopt more of a Marxist reading of *Elysium* than a transhumanist one, contending that in the film,

> the ownership, control and use of [various] innovations . . . secur[e] the interests of the already powerful. Brain-computer interfaces are used . . . to protect . . . intellectual property and financial secrets from earth's hackers; biometric surveillance maintains class divisions between Elysian citizens and earthly non-citizens; robots and drones are deployed [by] the Elysian state to monitor, police and sometimes kill the working poor; exoskeletons [more advanced than the one implanted into Max] are worn by the state's mercenaries . . . to enhance their power to kill rebellious and insurgent earthlings. In *Elysium*, technology is largely part of Elysium's power structure; the class divide between Elysium and Earth is expressed and sustained through a technological divide between Elysian rulers and earthly workers.

More important for our purposes is their argument that *"Elysium* highlights capitalism's ecological catastrophe" (Mirrlees and Pedersen 2016: 313). As they explain,

> The film's opening . . . visually tours viewers around Los Angeles 2154, showing them one giant sprawl of interconnected barrios interlaced with burning pits of garbage that spew smoke into the smog of an ozone depleted atmosphere. Skyscrapers and condominiums and apartments crumble, are stained with soot and overgrown with algae. Their dilapidated facades boast mangled remnants of advertisements for beauty products – perhaps relics from an earlier time when planned obsolescence was normal. As the camera shows us this ecological catastrophe, captions tell us what the planet has become: "In the late 21st century, Earth was diseased, polluted and vastly overpopulated." The planet has become this because the Elysian rulers transformed it into a factory for extracting value from nature and people in order to produce commodities for themselves, and then, upon realizing it was no longer

hospitable and habitable, they took flight to their "bell air in space" [*sic*], building and maintaining it by continuing to dominate earth's nature and workers. By depicting a future in which capitalism and the class system persists in spite of the earthly ecological and human catastrophe they cause, *Elysium* suggests that current neo-liberal solutions to our world's really present ecological problems (i.e.[,] the greening of markets plus eco-friendly technologies) are ineffective. By showing the ruling class insulating itself in outer space from the catastrophe of a destroyed planet and doing nothing to ameliorate capitalism's worst effects, *Elysium* suggests that capitalism negates environmental and human needs. (Mirrlees and Pedersen 2016: 313)

Similarly, although more succinctly, Giuliani (2021: 182, 206) states that "*Elysium*'s social critique [is that] the masses are left behind on desertified, polluted, violence-ridden Earth, while the chosen few live on a gigantic space habitat," and that "if you are given a chance at living on" the orbiting space station of Elysium, "you need to forget the ones you left behind in a dying Earth"—an *abject* Earth!—"and treat them as monsters endangering the well-being of the best among humankind." For Giuliani (2021: 16), *Elysium*, like *Code 46* (2003) and the Netflix television series *3%* (2016), "envision[s] new colonies, segregated spaces and carceral archipelagos that bear some resemblance to present-day *dispositifs*." All three (*Code 46*, *Elysium*, and *3%*), Giuliani (2021: 16) puts forward, are "*apparently* futuristic, but not really so" (emphasis added) because they possess "an uncanny correspondence with the real world"—an observation that resonates with Metz's (2013) claim that "with the growing gap between the rich and the poor at home and abroad, as well as major environmental change taking place, we are living in a real world that looks a lot like *Elysium*." This appears to be the point. When asked about his predictions for the future and what will transpire in 140 years, Blomkamp responded, "This isn't science fiction. This is today. This is now" (quoted in Smith 2013: 40).[24] All that is missing, Metz (2013) adds, is "space real estate." But as noted in the previous section, this may not be that far off—with the Jeff Bezoses and Elon Musks and other such (U)HNWIs responding to, demonstrating, and contributing to (indeed, *bringing about*) the abjection of the Earth with their "out of hand . . . bunker-fever" (Mahdawi 2024)—their fortresses and private islands and seasteading (see, e.g., Barba 2024; Garrett 2022; Jacob 2022; McClure 2022; O'Connell 2020, Rushkoff 2022a, 2022b, 2023; Schmidt 2024; Scrimgeour 2023; Shead 2021; Stone 2015)—as they work toward realizing their Elysium. We unpack this later, but first, an admission or a clarification.

What Do We Mean When We Say
"We" and "They"?

"We" are living in a time of monsters and catastrophes, as if propelled into a never-ending dystopian loop. The *finis mundi* is getting closer and closer and gradually becoming the only lens through which Europe and the West give meaning to "our" time. "We" fear invasions, a permanent state of terror and the ultimate environmental catastrophe—"our world" overflowing with chaos threatening the order that guarantees our safety, well-being, sustainability and progress. As in Saint John's apocalypse, the end of the world as "we" know it will erase Time and Space and irremediably harm the human body, bring back the unbounded violence that had been expelled from the space of reason. What is in danger is the very essence of *humans*, who are left unprotected and exposed to barbarity, epidemics and natural disasters against which borders, walls, colonies, segregated spaces, thicker identities and martial laws need putting in place: we will do all it takes to stop the spread of chaos and keep it "outside," even if it means sacrificing some for the good of many. Some are already paying the highest price, but it cannot be helped—their own lack of knowledge makes them vulnerable to disaster. If we manage to keep at a safe distance from toxic waste, viruses, environmental pollution, wars and other harmful effects of the same neoliberal capitalism we benefit from, the best of humanity will be safe.

So begins Gaia Giuliani in the introduction to her book *Monsters, Catastrophes and the Anthropocene: A Postcolonial Critique* (2021: 1). There is a lot to unpack in those opening sentences, but the paragraph seems like a fitting beginning for our discussion here. As Giuliani (2021: 5) describes, her "critique of monstrosity and catastrophe predominantly focuses on Europe and the West, whose imaginary of crisis—though differentially articulated in scientific, political, and popular culture within and across national boundaries —is shared by a transnational 'we' that, akin to an 'imagined community' [à la Benedict Anderson ([1983] 2006)], is grounded in common experiences of *history, geography* and *humanness*" (emphasis in original).[25] "The 'we's' perspective and worldview," Giuliani (2021: 5) continues, "instantiate the belief system of white hegemonic culture based on a hierarchical reading of bodies, cultures, social dynamics and historical processes that posits whiteness, hegemonic masculinity, bourgeois value and lifestyle, heteronormativity, Christianity and Western secularism (although with many internal differences) as standards." We (Brisman and South) would not disagree, but our focus here is on *a particular portion* of the "we"—those ultrarich who fear the "barbarity, epidemics and natural disasters," who have and will go to extreme lengths to create the "borders, walls, colonies, [and] segregated spaces" and who will "do all it takes to stop the spread of chaos and keep it 'outside'"—and who, to invert Giuliani's phrasing, will likely (and with few reservations) do so even if it means sacrificing many for the good of the few.[26]

Giuliani (2021: 5) describes that at the core of her book are "the (pluralistic) positionality of the 'we' and its cultural roots, incorporating diverse political dynamics, social processes and geographies from Europe and its national states, as well as from transatlantic ties to the rest of the West and the broader Global North." "As such," she maintains, "the roots of the 'we' lie in a vast realm of converging and diverging cultural elements, narratives and self-narratives, which [she] nevertheless see[s] as crystallising into a single voice at certain historical moments—as when homogenous narratives and policies on migration, the war on terror and environmental catastrophes are deployed to structure the way the 'we' conceives of and responds to the threat" (2021: 5). Giuliani (2021: 5) contends that "it is at times like those that the 'we' is made into a consolidated 'imagined community,'" and that "just as in the wake of 9/11, a shared history and a common future are invoked to legitimise emergency measures." It is "on the basis of a certain political and international acknowledgement of its 'common destiny,'" Giuliani (2021: 5) asserts, "that 'we' can operate as a semiotic *dispositif* [in the Foucauldian sense] capable of developing converging strategies and common actions against *monsters* and *catastrophes*" (emphasis in original). Again, we (Brisman and South) would not challenge Giuliani's proposition that at particular historical moments, certain "cultural elements, narratives and self-narratives" form a "single voice," although we might ask whether such crystallizing can have positive features (especially if reflective of organic solidarity, à la Durkheim)—and, if so, at what point does (or would) such consolidation create a "*monstrified* personification of Otherness" (2021: 3, emphasis in original) or simply a "monstrous Other." Our focus here is not on (what we assume to be) Giuliani's rather capacious (transatlantic, Western, Global Northern) "we" but on a much, much smaller "we"—an extremely wealthy "we" of which "we" (Brisman and South—and, one can assume, Giuliani too) are not a part.

In stating as much, however, we (Brisman and South) are well aware of our "politics of location"—"the socio-historical, geographical and cultural context" in which we are writing but also our "social 'location'" (Giuliani 2021: 5, 8)—a position alluded to in the previous chapter in our discussion of the Gothic in Latin American literature. In other words, we (Brisman and

South) recognize that, as privileged scholars living in countries of the Global North that have reaped the benefits of globalized modernity—and despite any modest "green" or "eco-friendly" lifestyle choices we have made—we (again, Brisman and South) are still part of the "small minority" that Giuliani (2021: 11) identifies when she writes that "mainstream narratives and official accounts of climate-change impacts and environmental catastrophes still refer to the risks posed by the last neoliberal acceleration of the Anthropocene as 'side-effects.' The depersonalisation of responsibility casts the Anthropocene as a product of 'human nature' as a whole, while it is, instead, a set of 'inter-related historical processes set in motion by a small minority' (Davis et al., 2019, p. 4)."[27] Indeed, we (Brisman and South) readily acknowledge—and concur with Giuliani (2021: 11) that:

> blanket blaming humanity as a whole, with no distinction of race, gender, class or nationality, has led to a general lack of accountability as well as the depoliticisation and normalisation of the crisis (Bettini 2013), as a result of which protests are silenced and those who flee disaster are criminalised, turned into *monsters* who do not accept a life of subjection and sacrifice and who cross walls, borders and segregated spaces to reach the (more) "protected" space of the "we," endangering it. In this frame, it is those who have benefited the least from value extraction and extractivism who would be sacrificed first in the event of an apocalypse that is being presented as nothing more than a crisis, a period of transition to a post-apocalyptic world in which logics and ontologies of the Anthropocene will once again prevail. Today as in the colonial past, racialised constructions of monstrosity and catastrophe are used as *dispositifs* to ostracise those who are perceived as threatening (Foucault [1976]; Nuzzo 2013, p. 56) and divert attention away from the *real* monster.[28] (emphasis in original)

In other words, in our identifying and indicting the monstrous treatment of nature (as we attempted to do in the previous chapter), we (Brisman and South) are mindful of global inequalities in the responsibilities for climate change and the burden of its impacts—that there is essentially an inverse relationship between countries' greenhouse gas emissions and vulnerabilities such that those most likely to experience the adverse impacts of climate change are and have been least responsible for its genesis (see, e.g., Althor et al. 2016). We do not wish to engage in "blanket blaming"—we do not, as we have written before, intend "to adopt an essentialist notion of humanity or to make gross generalizations about all humans being equally at fault"

(Brisman 2015: 295n13)—nor are we bidding to exonerate ourselves.[29] Seager (1993: 59) writes that "we have so degraded our environment, so stressed physical carrying capacities that the lives of millions of people on the planet (and certainly our cherished ways of life) are at risk. But, 'we'—an undifferentiated humanity—have not done so. Rather, large-scale environmental problems are the result of control exercised by people within very particular clusters of powerful institutions, that include, prominently, militaries, multinationals, and governments, which often act in collusion" (for a discussion, see Brisman 2015: 295n13). Here, we (Brisman and South) wish to underscore the exceptionally perverse way(s) in which the superrich, such as Jeff Bezos and Elon Musk, seem more interested in blasting into space, sending people to Mars, and colonizing the fourth planet in our solar system[30] than in using their capital (financial, intellectual, social) and resources (acquired through the legacies of colonialism on Earth) to help *repair* our planet.[31]

Watson (2015: 271) laments that

> the technology that made humans the masters of the earth has pushed its resources to the limits. Humans behave like masters and owners of the earth, but like all conquering armies who requisition provisions and lodging from conquered lands, *humans are in fact parasites* reliant on the very earth they occupy and exploit. Humans abused the earth's hospitality, and are now threatened by rising ocean levels, unbreathable air, polluted water, and species extinction. Just as earthly forces mastered humans in pre-industrial times, so the earth enslaved by technocracy once again asserts its mastery over humans, whose activities have exacerbated the effects of the earth's menacing floods, droughts and earthquakes. (emphasis added)

The argument that humans are "parasites" is one we considered in Chapter 1, where we explored the Anti-Creep Climate Initiative's (2022) unveiling of Thanos, the central villain in *Avengers: Infinity War* and *Avengers: Endgame*, as an ecofascist. One of the "everyday ecofascist myths" that the Anti-Creep Climate Initiative (2022: 16) challenges is the claim that "humans are like a virus or a cancer on planet Earth, and catastrophes like climate change or COVID-19 are nature's ways of defending itself."[32] We need not rehearse here why such "cheery nihilism," to quote Hunt (2023), is so disturbingly fallacious.[33] Our point is that humans—some more than others, some more recently than others (see, e.g., AFP 2015; Sierra Garcia 2020)—have, as Watson (2015) decries, abused our planet's hospitality and now seek another one. Paul Krugman, the American economist and former columnist for *The New York*

Times, claims that "even billionaires need a livable planet" (2020: 4), but we are not so sure they think so: it is as if the Jeff Bezoses and Elon Musks and other such (U)HNWIs belt out the lyrics, "I could fly a rocket ship to the sun but that won't help me fix world starvation" (by the punk band Fifteen),[34] and then, well, decide to do just that—devote their wealth and energy to building rocket ships to abandon this planet (and leave behind those who are starving—"the poors" or "the great unwashed" [Mahdawi 2024]). With this understanding, we turn to a consideration of how some of the world's richest people have sought and are continuing to seek "segregated" and "protected" spaces (on Earth, for now, at least) in the event of (an) apocalyptic climate change (see, e.g., Pielke 2019; Wallace-Wells 2022a, 2022b).

Escape Attempts

"Monsters," the abject, the altered Earth—all are sources of insecurity and apprehension. For some, the response is escape, withdrawal "to bespoke bunkers and private islands"—spatial, volumetric, and solid constructions that enclose and separate—where "those with means will attempt to insulate themselves from the panicked scramble for resources and solid ground" (Linnemann 2022: 65). This is not a new tendency, of course, and (literally) builds upon the historical alteration of landscapes to support fortifications, places of retreat, chambers, barrows, and tumuli of royal or religious significance, as well as coastal defenses and constructions that have reflected the "increasingly ecological character of modern warfare, which no longer aims at a single target but at the general destruction of habitats" (Fontana 2023: 170). Humans have always been "geomorphological agents" exploiting the "landscape and its subsurface to meet the needs of society" in ways "driven by changes in socioeconomic, technological, political and cultural parameters" (Price et al. 2011: 1057). These changes, however, have led us into a world of evolving "harmscapes" (Berg and Shearing 2018), "riskscapes" (Morello-Frosch et al. 2001), and "hazardscapes" (Mustafa 2005)—scenarios that, according to many, will not end well.

According to Amster (2003: 195, 197), "patterns of spatial exclusion and marginalization of the impoverished" have, indeed, been repeated throughout modern history but have strikingly re-emerged in recent years in ways that reflect narratives and fears of disorder, disease, and decay, prompting responses of "sanitization, sterilization, and quarantine." Fear of death, as suggested by the "mortality salience hypothesis," can "amplify nationalism and intensify bias" (Azarian 2016), as well as multiply symptoms, sources, and objects of abjection, all requiring "psychological and sociocultural defenses" to "assist in self-preservation (Kristeva 1982)" (Nations, Baker and Krszjzaniek 2017: 408). The period of paranoia and atomic anxiety of 1945 to 1963 was accompanied in film and television, as well as in comics and novels, by an explosion of images and narratives of devastation and decline, monsters and mutations but also government- and corporate-sponsored messages of reassurance—most optimistically that "the atom is our friend" and, more pessimistically but still with a positive core that, if things do go wrong, we can still survive (Moran 2022). The prospects for survival in the face of catastrophe have, of course, never been equal for all; for those who can afford to exert control over who or what is *within* and who or what is *without*, there has been a market for protection—for bunkers and barriers, gates and bridges (Greenberg 2003).[35]

Elsewhere (Lam, South, and Brisman 2023; South and South 2021), we have discussed the tendency toward pursuit of forms of self-protection and what Szasz (2007) calls "inverted quarantine" as embraced by middle-class eco-consumers and the "worried well," who can afford a certain lifestyle, food style, and home style. These are also, in order to afford such measures, the financially healthy, but their resources are limited compared to those of the wealthy elites (the UHNWIs mentioned earlier) who seek to buy their way out of problems, including present and future global troubles like climate change, by entering the market for artificial environments designed to provide protective and defensive responses to the ecological, military, and political threats of the Anthropocene. The superrich—the UHNWIs—may search for and find escape routes and "a way to get away" but never quite sever ties: they leave behind detritus and waste, and they need supplies and services. Even if these superrich create bunkers and fortified enclaves and private islands, the borders around those physical entities will not be "truly closed" because they will want to let in other "privileged bodies" (other superrich) and, presumably, people to serve them (Hennefeld and Sammond 2020: 11). They are both "consumers and producers of ecocide" (Lam et al. 2023: 337), as exemplified in the case of the new space tourism industry aimed at allowing the extremely wealthy to experience "escape," whether it is momentary (e.g., for leisure) or permanent (i.e., to flee a ruined Earth and resettle on another planet). The inequality and injustice of such escape from that which is seen as abject lies in the realization that if spent in other ways, the billions being invested in such ventures by these ultrawealthy (such as Jeff Bezos, Richard Branson, and Elon Musk) could be used to help heal the pain and problems of the impoverished Earth—making it all more the perverse that one of them (Musk) has been nominated for the Nobel Peace Prize (Zilber 2024). Instead, further damage and degradation will follow from massive extraction of resources and the generation of substantial new amounts of greenhouse gases and pollutants, emitted directly into the upper atmosphere (Gammon 2021), as well as from contributions to the collection of space junk circling the planet.[36]

From "Monstrous Nature" to Abjection to the Apocalypse

Before turning to Chapter 4 and our examination of nature and the *apocalypse* (or nature as contributing to the end of the world—or "the end of the world as we know it"), it might be helpful to revisit how we have situated the relationship of prevalent, if not *dominant* (primarily Western), depictions of the relationship between humans and the environment.

In Chapter 2, "Monstrous Nature and the Roots and Growth of Ecohorror," we suggested that the human/nature dualism leads to the notion and treatment of nature as "Other" and "monstrous." "Monstrous nature," then, is that which *humanity creates* (see Murray and Heumann 2016: xii). Essentially, when we view nature as "Other," we effectively designate it as "monstrous" and then treat it as "monstrous," when, in fact, *we* are the monsters. In response, nature "bites back"—or "stomps and smashes" (Rothman 2014, cited in Murray and Heumann 2016: 200)—or, at least, *appears* to do so—although such a conceptualization has come under criticism.

For example, orcas, the largest members of the dolphin family often known as "killer whales," rarely bother humans (Bradford and Pester 2022; Pappas 2021; Syed 2023):[37] they are a lot less dangerous to humans than white sharks (discussed in Chapter 2)—in part because "orcas don't encounter humans as often" (Munroe 2022), despite the fact that they are "the most widely distributed mammals, other than humans and possibly brown rats" (Bradford and Pester 2022). Indeed, as Cole (2023) points out, "their name [killer whale] is a bit of a misnomer." There have been no recorded instances of orcas killing people in the wild, although there have been a few fatal attacks by orcas in captivity (Bradford and Pester 2022; Ciccarelli 2020; Gill 2020).[38]

In June 2023, *The Guardian* reported that an orca had rammed a yacht in the North Sea near the Shetland Islands (Hoare 2023a). While such behavior had been observed in the Iberian orca population in increasing numbers since 2020[39]—with incidents occurring along the Spanish and Portuguese coastline from the Strait of Gibraltar to Galicia[40]—the cetacean-vessel "interaction" in June 2023 represented the first time that such an occurrence had transpired in northern waters, some 2000 miles (3200 km) from where it had first appeared

(Hoare 2023a; Hunt 2023; see also *Al Jazeera* 2023b; ESPN News Services 2023; Robledo 2023).

Given that the "violent" encounters appeared to be following a distinct pattern—with the orcas approaching the boats from the stern and striking the hull and biting and sometimes snapping off the rudders (Pare 2023)[41]—experts suggested that this was learned behavior (Hoare 2023a; Pappas 2022).[42] Attention turned quickly to *why* the orcas, the largest members of the dolphin family and the apex predators of the ocean, would engage in such behavior.

Some opined that the orcas may have been motivated by curiosity (see, e.g., Froelich 2020; Jones 2020b; McFall-Johnsen and Zitser 2023; Pappas 2022; Smillie 2020a, 2020b; White 2022g). Some submitted that the behavior was playful (Ciccarelli 2023; Hoare 2023a; Pag 2021; Pappas 2022)[43] or a fluke (Carty 2023; Watercutter 2023) or a fad or a trend (Pappas 2022; Pare 2023),[44] rather than "adaptive" (i.e., "useful") behavior (Beddington 2023; see also Salvoni 2023). Others proposed that it might be aversive (that could have begun after an incident with a boat, such as an entanglement in a fishing line [see Kwai 2023; see generally Froelich 2020; Jones 2020b; Smillie 2020a]), territorial or defensive (Ciccarelli 2023; Salvoni 2023; Syed 2023; see also Cole 2023; McFall-Johnsen and Zitser 2023; Thomson 2023)—perhaps as a sign of stress (Smillie 2020a, 2020b) or in response to trauma.[45] Dr. Alfredo López Fernandez, a biologist at the University of Aveiro (Universidade de Aveiro) and a member of the Atlanta Orca Working Group (Grupo de Trabajo Orca Atlántica), offered a more qualified analysis, stating, "It's not revenge. [The orcas are] just acting out as a precautionary measure" in order to protect themselves (quoted in Ciccarelli 2020, 2022a, 2022b; Osborne 2020a).[46] The preponderance of scientists agreed: the orcas were likely "not in their revenge era," Cole (2023) reported, but this did not stop many media outlets from "framing . . . them as 'attacks' motivated 'by revenge'" (Cole 2023).[47]

Thus, with "international headlines about 'rogue killer whales'" and "'orchestrated' orca attacks" accompanying videos shared "thousands of times on social media" (Gill 2020; see also Cavanagh 2020; Froelich 2020), the language used to describe such events and incidents became increasingly important.[48] Indeed, the headline for Salvoni's (2023) article in the *Daily Mail*, a conservative British middle-market tabloid, announced in bold lettering, "Killer whales are ramming boats off the coast of Spain in spate of deadly attacks to avenge orca matriarch Gladis after she was injured 'by boat or fishing net,' experts say"—despite the fact that there has not been a recorded instance of an orca (or orcas) killing a human in the wild (as already noted)—and despite the fact that *the article itself* did not mention any human fatalities.[49] Philip Hoare, the British writer and author of *Leviathan, Or, The Whale* (2008) and *Albert and the Whale: Albrecht Dürer and How Art Imagines Our World* (2021), questioned whether it was appropriate to use the word *attack* to refer to the actions of the orcas because doing so "is a human judgment; their actions are more likely to be defensive" (2023b).[50] Despite expressing reservations about describing the orcas' behavior with a particular choice of words, Hoare admitted to being "secretly excited at th[e] idea of nature fighting back," in light of the fact "at least 174 orcas have died in captivity since 1961, having been forced to swim aimlessly about in overgrown swimming pools without any peer interaction that defines them" (Hoare 2023b, citing Whale and Dolphin Conservation n.d.). Beddington (2023) also conceded that "we're taking great pleasure in projecting extremely human narratives and motivations on orcas," confessing to "lov[ing] the idea of orcas attacking boats," and noting the "very human-coloured notion . . . that orcas aren't just taking back the ocean but are somehow fomenting revolution, since the yachts they are ramming are so intimately associated with the ultra-wealthy."[51] Beddington (2023) then pointed to a post on Instagram that declared, "The orcas have done more for the working class than our elected officials ever have" (Abolish Golf Courses 2023)—a sentiment echoed on the Twittersphere by those who referred to the orcas as "anti-capitalist saboteurs."[52]

Hunt (2023), however, conveyed consternation with "the alacrity with which this 'us versus them' framing ha[d] sprung up—with 'us' often being used to group together people who think billionaires should pay more tax, and actual sea creatures." Such framing, Hunt (2023) put forth, "is telling of our profound disconnection from the natural world." "We have become most accustomed to viewing non-human life through a screen," she reasoned, and "as a result, our perspective tends to be distorted." Accordingly—and contra Beddington's (2023) seemingly more jaunty perspective—Hunt (2023) asserted that our detachment from the natural world and our mediated (and thus *limited*) experience with nonhuman animals means that "we become either over-familiar, projecting on to wild animals feelings and motives that they can't possibly share in our quest for 'relatable' content and characters; or entirely detached, as though we are just spectators of Earth's spectacle, standing apart." Indeed, "we're not witnessing killer whales 'fight back,'" Hunt (2023) maintained, "we are seeing their ongoing struggle to respond to changes driven by us. . . . This persistent idea that Mother Nature herself might rise up to reject and even undo the damage done by humans appeals because it *alleviates our sense of responsibility*, and *assuages our fears* that it's too late. But that glosses over not only the devastation that can't be reversed, but the suffering that is currently under way" (emphasis added).[53] "Whatever is behind the Iberian orcas' boat-ramming," Hunt (2023) continued, "these fractious encounters speak to increasing tensions, even outright conflict, between humans and the rest of animal life. The natural world can no longer be seen as separate to the one developed by humans, never mind a guard-rail against the latter's excesses and a cure for its ills: the impacts of human activity are too far-reaching and inextricable." "The least we can do," Hunt (2023) concluded, "if we're to express solidarity" with the orcas and the "orca rising" (or "orca uprising"; see *Al Jazeera* 2023b; Beddington 2023; Carty 2023; Cohen and Orwig 2023; Cole 2023; Hamilton 2023; Vlamis 2023) is to "be honest with ourselves about our part in [the] struggle."[54] Researchers, "not keen to speculate about something as multi-faceted and complex as orca behaviour," believed that we "set ourselves up to misunderstand the species entirely by trying to lump their behaviour into simple categories like good or bad, aggressive or playful" (Gill 2020)[55]—indeed, "while we may never fully . . . know why animals act the way they do" (Syed 2023)—"one thing is certain," Syed (2023) resolved, "our presence makes a difference."[56]

Hunt, then, might well see the suggestion of an "orca (up)rising"—of orcas "out for revenge"—or other such "provocative language," to use Gill's (2020) phrasing—as akin to the representation of nature "biting back" or "stomping and smashing" in ecohorror and thus problematic in that such perspectives and depictions *accentuate* or *contribute* to a human-nature divide. (Indeed, as Gill [2020] reported regarding incidents between orcas and boats off the coasts of Spain and Portugal, researchers worried that "the language used in news stories and social media posts—even by the coast guard, which had been 'adversarial and loaded,' might be 'a step in a slippery journey towards persecution of endangered orcas.'") If so, we would concur. When nature "bites back" (or "stomps and smashes") in varying ways in ecohorror films (as we discussed in Chapter 2), those films are not simply *reflecting* perceptions of (human-wildlife conflicts in) the real world. Rather, what happens is that we conflate cinema and reality and come to view nature as *more* monstrous. And because of this "monstrosity," we wish to reject it—cast it off. We are rejecting our mother (see Watson 2015),[57] much the way that the hybrid rejects the alien queen in *Alien Resurrection*, noted at the outset of this chapter.[58]

But it is not that simple. Kniss (2021: 70) argues that "humankind's harmful inclination [is] to either *fear* or *exploit*" nonhuman nature (emphasis added). In other words, it is not just that we see nature as monstrous and fear it and abject it/treat it as abject; rather, we may simultaneously fear nature and view it as monstrous *and* engage in exploitation *and* abjection. To put it another way, our abjection may emerge from our fear of it "biting back" *and/or* it may result from our overusing it/overexploiting it—and then, when we have no more use for it, discarding it (like a carcass) or parts of it.

How, then, have we demonstrated this abjection? Films like *Elysium* provide clues, as do the examples of the (U)HNWIs engaging in "bunkerization" and space tourism as forms of security and escape. It might be tempting to think that monstrous treatment *of nature* and the planet leads to various apocalyptic scenarios and, subsequently, the abjection of the Earth. The German science fiction thriller *Pandorum* (2009) comes to mind. The film opens with title cards, making reference to the history of human travel in space—beginning with 1969 ("Man Lands on the Moon") and 2009 ("Kepler Telescope Is Launched to Search for Earth Like Planets") indicating that in the year 2153, food and water shortages are common on Earth and that in 2174, with the world population having exceeded twenty-four billion and the planet's resources largely depleted, the sixty-thousand-person interstellar ark/sleeper ship *Elysium* is launched on its 123-year-voyage to the Earth-like planet of Tanis.[59] Early in the voyage, members of the crew receive a transmission informing them of Earth's destruction: "You're all that's left of us. Good luck, God bless, and God's speed" (see Brisman 2015: 292). *Pandorum*, then, would suggest the following progression or ordering:

monstrosity/monstrous treatment (e.g., overconsumption/misuse of natural resources) →
apocalypse (e.g., widespread conflict due to food and water shortages) →
abjection (e.g., leaving Earth for Tanis)

But this is not the only sequence or ordering. Giuliani (2021: 32) avers that "monstrosity appears to have signalled a limit, a boundary, or a border since the very beginning of human life. For centuries it was associated with representations of chaos, nature, and the *finis mundi*, the end of the world and of what was considered 'right' in Western society (Foucault 1961; Nuzzo 2013: 56)." In other words, this notion of monstrosity *equals* or *equates with* the end of the world (with no need for [a stage of] abjection).

More importantly, for our purposes, is that the

monstrosity/monstrous treatment → apocalypse → abjection

progression or ordering reflects a definition or understanding of apocalypse as a *catastrophe* or "widespread destruction" (Dictionary.com) or "great disaster" (Merriam Webster)—or a series thereof resulting in the collapse of civilization. But as Neocleous (2016: 66) reminds us, "'Apocalypse' comes from the Greek *apokalypsis*, meaning an unveiling or uncovering of truths normally hidden, and thus a kind of revelation or disclosure."[60] Moreover, Neocleous (2016: 67) continues, "the apocalyptic holds the promise of *hope*" (emphasis added). Similarly, Hall (2016: 252), discussing Wyndham's *The Day of the Triffids* (2008), notes that "the apocalypse in Wyndham's novel is not then a doomsday scenario, but a *revelation*, an uncovering of knowledge (ἀποκάλυψις *apokálypsis*, from ἀπο and καλύπτω meaning 'uncovering')" (emphasis added).[61]

With this in mind, we turn to Chapter 4 and different representations of the end of the world in literature and film. We focus on those that are or might be *revelatory*, rather than (just) *catastrophic* or *disastrous*.

Fuck Humans [Chapter 1] (Centro-Sagario, Grenada, Andalusia, Spain, September 2022)

Monstrous Nature [Chapter 2] (East Passyunk, South Philadelphia, Pennsylvania, USA, July 2023)

Monstrous "Nature" [Chapter 2] (Regency Centre, Lexington, Kentucky, USA, August 2023)

Dead Bird [Chapter 3] (Elizabeth Street Park, Lexington, Kentucky, USA, September 2023)

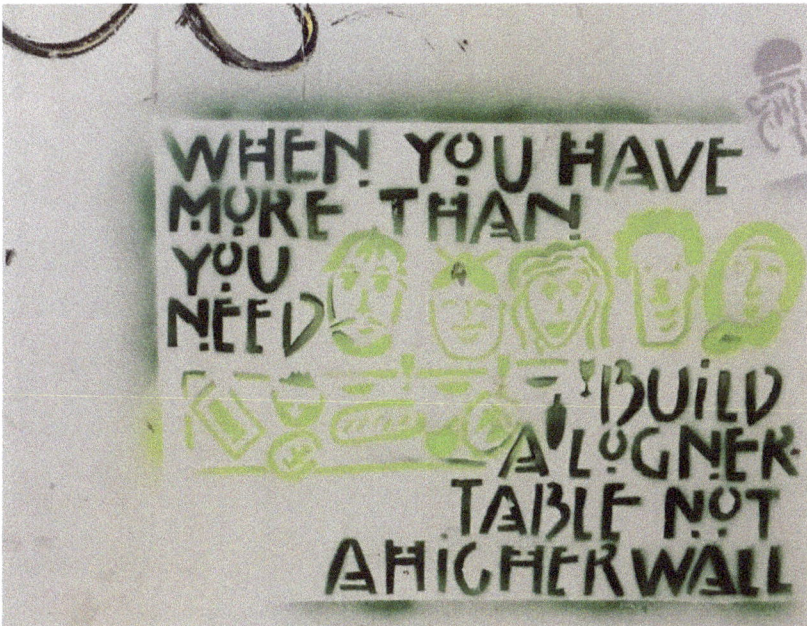

When You Have More Than You Need . . . [Chapter 3] (Oslo, Norway, September 2019)

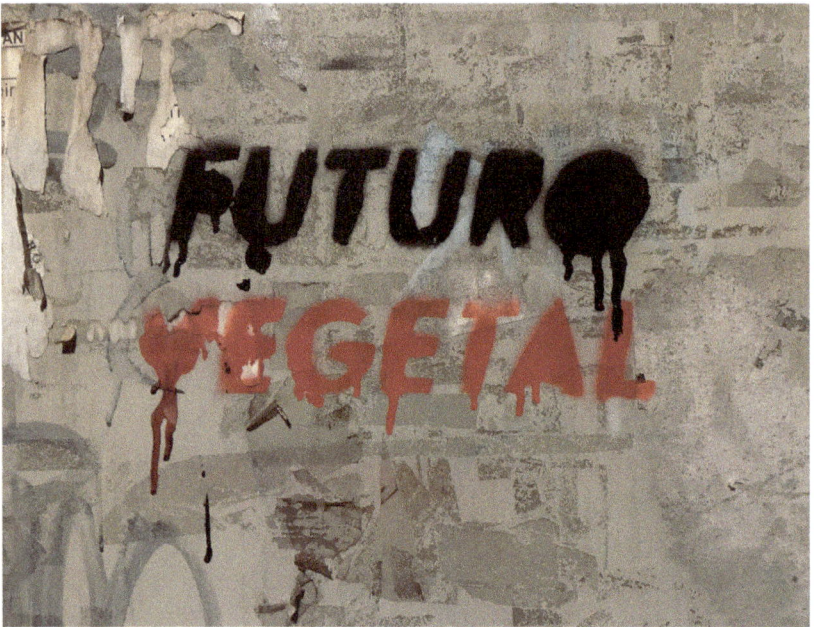

Futuro Vegetal [Chapters 4 and 5] (Grenada, Andalusia, Spain, September 2022)

4

Apocalyptic Imaginaries

Is the idea of the "apocalyptic" theological or cultural?[1] It can certainly be seen as a form of social imaginary (Taylor 2007: 171), whether rooted in religious texts and developments or in literary and other cultural forms (Collins 2014: 1). As Wojcik (1997: 1) suggests, it was only in the second half of the twentieth century that "traditional religious apocalyptic world-views" were challenged by parallel "widespread beliefs about a meaningless apocalypse." This latter version has been described by Rosen (2008: xv) as "neoapocalyptic" and lacking "the redemptive hope" of religious interpretations. This loss of hope—the familiarity of repeated failure to make things better—the "feelings of dissatisfaction with contemporary existence" (Renner 2012: 203)—provide the space for—and provoke thoughts about—"end times," in the sense of humanity running out of ideas for the salvation of self and the planet—and paying the price. A repeated metaphor and symbol to represent these "anxieties of the present" and the "extrapolation of consequences for the future" is the turn to the zombie as "the twenty-first century monster of choice, a ubiquitous symbol of any kind of systemic failure, from zombie banks in economics to zombie categories in social theory" (Schmeink 2016: 67).

It is perhaps along these lines that Paul Krugman (2012), the economist and Nobel laureate, adopts a definition of "zombie ideas" as "policy ideas that keep being killed by evidence, but nonetheless shamble relentlessly forward, essentially because they suit a political agenda" (see also 2020: 3). "The most persistent such zombie," Krugman (2020: 4) writes, "is the insistence that taxing the wealthy is hugely destructive to the economy as a whole, so that cutting taxes on high incomes will produce miraculous growth." As a distinguished professor and winner of the Sveriges Riksbank Prize in Economic Sciences in Memory of Alfred Nobel (otherwise known as the Nobel Memorial Prize in Economic Sciences), Krugman knows a thing or two about the connection (or lack thereof) between tax cuts for the rich and economic growth. The tax cuts → growth doctrine "keeps failing in practice," Krugman (2020: 4) explains, "but if anything has gained an ever-stronger hold over the Republic Party" it is, in his mind, "the ultimate zombie idea" (2012; see also 2020: 216), "shambling along, eating people's brains" (2020: 3).[2] Not only do "zombie ideas" defy death—like the zombies we discussed in Chapter 2—but the implication is that "zombie ideas" *infect others*—other healthy ideas (or people)—and *transform* them. Either that, or they simply eat people's brains, removing their capacity to think (and, presumably, reject ideas like the tax cuts → growth notion that has so often been refuted).

While "zombie *ideas*" continue to survive when there is no reason that they should (no living force or vitality to them), zombies, *as metaphors*, persist—and are actually pretty helpful as such. "Horror focuses our common fears and anxieties," write Carnes and Goren (2023: 6), "but takes them to disturbing extremes; what we often see in horror narratives is some fear come to life, given form and made into a sort of avatar." Accordingly, in Chapter 2, we discussed how monsters are products—or reflections—of the anxieties of their time and that zombies, in particular, have enjoyed a rebirth, if one will. Given that the "zombie apocalypse" is one of the ways in which we imagine "the end" (see Aistrope and Fishel 2020; Drezner 2014; Linnemann et al. 2014; Rahner 2019)—indeed, given that "zombies . . . are now synonymous with the apocalypse" (Staples 2017)—it is worthwhile beginning this chapter with zombies.

"That the zombie is ubiquitous in popular culture cannot be disputed," Lauro and Christie (2011: 1) declare at the outset of their volume *Better Off Dead: The Evolution of Zombies as Post-Human*, adding that "the zombie is more popular now than ever before."[3] Saunders (2012: 80) observes that in the first decade of the twenty-first century, there was "a marked increase in films, books, video games, and other forms of popular media associated with zombies, particularly the flesh-eating undead," noting that *Time* magazine (Grossman 2009) had anointed zombies as "the New Vampires" (replacing vampires as the "It monster" of the moment).[4] Similarly, Drezner (2014: 826, 825) asserts that "it does not take much effort to demonstrate that zombies have become increasingly popular in the twenty-first century" and that "whether one looks at films, songs, games, or books, the zombie genre is clearly on the rise."[5]

Why the resurgence? Why, according to Beale (2004: E1), were "zombie flicks . . . in vogue at the moment"—a few years into the twenty-first century? Dendle (2011: 178) claims that "after a slew of zombie films culminating in the late '80s, zombie movies ground to a virtual halt in the 1990s," and that "with some exceptions like Peter Jackson's *Braindead* (1992, released in the US as *Dead Alive*), studio-funded zombie movies were conspicuously in decline during this period." What can explain—or how do we account for—this revival?

To understand this change or turn, we would note that "since the beginning of time"—or, at least, humans' development of the concept of time—"humans have always been fascinated by death and have depicted it in an endless variety of ways" (Khapaeva 2020: 16) and that, as Young (2022: 6) remarks, "Cataclysms of one sort or another perpetually lurk in the darkest regions of our minds." Harris (2009) muses that "a fixation on the apocalypse is . . . nothing new. Depicting the destruction of the human race has a long tradition in American popular culture, as would be expected in a country that is still deeply religious—at least compared to much of Europe—and has its origins in being founded by Puritans fleeing persecution."[6] For Buell (1995: 296), "apocalypticism is an old American tradition," and one need only "look at American literary history [to] confirm[] its persistence through three centuries of American writing."[7] For Rosenthal (2000: 16), "every generation in our Western culture"—not just *American* culture—"has had its version of the Apocalypse, usually stimulated by war, famine or revolution, those leitmotifs of human history," while Adams' (2023) assertion is even broader: "For as long as complex human societies have existed there have been people predicting their imminent collapse." Murphy (2013: 50) takes things a step further, musing that "humans have been preparing for the worst for millennia" (for a discussion, see Brisman 2015: 288)—as illustrated by our discussion of elite bunkerization in Chapter 3. To be sure, many others have made similar observations about this allure and enthrallment—this infatuation with imagining calamities and envisaging the end of time(s). But this does not reveal why *zombies* have returned—assuming they ever disappeared in the first place.[8]

As noted in Chapter 2, for Saunders (2012: 80), "while nearly every culture has myths associated with reanimation of the dead, the current renaissance across multiple media, what might be deemed a 'zombie turn,' has little to do with premodern superstitions of walking corpses." Rather, he contends, "the current obsession with zombies, and particularly the looming (albeit unlikely) threat of human-zombie conflicts, is a reflection of the dangers of invasive alterity associated with uncontrolled spaces in the current era of globalization" (Saunders 2012: 80–81). "This shift," he continues, has been "especially prevalent in the United States following the attacks of 11 September 2001, as zombies have become phantasmal stand-ins for Islamist terrorists, illegal immigrants, carriers of foreign contagions, and other 'dangerous' border crossers" (Saunders 2012: 81, citing Muntean and Payne 2009 and Bishop 2009). Similarly, Drezner (2011: 825) states that "well more than one-third of all zombie films [of all time] have been released since the September 11, 2001, terrorist attacks (Bishop 2008)"—and that this is a *conservative* estimate. For Bishop (2009: 17), "wars and other tragedies affect cultural consciousness like the blast from a high-yield explosive or a massive earthquake." Situating the "steady rise" of studio and independent zombie movies since 2002 in history, Bishop (2009: 17) explains that "the use of atomic weapons at the end of World War II ushered in nuclear paranoia narratives like the films *Godzilla* (1954) and *Them!* (1954), and fear of the encroaching Communist threat inspired alien invasion stories like Jack Finney's novel *Invasion of the Body Snatchers* (1955) and the movie *Invaders from Mars* (1953)." Bishop (2009: 17) continues:

> The terrorist attacks of September 11, 2001, caused perhaps the largest wave of paranoia for Americans since the McCarthy era. Since the beginning of the war on terror, American popular culture has been colored by the fear of possible terrorist attacks and the grim realization that people are not as safe and secure as they might have once thought. This shift in cultural consciousness can be most readily seen in narrative fiction, particularly through zombie cinema.[9]

This makes a certain amount of sense. Young (2022: 8–9), the author of *Apocalypse Ready: The Manual of Manuals: A Century of Panic Prevention*, a compilation of official documents and guides for preparing for and responding to a wide range of disasters, which he curated from governmental archives from around the world, suggests:

> It is clear . . . that the 20th century was a period in which the world was persistently on the verge of experiencing one cataclysm or another. The exception was the final few years of the century. For those who grew up in the 1990s, threats such as a nuclear attack or a global pandemic seemed as outlandish as that of an extraterrestrial visitation. Indeed, the decade is now becoming recognized as something of a historical anomaly: for many in the industrialized Western world, it was a time characterized by relative peace, progress and prosperity.

With the break-up of the Soviet Union, the perceived threat of nuclear attack, which had been in place for some 40 years, lifted. Advances in medicine kept more infectious diseases under control than ever before, and new technology meant the detection and management of natural disasters was sounder than it had ever been. Best of all, the alien invasion that had been threatened by endless Hollywood B-movies had failed to materialize—despite the insistence of those who had observed alien craft—silver discs, cigar-shaped objects and black triangles—hovering in the skies, or had experienced close encounters of their own.

This lack of major global upheavals following the collapse of the Soviet Union has led to the 1990s being described as a "holiday from history."

As Young (2022: 9) continues, "Like all holidays, though, it had to come to an end. With the tragedy of the terrorist attacks on the United States in 2001, the 21st century was set up for a return to the world's 'normal' state of international turmoil, disorder and general peril." It is not that the public in the 1990s lived without anxieties or fears—whether manufactured or real (Beck 1992; Giddens 1991)—but that the scale and levels of reification were different—at least, for those living in the West/Global North.[10] As Bishop (2009: 18) puts forth,

Historically, zombie cinema had always represented a stylized reaction to cultural consciousness and particularly to social and political injustices, and America in the 1990s saw perhaps too much complacency and stability for zombie movies to fit the national mood. The Cold War was over, the Berlin Wall had fallen, Ronald Reagan's Star Wars defense system was proven unnecessary, and George H. W. Bush's Gulf War had apparently been resolved. In fact, aside from some skirmishes in third-world countries, Americans were largely insulated from global warfare. Furthermore, in the Clinton decade, sexual impropriety took headlines away from global genocide and tyrannical massacres. With nothing specific to react to or protest against, cinematic versions of the zombie genre declined steadily throughout the 1990s.

So, for St. John (2006), "it does not take much of a stretch to see the parallel between zombies and anonymous terrorists who seek to convert others within society to their deadly cause. The fear that anyone could be a suicide bomber or a hijacker parallels a common trope of zombie films, in which healthy people are zombified by contact with other zombies and become killers" (for a discussion, see Bishop 2009: 24). Moreover, Bishop (2009: 20) maintains, in order to appreciate "the post-9/11 social relevance of zombie cinema," it is necessary to examine and contemplate the genre and to distinguish it from other genres of horror. Bishop (2009: 20) explicates that "unlike many other tales of terror and the supernatural, the classical zombie story has very specific criteria that govern its plot and development." "These genre protocols," Bishop (2009: 20) continues, "include not only the zombies and the imminent threat of violent deaths"—which seems fairly obvious—"but also a postapocalyptic backdrop, the collapse of societal infrastructures, the indulgence of survivalist fantasies, and the fear of other surviving humans." While "these plot elements and motifs are present in pre-9/11 zombie films," Bishop (2009: 20, 24) admits, "they have become more relevant to a modern, contemporary audience" in the aftermath of the events of September 11, 2001,[11] where "the transmission of the zombie infection is a symbolic form of radical brainwashing"[12]—where "'your wife, your child, your best friend, your pastor, whomever, could suddenly become one'"[13]—a zombie, a suicide bomber, a hijacker, a terrorist.

This is all well and good—it may help explain why zombies have returned and supplanted other "monsters"[14]—but how does this perspective sit with Andrew Ross's (1991: 8) proposition that with the fall of the Soviet Union, "'apocalyptic fears about widespread droughts and melting ice caps ha[d] displaced the nuclear threat as the dominant feared . . . disaster'" (quoted in Hulme 2009: 63)?[15] Or, given that Ross was writing ten years *before* September 11, 2001, what do we make of the following from Dunne (2009)?

> Every age seems to invent a master narrative about its own demise. At the turn of the 20th century, the fear was of a violent struggle between races and civilisations. In the post-1945 world, the nightmare was of a nuclear holocaust. The narrative of demise that haunts us today is the threat that environmental harm holds for the planet and its ability to support human and other life forms.[16]

How do we reconcile this? Is the "master narrative" about the threat of zombies, which can be read as fears of anonymous terrorist attacks (discussed earlier) or as anxieties over unbridled immigration (see Bishop 2009)[17] or as (simply) more fathomable than (an analysis of) the end of capitalism (see Vint 2013; see also Grossman 2009),[18] *or* is the "master narrative" one of environmental harm? We present two possibilities.

One possibility is that zombie movies *are* ecohorror movies (or can be)—or that ecohorror films *are* zombie flicks (or can be). As Drezner

(2014: 829) observes, "a mob of reanimated, ravenous corpses is as inexorable a force as climate change," making zombies "the perfect avatar for the twenty-first century threat environment: they are not well understood by serious analysts, they possess protean capabilities, and the challenges they pose to states are very, very grave." Taking a slightly different tack, Lauro (2011: 231) suggests that M. Night Shyamalan's 2008 film *The Happening*, which we mentioned in Chapter 1 and in Chapter 2, "both is and is not a zombie movie. Of course, we cannot help but think of George Romero's iconic film when we watch the protagonists cross the Pennsylvanian countryside and hole up in a rural farmhouse." For Lauro (2011: 231–32), "*The Happening* can be claimed as a kind of zombie film because it features the two key aspects that we have come most recently to expect of the genre: the 'depersonalization' of people we once knew, and a vast, sudden, inexplicable epidemic" (quoting Dendle 2001: 4). With respect to the second of these—"the sense of onslaught, outbreak, or epidemic"—Lauro (2011: 232) explains that "no matter the zombie's origin story, whether it be the result of radiation exposure or a literal virus, zombie stories tend to involve a legion of newly transformed individuals, rather than a few lone specimens." She continues (2011: 232):

> Here, again, Shyamalan's film fits the criteria: there is an *epidemic*, albeit not of brain-eating zombies, but of suicide. As with the classic zombie, the afflicted in *The Happening* do not seem to recognize loved ones any longer. Instead, they utter some nonsensical or out-of-context words, as if the brain is resetting, and then they kill themselves in whatever way seems the most immediately expedient. Like zombies, they are automatons on autopilot, but instead of doing someone else's bidding or thirsting for blood, they are the death drive incarnate. There is the same kind of mindlessness exhibited in victims here as in the classic zombie. (emphasis in original)

Lauro (2011: 233–34) contends that in zombie films that involve a virus, the virus is often "not depicted as something completely natural that is in conflict with humans, but rather a mutation that begins with human tampering in a lab."[19] In *The Happening*, according to Lauro (2011: 234), "it is the evolution of the plants that is infused with danger, and this theme points to what may be the latest advance in the zombie narrative. If zombies in film and other popular media have often expressed our anxieties about humans over-reaching their natural sphere (from space exploration, to the development of nuclear weapons, to biotechnologies), then it seems only natural that one of the most pressing concerns as a civilization—the *environment*—would also begin to be reflected in the guise of zombie film" (emphasis added).

Lauro (2011: 234) suggests that the increased—indeed, *increasing* (we might add)—concern (or "panic," to use her word) about the environment has "given rise to the eco-zombie"—and that "one manifestation of this theme can be felt in those zombie stories, or apocalypse narratives more generally, where the earth, wiped clean of its human inhabits [*sic*], begins to reclaim its space. . . . The earth . . . would not miss us." Lauro's words, we would note, about the Earth beginning to "reclaim its space" sound eerily similar to the notion of "nature is healing," discussed in Chapter 3.[20] But Lauro (2011: 234) takes matters a step further by stating that "a more direct expression of humanity's antagonistic relationship with nature can be seen in the[] emerging narratives where the planet's response to our misdeeds is to foster the zombie epidemic."

The Happening, Lauro (2011: 234) claims, contains "a prominent ecological theme"—a "retaliatory strike for our crimes against nature"—and the "protagonists deduce halfway through the film that [the vegetation is] causing 'the event,'" whereby the plants and trees release "a kind of neurotoxin that kills the death-drive inhibitor in humans," causing humans to commit suicide: "the plants make the humans do the dirty work for them: we off ourselves."[21] We will return to notions of "the event" and the significance of "the event" later in this chapter in our discussion of apocalyptic depictions and the problem of time. For now, what is important is Lauro's (2011: 234–35) contention that Shyamalan's film possesses much of the flavor and features of zombie movies: "Many critics found the transparency of Shyamalan's environmentalist message cloying, but it is interesting to note that as a zombie film, this trend is far from novel. In fact, inducting the film into the zombie movie annals may even serve to justify this moral-toting narrative as *fulfilling the obligations of the genre*" (emphasis added). As Lauro (2011: 235) asserts, connecting us back to the theological and mythological origins of apocalyptic fears,

> At least since Romero, the zombie epidemic has served as a modern-day equivalent of the biblical plague; because zombies are so often raised from the dead by some misdeed of humanity, they pass judgment on our naïve vanity and Icarian hubris, delivering a punishment of mass proportions without reference to an angered deity but, nonetheless, with the implication that humanity has sinned . . . even if only against natural law.

Thus, Lauro (2011: 235) concludes, "the zombie is inherently an *ecological avenger*" (emphasis added):

> As a walking corpse, the zombie threat is one in which things of the earth, bodies that had been consigned to become a part of the planet, refuse to take it lying down. Whether the sin is . . . humanity's development of technology, weapons, and chemicals that pollute and poison the planet . . . the living dead may be little more than the planet's messengers, raised to exact revenge. So, we might say, whether the earth sends birds [as in Alfred Hitchcock's *The Birds* (1963)], or plants [*The Happening*], or our own dead mother [as in Edgar Wright's *Shaun of the Dead* (2004)] to do the bidding, there may be essentially no difference.

The proposition that zombie movies are or can be ecohorror movies (and vice versa) may help resolve the question of whether the "master narrative" of today is about the threats that zombies represent (e.g., economic collapse, global pandemics/infectious disease, terrorism, unchecked migration) or whether the "master narrative" of this age is one of environmental harm. Neither is—because they are the same. At the very least, the suggestion that zombie movies are or can be ecohorror movies (and vice versa) helps bolster the argument that the two assertions about "master narratives" are not in conflict. This gains further support when we consider Pihlström's (2020: 45–46) submission that "we could ourselves be regarded as monsters . . . we could, indeed, be reduced to monstrosity by being transformed into creatures consuming others' bodies. We are, after all, eating the world in order to continue our own lives."[22] Indeed, Pihlström's (2020) musings resonate with Doyle's (2020: 113) posthumanist approach to zombies and conclusion that zombie films "are narratives that prompt us to consider ecological crisis as we, like zombies, endlessly consume the planet's resources. This is to say that zombie stories allegorize the way that anthropocentrism encourages us to stand in the midst of a charnel ground without really seeing it and our place in creating it by bending the Earth, its resources, and its inhabitants to the insatiable appetites of human beings—and only some human beings at that."

Another possibility is that there might not be a *single* "master narrative" of this age. Instead, there might be "master narrative*s*" or powerful and competing narratives of fears and threats (of or from terrorism, economic decline, environmental catastrophe, etc.) with different groups/interests promoting their particular views of demise. This is the interpretation that we prefer; indeed, this seems to be one of Anson's points in her article, "'Master Metaphor': Environmental Apocalypse and the Settler States of Emergency," where she compares the 2016 armed takeover and occupation of the Malheur National Wildlife Refuge in Harney County, Oregon, by a right-wing militia group (Citizens for Constitutional Freedom), which invoked claims of federal government overreach and apocalyptic fears of white genocide, with the 2016–17 Dakota Access Pipeline Protests (#NoDAPL) at the Standing Rock Sioux Reservation by Native American water protectors. Noting "the uses and abuses of apocalyptic rhetoric," Anson finds that "apocalyptic stories of single disastrous moments shelter the settler state of emergency, protecting the logic of the settler colonial capitalism's continuous creation of and dependence upon the emergency event" (2020: 60, 61). The comparison, she claims, thus "clarifies the master metaphor lurking in the apocalyptic state of emergency—the ways apocalyptic emergency appeals reinforce the exclusionary violence and ecological devastation they so often seek to diagnose and disrupt" (2020: 61). While Anson's focus is on "apocalyptic appeals" that "entrench Western political structures," what is central for us is her substantiation of "the diverse and even divergent aspects of the literary mode" of apocalypse—that "the apocalypse can refer to an immense variety of storytelling traditions" (2020: 60, 61).

That there are "master narratives" (not one "master narrative") and "apocalypses" (or different ascendant or commanding visions of the—or *an*—apocalypse)—might be explained (at least in part) by Harris (2009), who reports that "the trend towards apocalyptic thought does not only reflect anxiety over a difficult period of history but, just as important, *changing times*" (emphasis added). "Indeed," Harris (2009) continues, "it is often the concept of change as much as the concept of destruction that triggers popular interests in apocalyptic themes." In support, Harris (2009) explains that "the first world war produced more apocalyptic popular culture than the second world war, despite the latter being on a much bigger scale. The key thing was that the first world war was new and different. That's why it triggered more apocalyptic thought'" (quoting Dr. Barry Brummett, the Charles Sapp Centennial Professor Emeritus in Communication at the University of Texas at Austin).

Harris's (2009) suggestion that "it is the fact that the world seems to be changing so quickly that is triggering apocalyptic themes in culture"—that apocalyptic thought is not only a reflection of "a difficult period of history" but of "changing times"—resonates with the opening statements of Levina and Bui (2013: 1) in their edited volume, *Monster Culture in the 21st Century: A Reader*:

> In the past decade, our rapidly changing world faced terrorism, global epidemics, economic and social strife, new communication technologies, immigration, and climate change, to name a few. These fears

and tensions reflect an ever more interconnected global environment where increased mobility of people, technologies, and disease have produced great social, political, and economic uncertainty. It is safe to say that, over the past decade, we have been terrorized by change. The speeding up of cultures, technologies, and environments . . . has also led to a surge in narratives about . . . zombies . . . and other monstrous bodies. Popular films and television shows . . . have allowed us to deal with the profound acceleration in changing symbolic, economic, and technological systems.[23]

Regardless of whether apocalyptic thought and visions reflect a rapidly changing world or a specific occurrence or a "difficult period of history," it is clear that "apocalyptic gloom sells" (Foster 2014: 2). As Foster (2014: 2) contends, "Death itself is the product most consistently sold to us, or the hope of escape from death. . . . In the end, our culture of narcissistic doom wants more than anything to create a climate of fear and isolation, in which we are forced to endlessly consume and die emotionally, as willing participants in late-stage capitalism." "Indeed," Foster (2014: 2) continues, "we have little choice in the matter; as society becomes increasingly stratified into the very rich and the very poor, human misfortune and visions of apocalyptic doom have become our principal source of entertainment"—or, in her words, "'apocotainment'—the apocalypse as entertainment for the masses."[24]

In the rest of this chapter, we focus on a particular type of "apocotainment"—on explicit environmental or climatic apocalyptic depictions—rather than on those involving pandemics (natural or human-caused), impact events (astronomical objects colliding with Earth), cybernetic revolt/AI takeover and technological singularity, or dysgenics and widespread human infertility—although there are lessons that can be learned from these other depictions; we will make passing reference to some of them. Our goal here is not to catalogue *all* environmental or climatic apocalyptic depictions in film or literature but to tease out some commonalities and, we would argue, problematic aspects of these visions.

Apocalyptic Depictions and the Cinematic Problem of Time

Killingsworth and Palmer (1996: 21) describe "apocalyptic narratives"—"a standard feature of environmentalist polemic (DeGregori [1983]; Emsley [1982])"—as "depicting the end of the world as a result of the overweening desire to control nature." To be sure, the hubristic aspiration and attempt to control nature is often the backdrop for various environmental endgames.

For example, in *The Colony* (2013), a Canadian science fiction action-horror film directed by Jeff Renfroe and set in 2045, the weather machines (in the form of climate modification towers) that control the Earth's warming climate have broken down, creating a cold planet of snow and ice, and forcing the remaining humans into underground bunkers/colonies (see Brisman 2015: 300; Howell 2013). Similarly, in *Snowpiercer* (2013), directed by Bong Joon-ho and set in 2031—seventeen years after an unsuccessful endeavor to reduce global warming with stratospheric aerosol injection (a method of solar geoengineering)[25] has created a new ice age—the remaining humans reside on a self-sustaining train that circumnavigates the Earth (see Denby 2014; Martí 2020; McClanahan, Brisman and South 2017; Schmidt 2014; for a review of the American television series based on the film that premiered in 2020, see Hale 2020; Itzkoff 2020).

Both *The Colony* and *Snowpiercer* portray worlds that have been environmentally devastated as a result of efforts to address global warming. In both films, humans have tried to "control nature" and have failed in doing so. What is not clear in the films is whether the human-induced climate change that triggered a new ice age (weather machines in *The Colony*; stratospheric aerosol injection in *Snowpiercer*) resulted from human attempts to "control nature" *in the first place*, or whether humans were simply unconcerned, unmoved by their actions that degraded the environment. In other words, it might have been anthropocentrism and arrogance, or it might have been indifference that warmed/degraded the planet. (Regardless, it was our monstrous treatment of nature and our abjection of the Earth, our mother.) But it was definitely an effort to *control* nature and "rectify" a changing and increasingly "hostile" environment (brought about by humans *for whatever initial reason*) that resulted in the conditions present in the films—where the Earth really could not sustain human life, other than in bunkers/colonies or on a fast-moving train.

On the surface, it would seem that *The Colony* and *Snowpiercer* illustrate Killingsworth and Palmer's (1996) notion and point about "apocalyptic narratives." In fact, the two films might be better thought of as *post-apocalyptic* (see Denby 2014). But we are getting ahead of ourselves.

We conceptualize the following progression:

ecocide → misericordia → apocalypse → post-apocalypse

What we wish to suggest is that many depictions of environmental "end times" present what we consider to be "incomplete narratives"—only a part or parts of the progression. We begin by offering brief explanations of each of these categories and cinematic and literary instances that represent them. We then turn to several literary examples, which, we argue, encompass more of this timeline and variations on this timeline, before explaining the problems with such truncated stories.

Ecocide

The concept of "ecocide" has a longer history than is often assumed, dating back to the 1970s, but it has gathered increased attention in recent years as the scale of destruction affecting the environment and biodiversity has become more obvious and more pronounced. The source of such impacts is, of course, human activities, leading the late Polly Higgins, a U.K.-based lawyer, to propose an amendment to the 1998 Rome Statute, creating the crime of "ecocide," which was to be defined as "the extensive damage to, destruction of or loss of ecosystem(s) of a given territory, whether by human agency or by other causes, to such an extent that peaceful enjoyment by the inhabitants of that territory has been severely diminished" (Higgins et al. 2013: 257, quoting Higgins 2010).

Today, there are numerous documentaries about harms to the planet caused by humans and, in recent years, many have made direct reference to the idea of "ecocide." Not many fictional depictions, however, have *focused on* ecocide, although plenty of films depict our "ecocidal tendencies." Examples here might include *Days of Thunder* (1990), *Driven* (2001), and the *Fast & Furious* media franchise[26]—all of which demonstrate our fascination with car culture and speed and our profligacy with fossil fuels. In *Cloudy with a Chance of Meatballs* (2009), the animated science fiction comedy film, the "Flint Lockwood Diatonic Super Mutating Dynamic Food Replicator" (or "FLDSMDFR") transforms water into food, but it requires a tremendous amount of energy and results in tremendous food waste that eventually creates an avalanche. The FLDSMDFR eventually gains sentience, developing "food storms" around the world that destroy cities and landmarks. For children, the film is light-hearted; for adults, it should be a scary movie about climate change and our poor environmental stewardship (Lowry 2021). All of these films lend support to Du Rées's (2001: 16) observation that "a certain level of environmental damage is accepted in modern society since it serves to provide for other social interests"—entertainment, private vehicle ownership, and food on demand without consideration for food miles and leftovers in landfills. Perhaps the perfect example of a twenty-first-century blend of machine and magic is the creation of cryptocurrencies, requiring the use of enormous amounts of energy, with side effects of carbon production and water waste, to create virtual and digital "money" like Bitcoin (Chamanara et al. 2023; UNU 2023).

Misericordia

In Chapter 3, we noted how in *Pandorum*, the German science fiction thriller, the crew on the spacecraft *Elysium*, which is headed to the planet of Tanis (which can support human life), learns of Earth's destruction. It is not clear what has caused the end of Earth, but we know from the film's opening title cards that in the year 2153, food and water shortages have become common-place (and that the "Paleo 17" space probe landed on Tanis), and that twenty-one years later (in 2174), the "battle for Earth's limited resources reache[d] its boiling point," leading to the launching of the *Elysium*. What we can infer from this timeline is that some degree of ecocide led to the conditions in the mid- to late twenty-second century.

We also noted at the end of Chapter 3 and at the beginning of this chapter that "the apocalypse" is often associated with a "great disaster" and the "end of time(s)" or the "end of human civilization" or the "end of human life (on Earth)."[27] Under this conceptualization, then, the apocalyptic moment or event in *Pandorum* would be *Earth's destruction*, with the rest of the film devoted to the *post*-apocalypse. How, then, should we conceptualize the inter-vening period?

For Professor Manuel Peter Eisner (2012) of the Institute of Criminology of the University of Cambridge, "'misericorde' was the name given to a knife used on battlefields to kill people with wounds." Professor Eisner has extended its meaning to "reflect[] a society with a very limited ability to save the life of people even with minor injuries" (Eisner 2012). We have reformulated it as *misericordia*—the period between humans' ecocidal acts and omissions and the "end of the world" (or the end of the world *as we currently know it*). During this period, ecocide may continue, as society collapses. The "end," then—the apocalypse—may be the result of ongoing ecocide (and society's inability to change its ways to avoid it), or it may be the result of something else (e.g., war) stemming from societal collapse. So, in *Pandorum*, *misericordia* is occurring during the years between 2153 and 2174 (and likely before and some period after).

To offer another example: in *Mad Max* (1979), set in future Australia, after the Earth's oil supplies have been nearly exhausted, the forces of law and order have begun to break down due to energy shortages. (This becomes more clear, actually, in the 1981 sequel, *Mad Max 2: The Road Warrior*.)

Violent motorcycle gangs have been terrorizing the remaining population, looting, stealing fuel, and foraging for scraps. The plot focuses on Max Rockatansky (played by Mel Gibson), a young police officer in the poorly funded Main Force Patrol (MFP), one of the few remaining police agencies, which has been created to take control of the deserted back roads and protect the remaining outback communities. Some might consider this an *apocalyptic* film or even *post-apocalyptic* in that the *apocalypse* occurred when humans started running out of fossil fuels. We, however, would suggest that it demonstrates *misericordia* in that it precedes the *total* breakdown of society: we do not receive a full picture of what happened before (the *ecocide*), but we can imagine what *might* lie ahead: the *apocalypse*—or an *apocalyptic event*—and the *post-apocalypse*.[28]

Apocalypse

A lot of films are often referred to as "apocalyptic," but here we refer specifically to those depicting attempts to *prevent* an apocalyptic event or to those representing *the experience* of the impact event. Examples of the former, although not ones stemming from human licentiousness, might be Michael Bay's *Armageddon* (1998), starring Bruce Willis, Billy Bob Thornton, Ben Affleck, and Liv Tyler, among others, and Mimi Leder's *Deep Impact* (1998), starring Robert Duvall, Téa Leoni, Elijah Wood, and Morgan Freeman. In both of these films, the would-be "apocalypse event" does not involve environmental or climatic disasters as a result of the lack of human restraint (legal or moral) regarding nature and the Earth's resources but last-minute attempts *to prevent* "impact events" (astronomical objects colliding with the planet). With respect to the latter—*the experience* of the impact—Roland Emmerich's *The Day After Tomorrow* (2004), with Dennis Quaid and Jake Gyllenhaal, portrays sudden, violent catastrophic weather, which includes a massive snowstorm in New Delhi, a powerful hailstorm that strikes Tokyo, and a series of tornadoes that devastate Los Angeles. The audience learns that the buildup of greenhouse gases in the atmosphere has increased surface ocean temperatures and reduced salinity, which has disrupted the thermohaline circulation in the Atlantic Ocean, causing temperatures in New York City to plummet and the Statue of Liberty to become buried in snow (see Brisman and South 2013a). *The Day After Tomorrow* focuses on efforts to endure these various catastrophic weather events—specifically, those in New York City. There is no consideration, however, as to what happens after they do, but civilization as we know it—at least, civilization in the Northern Hemisphere—has changed dramatically.[29]

Post-Apocalypse

The time frame for a *post-apocalyptic* film might be immediately after a cata-clysmic occurrence or some period of time after the catastrophe. In some instances, the *post-apocalyptic* story focuses on the psychology of the remain-ing humans (in literature, we might think of J. G. Ballard's 1962 novel *The Drowned World*, in which most of the Earth has become uninhabitable as a result of global warming);[30] in other instances, the *post-apocalyptic* story centers on efforts to seek out or perpetuate humanity on the planet (again, in literature, we might contemplate Nevil Shute's 1957 novel *On the Beach*)[31] or on attempts to return to Earth after some (environmental) calamity, such as in M. Night Shyamalan's *After Earth* (2013), with Will Smith, Jaden Smith, and Zoë Kravitz. *Post-apocalyptic* fiction may also describe or picture non-technological future worlds, where only isolated elements of society and select technologies remain, or future worlds where humans have evacuated Earth to other planets or space colonies, as seems to be the goal of some of the UHNWIs described in Chapter 3.

Waterworld (1995), starring Kevin Costner, Dennis Hopper, and Jeanne Tripplehorn, begins with the globe in the Universal Pictures logo morphing into a world with the continents submerged under water. An ominous voice states: "The future: The polar ice caps have melted, covering the Earth with water. Those who survive have adapted to a new world." The film focuses on a world (circa 2500) that is covered by water due to a drastic rise in sea lev-els. The human population has been scattered across the ocean(s)—although the Earth appears to be one big ocean at this point—in individual, isolated, floating communities consisting of artificial islands and mostly dilapidated sea vessels. It has been so long since the events that submerged the continents that humans have forgotten that these ever existed; the notion of humans living on "Dryland" is considered a myth. There is, however, no mention as to how the icecaps melted, causing sea levels to rise, or what happened in the years when the continents were gradually submerged.

One of the few films that actually presents some element of the miseri-cordia → apocalypse → post-apocalypse progression is in the opening of *Pandorum*, discussed earlier in this chapter and also in Chapter 3. But for the most part, Hollywood films present just one step or stage in this progres-sion. To some extent, this might be expected: it is hard to condense years of cause and effect in under three hours. And admittedly, the purpose of these films is to entertain (as with the movies produced by the MCU, discussed in Chapter 1)—even if carrying a subtext as in *The Day After Tomorrow*, where the vice president of the United States, Raymond Becker (played by Kenneth

Welsh), is fashioned so similarly to Dick Cheney (see Ebert 2004; Orr 2004), the devout climate denier (see, e.g., Schor 2008), who was vice president of the United States at the time the film was released, that it would be hard to miss the environmental and political message. While collectively, the films (and novels) mentioned earlier might comprise a premonitory puzzle or tale, individual films do not engage in the kind of cinematic ordering and progression that we identified. Let us consider whether a different dynamic unfolds in literature.

Apocalyptic Depictions, the Cinematic Problem of Time, and Literary Solutions

Our first example, Douglas Coupland's *Player One: What Is to Become of Us* (2010), follows four characters in the lounge of an airport bar—Karen, Rick, Luke, and Rachel—in addition to four minor characters and "Player One," a fifth main character—"more of a ghost than a soul" (2010: 42)—who watches, re-narrates, and comments on the events that transpire to the (other) four main characters over the course of a real-time, five-hour story but from the vantage point of an outside observer. While the characters interact in the airport cocktail lounge, crude oil prices go up—to US$251.16 (2010: 53) and then to US$900 a barrel, "but in reality," as Rachel points out, "it's no longer for sale" (2010: 91). Chaos ensues—explosions, rioting, murder. But in the end, order is restored: told from the combined point of view of Rachel and "Player One," we learn (in the final part of the fifth chapter/fifth hour—a sort of epilogue that reveals the fate of the rest of the characters)—that "it will begin to rain, and the chemicals outside the lounge will crackle and fizz and drain away. Gas will be rationed and doled out by the government, and it will never go below $350 a barrel again" (2010: 212). Essentially, *Player One* takes place *during* a global disaster—when oil prices skyrocket. There is not really a *weather* event or *climatic* event, but there is an *environmentally related* event, and we see a little bit how an "apocalyptic event" might unfold: in the third chapter, Karen speaks with her daughter (Casey) on the phone; in response to Karen's question, "Sweetie, are you okay?," Casey replies, "We're outside the Husky station down at the crossroad. It's been one great big hockey riot for the past half-hour. There's no gas left. Everyone's going apeshit. I've been taking pictures." That Casey does not appreciate the severity of the situation suggests either "normalcy bias," which Young (2022: 14) defines as "a psychological quirk that creates a period of initial disbelief or denial during a time of extreme crisis, thereby causing people to fail to appreciate the danger they are in and to fail to act appropriately" (which we will return to later in this chapter), or "crastinal blindness," which Coupland (2010: 219) describes as "the inability to think past tomorrow."[32] That order is restored signals that misericordia has been avoided.

Our second example, David Graham's *Down to a Sunless Sea* ([1979] 1981), told in the first person by Jonah Scott, a British pilot for "Air Britain," takes place in the near future (October 1985). The United States has unraveled into the equivalent of a bankrupt "Third World" country—at least, what would have been called a "Third World" country when the book was written (see Chapter 3)—after it fritters away its oil reserves, leading to the collapse of the dollar. Reflecting on the United States earlier in the decade, Scott explains that the Americans "had enormous reserves of oil, right under their feet—and used it, down to the last drop, anywhere they could. . . . Americans used more energy in seven decades than the rest of the world together. They had one gorgeous lifetime of the biggest cars. . . . And then the oil ran out" (Graham [1979] 1981: 16). "The lack of forward planning," Scott continues, "the persistent refusal to implement a conservation policy made the final result certain. Most Americans believed it could never happen—and when it did happen, it was the sheer velocity of collapse that was so appalling." Returning to the present (the mid-1980s), Scott tells us that without oil, but with a weak currency, food cannot be distributed, leading to widespread hunger and looting. Manhattan, for example, is a "dying city," with "no power, no elevators, no comforts" and a population consisting of "thieves, rapists, hopheads, muggers, stickup and second-story men" (Graham [1979] 1981: 12, 22).

Scott flies a planeload of people from New York to London. En route, the plane learns that Israel has attacked Beirut, Damascus, and Cairo with nuclear weapons in retaliation for their poisoning of Tel Aviv's water supply.[33] Israel's strike triggers a worldwide nuclear holocaust, with the USSR and China attacking the United States and its allies. The survivors on the plane eventually land at McMurdo Station in the Antarctic, where they begin to rebuild a world of peace based on cooperation and an absence of nationalism—"no more Russians, no more English, no more Americans—just people" (Graham [1979] 1981: 304).[34]

What we find striking about this book is that not only does it depict *misericordia*—a(n) (American) society with a very limited ability to care for its unfortunate—but it also describes an *apocalyptic* event (nuclear holocaust), an attempt to navigate (literally) the event, and a *post-apocalypse* (life in Antarctica). One could argue that the book also hints at *ecocide*—the excessive consumption of fossil fuels that leads to the United States sapping all of its oil reserves. One could also maintain that with its "domestic oil fields . . . depleted" and with the United States unable to buy any oil with "worthless dollars" (Graham [1979] 1981: 33), an "initial" or "first" series of apocalyptic events occurred:

> Until the satellite ground relay stations in America went off the air, viewers all over Europe and the rest of the world followed the collapse of a nation. Riots spread to Seattle, Dallas, New Orleans and the great cities of the Midwest; that old hellhole Watts erupted into downtown Los Angeles—and the one common denominator was hunger. With food supplies into cities halted, the starving mobs stopped at nothing: warehouses, shops, hotels, bars. . . . There was to be seen the first great schism in the American population: the hungry but still civilized segment of the people began to leave the cities, walking, cycling, but not driving . . . there was no more gasoline, and every road and avenue was choked with abandoned cars. Those who stayed were used to living by their wits; the homeless, poor, criminal and insane went on the greatest looting spree of all time. It was only when they realized that a suitcase containing a million dollars would not buy one loaf of bread, one can of beans, that they began looting for food, not valuables. (Graham [1979] 1981: 33–34)

In other words, the book may illustrate ecocide → misericordia → apocalypse → post-apocalypse *or* ecocide → apocalypse #1 (rioting, food supplies halted, starving mobs) → misericordia → apocalypse #2 (nuclear holocaust) → post-apocalypse. Regardless, our point is that *Down to a Sunless Sea* offers detail, depth, and complexity to each "step" or "stage," even though the bulk of the story occurs *during* an apocalyptic event. We will elucidate why this is significant after our third example.

Our third example, James Howard Kunstler's *World Made by Hand* (2008), set in Union Grove, New York, a little north of the state capital of Albany, is, in the words of one reviewer, a "semidystopic dramatization of what small-town American life might be like in the wake of major terrorist bombings and industrial decline on U.S. soil" (Cheuse 2008b). Like *Down to a Sunless Sea*, *World Made By Hand* (2008) has a male narrative protagonist—in this case, Robert Earle, a former software executive "haunted by the ghosts of [his] family: wife Sandy, gone from an outbreak of encephalitis, daughter Genna, taken by the [Mexican] flu, and son Daniel, who left home and did not return" (Kunstler 2008: 14). "I wished I knew whether he was alive and well and where he had gone and been to," Earle laments, "but there were no more phones or mail as we once knew them. I tried to avoid nostalgia because it could destroy you" (Kunstler 2008: 14). The residents of Union Grove, like Earle, must cope with a world without cars, gasoline, or electricity—or black pepper or cinnamon (Kunstler 2008: 24; for a discussion, see Leone 2008): this is a world wrecked by "climate weirdness" (Kunstler 2008: 181)—"the Everglades are drowning" (Kunstler 2008: 142)—and the economic and social upheaval of "peak oil" (see Cheuse 2008a; Leone 2008)[35]—a situation that Jonah Scott recounts in *Down to a Sunless Sea* and that starts to unfold in *Player One*. At one juncture, we hear that "New York City is finished. . . . They can't keep order there, and you can't have business without order. It'll take a hundred years to sort things out and get it all going again" (Kunstler 2008: 142). A few pages later, we learn about "civil disorders in Philadelphia and Baltimore, refugees fleeing, what you folks call pickers, bandit gangs. Pennsylvania became a desperate place. After awhile, it was like cowboys and Indians"—and hear that old (or, perhaps, just simmering) "grievances and vendettas" (re)emerged: "poor against whatever rich [were] left. Black against white. English-speaking against the Spanish. More than one bunch on the Jews" (Kunstler 2008: 148, 149). Millions have died from epidemics ("common antibiotics were in short supply" [Kunstler 2008: 23]) and terrorism: a bomb in Washington, another in Los Angeles—an "act of jihad [that] was extraordinarily successful. It tanked the whole U.S. economy" (Kunstler 2008: 23). Throughout the novel, we are reminded that "the law is on the run" (2008: 8)—"No real police, courts. No state governments" (2008: 206)—and "no social safety net" (2008: 229)—"no *official* safety nets . . . no more social services, no life insurance, nothing but the goodwill of neighbors" (2008: 70, emphasis added). In Leone's (2008) summary, "a phantom government exists, but nobody can recall the last election."

The novel draws a contrast of life in Union Grove with that of "Karptown," ruled by the kingpin Wayne Karp, a "colony of former NASCAR-loving freaks," in the words of Leone (2008), comprised of "scrappers and thugs who salvage and steal from around the county" (Brisman 2015: 287); a religious group or collective called the "New Faith Church," led by Brother Jobe; and a self-sufficient English manor–style arrangement lorded over by a wealthy farmer, Steven Bullock (see Brisman 2015: 287). Each of the groups, then, represents the different paths or ways in which society might unfold in the aftermath of a series of cataclysmic events and the breakdown of modern social norms: cooperation and community, in the case of Union Grove; a kind of "Social Darwinism"/"only the fittest survive" reminiscent of William Graham Sumner (see Reich 2011) or Donald Trump (see Chait 2017), as with Karptown; religious devotion to a cult of personality, in the example of Brother Jobe; and a sort of "pseudo-feudalism," in the form of Bullock's farm.[36] As one might expect, tensions and violence occur within and between the groups, although in the end, the groups that emphasize unity and support fare better than those organized around exploitation.

In many respects, *World Made by Hand* could be considered *post-apocalyptic* in that it describes life after society or the world as we know it. In fact, there is an acronym for this, although it does not appear in Kunstler's book— "Teotwawki" (which stands for "the end of the world as we know it") (Foster 2014: 26, citing O'Brien 2012; Weiss 2024), which we noted in Chapter 1.[37] Indeed, at one juncture, Earle makes a trip to the capitol building in Albany, where he encounters ransacked filing cabinets, papers strewn about, and the acting lieutenant governor slumped at his desk. To a surprised Earle, the acting lieutenant governor explains: "I guess you could say we're keeping the chairs warm . . . under the theory that this . . . eventually comes to an end" (for a discussion, see Leone 2008).[38]

Taking Coupland's *Player One*, Graham's *Down to a Sunless Sea*, and Kunstler's *World Made by Hand* as a group—and there are, to be sure, many more examples that we could discuss—we would suggest that literature seems to offer a more complete picture of the ecocide → misericordia → apocalypse → post-apocalypse sequence than film. The reason should be obvious: as noted earlier, there is only so much that writers and directors can fit into a three-hour film. The more important issue pertains to *why* this is problematic.

To answer this question, it may be helpful to return to zombies for a moment. Drezner (2014: 835) remarks that "in almost all zombie films and fiction, the plot is depressingly similar. Flesh-eating ghouls are introduced in minute one. By minute ten, the world is a postapocalyptic hellscape." "The implication," Drezner (2014: 835) continues, "is that if zombielike threats emerge, both the state and civil society *will break down almost immediately*" (emphasis added). For Drezner (2014: 835), "the assumption is so baked into the traditional zombie narrative that some of the most prominent examples in the genre—*28 Days Later*, *The Walking Dead*—do not even bother to show *how* society breaks down. They simply flash forward to the end of the civilized world" (emphasis added).

A similar insinuation—that state and civil society will collapse almost instantly—coupled with the absence of the misericordia process or stage—also occurs in environmental or climatic cinema. In *The Colony* and *Snowpiercer*, viewers learn about failed efforts to address Earth's warming climate and then are catapulted into worlds of snow and ice: in the words of Schmidt (2014), describing *Snowpiercer*, the setting is "an elegant ice age rather than a humid melting," because "chemicals released into the atmosphere to cool our warming planet perform too well, rendering Earth an uninhabitable snowball." But, as Schmidt (2014) continues, "*Snowpiercer* does not depict the original disaster directly. Like many films in this genre, it expends creative energy imagining the social dystopia that follows the apocalypse." *Waterworld* (1995), in comparison, skips any mention altogether of human efforts to retard or reverse the melting of the polar ice caps, jettisoning moviegoers into a planet of water five hundred years in the future. The message or impact of this narrative leap is twofold.

First, as Denby (2014: 94) explains in his review of *Snowpiercer*, "The disaster is just a given, which suggests a more banal explanation for the end of days. . . . In movies, the death of a single person is still a tragedy; the death of the human race is entertainment."[39] Denby (2014: 94) contends that *Snowpiercer*, like other films where "the world is about to end—or, at least, humanity is about to be destroyed"—movies such as *Waterworld* (1995), *The Day After Tomorrow* (2004), *I Am Legend* (2007), *The Road* (2009), and *World War Z* (2013)—is not "overtly or even covertly political." Nevertheless, the notion of the disaster as "a given" instills a sense of inevitability, which underscores that such films—and, really, any real-life cataclysm or upheaval (environmental or otherwise)—are about *survival*. We will return to this matter shortly.

Second, such depictions (where the disaster is "a given" and state and civil society collapse almost instantly) condition us to think about *an event*—all of a sudden, the Earth is blanketed in snow or covered in water. Even *The Day After Tomorrow*, whose story unfolds over the course of a few days, conceptualizes the environmental impact of global warming as one discrete, violent weather occurrence (albeit after the "warnings" of catastrophic storms in New Delhi and Tokyo and tornadoes in Los Angeles). This treatment of climate change as instantaneous—akin to the snapping of one's fingers (to evoke Thanos in *Infinity War* and *Endgame*, discussed in Chapter 1)—shifts our individual and collective attention not just from *mitigating* the effects of climate change or even *adapting* to them but to *survival*.

Douglas Rushkoff (2022a), the American media theorist, recounts meeting with "a group mysteriously described as 'ultra-wealthy stakeholders,' out in the middle of the desert"—"five super-wealthy guys—yes, all men—from the upper echelon of the tech investing and hedge-fund world. At least two of them were billionaires." Rushkoff (2022a) describes how the meeting—at first, he thought it would be *a conference* with the "tech elite" on "the future of technology"—centered on issues of security for (their) underground bunker systems after "the event": "The event. That was their euphemism for the environmental collapse, social unrest, nuclear explosion, solar storm, unstoppable virus, or malicious computer hack that takes everything down."

Essentially, for the "ultra-wealthy stakeholders" to whom Rushkoff (2022a) spoke, it did not matter *what* "the event" would be. All that mattered was that there *will be an event* for which they aim to be prepared. This means being safe, secure, and protected from the "abject Others"—"the poor"—and "wretched social masses," discussed in Chapter 3. What we wish to stress is that in many apocalyptic scenarios—and in environmental or climatic ones, in particular—there may not be *an event* but *events*—ones that are spread out over time. Hollywood condenses these, which sends a distorted—and, we might add, perverse—message: you are a sucker if you are not ready.

For Elon Musk, quoted in Woolf (2016) and discussed in Chapter 3, "there [a]re 'two fundamental paths' facing humanity today. 'One is that we stay on Earth forever and then there will be an inevitable extinction event. . . . The alternative is to become a spacefaring civilization, and a multi-planetary species.'" For those who are not as financially well-off as Musk and who cannot quite afford their own "Heart of Gold" spaceship—or a seat on Musk's (see Wall 2016; Woolf 2016)—there are the types of "doomsday bunkers" described by Rushkoff (2022a). For others, "preparedness" (or "self-reliance," as some prefer; see O'Brien 2012) can range from stockpiling a year's supply of chopped wood, rice, wheat, and other items/staples to "just" seventy-two-hour emergency kits. And, of course, plenty of guns. As James Wesley Rawles, editor of SurvivalBlog ("The Daily Blog for Prepared Individuals Living in Uncertain Times Since 2005"), states: "I don't want to wake up and find out that I'm the go-to guy—literally" (quoted in O'Brien 2012).[40]

Dreams, Nightmares, Hardships, and Heroes

Trimble (2019: 4) points out that "Black women, white mothers, and children are typically relegated to the narrative margins of apocalypse films." In addition, such films often do not provide us with an image of *what could be*—what could be different or better. The same criticisms cannot be said for literature. Let us consider but one example: the children's book *Just a Dream* (1990), by Chris Van Allsburg. *Just a Dream* tells the story of Walter, a young boy who litters and refuses to separate trash from recycling—a child who cannot comprehend the purpose or joys of environmental stewardship and who dismisses his neighbor, Rose, a little girl delighting in watering her recently planted tree. One evening, Walter watches a television program that portrays "a boy who lived in the future"—one who "flew around in a tiny airplane that he parked on the roof of his house" and who had "a robot and small machine that could make any kind of food with the push of a button" (Van Allsburg 1990: [7]). The narrator explains that when Walter went to sleep that night after watching the television show, he did so "wishing he lived in the future" so that he could have "his own plane, a robot to take out the trash, and a machine that could make jelly doughnuts by the thousands" (Van Allsburg 1990: [8]). Walter falls asleep, and his wish comes true. He travels in his bed to the future, where he wakes up in the middle of a huge dump. The houses on his street are half-buried in bulging trash bags. Walter thinks this is "just a dream" and goes back to sleep.

Walter wakes a second time, now finding himself in his bed perched in the branches of a tall tree. Many of the trees around the one in which Walter is caught have been chopped down. Walter learns that the trees are being felled for something "very important"—for the "QUALITY TOOTHPICK COMPANY" (Van Allsburg 1990: [16]). Walter falls back asleep. . . .

> Walter couldn't stop coughing. His bed was balanced on the rim of a giant smokestack. The air was filled with smoke that burned his throat and made his eyes itch. All around him, dozens of smokestacks belched thick clouds of hot, foul smoke. (Van Allsburg 1990: [20])

Next, Walter travels to the mountains, where he encounters hikers traipsing to the HOTEL EVEREST, located "on the top of Mount Everest" and adorned with a flashing yellow sign (Van Allsburg 1990: [24])—and then to the "open sea," where fishermen celebrate catching a small fish ("Our second one this week!" (Van Allsburg 1990: [28]))—one so tiny that Walter asks, "Aren't you supposed to throw the little ones back"? (Van Allsburg 1990: [28]).

The rocking of Walter's bed puts him back to sleep, but he awakes to. . . .

> a loud, shrieking horn . . . cars and trucks all around him, horns honking loudly, creeping along inch by inch. Every driver ha[s] a car phone in one hand and a big cup of coffee in the other. When the traffic stop[s] completely, the honking gr[ows] even louder. (Van Allsburg 1990: [32])

It is important to remember, here, that Van Allsburg's book was published in 1990. Thus, when Walter wonders, "Where are the tiny airplanes, the robots?" and ponders, "This can't be the future," he is—or would have been—quite wrong: this seemingly futuristic world in 1990 is our *past* world in the mid-2020s: drivers today use their personal mobile phones/devices, rather than car phones, which fell out of favor fifteen or so years ago (fifteen years *after* Walter's dream, that is).[41]

Walter's subsequent trip takes him to the Grand Canyon, where he sees a "dull yellow haze" and gazes into a "fogged distance" and where he encounters a woman on a horse, who offers to sell him postcards that "showed the canyon in the old days" (Van Allsburg 1990: [36]). From here, while lying in his bed flying through the night sky, Walter talks to a duck—part of a flock that has been flying for days, seeking a pond where they had always stopped to eat.

Walter then wakes up in the present feeling terrible: "The future he'd seen was not what he'd expected," and the "robots and little airplanes didn't seem very important now" (Van Allsburg 1990: [42]). Looking out of his bedroom window at the trees and grass in the early morning light, he jumps out of bed, races down the street (still in his pajamas), and locates his litter from the previous day. He then sorts the items he had lazily placed in the rubbish bins.

A few days later, Walter plants a tree with his father (in close proximity to Rose's) and then, later that night, goes to sleep. He wakes to find his bed standing in the shade of two tall trees. Walter looks up at the blue sky, notices laundry hanging from a clothesline flapping in the breeze, and observes a man pushing "an old motorless lawn mower" (Van Allsburg 1990: [48]). "This isn't the future," Walter thinks to himself. "It's the past" (Van Allsburg 1990: [48]). Walter soon discovers that the man is Rose's great-grandson, that one of the trees had been planted by Rose and that "this was the future" (Van Allsburg 1990: [48]). It was "a different kind of future"—one (still) without robots or tiny airplanes—or even clothes dryers or gas-powered lawn mowers—but one that he liked and that made him smile (Van Allsburg 1990: [48]).

More than ten years ago, Schmidt (2014), writing on the uptick in cinematic dystopia (with the release of *Divergent* [2014] and *The Hunger Games: Mockingjay—Part 1* [2014]), commented that while "cinema has long been drawn to science fiction and the challenge of visualizing the unimaginable," many dystopian and post-apocalyptic films (including *Snowpiercer*, which had been released the year before) "are concerned with environmental apocalypse, or . . . unfold in the aftermath" but "offer no solutions and little consolation." Although ostensibly a children's storybook, *Just a Dream* is no less "nightmarish" (to borrow from Schmidt 2014). But unlike the films discussed earlier, it does proffer an alternate vision of what could be, of a different trajectory with hints for how to achieve it, and it thereby fosters a sense of hope.

Indeed, many films on the ecocide → misericordia → apocalypse → post-apocalypse spectrum extend (read: trumpet) announcements about human resiliency and, more specifically, survivalism (often based on principles of survivalism). This should come as little surprise. As Young (2022: 15) writes in his "manual of manuals"—his compilation of official governmental documents and guides for preparing for and responding to a wide range of disasters—"Western democracies tend[] to focus on the individual and the actions they could take to protect themselves, their immediate family and their property."[42] To be sure, "a 'survivalist' theme often runs parallel to and occasionally intersects with American or Western preoccupation with end-game scenarios. For example, one of the characters in Barbara Kingsolver's novel *Flight Behavior* asserts: 'Humans are in love with the idea of our persisting. . . . We fetishise it, really. Our retirement funds, our genealogies. Our so-called ideas for the ages' (2012: 282)" (Brisman 2015: 288n6).

It has not always been this way. In his analysis of Susan Sontag's "The Imagination of Disaster" (1965), Broderick (1993: 362) reflects on Sontag's recognition of "the dominance of an aesthetic of *disaster* (with monsters as metaphors of nuclear energy) and a fear of global atomic death which could occur universally and at any moment" (emphasis in original). As Broderick (1993: 362) contends, "The sub-genre of SF cinema which has entertained visions of nuclear Armageddon concerns itself primarily with *survival* as its dominant discourse" (emphasis in original). For Broderick (1993: 362), from "the early post-Hiroshima films of the '40s which anticipated global atomic conflict and the cautionary tales of short and long-term effects in the '50s through to the hero myths of apocalypse in the '80s, a discernable shift away from an imagination of disaster toward *one of survival* is evident" (emphasis added). So, in turn, for Schmidt (2014), whereas filmmakers in 1955 were "preoccupied with the spectacle of apocalypse (as in a film like *Day the World Ended*) . . . by 1985, a film like *Mad Max 3: Beyond Thunderdome* was much more concerned with the struggles of surviving in a post-apocalyptic dystopian society."[43]

While Schmidt (2014) might have invoked an example from some years earlier (the "struggles of surviving" are no less pronounced in *Mad Max 2: The Road Warrior* than in *Mad Max 3: Beyond Thunderdome*), the point is that most films that fall in the latter half of the ecocide → misericordia → apocalypse → post-apocalypse sequence "centre on a rugged hero figure." "The protagonists with whom we are conditioned to identify in these movies are the survivor types. As survivors of an apocalypse, they give us hope that we can survive hardships" (Harris 2009, quoting Jamsheed Akrami, a filmmaker and Professor at William Paterson University in Wayne, New Jersey).

But "the hope"—if one can call it that—is a very specific kind of "hope" for a very specific few—a very particular "hope" for a very explicit segment of the population: a white male seeking to fulfill his patriarchal role as "a central father figure" (Harris 2009). This leaves Trimble (2019: x) to ask, "if able-bodied men are the model survivors, what does this mean for the rest of us?" Relatedly, Trimble (2019: x) wonders, "What will we do with our supplies if our neighbors don't have any?" Most films avoid such questions by consolidating "the few" to the heteronormative nuclear family (or a male in a protective role looking after a child/younger person) and treating "the neighbors" and friends (essentially, anyone else) as either a marauding threat (such as in *The Road* [2009]) or as sacrificial lambs to assist the protagonists and advance the plot (as in *Children of Men* [2006]).

To return for a moment to zombies, Staples (2017) writes, in his appreciation of George Romero, who passed away on July 16, 2017, that Romero's "broader theme" was "how mutual contempt and tribal self-interest so often prevent people from banding together in the face of a mortal threat. The flesh-eating dead, at least, come together in mindless self-interest," whereas in *Night of the Living Dead* (1968), "the embattled residents of the farmhouse bicker and betray one another even as darkness closes in. Mr. Romero viewed them as a metaphor for a society so deeply invested in petty enmities that it failed to see it was being swallowed alive."[44] In other words, films like Romero's *Night of the Living Dead* and others involving "the-living-dead-as-metaphor" (Gleiberman 2017) often convey what much environmental and climatic disaster films do not—that *community* and *cooperation* trump *individualism* and *self-interest* (although neither Romero's zombie films nor environmental and climatic disaster films offer anything like *Just a Dream*).

Essentially, films depicting one or more steps or stages in the ecocide → misericordia → apocalypse → post-apocalypse sequence do not offer glimpses of a different or, perhaps, better future. Instead, we encounter stories of *survival*—usually because of rugged (male) individualism—that pronounce a commitment to patriarchal and heteronormative values. (We rarely meet Black lesbians or nonbinary individuals leading the way, navigating obstacles, kicking butt, and "making it through" the quest.) Seldom do we experience the potentials of cooperation and the pitfalls of tribalism.

As fiction goes (albeit in literature, rather than cinema), Kunstler's *World Made by Hand* does offer us a view of a different future. In his review, Cheuse (2008b) writes that while "things in Union Grove get worse before they improve, and certainly the world never returns to the level of technological accomplishment of our day [the first decade of the twenty-first century], . . . in the end, the beauty of Kunstler's brilliant cautionary fiction, aside from the charming narrative with its many convincing details of life after apocalypse, is that most readers will admit that Earle's world, the world made by hand, after all the terror bombs and bad actors and missing luxuries are dealt with, sounds as least as unpredictably pleasing as our own."[45]

Kunstler's story becomes more compelling if one situates it in his larger intellectual or literary history. In *The Geography of Nowhere: The Rise and Decline of America's Man-Made Landscape* (1993), a work of nonfiction,

Kunstler explores the relationship of the automobile to American society, civic planning, and suburban sprawl. In *The Long Emergency: Surviving the Converging Catastrophes of the Twenty-First Century* (2005: 3, 17), another work of nonfiction, Kunstler argues, *inter alia*, that "the American way of life—which is now virtually synonymous with suburbia—can run only on reliable supplies of dependably cheap oil and gas," that "the price and supplies of fossil fuels will suffer oscillations and disruptions" (leading to economic and social upheavals) in a period that he refers to as "the Long Emergency," and that "life will become"—it will *need* to become—"intensely and increasingly local," somewhat like Union Grove.[46] Effectively, Kunstler's nonfiction (such as *The Geography of Nowhere* and *The Long Emergency*) provides us with views of ecocide and our path to misericordia and the apocalypse; Kunstler's fictional work *World Made by Hand* offers us a post-apocalyptic vision and setting. The former—the nonfiction (Kunstler 1993, 2005)—offers some descriptions and prescriptions for how to avoid the cataclysms and catastrophes that precede the latter—the fiction (Kunstler 2008).

In many respects, *Just a Dream* accomplishes in fewer than fifty pages what Kunstler (in three books) or movies (in two-to-three hours) do not: Van Allsburg narrates ecocidal acts/omissions, portrays apocalyptic environmental harm, and then provides both a different/better future and suggested steps toward achieving this different/better future before it is no longer a possibility. *Just a Dream* may neither contain an image of misericordia nor extend environmental catastrophe into the post-apocalypse, but perhaps that is the point: the ecocide → misericordia → apocalypse → post-apocalypse sequence is not inevitable. Unfortunately, it will take more than just picking up one's own litter, separating recyclables from rubbish, and planting trees, as Walter does after his nightmare. But the future of humanity and our place in this world may not rest on the broad shoulders of hirsute adult humans with Y chromosomes and guns.

Taking Stock: Ambiguity, Ambivalence, and Apocalyptic Imaginaries

"Environmental discourses have long been clothed in the language of Apocalypse," Hulme (2009: 63) writes in his helpful account, *Why We Disagree About Climate Change: Understanding Controversy, Inaction and Opportunity*. But this was not always the case. As Buell (1995: 301) reveals, "For the first two centuries of settlement, American environmental thought remained *millennial* rather than *apocalyptic*, driven by the vision of wilderness as an inexhaustible resource waiting to be transformed into productive farms, towns, and cities, in the spirit of the biblical promise that the desert shall blossom as the rose" (emphasis added). "Only by gradual degrees, during the nineteenth century," explains Buell (1995: 301), "did the sense of environmental endangerment gather force and begin to challenge this gospel of plenty." In fact, as Buell (1995: 301) points out, "only during the past two or three decades, and scarcely even then, have larger numbers of Americans declared themselves willing to curtail their taste for abundance to alleviate pressure on the environment."

From here, Buell (1995: 308) outlines the discourse (rather than the social history) of environmental apocalypticism, concluding with the following: "As ecocatastrophe becomes an increasingly greater possibility, so will the occasions for environmental apocalyptic expression and the likelihood that it will suffuse essay, fiction, film, sculpture, painting, theatre, and dance in unprecedentedly powerful, mind-haunting ways"—some of which we have attempted to highlight and consider in the previous sections of this chapter. Buell (1995: 308) then asks: "Can our imaginations of apocalypse actually forestall it, as our fears of nuclear holocaust so far have? Even the slimmest of possibilities is enough to justify the nightmare."

Buell's (1995) question, which we reformulate ever so slightly, is what animates the rest of this penultimate part of this chapter: what impacts have our imaginations of environmental apocalypse actually had? What effects has the rhetoric of apocalypticism had? We consider arguments suggesting positive dimensions to environmental apocalyptic imaginaries as well as what we might consider to be negative or counterproductive components of such depictions and visions.

Positive Aspects of Environmental Apocalyptic Language and Imagery

For Young (2022: 13), "popular culture has a role to play in how we interpret information." Films afford us the opportunity "to imagine how a disaster might play out without having to experience it for ourselves"—to "peer into the abyss from a safe distance," proposes Rahner (2019: 63). Because "Hollywood has tackled every kind of cataclysm, from pandemics (*Contagion*, *World War Z*, *I Am Legend*) to nuclear war (*Threads*, *The Day After*, *Dr. Strangelove*), natural disasters (*Twister*, *Supervolcano*, *The Wizard of Oz*) and alien invasion (too many to mention)," Young (2022: 13) argues, "the depiction of cataclysms on screen can help to prepare the public for the real thing: they allow audiences to face their fears in a safe environment, think about how they would act in the same situation and discuss the scenario with others."[47] Young's (2022: 13) suggestion that "on-screen" cataclysms can prime us for "the real thing" resonates with that of Rahner (2019: 62), who quotes Biskind, author of *The Sky Is Falling: How Vampires, Zombies, Androids, and Superheroes Made America Great for Extremism* (2018), for the proposition that "apocalyptic fantasy movies and TV shows . . . are 'dress rehearsals for a show we hope will never open.'" In a related vein, Vlahos (2013) contends that contemplating the zombie apocalypse (or for our purposes, an/the environmental apocalypse) functions as a "form of shared emotional preparation—a collective therapy— for facing bad things to come," adding that, ironically, this meditation may be "society's only working pathway to real-world, worst-case strategic analysis" (quoted in Drezner 2014: 832).[48]

Taken together, then, Young (2022), Rahner (2019), and Vlahos (2013) find value in apocalyptic fantasies for their capacity to condition or groom audiences for "bad things" that may be on the horizon (although whether the "bad thing" is the "the real thing"—the cataclysm depicted on the screen—or some *other* "bad thing" likely depends on the nature of the calamity: alien invasions and zombie uprisings are less likely than tornados, floods, and pandemics). This seems plausible, but we would underscore that the statements quoted earlier refer to *emotional* "preparation" and "preparedness." None of the authors seem to suggest that the films offer anything remotely akin to the purportedly practical information available on Rawles's website SurvivalBlog (discussed earlier), although somewhat disturbingly, Drezner (2014: 837) finds that "as zombies have acquired more cultural cachet, the [National Rifle Association] and its supporters have leaned even more heavily on the millenarian argument to protect gun rights (Patrick 2014)"—which is a rather elaborate way of proposing that zombie movies encourage gun ownership.

Both Bishop (2009) and Schmidt (2014) offer additional perspectives worth our consideration here. For Bishop (2009), the issue is less that apocalyptic scenarios "prepare the public for the real thing" to come or operate as "dress rehearsals" for a show we do not want to experience than the fact that apocalyptic narratives might help prepare audiences *for reality*. Bishop (2009: 24) recounts how Peter Dendle, a Professor of English at Pennsylvania State University Mont Alto and author of *The Zombie Movie Encyclopedia*, "was approached in the summer of 2005 by a law student who had survived the horrors of September 11 firsthand. Although the experience was understandably shocking, this student claimed he had been emotionally prepared for the tragedy not by his family, community, or government, but by his long appreciation for zombie movies." With this in mind, Bishop (2009: 24) speculates that "perhaps zombie cinema"—and, again, we would include a wider range of apocalyptic cinema—"is not merely a reflection of modern society, but a type of preemptive panacea, and that potential gives the genre both cultural significance and value."

For Schmidt (2014), as discussed earlier, while speculating on the reasons for an apparent increase, at the time, in dystopian cinema and post-apocalyptic situations (pointing, specifically, to *Snowpiercer*, *Divergent*, and *The Hunger Games: Mockingjay—Part 1*), observed that such movies "seem[ed] [both] more urgent and more extreme" but were bereft of solutions or offered little in the way of comfort. This led Schmidt (2014) to inquire: "Why . . . do we shell out 12, 13, 14 dollars for films that seem designed only to frighten and depress us? What species of entertainment, much less relief, do these nightmare scenarios offer?" Schmidt (2014) speculated that "these films allow us to reflect on the harsh realities of our present moment, on conditions that are difficult to confront head-on. Though ostensibly set in the future, the post-apocalyptic mode can function as a window on, and critique of, the present"—perhaps in the way that Neill Blomkamp, the writer, producer, and director of *Elysium*, discussed in Chapter 3, viewed his film as a commentary on today/contemporary society.

Causes for Concern: Negative Aspects of Environmental Apocalyptic Language and Imagery

Earlier in this chapter, we made the case that many (cinematic) depictions of environmental "end times" present what we referred to as "incomplete narratives"—only a part or parts of the ecocide → misericordia → apocalypse → post-apocalypse sequence. Often, such "incomplete narratives" treat "the disaster" as "a given" (instilling a sense of ineluctability)—and as "an event" (a *discrete* event)—whereby the Earth is suddenly flooded or buried in snow. As a result, we argued, audiences receive the message that real-life cataclysms or upheavals (environmental or otherwise) cannot be avoided or mitigated— and that *adaptation* means *survival* (of the few, almost invariably led by men) in a somewhat zero-sum game. In contrast, some literature proffers alternate (hopeful) visions of what could be—of a different trajectory that either averts the ecocide → misericordia → apocalypse → post-apocalypse sequence (with hints of how to follow/forge this path [e.g., *Just a Dream*] or fosters "unpredictably pleasing" worlds in the aftermath of widespread devastation, destruction, and death [e.g., *World Made by Hand*]).

To be sure, these are not our only misgivings about or criticisms of apocalyptic imaginaries and, notwithstanding some of the potential positive aspects noted in the previous section, we identify two additional concerns.

First, while the notion of "the disaster" (or "the disaster *event*") as "a given" can infuse a feeling of inescapability ("we are all at risk"), the opposite may also occur. As Young (2022: 14) contends, films may have "a detrimental effect on the public's perception of risk." As an example, Young (2022: 14) points to tornadoes, "which are almost universally depicted as taking place in rural locations" but which "in reality . . . can occur anywhere." Moreover, Young (2022: 14) asserts—and this relates to our objections to the "rugged hero" representation—"the fact that our heroes frequently survive, despite the odds, . . . serves to downplay the risk involved in major disasters." As Young (2022: 14) explains, this "plays into a human flaw, a cognitive bias, that is a key problem with which emergency planners are familiar." This "cognitive bias" or "normalcy bias" (mentioned earlier) is a "psychological quirk that creates a period of initial disbelief or denial during a time of extreme crisis, thereby causing people to fail to appreciate the danger they are in and to fail to act appropriately" (Young 2022: 14). It is, as Young (2022: 14) continues, "what leads people to gather at the beach and stare out to sea moments before a tsunami; it is why we do not evacuate as a volcano is erupting, and why many of us ignore flood and tornado warnings." Importantly, "this underestimation of risk has been found to lead to less obvious consequences during natural disasters, too," where studies have found that "during severe flooding, male drivers take particularly dangerous and inappropriate actions, such as attempting to drive through water" and that, in fact, "more than half of all flood deaths in the United States are drivers who have made poor decisions" (Young 2022: 14). In other words, cinematic depictions and stories of survival may result in misguided assessments of one's own invincibility. Helen Hunt and Bill Paxton may be able to outrun a tornado in *Twister* (1996); most of us cannot.[49]

Three decades ago, Buell (1995: 285) asserted that "apocalypse is the single most powerful master metaphor that the contemporary environmental imagination has at its disposal. . . . The rhetoric of apocalypticism implies that the fate of the world hinges on the arousal of the imagination to a sense of crisis" (for an assessment, see Anson 2020: 68). While environmental apocalypticism remains powerful, we are not so certain that it has been so in the ways that Buell (1995) described. And this leads us to our second point. For Buell (1995: 285), apocalyptic imagination can be "used to anticipate and, if possible, forestall actual apocalypse." But in the ensuing decades, commentators across the political spectrum have questioned the motivating potential of "apocalyptic doom" (Foster 2014: 2). Indeed, Anson (2020: 60) observes that "narratives of apocalypse" and predictions of what might precede or follow it—"too often overwhelm, immobilize, and instill a sense of futility."

McCright (2007: 208–09) notes that "most of the anti-environmental coun-termovement has criticized climate science for promoting gloom-and-doom scenarios (Bailey 1993)"—the implication being that the public—or the American public, at least—has become scared, overwhelmed, and fatigued by repeated doomsday messaging.

Similarly, Bret Stephens (2022), the conservative columnist for *The New York Times* and self-proclaimed "agnostic on the causes of climate change" whose views on global warming came under fire when he was first hired by the newspaper (see, e.g., Calderone and Baumann 2017; Readfearn 2017), decried "apocalyptic environmentalism" early in his tenure at *The New York Times*, asserting that "if environmental alarmists ever wonder why more people haven't come around to their way of thinking, it isn't because people like me occasionally voice doubts in newspaper op-eds. It's because too many past predictions of imminent disaster didn't come to pass. That isn't because every alarm is false—many are too real—but because our Promethean species has shown the will and wizardry to master it, at least when it's been given the means to do so" (Stephens 2018). Several years later, Stephens (2022) described how at one point, he felt that "the sever-ity of the threat seemed to [him] wildly exaggerated and that the proposed cures all smacked of old-fashioned statism mixed with new-age religion." He asked: "Hadn't we repeatedly lived through previous alarms about other, allegedly imminent, environmental catastrophes that didn't come to pass, like the belief, widespread in the 1970s, that overpopulation would inevitably lead to mass starvation? And if the Green Revolution had spared us from that Malthusian nightmare, why should we not have confidence that human ingenuity wouldn't also prevent the parade of horribles that climate change was supposed to bring about?" (Stephens 2022).[50] Reflecting on his evolving thinking, Stephens (2022) maintained that while "expensive efforts to curb greenhouse gas emissions in Europe and North America seemed particularly fruitless when China, India and other developing countries weren't about to curb their own appetite for fossil fuels," he was bothered by "a millenarian fervor . . . about climate activism, with its apocalyptic imagery (the Statue of Liberty underwater) and threats of doom unless we were willing to live far more frugally." Eventually, Stephens (2022) came to "accept the danger we face," concluding his piece with a number of suggestions for devising effective climate policies in the current socio-political landscape. One of these ("*Be honest about the nature of the challenge*") advises that "talk of an imminent climate catastrophe is probably misleading, at least in the way most people understand 'imminent.' A continual drumbeat of alarm may do more to exhaust voters than it will to rouse them."

Essentially, for Stephens (2018, 2022) as for Anson (2020) and McCright (2007)—and contra Buell (1995)—apocalyptic depictions, discourse, imagery, and rhetoric can overwhelm and scare, leading to exhaustion and fatigue. More worrisome is Drezner's (2014: 836) contention that "if citizens think that we're teetering on the brink of chaos, the apocalyptic mindset can, in and of itself, help *bring about* the very disaster it fears"[51] (emphasis added). Drezner's (2014) claim may be a little extreme, for "mindsets" are just that: they exist *in the mind*, but they do not *do* anything. They are individual or collective attitudes regarding, *inter alia*, culture, outlook, philosophy, values, and worldview. They may influence behavior—prompt action or inaction—but by themselves cannot "bring about" anything; an "apocalyptic mindset" certainly cannot "bring about the very disaster it fears." Nevertheless, *an* or *the* apocalyptic imagination or mindset, rather than "anticipating" and possibly "forestalling" (*an* or *the*) actual apocalypse may have the opposite effect. As Ryzik (2017) reports, "The kind of high-stakes film that Hollywood loves to produce," such as *The Day After Tomorrow*, discussed earlier, which shows Manhattan as a "frozen dystopian landscape," or *Geostorm* (2017), in which "the climate goes apocalyptically haywire" due to malfunctioning satellites designed to control the global climate, tend to "backfire[], driving people further into denial and helplessness; instead of acting, they freeze." Indeed, "when climate change is depicted on screen," Ryzik (2017) laments, "it's often in an onslaught of fire and brimstone, an apocalyptic vision that hardly leaves room for a hopeful human response."

In sum, environmental apocalyptic imagery and language across media—whether in newspapers, in environmental movement literature/marketing/publicity, or on movie theater screens—may tire, rather than inspire, paralyze rather than rouse. "Intimations of doom have failed to motivate us," Soloski (2024) reports, and "the old ways of frightening people into action haven't worked" (Scott 2023: 14).[52] "If you really want to mobilize people to act," adds Andrew Hoffman, the Holcim (U.S.) Professor of Sustainable Enterprise at the University of Michigan and author of *How Culture Shapes the Climate Change Debate* (2015), "you don't scare the hell out of them and convince them the situation is hopeless" (quoted in Ryzik 2017). With this in mind, Ryzik (2017) asks, how, then, do we "hope to find the sweet spot between jolting audiences and inspiring them"?[53] In the next chapter, we return to this question of how to balance making (the) threat(s) of catastrophic or cataclysmic environmental harm (or "potentially imminent tipping points," to use Stephens's [2022] preferred language) seem serious enough and close enough in time and space for people to care and act with ensuring that people are not oversaturated with apocalyptic imaginaries so that it (the apocalypse) seems inevitable/so that they do not eschew conservation or mitigation for doomsday preparation.

End Times and Endings

Von Mossner (2012: 42) notes a "remarkable increase in disaster science fiction films in recent years that directly or indirectly evoke potential future ecological catastrophes as a consequence of present human behavior." We would not disagree, although we would underscore that such films rarely demonstrate or otherwise depict *the actual connections* between specific "present human behavior[s]" and the potential ecological catastrophes. Indeed— and as we have argued—most "disaster science fiction films" portray only one or two steps in the progression (although *regression* might be a better word) of ecocide → misericordia → apocalypse → post-apocalypse. Moreover, many of these films (novels tend to be less guilty of this) show or make reference to *an event*—a *discrete event*—rather than a process. To some extent, this is to be expected: "Emissions from fossil-fuel combustion, from land use change, from industrial manufacturing—they all alter the climate system, but in different ways, at different space and time scales and with different effects" (Hulme 2014: 124)—a "slow violence," to use Nixon's (2011) phrasing.[54] Again, as we have acknowledged already, film cannot encapsulate this very well in a two-to-three-hour timeframe; literature is slightly more effective.

To return to our discussion at the outset of this chapter, "we have a long history of apocalyptic predictions" (DeGregori 1982: 206) and "apocalypticism is among the most enduring human obsessions" (LaFrance 2024), although the end-time stories and visions change.[55] On the surface, it may not seem to matter whether one depiction or type of unease is more prevalent or salient than another. As Biskind (2018: 20) suggests, "Nothing entertains like disaster, according to conventional wisdom, but now it seems as though nothing entertains *but* disaster" (emphasis added). It also seems as if nothing *sells* like disaster. In his exposé on the booming business of doomsday luxury accommodations, O'Connell (2020) paraphrases Robert K. Vicino, founder and CEO of the Vivos Group (also known as just "Vivos"), a California-based company that builds gigantic underground shelters (made out of concrete and steel) designed to withstand explosions of up to half a megaton and protect "those *Americans* who cared to protect themselves and their families from a variety of possible end-time events" (emphasis added): "apocalyptic unease [is] basically a volume game. If you [don't] like one terrifying dystopian scenario, [there are others] that might be more your thing."[56]

For the ultra-wealthy discussed in Chapter 3, it may, indeed, not matter which "dystopian scenario" befalls us. And, in some respects, it may not matter much to those least fortunate either. But as Hurley and Sinykin (2018: 451) reveal, to think of the apocalypse as an "imagined future" misses the point. "Apocalypse is not singular and universal, but rather plural and particular," they write, and if this is so, "then we must ask not only when, but—because it is, among other times, *now*—where is it happening, and to whom, and by whom?" (Hurley and Sinykin 2018: 453, emphasis in original). "We must ask, with regard to the apocalypse," Hurley and Sinykin (2018: 453–54) continue, "questions posed by slow violence, structural violence, environmental violence and colonial violence. The Indigenous people of Tuvalu are already living the climate change apocalypse. Marshall Islanders, Iraqis, Belarussians, and downwinders across the globe are already living the nuclear apocalypse. Native nations in North America are already living the zombie apocalypse."

Reflecting on the occasion of the "Great North American Eclipse" in early April 2024, LaFrance (2024) ruminated, "Only rarely do we have shared experiences that are cosmic in scale—whether meteor showers, earthquakes, eclipses, or comets—ones that remind us, if briefly, that we are living on a planet that's simultaneously spinning on its axis and corkscrewing its way through the vast wilderness of outer space." To this we might add, whether humanity, and the planet as a whole, will encounter an apocalypse "cosmic in scale" remains to be seen; that *some* of humanity has already encountered apocalypse*s* (enormous and immense in their own worlds) and will continue to do so is without question.

5

Conclusion

Goodbye, Earth (?)(!)

In the previous chapter, we identified Chris Van Allsburg's *Just a Dream*, a children's storybook, as a rather effective story containing not just an account of ecocidal acts/omissions and portrayals of apocalyptic environmental harm(s) but also a vision of a different/better future, along with some modest measures toward realizing this different/better future before it is too late. We find it fruitful to again look to children's literature.

Goodbye, Earth! (2019), written in rhymed verse by nine-year-old Zayne Cowie (with help from Pamela Drukerman, Leah Varjacques, and Julie Lunde), bewails a warming planet: "One degree warmer's our demise/And we're on track for more to rise,/Carbon at an all-time high,/Ice sheets about to liquefy." Cowie expresses grief that he will not be able to see "Pacific islands, northern lights,/Himalayas, desert nights," and mourns the loss of cities like New York and Miami "swallowed by the sea!" He then castigates "grown-ups" for this "climate mess" through *actions* (leaving the "Paris accord," while choosing "big cars, fast food, and coal") and *inactions* ("With storms and droughts, and mass migration,/you're still stuck in conversation?"). Cowie acknowledges that kids cannot vote ("we don't pay tax/or donate to your super PACs"), but attempts to keep things simple and urges one initial measure: cutting down on carbon emissions by investing in renewable energy. His parting message:

> *We've said our bit, now you get cracking.*
> *No more pipelines, no more fracking!*

We may be kids, but we are pissed.
We're fighting now just to exist!

If we don't protect all it's worth,
Prepare to say: Goodbye Earth!

While *Goodbye, Earth!* rebukes adults, in general, for failing to address climate change, the book does chastise politicians concerned about "spending bills and budget fears [and] re-election each two years." And it takes a thinly veiled jab at Donald J. Trump, who said he would "make our country great."

In comparison, *Goodbye Earth: A Children's Book for Grownups Who Persist* (2017), by Nancy Caye Jones, is really just an indictment of the forty-fifth president of the United States. Although Donald J. Trump's name does not appear in the text, his image does (with illustrations by Andy Rubin), and Jones makes frequent reference to various lowlights of his time in the political arena (e.g., "Make fun of someone who's disabled?/Pick on women? Get Latinos labeled/rapists, thieves or something worse?/Build that wall from Mexico's purse?"). For Cowie, "The Earth's in trouble" because of myopic actions—and lethargy and inaction—by "grown-ups," and the solution begins with a reduction in carbon dioxide emissions and a switch to renewable energy sources; for Jones, the problem rests with one person, and the solution is to confront him:

Let's take a breath while we still can
and stand up strong against this man
who loves to bully in the night,
who cannot bear the smallest slight.
While there's still time don't let him plunder
all our land and rip asunder
treaties to protect the air
that say all nations need to share
the efforts to reverse the trend
that leads us to the very end.
      Don't let him kill the EPA.
      Don't let life just fade away.

Let us take one last example. In *Goodbye Earth, Hello Moon* (2008), geared toward children ages 5–6, Gabriel Meil and Emily Rylander describe what appears to be a normative world: "There were monkeys in trees,/Bears sleeping on mountains, Penguins on ice, Whales spitting up fountains." Until, that is, a group of penguins realize that "it got a lot hotter!"—that "there's rain in the desert" and "flooding galore" and that their "glacier's too small" and "not cold anymore." The penguins decide to "have an adventure" and invite their friends. While one appears to be writing a letter and also calling or texting on a flip phone, another packs fish in a suitcase. Soon the penguins are aboard a boat that looks more like a cargo ship than an ocean liner, waving goodbye to Tierra del Fuego. Turtles say, "Au revoir, Zanzibar," while primates wish farewell to the equator. For camels, it is "Sayonara, great Sahara!" as fish burble, "Ciao ciao, Palau." From here, the animals float "up into the sky" in hot air balloons, blimps, and zeppelins:

The turtles and tigers,
birds and baboons,
said, "Goodbye Earth."

"Hello Moon!"

In the last images of the book, we see the animals frolicking in space as they might have on Earth, albeit with astronaut helmets—presumably to provide them with pressurized atmosphere and protection against radiation.

Of the three "Goodbye Earth" books that we have considered,[1] Meil and Rylander's is the only one not to include humans or any sense of *anthropogenic* causes of global warming and climate change. In this sense, it might seem like the most benign of the books—especially when one considers the promotional description:

Addressing a world that is changing due to rising temperatures, this story highlights the cheeky responses of many different animals as they leave their endangered habitats to travel to the moon. A hilarious romp through the issue of global warming, the superb illustrations and smart writing of this beautiful picture book will entertain children and engage adults with its irreverence and beauty. Through a careful use of humor, this uproarious tale manages to address the problem of global warming without being scary or preachy, and features a surprise ending that is both fun and hopeful.

While Meil and Rylander's book is not sermonizing—indeed, there is a total absence of any moralizing message—it is hardly "hilarious" or "uproarious." In fact, *it is scary* because (1) it depicts a world without *any* humans; (2) it suggests that this (posthuman) world will continue to have adverse impacts on biotic factors in Earth's ecosystems; and (3) its way of "address[ing] the problem of global warming" is downright Muskian or Bezosian—leave Gaia for another celestial body.

Cheeky? Irreverent? Meil and Rylander's version of "Goodbye Earth" is positively *horrifying.*

Horror.

"Horror is a powerful word," write Rust and Soles (2014: 509)—and one that has permeated our discussions in this book. As Rust and Soles (2014: 509) explain,

> [Horror] evokes feelings of loathing, repugnance, aversion, dread, and outright terror. Horrific events take place in our world every day, so it is only natural that these events find their way into our collective imagination through literature, cinema, and other forms of art and popular discourse. These days, phrases like global climate change, the sixth extinction, and environmental injustice alert us to the horrific events poised to alter life as we know it on this planet. As literary and film scholars, we find that as we read texts, our sense of horror is amplified by considering the relationship between textual horrors and those in the material world. When one considers the terrors that humanity hath wrought upon the planet, particularly over the past two centuries, it is easy to be scared.

And we should be scared.

Indeed, Tidwell and Soles (2021: 5) remind us that

> Greta Thunberg's call for fear rather than hope provides . . . a useful perspective. At the World Economic Forum in January 2019, the climate activist said, "Adults keep saying we owe it to the young people to give them hope. But I don't want your hope, I don't want you to be hopeful. I want you to panic, I want you to feel the fear I feel every day. And then I want you to act, I want you to act as if you would in a crisis. I want you to act as if the house was on fire, because it is." This call for a negative affective response to climate change highlights the power of fear to create change. Fear is not simply a reflection of deep-seated hatred. Sometimes it is justified and necessary.[2]

As we suggested toward the end of Chapter 4, fear (independently and intertwined with apocalyptic imagery and language) can be motivating or paralyzing.[3] We will explore this. For now, we try to move more in the direction of the prior than the latter—more toward inspiration than incapacitation—by offering our conclusion in the form of five points. In so doing, we shift from the analytical, critical, and descriptive approach of our previous chapters to a more *prescriptive* one.

1. There are no monsters "out *there*." We, humans, *create* our monsters: it is a process of *othering*—othering people, othering nonhuman nature.[4]

Pihlström (2020: 35) clarifies that "while very few of us believe . . . monsters to be real—and certainly there are no good scientific or any other reasons to do so—merely imagining their possibility in fictional contexts may be philosophically highly relevant and may illuminate deep problems concerning our ethical relation to the world in general and other human beings in particular."[5] Indeed, as Marcus (2024) notes, "Every generation births its own monsters," and so, too, does "culture gives birth to a monster before our eyes . . . the monster is an incorporation of the Outside, the Beyond" (Cohen 1996: 9, 7).[6] Indeed, as Kniss (2021: 68) observes, "th[e] characterization of nature as Other lies at the heart of society's fear of the natural world."[7]

This is not new. As Giuliani (2021: 9) reminds us, "Since early Modernity, ideas of *monsters* and *catastrophes* as external beings and events have been reinforced by the assumption that Europe and the West are isolated, under attack and faced with a threat coming from what is perceived to be an *incommensurable* and *ontologically dangerous* outside, a place of darkness (Conrad 1899)" (emphasis in original). But it does seem to be more pronounced in the last quarter century. As Giuliani (2021: 3) explains, in language that resonates with our comments in Chapter 4 regarding (the) cultural representations of September 11, 2001:

> the September 11 attacks on the safe space of the "we" clearly involved different dynamics from *symmetric* warfare, and the "war on terror" that followed brought into international relations modes of warfare that had been typical of colonial wars. A new kind of enemy emerged, a *monstrified* personification of Otherness produced by the conflation of enemy and monster in the figure of the terrorist, to whom, as in colonial wars, no protection nor legal status was granted. . . . Today, the monster is feared to have returned in the guise of masses of migrants, refugees and terrorist cells striking back from both within and outside the *bios* [social organization]. At the same time, nature is striking back, too, and making issues of climate change, ocean acidification, air pollution, toxic waste and devastated land invade the space of the "we," threatening its *zoe* [biological structure of life]. (emphasis in original)

It follows, then, that if we create (our own) monsters—indeed, if "it is *easy* to create monsters of those who differ from the predominant view"—then "seeing them *as monsters* makes it easy to exploit, oppress, and even kill them" (Senf 2020: 78, emphasis added). This, in turn, leads Giuliani (2021: 2) to put forth that monsters are "expendable"—because, as she explains, "it is against them that the order is built and maintained lest they challenge social and political assumptions, eventually undermining the endurance of the body politic."[8] Exemplifying Giuliani's point, albeit in far less elegant words, Donald J. Trump, in his efforts to return to office, cast those individuals attempting to cross the southern border into the United States as "violent criminals": "The migrants are hurting people. . . . They talk about the beautiful dream of migrants. It sounds so nice, you know, like in a fairy-tale book. But some of these people are monsters" (quoted in Gold 2024a).

Essentially, in the Gothic imagination, which we discussed in Chapter 2— and for contemporary MAGA border politics—the monster (in the form of "the migrant") "is representative of social traumas, for which it is also blamed" (Skott et al. 2021: 389, citing Ingebretsen 2001). "Monsters define the boundaries of normal and other," Skott and her colleagues (2021: 389) explain, and so "'by locating monsters off the social map, we are locating ourselves on it' (Ingebretsen 2001: 5)," but for Trump and his supporters, the goal is to *relocate* the migrants-as-monsters *physically* and *quite literally* off the *geographic* map of the United States.[9]

As we have attempted to articulate in this book, this "othering" of other people and then treating them as monsters resembles—or is consistent with— the "othering" of nonhuman nature, which we then also treat as monsters/ as monstrous, and which we depict as such in popular cultural representations.[10] Thus, for Keetley (2021: 35–36), "[Algernon] Blackwood's 'The Man Whom the Trees Loved' and [Lorcan] Finnegan's *Without Name* show that the vegetal world—trees in this case—can act as 'monsters.' Indeed, we make them into monsters by pushing them from the center of our world 'to the furthest margins of geography and discourse.'" Correspondingly, and as we have explored in earlier chapters, "human desecration of the Earth may create the very monsters that drink their blood" (Murray and Heumann 2016: 42)—or, in the example of *The Happening*, human desecration of the Earth may lead the Earth to cause humans to shed their own blood.

Our monstrous treatment of nature—our treatment of nature *as* monstrous—leads Murray and Heumann (2016: 207) to conclude that "the true monster in the Anthropocene age . . . [is] humanity itself."[11] We would concur—to an extent: yes, we create monsters (whether it is other people—immigrants, terrorists—or nature); and yes, we, humanity, have been and continue to be monstrous in our behavior toward nature and the environment. But, as we attempted to underscore in Chapter 3, some of us are more guilty than others; blame should not be apportioned equally.[12]

2. The monsters that we create demonstrate things; they have metaphorical value.

Dixon (2008: 672) contends that "though each age and time has its own particular monsters to contend with, this experience can tell us something about our *past,* insofar as the fear and anxiety the monstrous provokes bring to light a way of life that has but the semblance of order" (emphasis added; for a discussion, see Saunders 2012: 101n34, and accompanying text).[13] As we have endeavored to show throughout this book, monsters also reflect our *current* anxieties: "horror movies can teach us *about ourselves* and *each other*" (Fineman 2017, emphasis added)—and, as we noted throughout Chapter 2 and Chapter 4, "horror-movie monsters can become allegorical stand-ins for what scares us" (Fineman 2017, quoting Monica Castillo, who was then a film writer for the *Watching* newsletter at *The New York Times*).

For Giuliani (2021: 14), "migrant landings on Europe's southern shores are often represented as *alien* invasions requiring military force (as in the case of the Hungarian-Serbian, Turkish-Greek and Croatian-Bosnian Herzegovinian borders)" (emphasis in original). "This same iconography," she explains, is "allegorically rendered in apocalyptic films, where the figures of the hungry, angry and bloodthirsty terrorist alien and rabid monster (the *fast running and devouring rabid undead*) are familiar to audience members from representations in mainstream visual and print media (Santos et al. 2018; Giuliani et al. 2020a)" (Giuliani 2021: 14–15, emphasis in original). "Moreover," Giuliani (2021: 15) continues, "widely circulated images of the environmental catastrophe and mainstream narratives of the Anthropocene populate media and film narratives in which a planetary catastrophe is brought about by a planet-to-planet collision, the sun's cooling, climate change, epidemics, or human genetic mutation." The end result is that "mass migrations, terrorism and environmental catastrophe, in particular, often figure in contemporary horror films about contagious diseases, economic downturns, planetary apocalypses, genetic mutations, or weapons of mass destruction, in which zombies, aliens and mutants allegorise some of the characteristics of the ongoing transformations (Brioni 2013)" (Giuliani 2021: 35). Thus, it seems, whatever its form—an angry/bloodthirsty/hungry alien/monster/zombie or some other "creature"—such imagery and iconography "reflect real anxieties about the natural world and its existence outside of human control" (Tidwell 2018: 115). Perhaps even more disturbing, for our purposes, is that in some ecohorror (such as *The*

Happening, discussed throughout this book), the *entire planet*—the *whole world*—is depicted as malevolent and vengeful—at least, toward its *human* inhabitants (see Ulaby 2008).

Just as monsters can reveal something about our *past* and expose (or shine a spotlight on) our *current* anxieties, they can also serve as "luminous warnings" (Skott et al. 2021: 395, citing Ingebretsen 2001)[14]—as *"portent[s]*, directing us to a future that exceeds prediction" (Dixon 2008: 672, emphasis added). Thus, Godzilla, mentioned in Chapter 2, "represents a *cautionary symbol* of the dangerous consequences of mistreating the natural world— monstrous nature on the attack" (Murray and Heumann 2016: xi, emphasis added), while for Collins and Bond (2011: 190), "zombies, and apocalyptic fiction generally, can function as jeremiad, a warning to its audience to repent and reform."

3. These "representations have material consequences" (Alaimo 2001: 279).

In much the way that Hall (1981: 233) avers that "cultural domination has real effects—even if these are neither all-powerful nor all-inclusive," we would stress that portrayals of nature as monstrous are not benign: they have real-world impact(s). Tidwell (2018: 116) notes that "although discussions of ecohorror"—and, we would add, monstrous nature—"have often emphasized attacks by the natural world or invasions . . . this emphasis is built upon a presumed separation between humanity and the non-human world." "Human and non-human are not separate, however" (Tidwell 2018: 116), and thus (certain) representations that suggest as much can reinforce the perception and belief that they are. In other words, "when films . . . portray nature as monstrous—as something that literally threatens human life and figuratively threatens the bounds of human subjectivity—they insist on solid divisions between nature and culture" (Alaimo 2001: 280).[15] When such representations "vilify nature," Alaimo (2001: 280) contends, they can serve to "justify[] the slaughter of creatures we construct as repulsive"—or the destruction of the environment. This can become cyclical and provide cultural reinforcement: nature is vilified in representations, thereby justifying its destruction; once destroyed or degraded, it is treated as abject, encouraging further disregard.

For Alaimo (2001: 292), certain "films that represent nature as monstrous present a particular threat to environmentalism, as they directly contradict the ethos of environmentalism"—and, we would add, undercut the efforts of green criminologists and other scholars working across the humanities and social and natural sciences. Indeed, as Alaimo (2001: 292) continues, whereas most environmentally oriented media, such as "advertisements, television programs, or direct-mail campaigns encourage us to realize our connection to and take responsibility for ecosystems as far away as the Amazon or the Arctic, monstrous nature demands just the opposite."

4. We can and should challenge these representations.
Murray and Heumann (2016: 192) claim that "cinema has the potential to bring environmental issues such as climate change to the forefront. But the cinematic mechanism also has the potential to obscure that message with spectacular beauty." With this in mind, we put forth some suggestions.

First, we encourage scholars to continue to scrutinize how we represent nonhuman animals, plants, and nature as a whole because these representations function both as *mirrors* and as *guides*. As Parker (2016: 223) submits, "Fictional depictions of the natural world are hugely important as they both reflect and influence our views of nature itself."[16] Relatedly, Phillips (2021: 115) suggests that "popular films, like political speeches and Twitter tirades, are all circulating texts that carry with them invitations for us to feel." His stated goal in examining these "political feelings in popular culture" has been to offer suggestions for how "to reflect on these invitations and decide for ourselves which feelings we will embrace and which we will refuse" (Phillips 2021: 115).[17]

We contend that more is needed than just "reflecting on" feelings (and embracing some and rejecting others). For Foy (2010a: 14), "although true activism requires mobilized engagement to inspire change, the empowerment of political dissent via mass media and popular culture . . . provides an argument that true public, democratic action is occurring through popular culture. We merely have to tune in to join the conversation." This, too, seems insufficient to us: more is needed than just "tuning in" and "joining the conversation." Rather—and this leads us to our second proposition—we urge scholars to continue to *challenge* the representations of nonhuman animals, plants, and nature, so that the challenge becomes an "intervention" in the McGregorian (2022: 1) sense—as "an act of interposing or interfering in an affair so as to affect its course or consequences"—much as the Anti-Creep Climate Initiative has done in terms of exposing the ecofascist myths in popular cultural forms (see Chapter 1) and as we suggested one might do with *Black Panther* and *Wakanda Forever* and *Infinity War* and *Endgame*.

Mirrlees and Pedersen (2016: 306), in their meditation on *Elysium*, write: "Against the notion of popular culture being either a manipulative instrument used by capitalist elites to ideologically brainwash the masses or a direct expression of working class experiences, Hall (1981: 239) conceptualized popular culture as a terrain of hegemonic and counter-hegemonic struggle: 'popular culture is one of the sites where the struggle for and against the powerful is engaged. It is partly where hegemony arises, and where it is secured.'" Whether the MCU and lots of other contemporary popular cultural forms are "manipulative instruments" rather than "direct expression[s] of working class experiences" or experiences of environmental degradation and destruction may be subject to debate, but we do insist that *green cultural criminologists* (and those working in related projects) can help engage in this counter-hegemonic struggle.

More directly, Tidwell and Soles (2021: 4) remind us that "as with horror writ large, ecohorror's focus on fear (or ecophobia) often generates a troubling ambivalence. Despite many creators' audience members' very real concerns about environmental issues and their desires to prevent the worst from happening, ecohorror runs the risk of reinforcing fearful responses to the nonhuman or—equally dangerous—leading to a feeling of hopelessness"— a concern we raised with apocalypticism in Chapter 4. Ecohorror is—and, again, the same holds true with "end times" language and imagery—"not primarily a call to action" (Tidwell and Soles 2021: 4). "Even the most pointed ecohorror critique of environmental degradation," they submit, "is ultimately couched in mere entertainment" (Tidwell and Soles 2021: 4).

We see our task as being to help remove the veil of entertainment—to demonstrate how and why monstrous horror and ecohorror, representations of the Earth as abject, and apocalyptic imaginaries *can be* and *should be* a "call to action." Murray and Heumann (2016: 192) remind us that "monstrous cinema and its cli-fi offshoots may present important environmental messages, but they also must entertain viewers with spectacular effects to attract the audiences needed for big profits. And these awesome cinematic presentations may actually *obscure* the ecological points on display" (emphasis added).[18] What we call for here is a concerted effort to *illuminate* what is obscured—and to fulfill the potential that film has "to move audiences to both awareness of and action to address climate change [and other environmental issues]" (Murray and Heumann 2016: 206). If "works of horror encode instructions" for viewers (or readers) in how we might "react to the monster" (Keetley 2021: 26, 27, citing Carroll 1990)—or, alternatively, how we *should not*—then we must help *decode* these messages or lessons.

5. Just as there are no monsters "out *there*," there are no superheroes—at least, not in the sense that MCU conceptualizes and markets them.

There is no Captain America or Captain Marvel or Iron Man, no Hulk, no Thor.[19] As problematic as the MCU might be, movies like *Infinity War* and

Endgame do provide some guidance: even superheroes—strong ones, big ones, green ones, and ones that fly—work better and are more effective working *as a team*—a message made clear in *World Made by Hand* (Kunstler 2008).[20] At the risk of sounding corny or cheeky, we need to be our own Avengers.[21] We *must* be our own Avengers. Except that instead of seeking to punish some extraterrestrial lifeform for threatening our planet, we need to pursue redress for the harms *we* (humans) have caused.[22]

Townsend (2018), in her critique of *Infinity War*, writes:

> In the fight between growth and entropy, population isn't the defining issue. The solution has never been as simple as "less people." [*sic*] Consumption, productivity, energy-return-on-investment, peace, pace of technological advance, circularity, lifestyle, economics and even the stories we tell ourselves combine into a wicked mesh of factors with unexpected plot-twists and cliff-hanging outcomes. In fact, throughout the marvel odyssey[,] *the real enemy has been simple answers.* (emphasis added)

Townsend (2018) continues:

> Almost all of the "heroes" started out believing that their super-human powers were enough to guarantee change. But each of then [*sic*] had *to learn compromise, innovation, negotiation and teamwork instead.* Often the movies' denouements are far from perfect and with solutions that have unexpected ramifications (like flattening cities whilst fighting off aliens). Each one of the Avengers are [*sic*] dealing with the fallout from saving the world. (emphasis added)

Townsend (2018) concludes:

> Sustainability isn't simple. Thanos says that with a "click of his finger[,]" he can save the universe. It's going to take harder work than that. That's ultimately Thanos's failure, the belief that sustainability can happen in one fell swoop or single answer, rather than being everyday, constant and unending work to keep the balance and find new solutions in the face of unexpected new problems.

Ultimately, we, humans, are going to need to shift quickly and dramatically from the "go it alone" attitude that is ingrained in much Western (and certainly much *American*) culture (see, e.g., Kanthak 2023, citing Caputi 2013;

see generally Cassino 2023; Hirschmann 2023)—as exemplified, *inter alia*, by the "rugged hero figure" of the *Mad Max* media franchise and *The Road* (2009), as well as in "prepperist" and "survivalist" fantasies and behaviors described earlier in this book.

While "humanity may contribute to the malevolent elements of nature on the big screen," Murray and Heumann (2016: xviii) write, "these films also suggest that embracing interdependent relationships with nonhuman nature may save us all." Regardless of the popular culture form, we must help make sure that this message is clear so that these relationships are fostered. Two decades ago, Giroux (2006: 191–92) concluded: "To confront the biopolitics of disposability, we need to recognize the dark times in which we live and offer up a vision of hope that creates the conditions for multiple collective and global struggles that refuse to use politics as an act of war and markets as the measure of democracy. Making human beings superfluous is the essence of totalitarianism, and democracy is the antidote in urgent need of being reclaimed." His message is no less critical now.

Notes

CHAPTER 1

1. In their introduction to their edited volume, *The Politics of the Marvel Cinematic Universe*, Carnes and Goren (2023: 5) explain that "scholars of popular culture investigate important 'texts' (which in this context mean not just written words but also films, TV shows, music, performances, and other media) and interpret the images and ideas presented in them." In *Monstrous Nature and Representations of Environmental Harms: A Green Cultural Criminological Perspective*, we employ the word *forms* as Carnes and Goren use the word *texts*—that is, rather capaciously.

2. For example, in August 2018, in an interview with *The Film Stage*, Ethan Hawke, the actor, film director, and screenwriter, commented:

> Now we have the problem that they tell us *Logan* is a great movie. Well, it's a great superhero movie. It still involves people in tights with metal coming out of their hands. It's not Bresson. It's not Bergman. But they talk about it like it is. I went to see *Logan* cause everyone was like, "This is a great movie" and I was like, "Really? No, this is a fine superhero movie." There's a difference but big business doesn't think there's a difference. Big business wants you to think that this is a great film because they wanna make money off of it.

3. The philosopher Timothy Morton draws a distinction between "disasters" and "catastrophes," claiming that "disasters are what you witness from the outside. Catastrophes involve you, so you can do something about them" (2021: 29). For a different perspective, see Giuliani (2021: 9–10). We leave a consideration of this alleged difference for another day, taking the position that when it comes to the environment, neither is good or desirable.

4. For those interested in an overview of such contrasts and cultural divides, see Fisher (2013); see also Eden Gallery (2021).

5. In another kind of cultural studies analysis, we might say more about the interlocking ownership of film and streaming companies that produce so much of the media that present worldbuilding and mythmaking for contemporary entertainment (see, e.g., Pitre

2023). As *The Economist* (2015) put it, "Disney is making a fortune and safeguarding its future by buying childhood, piece by piece." To limit ourselves to the present case, note that Walt Disney Pictures, which was responsible for *Monsters, Inc.* and *Monsters University*, is a subsidiary of Walt Disney Studios; Walt Disney Studios Motion Pictures is an American film distribution studio within the Disney Entertainment division of The Walt Disney Company. Walt Disney Studios Motion Pictures (previously, Buena Vista Pictures Distribution, Inc.) handles theatrical and occasional digital distribution, marketing, and promotion for films produced and released by Walt Disney Studios, which includes Walt Disney Pictures, Walt Disney Animation Studios, Pixar Animation Studios, Marvel Studios, Lucasfilm Ltd., and 20th Century Studios. The Walt Disney Company acquired Marvel Entertainment and its subsidiary, Marvel Studios, in 2009 (see Carnes and Goren 2023). For a visual, see, e.g., Aguilar (2019). For a discussion of The Walt Disney Company's approach to "brand management" as well as "Disney Drudgery"—labor and working conditions at the company—see Pitre (2023); for a criminological discussion of The Walt Disney Company and the Walt Disney World Resort, see Lloyd (2023).

6. The film's first twenty-four hours of presales (advance ticket sales) exceeded those of any other MCU title (D'Alessandro 2018; Lane 2018).

7. At the time, these figures represented the fifth-largest opening weekend ever—behind *Star Wars: The Force Awakens* (2015), *Star Wars: The Last Jedi* (2017), *Jurassic World* (2012), and *The Avengers* (2012) (Sow and Sy 2018). These amounts also denoted the highest opening of all time for a film in February, as well as for a film released over President's Day weekend (Sow and Sy 2018). According to Ryan Coogler, the director and screenwriter for both *Black Panther* and *Wakanda Forever*, the two films "made $2 billion at the box office, which is what matters the most to corporations" (quoted in Ugwu 2022). This financial success should not come as a surprise. Carnes and Goren (2023: 1) assert that "the financial success of [MCU] is unparalleled in modern media history," and that "eight of the twenty-five highest grossing films of all time are MCU movies."

8. The "resource curse," also known as the "paradox of plenty," refers to the phenomenon whereby an abundance of fossil fuels and minerals generates *less* economic growth, *less* democracy, higher levels of corruption, greater degrees of ineffective governance, and more political violence (see, e.g., Brisman and South 2013b; Brisman, South, and White 2013; Clark 2013; South and Brisman 2013a).

9. Sow and Sy (2018) also note that Botswana has attempted to escape the "resource curse" by engaging in economic diversification and a fiscal rule that separates expenditures from revenues so as to protect expenditures from fluctuations in diamond prices.

10. Phillips (2022) adds that in the 1960s, "a group of Black Panthers with guns protested at the California Statehouse, proclaiming, 'The time has come for Black people to arm themselves.'" In fact, on May 2, 1967, a group of thirty Black Panthers walked into the California State Capitol to protest against a bill that would prohibit individuals from carrying loaded firearms in public spaces—a measure that they felt would infringe on Black people's right to bear arms at a time of increased police attacks by police officers (Dumont 2022; Wing 2016). The bill passed both the California State Assembly and the California State Senate—with the *support* of the National Rifle Association (NRA)—and was signed into law on July 28, 1967, by California Governor Ronald

Reagan (Dumont 2022; Wing 2016). Wing (2016) muses that the NRA "apparently believed that the whole 'good guy with a gun' thing didn't apply to black people." Similarly, Dumont (2022) reports that in the late 1960s, "the rising presence and influence of the Black Panther Party in California [had begun] to make some California lawmakers, law enforcement, and the NRA nervous. . . . And while the NRA was brazenly against the rights of Black Americans to bear arms, when it came to white conservatives, the NRA became flagrant supporters of gun rights—fueling the present gun rights movement."

11. Ugwu (2018) notes that *Black Panther* draws a contrast not only between T'Challa's preference for isolationism and Killmonger's promotion of violence, but T'Challa's "African-ness" and Killmonger's identity as an African-American.

12. As Hirschmann (2023: 173) explains, in the MCU, vibranium is a "limitless resource" that can be "mined without environmental damage of any sort" and that it "seems to yield, through its energy-manipulating properties, an equally limitless source of innovation and nonpolluting power."

13. In an interview with George Gene Gustines (2017), Ta-Nehisi Coates, who wrote the *Black Panther* series for Marvel Comics from 2016 to 2021, reflects on "the decision to create Black Panther," stating, "It was not an apolitical decision to have this black character in Africa, in this advanced nation, and have him be highly intelligent. All of these were political decisions."

14. At present, *Wakanda Forever* holds the record for the highest-grossing movie opening in the month of November (Hale 2022).

15. In her chapter "Environmentalism and the Marvel Cinematic Universe: *Spider-Man: Far from Home* as a Cautionary Tale," Hirschmann (2023: 180n2) acknowledges that although she enjoyed *Spider-Man: Far from Home* (2019) "a great deal" and that she "increasingly bec[a]me a fan of the MCU during the pandemic lockdown," she is aware that her criticisms in the chapter "may appear to communicate the opposite because [she is] engaged in a process of critical analysis of a particular theme." As such, she writes, "I want to stress that I love the escapism that such movies provide, and the raw entertainment, as much as anyone. But I do believe that the political implications of the movies' texts are fair game for political theoretical analysis." Our green cultural criminological analysis is undertaken in a similar spirit.

16. For a discussion of *Black Panther*'s "groundbreaking use of Afrofuturism," see Phillips (2021: 94); see also Wallace (2018).

17. For a discussion of the Mesoamerican influences and inspiration in *Wakanda Forever*, as well as the film's Indigenous representation, see Blanck (2022); Guerrero (2022).

18. For Phillips (2022), "the villains of the 'Black Panther' films aren't clear-cut enemies but victims of structural racism: Killmonger in the original and Namor in the sequel are righteously angry men of color who are responding to the ways their communities have been damaged by great -isms (including capitalism, colonialism, and, again, racism)."

19. As an aside, one can only imagine the backlash in the United States from proponents of the far-right "great replacement" conspiracy theory, who promote paranoid narratives of "White extinction" (see, e.g., Arango et al. 2019; Blow 2018; Cavin 2022; Montanaro 2022), had Public Enemy's "Fear of a Black Planet" been part of the soundtrack!

20. As Muffett and Bruch (2011: 4) observe, "well-managed resources can help fund reconstruction efforts and help bring order from chaos." Likewise, Lujala and Rustad (2011: 19) contend that "high-value natural resources have the potential to promote and consolidate peace." For a related discussion, see Brisman, South and White (2015).

21. Carnes and Goren (2023: 2) acknowledge that "because the MCU caters to immensely broad domestic and global audiences, MCU content can . . . be powerfully *constrained* by real-world politics. Stories and plots often conspicuously tiptoe around political issues that might divide audiences or somehow drive down ticket sales" (emphasis in original). "As Marvel Studios works to ensure that its films appeal to vast domestic and international audiences," Carned and Goren (2023: 3) continue, "the MCU can be a driver of contemporary political and social currents, but the MCU can also be *driven* by those same forces" (emphasis in original). While we are certainly aware that MCU—and media franchises, more generally—feel they need to tread softly when it comes to certain cultural, political, and social issues, we contend the film industries (and entertainment conglomerates, more broadly) are often *too apprehensive—too risk-averse*—and that they could make more compelling movies and media products by being more adventurous and less pusillanimous. Engaging with attendant cultural, political, and social issues does not mean propagandizing; attention to context, history, and nuance does not equate with indoctrination (see generally Brisman 2024). Identifying media studios' missed opportunities and teasing out what these companies might have done or might do differently with their popular cultural forms are key tasks of green cultural criminology.

22. To be sure, *Black Panther*, *Wakanda Forever*, *Infinity War*, and *Endgame* are not the only MCU films that involve ecological issues. According to Townsend (2018),

> Over 10 years and 19 films[,] Marvel has played with environmental themes. The trash planet of Sakaar [in *Thor: Ragnarok* (2017)] into which the whole universe dumps its waste "out of sight" is a direct analogy of the trash ships of today. The Tivan Corporation mines the giant head of a deceased Celestial for brain tissue and spinal fluid to sell on the black market (a rather nifty example of the circular economy [or macabre example of organ harvesting]). Even [Tony] Stark himself invented a new element (and unlimited clean energy source) in his basement particle accelerator.
>
> In fact, the whole Marvel Cinematic Universe story arc wrestles with resources, energy, social equity and long-term survival. It clearly operates within the same rules of entropy as ours (except for the magic bits) and throws up the same problems. But this outing takes that theme front and center. *Avengers: Infinity War* could be renamed The Sustainability War.

For an excellent examination of environmentalism in *Spider-Man: Far from Home*, as well as *Infinity War* and *Endgame,* see Hirschmann (2023).

23. On allusions to the Malthusian growth rate in *The Happening* (2008)—a film discussed in Chapter 2—see Foy (2010b); on the "Malthusian culling of the lumpen poor" in *The Purge* media franchise, see Linnemann (2022: 76). Whether and how Malthusian themes have emerged in other contemporary films is worthy of examination but outside the scope of this chapter.

24. Brody (2018) quips that "each one [of the small, gem-like stones] endows its bearer with one particular power, but whoever collects all six (as if they came in boxes of breakfast cereal) gets total, unprecedented, presumably irresistible control of the universe."

25. Swift's satirical essay "A Modest Proposal" (in full, "A Modest Proposal For Preventing the Children of Poor People From Being a Burthen to their Parents, Or the Country, and For Making Them Beneficial to the Publick") propounds that a pragmatic and reasonable solution to alleviating poverty in Ireland is to "mak[e] these children sound and useful members of the commonwealth" by selling them to English landlords as *food*—"a most delicious nourishing and wholesome food, whether stewed, roasted, baked, or boiled" (Swift 1729). As Townsend (2018) explicates, "With excruciating rationality Swift outlines the economic and social benefits of his plan: reduced population, improved treatment of women (as the producers of the new resource), and the health benefits of fresh meat. The horror of his proposal is obvious, but the real squirting discomfort comes from his flawless economics. Remove the word 'babies' and every word sounds practical and even compassionate"—much like Thanos's promise.

26. In some respects, *Infinity War* evokes *Soylent Green* (1973) where, as Murray and Heumann (2016: 197) remark, "In a world completely overrun with humans, food sources for the masses come in the form of 'soylents,' including the infamous soylent green: people. *Soylent Green* provides a picture of what would happen on Earth if Paul Ehrlich's predictions came true: 'Population will inevitably and completely outstrip whatever small increases in food supplies we make,' Ehrlich asserted in 1970 (Collier 1970, 189)."

27. Wang and Zhang (2023: 191) argue that "many Phase One and Two antagonists [the MCU films that were released between 2008 and 2011 and between 2013 and 2015, respectively] are one-dimensional, their backstories and motives are somewhat predictable, and their character development is brief." Since Phase Three—the MCU movies that were released between 2016 and 2019—they continue, "the antagonists have symbolized prevalent cultural and social anxieties. The Phase Three villains have moved beyond the one-dimensional bad buy motivated by greed, revenge, or ambition and have increasingly served as stand-ins for some of the grand challenges facing humanity" (Wang and Zhang 2023: 182). Thanos's goal in *Infinity War* is not to destroy the world and thus fits Wang and Zhang's (2023) description. In *Endgame*, however, Thanos (rather disappointingly) becomes more of a run-of-the-mill "bad guy"—much more akin to the pre–Phase Three villains. For example, in *Endgame*, Thanos threatens, "I will shred this universe down to its last atom. And then with the stones you've collected for me create a new one teeming with life that knows not what it has lost but only what it has been given. A grateful universe." Later, he announces, "In all my years of conquest, violence, slaughter, it was never personal. But I'll tell you now, what I'm about to do to your stubborn, annoying little planet. . . . I'm gonna enjoy it. Very, very much." As Fullerton (2019) explains, the Thanos in *Endgame* "seemed more openly villainous than the version we grew to know over the course of Infinity War, swapping his unusual plan of balancing the population with a less evocative idea of destroying then reforming the galaxy, and crowing about how he'd enjoy destroying the Avengers' 'annoying' planet— a far cry from the quieter, more understandable Thanos we'd spent so much time with in Infinity War." In this way, Thanos resembles the mutant, Apocalypse (En Sabah Nur) in *X-Men: Apocalypse* (2016)—"an invincible and immortal figure determined to take control and rain down pain on the world . . . hoping to clean the world of unworthy humans and start it anew" (Zakarin 2015; see generally Kenny 2016). As the actor Oscar Isaac, who plays En Sabah Nur, explains, "He [En Sabah Nur] is the creative-slash-destructive force of this earth. When things start to go awry, or when things seem like they're not moving towards evolution, he destroys those civilizations" (quoted in Stack

2015). Or, as Stack (2015) adds, "Think of him as a god who does gut renovations." For an overview of every "phase" in the MCU to date (as of February 2024), see Sandwell and Longridge (2024).

28. The word *manifesto* implies something far more coherent than the rambling words of those who engage in mass shootings. Moreover, using the word, "manifesto," elevates the ideas of the shooters-writers, giving them more credibility than they are due. On the use of the word *manifesto* in such contexts, see, e.g., Cavin (2022); see also Belew (2019), who in her article on the shooting in El Paso, clarifies that "by manifesto, [she] mean[s] a document laying out political and ideological reasons for the violence and connecting it to other acts of violence." For more on the shooting itself, see Arango, Bogel-Burroughs, and Benner (2019).

29. Ecofascism has ties with/to deep ecology and German romantic nationalism, and in an alliterative accession to her argument and definition, Anson (2020: 69) adds that "ecofascism is the bedrock of American environmental thinking, as nature's nation nationalized a nature tradition that relied on claims of the naturalness of racial hierarchies and romantic appeals to 'natural law' to justify genocide." For Mann (2022), "the problem with demanding a precise definition of fascism is that it exaggerates both the 'exceptional' character of fascist politics, and the distance between us and its historical calamities. In thinking about fascism, we can't just be on the lookout for its original form as it emerged in interwar Europe—dandies and thugs pursuing the renewal of the racial-national body through party-organised violence and imperialism." We could query whether a similar argument could be made for demanding a precise definition of "*eco*fascism."

30. The Anti-Creep Climate Initiative (2022) defines "ecofascism" as "environmentalism that 1. Advocates or accepts violence and 2. Reinforces existing systems of power and inequality. Ecofascism suggests that certain kinds of people are naturally and exclusively entitled to control environmental resources. Ecofascism offers the same old s*** but worse." Similarly, Andrews (2019b) describes how "ecofascism" refers to "the use of fascist means (subjugation, violence, misinformation) to achieve ecological goals (conservation, climate action)," noting that "so-called eco-fascists aren't trying to challenge the power structures that created climate change in any meaningful way: they're simply trying to lash out at those more vulnerable than them [*sic*]." Sierra Garcia (2020) explains that "ecofascism" (or "ecofash") entails "the promotion of authoritarian, fascist ideologies for environmental good," adding that "[m]inimizing or even encouraging human death and suffering so long as it helps the environment is an excellent example of th[is] dark ideology." For additional, accessible, and easy-to-understand explications of ecofascism, see, e.g., Corcione (2020); Fox (2021); Guidi (2022); Kamel, Lamoureau, and Makuch (2020); Mackay (2020); Manavis (2018, 2020); Mann (2022); Mason (2021); Walsh (2022); Wilson (2019); see also Amend (2019); Joshi (2020); Seymour (2023); Smyth (2019). For an in-depth exploration, see Moore and Roberts (2022). For a consideration of whether "MAGAism is the antechamber to an American-style fascism," and on a comparison of fascism in Italy (in the 1920s through the 1940s) and Germany (in the 1930s and 1940s) to "the MAGA world," see Fraser (2024).

31. Although, as mathematicians have discovered, even odds in a coin toss are not really 50/50 (see Klarreich 2004; Lewis 2012).

32. Doing so might also have helped illuminate "the disproportionate impact different people and societies have on the environment, and its questionable assumption that human society and 'the planet' [or the universe, in Thanos's case] are somehow

discrete and utterly separate actors" (Sierra Garcia 2020)—an issue to which we return in Chapter 2—as well as how many environmental risks and burdens are not distributed uniformly across groups of people (see, e.g., United States Environmental Protection Agency 2021; see generally Andrews 2019b; Giuliani 2021: 10). Mike Davis (2010: 37) observes that "global warming is not H. G. Wells's [*The*] *War of the Worlds*, where invading Martians democratically annihilate humanity without class or ethnic distinction." As Davis (2010: 37) reminds us, "Climate change . . . will produce dramatically unequal impacts across regions and social classes, inflicting the greatest damage upon poor countries with the fewest resources for meaningful adaptation." For a discussion of how climate change will exacerbate social and economic inequalities, see, e.g., Bettini (2013); Brisman, South and Walters (2018a, 2018b, 2020).

33. "In fact," Andrews (2019b) continues, "it's not a strategy at all: It's a farce to cover up bloodlust, a cry for attention, or both."

34. Wilson (2019) writes that "openly anti-human . . . viewpoints . . . offer a ready basis for authoritarian, genocidal responses to ecological disaster." Andrews (2019b) echoes this sentiment:

> The strongest indicator of a person's consumption—and their carbon footprint—is wealth. The reason you don't see anyone calling to keep out billionaires is that demographic changes also stoke a protectionist fear: that a rich country needs to protect its supposedly threatened resources from those perceived to be needy newcomers.
>
> Not surprisingly, racism, sexism, classism, and ableism have long fed into the history of the 'population control' movement. And tragically, some people have taken this kind of thinking to even more destructive extremes.

On how Thanos evokes fears of "the rise of authoritarianism," see Wang and Zhang (2023: 187).

35. In a variation on this exercise, Hirschmann (2023: 175) describes the massive destruction caused by invasive plants and insects—sometimes brought intentionally from one continent to another—such as with the Japanese knotweed and mile-a-minute weed that "migrated" to the United States as ornamentals—before suggesting that "removing humans from the planet will not help suppress those invasive populations or help native species thrive." "Indeed," she continues, "humans are needed to undo the damage they have done through ecologically defensive action. If, rather than eliminating people randomly, Thanos *selectively spared* those who struggle to remove non-native invasives and plant native species and instead targeted corporate polluters, one could argue that there was some reason to his method. But in a random selection, why would he not expect that surviving corporate heads would view this as an opportunity to gain greater competitive advantage, leaving them carte blanche to continue polluting?" (Hirschmann 2023: 175–76; emphasis added). Thanos's "misguided solution to environmental desolation . . . communicates a subtle message to the attuned viewer that people are the problem, not the solution" (Hirschmann 2023: 179). "Instead of selecting people at random in a consumerist, bottom-up philosophy," Hirschmann (2023: 179) resolves, "Thanos's plan would be less maniacal if it was part of a strategy to reduce pollution and encourage renewable energy by targeting the governments and corporations that have the power to enact such changes (Rowlands 2001: 19). People are not the primary causal problem even if they are the problems' technical endpoint and vehicle: corporations and governments are."

36. A parallel real-world question is, if we (or, rather, the "superrich") can spend billions putting bits of electronic equipment into an orbit around the planet—or blasting themselves and other "ultrarich" into space—why cannot we (or, rather, they) spend billions to apply science to reducing disease, hunger, and global warming? We return to this discussion in Chapter 3 (see also Lam et al. 2023, 2025).

37. Wang and Zhang (2023: 191n3) note that "critics have questioned why Thanos chooses to kill half the life in the universe instead of doubling the universe's resources, placing half the population in an alternate universe, or other extraordinary solutions that would solve the problem without so much death."

For example, one Twitter contributor, "America Is Musty" (@DragonflyJonez), put it rather succinctly, tweeting on April 28, 2018, "Thanos wanted to kill half the universe bc there's not enough resources to go around but genocide ain't the answer, man. Why not just make it rain potatoes or some shit. All of this could've been prevented if only he'd watched Cloudy With A Chance of Meatballs"—to which "SnackGPT" (@bajetown-reppa) replied (favorably), "Homie has a glove that makes him basically omnipotent but he can't make some big ass vegetable gardens . . . Foh." (*Cloudy with a Chance of Meatballs* [2009] is an American computer-animated science fiction comedy film directed by Phil Lord and Christopher Miller, produced by Sony Pictures Animation Inc. and Columbia Pictures [distributed by Sony Pictures Releasing], and based on the 1978 children's book of the same name [written by Judi Barrett and illustrated by Ron Barrett (1978)], in which a scientist invents a machine that can make food fall from the sky.)

To offer another example, Olorunnisola (2023) asks, "why didn't Thanos just double the resources with The Infinity Stones? Or create new planets to accommodate additional life, if needed." He then responds: "Simple: because it would have made it easier for people to use and waste them in the same way they always have, aggravating the imbalance he perceived already existed in the cosmos." Thus, taking Olorunnisola's (2023) points into consideration, a kinder, gentler Thanos would have increased resources, improved distribution of those resources, and then reduced the forces driving overconsumption—assuming that other beings/lifeforms/peoples/species possess similar imperatives and urges of profligacy of many humans.

38. On this point, Olorunnisola (2023) underscores "the temporary nature of [Thanos's] solution," explaining that "since the population boom of the Industrial Revolution, when the human population reached its peak of 1 billion in 1804, it has only grown exponentially [*sic*]. At the time of Thanos's snap, Earth's population was 7.6 billion. . . . at a 1% annual population growth, which is Earth's current growth, the effects of Thanos's snap will be reversed in 69 years." This leads Olorunnisola (2023) to wonder "if six decades of 50% humanity thriving in full bellies, clear skies, and environmental abundance is worth a lifetime of grief and pain."

39. Olorunnisola (2023) picks up this line of thinking: "Thanos wiped out 50% of all living creatures, including animals and plants. . . . this does not limit the depleting impact of humans on earth; it just halves the resources for the remaining 50% of life." But "let us assume," Olorunnisola (2023) continues, that "Thanos erased only humans and spared all plants and animal life. His logic [still] remains flawed. Here's why: the problem is not overconsumption without the availability of renewable sources of energy. This is the angle Thanos should have [taken]. His solution to the universe's extinction threat should have been in line with *provision*, not *elimination*" (emphasis added)—a point alluded to earlier.

40. Fullerton (2019) makes the important point that "it's not like *both* films could be about Thanos (this one [*Endgame*] spends a lot more time with the six original Avengers). Arguably it's the success of the first film in humanising the villain that makes him feel a little thinner here [in *Endgame*]" (emphasis in original).

On the "'muddled middles' of monster movies"—"how viewers may pleasurably identify with monsters in the middle of a monster movie, even if that identification is accompanied by fear and does not last through the closure provided by the end of the film," see Tidwell (2021: 62, quoting Alaimo 2001: 94).

On the emotive responses of the audience in relationship to those of the characters in the horror genre—on how "in works of horror the responses of characters often seem to cue the emotional responses of the audience"—see Carroll (1987: 52); see also Aistrope and Fishel (2020).

41. Welsh, Fleming, and Dowler (2011: 459) report that "fictional media sources, including film and television, may . . . have persuasive effects on public attitudes and beliefs (Appel 2008; Appel and Richter 2007)." Appel's (2008) cross-sectional studies in Germany and Austria, for example, found that "those who watch a lot of fictional stories on television tend to perceive the world as a just place, a place where people get what they deserve." For Appel and Richter (2007), "fictional narratives conveyed by books, movies, and—perhaps most importantly—television programs play an important part in everyday life and, therefore, in the socialization of children, adolescents, and adults," and their study led them to suggest that "fictional narratives can have a persistent implicit influence on the way we view the world, and that these effects may last longer than the effects of typical explicit attempts to change beliefs by presenting claims and arguments." Testing whether exposure to gay men on the television sitcom *Will & Grace* can influence attitudes toward gay men more generally, Schiappa, Gregg, and Hewes (2006: 20, 31) conducted a study of university students, examining the relationship between number and intimacy of gay contacts, parasocial interaction ("the phenomenon that viewers form beliefs and attitudes about people they know only through television, regardless of whether such people are fictional characters or real people"), and viewing frequency of the show; their results indicated that "viewing frequency and parasocial interaction predict lower levels of sexual prejudice toward gay men." More recently, in a conversation about Alex Garland's *Civil War* (2024), David Rooney, chief film critic of *The Hollywood Reporter*, proposed that "perhaps a sizeable slice of the American public needed movies like those [Jonathan Demme's *Philadelphia* (1993), Ang Lee's *Brokeback Mountain* (2005), and Gus Van Sant's *Milk* (2008)] that were more humanist than radical—not to mention TV like *Will & Grace*, which could be mischievously edgy but rarely provocative—to get comfortable enough to broach the idea of marriage equality"—comments that resonate with Schiappa, Gregg, and Hewes's (2006) findings. (On how *Will & Grace*, with its openly gay characters, evidence how "entertainment media is . . . a site where politically relevant messages are sent and received," see Carnes and Goren [2023: 5].) Essentially, while some individuals may seek television programming and films that are consistent with their prior beliefs and socialization (see Segrin and Nabi 2002)—meaning that such media can strengthen existing attitudes—fictional narratives (especially those containing fact-related information) can induce profound changes in viewers' (or readers', in the case of Appel and Richter [2007]) real-world beliefs. As Carnes and Goren (2023: 2) declare, "The MCU . . . is . . . a product of contemporary politics and society. Many of its stories seem to be direct responses to

the pressures and problems of the day. Racial injustice, environmental catastrophe, and political misinformation aren't just contemporary social ills, they're also key thematic elements of recent MCU blockbusters like *Black Panther*, *Avengers: Endgame*, and *Spider-Man: Far From Home*." But as per the Spider-Man proverb known as the "Peter Parker Principle" (see Stahl and Nelson 2024), "with great power comes great responsibility." While there may be some debate as to what responsibilities, if any, MCU has to engage with "the pressures and problems of the day," it is clear that MCU has great power, should it choose to wield it in ways that might help audiences navigate and ameliorate "contemporary social ills." In other words, while MCU's protagonists may be superheroes, as a media franchise, it is rather staid and unadventurous, reinforcing support for the status quo, instead of prompting more sophisticated thinking about racial injustice, environmental catastrophe, and political misinformation that could influence (positively) attitudes and beliefs. Maybe this should not come as a surprise. Carnes and Goren (2023: 11) note that "superhero stories often focus on *restoring the status quo* rather than addressing the world's existing problems and injustices and ultimately changing the world for the better" (emphasis in original). As such, they continue, "superhero stories might not nurture—and might actually *limit*—political and social imagination by implicitly presenting the status quo as the ultimate good, worth preserving and thereby discouraging people from imagining different and better futures" (emphasis in original).

42. According to Maya Phillips (2019), "Though some fans complain about substandard movies and ever-lengthening runtimes, audiences remain invested in the MCU: 'Avengers: Infinity War' was the fourth-highest-grossing movie of all time, closely followed, in the top ten, by 'The Avengers,' 'Avengers: Age of Ultron,' and 'Black Panther.'" Kendall R. Phillips (2021: 98), no relation, notes that "with a global box office take of over $2 billion, [*Infinity War*] was by far the most successful film of 2018. It also earned the highest opening weekend and single weekend gross and was the fastest film to reach the $1 billion mark" (citing McClintock 2018). *Endgame*, which premiered almost exactly one year after *Infinity War*, would become "the highest grossing film in history with a staggering $2.8 billion" (Phillips 2021: 110, citing Mendelson 2020).

43. For a discussion of online hashtags such as #thanoswasright and a defense of Thanos's beliefs and reasoning, see Wang and Zhang (2023: 187).

44. See Giuliani (2021: 113), who contends that "science fiction has long been regarded as a product of far-right or even neo-fascist cultures for indulging white or Western (neo-colonial) supremacy and genocidal fantasies against both the external enemy and the internal other." Cf. Phillips (2021: 76), who identifies "an inherent conservatism in the superhero story," and who quotes Reynolds (1992: 77) for the proposition that "the superhero has a mission to preserve society, not re-invent it."

45. On the work and impact of the Anti-Creep Climate Initiative, see, e.g., Anson et al. (2022); Ivakhiv (2022); Taylor (2022).

46. In "Glare of Disdain," Gene Lueng Yang (2016), the cartoonist and graphic novelist, paraphrases Sims Bishop's words: "Books can be *windows* into other people's lives and *mirrors* of our own" (emphasis in original). The sentiment, however, remains.

47. As an example, Kwame Alexander (2016: 33), the American poet and children's book author, has proclaimed:

> If we don't give children books that are literary mirrors as well as windows to
> the whole world of possibility, if these books don't give them the opportunity to

see outside themselves, then how can we expect them to grow into adults who connect in meaningful ways to a global community, to people who might look or live differently than they. You cannot.

For a discussion, see Crandall (2022). For a similar perspective, see Krotz (2023: v), who discusses the work of the Georgian Bay Métis writer, Cherie Dimaline, and the importance "for Indigenous youth to see themselves in 'stories that matter.'"

48. They add that "with the advent of fake news, it might even be a whole lot more confusing—and dangerous—than that" (Jewkes and Linnemann 2018: 66).

On the criminal justice system as a "funhouse mirror" at a carnival that distorts viewers' perception of the system and the operation of the law—with some parts grossly enlarged and others greatly narrowed or shrunken—see Brisman (2016: 157); Brisman (2022: 159–60). On the importance of writing to organize one's thoughts and how one feels—and to "record the truth before [one's] anxiety twists everything like a funhouse mirror," see Dimaline (2023: 29).

For a slightly different use of the idea of "hall of mirrors," where the underlying phenomenon being described, rather than the news cycle reporting on it, is chaotic, confusing, and distorted, see Goldberg (2023: SR2), who writes:

> As a few bleak anecdotes illustrate, it is often impossible, in real time, for out-siders to know what is happening in the ceaselessly reigniting war between Israel and the Palestinians. This was true even before social media and before Elon Musk acquired Twitter and turned it into the cesspool of misinformation, trolling and hysteria now called X. But today countless people are plugged into a frantically churning news cycle, trying to instantly metabolize a conflict that is a *hall of mirrors* in the best of times and is now careening toward a possible regional war, with all the propaganda and mass panic that entails. It's an epistemological catastrophe that is putting people's lives in danger. (emphasis added)

49. This is sometimes popularized as "the end of the world as we know it," often referred to as "Teotwawki" by "preppers" and "survivalists" (see, e.g., Foster 2014: 26, citing O'Brien 2012; Weiss 2024).

50. For a helpful note on interdisciplinary scholarship on "monsters," "monstrosity," and the "monstrous" involving a wide range of creatures/lifeforms (e.g., aliens, humans, vampires, zombies) across various genres (e.g., films, novels, poetry, television), see Carrier (2023: 109n2). On how "police are in the business of fighting monsters" and on "the intimate and abiding connection" between monsters and the police, see Linnemann (2016: 43, 44); see also Neocleous (2014).

CHAPTER 2

1. Arachnophobia is so pronounced that in Sophie Corrigan's *The Not Bad Animals*, a children's book in which forty-two disesteemed creatures attempt "to set the record straight because [they're] fed up with the lies [humans] have been spreading" (2020: 4), the spider appears on the first double-page spread. Beginning with the spider, Corrigan presents the case for considering each animal "creepy" and "crawly" and "terrifying" before endeavoring to demonstrate that these "rumors" are "just plain MEAN" and that animals are "NOT bad at all . . . just misunderstood" (2020: 4, 5, capitalization in

original). Humans/readers learn, *inter alia*, that "spiders are SO good for the environment. They eat bugs, recycle their own webs by eating them, and are a vital source of food for birds, frogs, lizards, and even other spiders" (Corrigan 2020: 9, capitalization in original).

2. James (2015: 123) notes that for "some writers . . . the idea of wilderness, conceived of as an area untrammelled by man, is culturally specific, the product of distinctively Western assumptions about, amongst other things, masculinity, religious evangelism and the moral permissibility of subjugating indigenous peoples." Elsewhere in this chapter, we provide a brief overview of the history of the social construction of "wilderness." For now, we note that the term *wildlife* is problematic for some green criminologists. For example, Sollund (2020: 523n5) writes, "To refer to animals that are not domesticated as 'wildlife' is anthropocentric in that this alienates them and treats them as 'other' or different from domesticated species and humans. The term 'wildlife' suggests that animals that are not under human control are somehow acting only according to their needs. Much 'wildlife' poses no threat to humans"—a point to which we return later—"but the term," Sollund continues, "suggests that such animals may be dangerous or harmful to humans—a perspective that often leads humans to kill or mistreat such 'wildlife.'" For a discussion, contrast Runhovde (2020: 550n3) and Sollund (2017: 80n4) with Nurse (2015: xi).

3. The "ecophobia" that Estok (2009: 208) describes—and decries—is

as present and subtle in our daily lives and literature as homophobia and racism and sexism. It plays out in many spheres; it sustains the personal hygiene and cosmetics industries (which cite nature's "flaws" and "blemishes" as objects of their work); it supports city sanitation boards that issue fines seeking to keep out "pests" and "vermin" associated in municipal mentalities with long grass; it keeps beauticians and barbers in business; it is behind landscaped gardens and trimmed poodles in women's handbags on the Seoul subway system; it is about power and control; it is what makes looting and plundering of animal and nonanimal resources possible. Self-starvation and self-mutilation imply ecophobia no less than lynching implies racism.

For a discussion, see Hillard (2009); Kniss (2021); Parker (2016); Tidwell and Soles (2021).

4. Kweku (2017) reminds us that "movies that operate in the world of the fantastic can be an escapist retreat. But just as often, instead of withdrawing from their own era, they embody its concerns and preoccupations. Watching science fiction and fantasy movies is like reading the dream journal of the collective subconscious." Thus, for Harris (2009), writing almost a decade earlier, "summer movies are always famed for big setpiece special effects and explosive finales," but that "as America fights two foreign wars and deals with an economic meltdown, Hollywood's 'dream factory' has taken a decidedly nightmarish turn."

5. We return to apocalyptic depictions in Chapter 4.

6. Two "insect documentaries that vilify and/or glorify the insects on display by underlining similarities between the behaviors, culture, emotions, and even appearances of humans and insects" are *The Hellstrom Chronicle* (1971) and *Beetle Queen Conquers Tokyo* (2009) (Murray and Heumann 2016: xix). According to Murray and Heumann (2016: xix), the former constructs insects as monsters, while the latter constructs humans as "model 'persons' . . . to promote an environmental message that either warns humans

about their mistreatment of the natural world or encourages insect preservation through the protection of the natural world."

7. Examples here include *Damnation Alley* (1997), *The Nest* (1988), *Mimic* (1997), *Bug* (1975), and *Cronos* (1993). *Damnation Alley* and *The Nest* present cockroaches as "horrific monsters that must be destroyed, perhaps because they too closely resemble the malevolent side of humanity," whereas *Mimic* and *Bug* "examine the destructive repercussions of genetic engineering meant to alter cockroaches for human benefit" (Murray and Heumann 2016: xix). For Murray and Heumann (2016: xix), "*Cronos* (1993) more explicitly highlights the symbolic value of the cockroach as a seemingly immortal survivor." As the authors explain, all five of these films "demonstrate a similar perspective on the cockroach," insofar as they "suggest[] that manipulating nature, even for beneficial results, ultimately leads to destructive ends" (Murray and Heumannn 2016: xix).

8. For Murray and Heumann (2016: xx), "two recent European comic vampire films"—*Strigoi* (2009) and *The Pack* (*La meute*) (2010)—"illuminate the interconnected relationship between blood, soil, and vampirism" and "highlight[] the environmental underpinnings of the vampire myth in relation to a shattered ecology or home." Roberto Rossellini's *Germany Year Zero* (1948) and Guillermo del Toro's *The Devil's Backbone* (2001) "demonstrate the monstrous metamorphosis an environment destroyed by war causes children" (Murray and Heumann 2016: xx).

9. *Land of the Dead* (2005) and *Warm Bodies* (2013) function as "evolutionary narratives of survival and reproduction and ultimately endorse interdependent relationships between humans and the zombies they become"; Murray and Heumann (2016: xxi) advance the argument that "the most successful evolutionary narratives stress *cooperation* between species instead of war" (emphasis added). Two Troma Entertainment series—*The Toxic Avenger* (1984–2023) and *Class of Nuke 'Em High* (1986–2017)—can reveal "the consequences of disturbing a pristine ecosystem and offer a viable solution to greedy humans' exploitation of the natural world" (Murray and Heumann 2016: xxi). The *Frontline* documentary *Poisoned Waters* (2009), Barry Levinson's "found footage" horror movie responses in *The Bay* (2012), and Shane Carruth's *Upstream Color* (2013) all illustrate "the repercussions that humanity and the nonhuman environment face when we choose tragic evolutionary narratives rather than interdependence" (Murray and Heumann 2016: xxi).

10. Examples here include (1) *The Texas Chainsaw Massacre* (1974), (2) *The Hills Have Eyes* (1977), (3) *Motel Hell* (1980), (4) *The Lone Ranger* (2013), (5) *Blood Diner* (1987), (6) *Ravenous* (1999), (7) *American Psycho* (2000), (8) *Trouble Every Day* (2001), (9) *Jennifer's Body* (2009), (10) *American Mary* (2012), (11) *RoboCop* (2014), and (12) *Elysium* (2013). Murray and Heumann (2016: xxii) regard the first four of these as "cannibal horror films" that "make similar statements about our desecration of the natural world"; the authors look to films 5–9 in order to contemplate "cannibalism within a gendered framework that complicates colonial fantasies of land, women, and wendigo." *American Mary* (2012) represents a "feminist body horror film," while *RoboCop* (2014) and *Elysium* (2013) are "masculine human-weapon films" or "body-modification films" that "replicat[e] the natural world they seem to transcend" (Murray and Heumann 2016: xxii).

11. For more on "Gothic ambiguity"/how ambiguity permeates "the Gothic," see Sothcott (2016: 435, 437, 438, 439, 440, 441, 442, 443).

12. On "the longing for the 'sacred suspension of ordinary rules' and a secret admiration of the transgressive—the enduring human fascination with forbidden people, places, and things," see Linnemann (2016: 68, quoting Žižek 2011: 8). Such "longing"

seems to be a universal across the cultures of communities around the world. Indigenous peoples draw upon connections to the wildlife and landscapes that they and their ances- tors inhabit, and legends and myths can be both entertaining and instructional (Sepie 2017). For example, Dimaline (2023: 24) explains that stories of the Rougarou—a wolf- or dog-like creature that usually walks and talks like a man and who lives in Métis communities and some Cajun settlements—were "used as a way to deter anxiety while still doing the necessary work of invoking the desired feelings and behaviours." As Dimaline (2023: 24) continues, "These stories were also a way for the old women to get their point across without being ignored by their listeners. We took them seriously but we also enjoyed the thrill of being scared while remaining safe without their reach."

Skott and colleagues (2021: 390) write that "monsters . . . cross boundaries and cat- egorical distinctions, which both fascinates and frightens us (Ingebretsen 2001; Sothcott 2016)," and that which "simultaneously fascinate[es] and repuls[es], as a rejected aspect of oneself" is "the abject," which ambiguously blurs or crosses the border between "subject and object" (Hall 2016: 245; see also 2016: 250). (In a similar fashion, Hook [2012: 133] draws on Fanon's [(1952) 2008] idea of the "phobogenic object of racism" to argue that "the target of racism remains criss-crossed not only with relations of disgust, repulsion and denigration, but also with potent relations of allure, exoticism and desire. Each such aspect of this ambivalent object-relationship needs to remain in place if we are to understand anything of the volatility of racist affect: the multiple paradoxes of anxiety yet attrac- tion, contempt yet desire, abjection yet sexual curiosity.") This, as we expound elsewhere in the chapter, may help explain our feelings and reactions to Frankenstein, Dracula, and other figures of/in horror (e.g., the zombie) because they possess some distinctly human aspects/characteristics/features, but also some that are manifestly and markedly not; faced with this blurring or crossing—with that which "'does not respect borders, positions rules'"—and fixating on those/their differences, we reject these figures (Hall 2016: 250, quoting Kristeva 1982: 4). We return to "the abject" and abjection in Chapter 3.

13. On how villains in the MCU—discussed in Chapter 1—"have often been char- acters that evoke our most poignant social anxieties," see Wang and Zhang (2023: 190). On "the way monsters recast collective anxiety in fictional form" and how "we can read the dominant worries of an era in its monster stories," as well as on the "therapeutic aspects" of monster culture and monsters as "offer[ing] catharsis," see North (2014). Sothcott makes a similar point, describing how "the Gothic" projects—or reflects—a culture's anxieties, fears, and horrors (2016: 433, 434, 435, 436, 438, 441, 442, 443), and how it serves a "cathartic" function (2016: 434, 436, 443). Such recasting of collec- tive anxiety in fictional form—such reading of dominant worries—such projects and reflections—need not be complex. Senf (2020: 79) proposes that "[e]ven when popular works are themselves simplistic or are read in simplistic ways, they often reveal a great deal about the culture that produced them." Senf (2020: 65, 66) takes the additional step of encouraging the academic study of popular culture, more generally, because "it targets who we are at a particular moment"—especially if we are sensitive to "the histori- cal contexts in which art and popular culture are produced."

14. Levina and Bui (2013: 10) argue that "popular representations of monstrosity in the twenty-first century reflect anxieties and fears over physical, economic, and political boundaries in the globalized world." We return to this dynamic in Chapter 4, but for now, we offer the following notes and comments. Ulaby (2008) reports that "horror always seems to reflect the anxieties of its time" and, more specifically, that the

popularity of zombies in the post-9/11 2000s has been considered as a reflection of current worries (Saunders 2012; see also Drezner 2014). Aistrope and Fishel (2020: 637–
38) observe that "the zombie is a stand-in for the terrorist or radical enemy other."
Similarly, both Chomsky (2014) and Onstad (2008) reflect on links between social
fears, upheavals, and popular imagery concerning such threats. Likewise, Saunders
(2012: 80) remarks that "while nearly every culture has myths associated with reanimation of the dead, the current renaissance across multiple media, what might be deemed
a 'zombie turn,' has little to do with premodern superstitions of walking corpses."
Rather, he argues, "the current obsession with zombies, and particularly the looming
(albeit unlikely) threat of human-zombie conflicts, is a reflection of the dangers of
invasive alterity associated with uncontrolled spaces in the current era of globalisation. This shift is especially prevalent in the United States following the attacks of 11
September 2001, as zombies have become phantasmal stand-ins for Islamist terrorists, illegal immigrants, carriers of foreign contagions, and other 'dangerous' border
crossers. . . . zombie 'uprisings' are . . . used as a narrative tool for exposing concerns
about international relations and domestic social problems" (Saunders 2012: 80–81;
for a discussion, see Neocleous 2016: 47). (We return to these statements by Saunders
[2012] in Chapter 4.)

For Giuliani (2021: 35), "In our times, monsters and cannibalistic monsters have
returned as assemblages of images and imaginaries inherited from the history of Western
representations of the Other, often through allegories that apparently were only the
product of a certain moment in history and a specific context." On this point, see
Tcareva (2020: 83), who identifies how, in literature and art, "the trope of cannibalism . . . is most often discussed in terms of two familiar, polar opposite images: the
colonial image of a barbarian on a far-away island, or the contemporary image of the
'civilized,' urban cannibal. In European literature of the nineteenth and early twentieth
centuries, scholars argue, the trope of consuming human flesh tends to serve the quite
straightforward purpose of othering those who are racially, ethnically, or socioeconomi-
cally different from the white bourgeois middle class." Tcareva (2020: 84, citing Brown
2013) also "suggests that the literary function of the figure of the cannibal mutates and
changes to reflect the particular fears of a given time and place," and she demonstrates
how "true cannibalism does not refer to the act of consuming the flesh of one's own
kind, but functions as a metaphor for the exploitation and subjugation of one's fellow
citizens, for living a life of luxury at the expense of others."

Correspondingly, albeit in more plain-spoken terms, Bould (2021: 28–29) opines,
"Whether it is alienation, consumerism, conformity, rich people, poor people, people
of colour, people of pallor, immigrants, nationalists, white supremacists or Trumpians,
zombies are allegorical as fuck."

For in-depth analyses of the rise of the walking dead and zombie culture, see, e.g.,
Olney (2017), Rutherford (2013); see also Bishop (2010), Boluk and Lenz (2011),
Keetley (2014), and Lauro (2017)—all part of a series entitled "Contributions to
Zombie Studies," published by McFarland & Company, Inc., which, as of February
2025, contains twenty-nine books. For a discussion of research on zombie films prior
to 1968 (before George A. Romero's *Night of the Living Dead*), as well as those post-
1968, see Murray and Heumann (2016: 83–85); for a discussion focused just on films
embracing the "genre conventions" inaugurated by Romero (post-1968), see Bishop
(2009: 18–24).

On the history of zombies and specifically Americans' fascination and obsession with them, see, e.g., Arablouei and Abdelfatah (2019); Fashiontribes.com (2007); Hill (2019); Kaplan-Levenson and Abdelfatah (2019); North (2014); see also Onstad (2008).

For an examination of why zombies have become so prevalent in popular culture, in general, and in mainstream security politics, in particular, see Neocleous (2016). On the general growth in scholarly investigation and research on zombies, see, e.g., Drezner (2014: 826); Lauro and Christie (2011: 237n1). On criminological engagement with the zombie trope, including zombification and fears of a "zombie apocalypse," see Linnemann (2016, 2022); Linnemann and Wall (2013); Linnemann, Wall, and Green (2014); see generally Fredriksson (2019).

15. Indeed, as Aistrope and Fishel (2020: 645) remind us, "While fearful stories are as old as human society, the modern horror genre originally emerged, under the rubric of Gothic fiction, during the late eighteenth century, as a reaction against the forces of Enlightenment, which had, at least in some minds, disenchanted the world and unleashed a maelstrom of unintended calamities that were not adequately captured in prevailing narratives about progress and mastery." In a similar vein, Skott and colleagues (2021: 387) explain: "Dating back to works, such as Horace Walpole's *The Castle of Otranto* ([1764] 2014) and Mary Shelley's *Frankenstein* ([1818] 2013), the Gothic emerged as a reaction to the Enlightenment ideals of order, rationality, and rules. The Gothic imagination deals with extreme contrasts, the erosion of boundaries, and an emphasis on the ambivalence and uncertainty that contribute to an infinite spectrum of the 'real' and imagined." Sothcott (2016: 431–32) points to the same origins and influences: "It is difficult . . . to identify a period since the publication of Walpole's *Castle of Otranto* (1764) when [the Gothic] has not inspired the popular culture of modern society. Count Dracula and his vampiric brethren, Frankenstein and similar abject mutations of scientific excess, the werewolf and ghost, witches, ghouls."

16. Cronon (1995) is excerpted in Cronon (1996). There are, of course, many other accounts of the Western notion of "wilderness"—what Callicott and Nelson (1998; Nelson and Callicott 2008) refer to as the "received wilderness idea." For example, James (2015: 120–23) offers "[a] very short history of the received wilderness idea," drawing heavily on Nash (1982), as well as "sceptical responses" (2015: 123–26). Our goal here is not to chronicle this discussion/history/lineage but to make the point that just as people have fought over lands deemed "wild," the concept of "wilderness" (e.g., what it includes, what it excludes) has (also) been constructed and contested.

17. As Loskutoff (2018: SR4) observes,

> Civilization itself is an attempt to protect us from this feeling [of being consumed by nature or, in his case, a grizzly bear]. From its earliest iterations in fire-starting and cave-dwelling to its current zenith in the construction of megalopolises, as well as the careful documentation of every birth and the methodical laying bare of each strand in every helix, civilization is a way of setting ourselves apart from the prey we once were. Building walls, both physical and informational, to keep out the bears.

18. James (2015: 121) concurs, explaining that the Pilgrim Fathers thought that the "wild lands" of the New World "harbour[ed] strange and terrible beasts: not just grizzlies, rattlesnakes and the always-watching malevolent natives, but also 'Dragons,' 'Droves of Devils' and 'Fiery flying serpents' (Nash 1982: 29)." See also Kniss (2021: 72–73).

19. Compare Cronon's description with that of Amitav Ghosh (2016: 22), who, in *The Great Derangement: Climate Change and the Unthinkable*, reflects on how "the nineteenth century was indeed a time when it was assumed, in both fiction and geology, that Nature was moderate and orderly."

20. As Skal (2012: xi) reminds us, "Speak of monsters and you're soon speaking about all kinds of things. Shelley's *Frankenstein* can't be fully appreciated without a larger understanding of the tension between the self-satisfied Enlightenment and Romantic radicalism; *Dracula* doesn't start to make sense as a cultural document without at least a basic understanding of Darwinism's impact on Victorian thought and society." Along the same lines, Sothcott (2016: 436) reflects on how "the eighteenth-century Gothic" might be seen as "an attempt to resolve feelings of guilt arising from a paradoxical yearning for the splendours and nobility of pre-modern Europe dominated by the Catholic Church with simultaneous celebrations of its decline wrought by, amongst other influences, the modernizing impetus of ascetic Protestantism (Miles 2002)." The nineteenth-century Gothic, Sothcott (2016: 436) continues, might be considered as "a register of . . . unease regarding the rapid urbanisation of society" or of "newly experienced fears, following the emergence of Darwinian science" regarding the "possibility of human evolutionary regression (Hurley 2002; see also Rafter and Ystehede 2010)"—or as a reflection of "anxieties wrought by changing gender relations and the culture shock of nineteenth century colonial encounters with other 'races' (Punter 2000)."

21. This stands in contrast to some scholars' claims about the zombie, noted earlier. As Saunders (2012: 86) reminds us, "In most cases, the zombie—unlike the seductive vampire, the duplicitous werewolf, or the pitiable Frankenstein's monster—lacks any traits evoking humanity (other than its 'human'-like shell). The prototypical zombie walks slowly and in a stilted fashion, compelled forward by some unearthly force that cannot be reasoned with or stopped: even a dismembered zombie and its constituent parts will continue to crawl forward, seeking its prey." Similarly, Sothcott (2016: 435) puts forth that "the zombie . . . is something of a marginal Gothic figure—a relatively recent addition to the menagerie of Gothic 'monsters'—with no positive redeeming features. Responses to the zombie are invariably negative: there is no charm in becoming a shambling wreck of former humanity. Yet other Gothic characters enjoying an equally powerful resonance today (the vampire, the werewolf, the doppelganger for example) are fundamentally more ambiguous in character. There is something erotically charged about the vampire, something comfortingly sensuous about the werewolf, something mysterious about the doppelganger that renders them more than just representations of monstrosity but also channels of cultural value." Correspondingly, Doyle (2020: 98, 99) observes that "while auteurs of the zombie subgenre of horror could have attributed any number of biological processes to the zombie, it is the endless urge to consume—often described as animalistic—that characterizes the zombie" and that "in making zombies sound less human and more 'animalistic,' film and television sound editors imply that the animal is the antithesis of the human, an ultimate other against which humanity is defined." For a related perspective, see Linnemann (2016: 28, 149), who describes "zombification" as "the mediated transformation of a human being into a disposable object," and who explains how "meth heads" are treated like "zombies"—"the lowest common denominator, disposable enemies." S. G. Browne's *Breathers: A Zombie's Lament* (2009) represents an exception: the story is told from the point of view of Andy Warner, a reanimated/newly revived zombie who falls in love with another zombie and pursues "zombie activism" (Saunders 2012: 88).

22. Although as Rafter and Ystehede (2010: 264) point out, Bram Stoker described—or classified—Count Dracula as "a criminal and of criminal type. Nordau and Lombroso would so classify him."

23. Pihlström (2020: 37) adds that "the 'in-betweenness' is multifarious: traditional vampires such as Bram Stoker's Count Dracula, for example, are in-between not only in life and death, but also in East and West, in primitive pre-modernism and in the modern technological world, and so forth (see also Botting 1996, p. 150)."

24. Ellison and Adamec (2018: xxiii) begin the preface to their edited volume, *Carnivorous Plants: Physiology, Ecology, and Evolution*, by noting that "the idea of 'killer' plants is a staple trope of science-fiction novels, horror films, and Broadway shows." To be sure, "real life" carnivorous plants do not consume (flesh) *out of revenge* (see Williams 2022; for a descriptive synthesis of plants and fungi that possess compounds that could kill humans, see Carlson 2022), although some plants do emit odors of decaying meat or rotting flesh (see, e.g., "Guardian staff and agency" 2021; Puglise 2016; Simons 2020; Weston 2023; United States Botanical Garden 2024; see also Malabrigo et al. 2023). Nor is this the case with most movies—*Treevenge* and *The Ruins* notwithstanding: even when cinematic plants (or fruits) do develop or exhibit a taste for human blood, they tend not to be motivated by retribution. *The Guardian* (1990) involves a young couple with a newborn baby boy who do not realize that the nanny they have hired is actually a magical nymph (a hamadryade) who sacrifices infants in her care to an evil tree. Other examples include the horror comedy films *The Little Shop of Horrors* (1960) and *Little Shop of Horrors* (1986) (based on the 1982 stage musical adaptation of the same name), and the parody film *Attack of the Killer Tomatoes* (1978).

While *The Happening* (2008), mentioned in Chapter 1 to this book, does not involve *bloodthirsty* plants seeking to retaliate, "nature [does] turn[] against us" in the movie, and the film is intended as "a warning to heed the clarion call of impending environmental catastrophe" (Foy 2010b: 180, 181). Keetley (2021: 36n4) maintains that "*The Happening* actually leaves nature's motives unclear," and Tidwell and Soles (2021: 15–16n15) support Keetley's position that "the threat shown in the film—plants and their agency—has no clear explanation or agency behind it." The claims of Keetley and Tidwell and Soles notwithstanding, the more popular belief seems to be that in *The Happening*, in which an inexplicable airborne neurotoxin causes those infected to commit suicide—"nasty payback from the natural world," writes Dargis (2008) in her review—"the film's horror stems from the idea that human behavior may provoke deadly environmental reactions that are neither foreseeable nor easily comprehensible" (Williams 2016: 238). At the end of the movie, Dr. William Ross, Department of Botanical Toxicology, University of Chicago (played by Stephen Singer), states in a television interview:

> As everyone knows by now, traces of the neurotoxin have been found in some plants and trees. Now most environmentalists feel that this event is like—like the red tide in the ocean, but instead of algae killing fish, this happened on land. Plants and trees just can't pick up and move when they feel threatened, like other species. They have only one option: to rapidly evolve their chemistry. . . . I believe—All right? And this is just my opinion. That this was a prelude—A warning, like—like—like the first spot of a rash. *We have become a threat to this planet.* I don't—I don't think anybody will argue that. And this is a warning. (emphasis added; for a discussion, see Foy 2010b: 180, 183n6; Murray and Heumann 2016: xv)

Essentially, both *The Happening* and *The Ruins* "posit that horrors . . . exist in ostensibly quiet and serene environments" and both "feature[] plants as the principal monster terrorizing humanity" (Williams 2016: 228, 227). In the latter, vengeful vines devour human flesh; in the former, as noted earlier, plants emit a neurotoxin that induces a pandemic of suicide—in other words, causing humans to bring about their own bloody ends in response to ecological encroachment and environmental exploitation (see also Lauro 2011). See also note 21 in Chapter 4, on the remarkable real horror of the method of self-propagation developed by the fungus *Ophiocordyceps unilateralis*.

25. For Keetley (2021: 24), "tentacular ecohorror" functions as a third category of ecohorror, somewhat distinct from "the animal-oriented revenge-of-nature narrative" and "the vegetation-dominated plot of the concealing mass." Keetley (2021: 30–31) further distinguishes two "movements" of "tentacular ecohorror": "the first movement of tentacular ecohorror is the encounter with the impersonal nature that asserts its own life with rustling insistence, the second movement is the human's entanglement with this nature. Nature reaches out its tentacles, rendered all the more alien in their startling agency."

26. This represented a shift from Beccaria. Whereas Beccaria considered crime to be the result of a *rational* calculus (see, e.g., Beirne 2017: 15–18), Lombroso viewed crime as *anything but* rational—the product of genetic throwbacks (see, e.g., Posick and McBride 2017: 28–32; Skott et al. 2021: 386).

27. The idea that monsters may be more terrifying because they retain an outward presentation of ordinariness and likeability finds purchase in Travis Linnemann's enthralling monograph *The Horror of Police* (2022), where he recasts the police not as "monster-killers" or "evil-hunters" but as monsters *themselves* (for a review, see Damm 2023).

In a different vein, Khapaeva (2020: 2) notes, "In the late 1980s–early 1990s, a radical shift occurred in popular culture: the monster evolved from a grotesque criminal to a cult figure. In this decade, the image of the zombie, cannibal, serial killer, and vampire began to merge into an image of one compelling *idol-monster*" (emphasis in original). "Today," Khapaeva (2020: 2–3) continues, "bloodsucking vampires are described as 'perfect' and 'godlike' in most vampire sagas," such as in the *The Twilight Saga* based on the book series by Stephenie Meyer. Such monsters are decidedly *not* terrifying because they retain an external presentation of ordinariness. Rather, Khapaeva (2020: 3) explains, "[t]he idol-monster, with whom the audience is supposed to enthusiastically identify, . . . appear[s] in the role that was previously reserved for human protagonists."

28. See Khapaeva (2020: 19), who writes that "the idea that the difference between humans and monsters is ambiguous and that the murderous monster is actually the Other and thus deserves our sympathy has become an important message of the popular culture products [fiction and movies]" (citing Auerbach 1995).

29. In *Venom: Let There Be Carnage* (2021), another MCU movie, Woody Harrelson plays Cletus Kasady, a serial killer. At the beginning of the film, in an interview with Eddie Brock (Tom Hardy), an investigative journalist who is also the host of an alien symbiote Venom, Kasady asks Brock to deliver a message to all of his "fans" and then remarks that "people love serial killers." For Brock, Kasady is a criminal who "bear[s] little resemblance to 'us'" (Garland 1996: 461); Kasady, however, claims that the two of them are "the same." This proves portentous because later, Kasady bites Brock's hand, ingests a small part of the symbiote, and becomes the host of Venom's spawn, Carnage. In this way, Kasady becomes like Brock—capable of retaining an outward presentation of

ordinariness while hiding their "true nature." Interestingly, when Venom leaves Brock's body and goes off on his own, he attends a costume party/rave, where he is adored and complimented by other nightclubbers for his "amazing" costume (see Gribbin 2021; Shuster 2021). At one moment, Venom grabs the microphone and preaches an end to "this cruel treatment of aliens" and the need to "be able to live together upon this ball of rock. . . . Free to be who we be!" all to resounding cheers and calling into question who or what is "monstrous."

Essentially, Kasady exemplifies Garland's notion of "criminology of the other," and when Kasady becomes host to Carnage, he *genuinely* becomes an "Other"—a human/symbiote hybrid. When Venom detaches from Brock (his host), his outward appearance is that of an "alien other." But because he attends a "coming-out party" where *everyone* is in costume, he is embraced. Basically, rather than being rejected (and rejection is a common theme in the film, as well as in the first film, *Venom* [2018]), Venom is loved, and it is society's xenophobia and homophobia that are considered to be—and treated as—monstrous and abject.

30. What is significant for Skott and her coauthors (2021: 388) is how "Gothic narratives may have a significant impact on the development of public policy." As they explain, "The spread of the Gothic has not been restricted to shaping media reports of sensationalist crime; rather, Gothic narratives have also been constructing the perception of criminal transgression and justice, more generally" (Skott et al. 2021: 388). Drawing on Valier (2002: 321), Skott and her colleagues (2021: 388) point out that "punitive populism is built on Gothic tropes, which are 'embedded in the practices of the institutions of crime control and punishment themselves.'" "Sensationalist crimes," then, are "no longer considered anomalies, but permanent insidious features with repetitive themes of haunting and dereliction, from which, in true Gothic spirit, there is no rescue or escape (Valier 2002: 323)" (Skott et al. 2021: 388). Moreover, Skott and colleagues (2021: 388) continue, "The populism of today does not simply come from mass-mediated stories, but instead reflects *cultural anxieties* and a longing for categorical certainties in the vertiginous conditions of late modernity (Sothcott 2016; Valier 2002; Young 2007)" (emphasis added)—a point we make earlier in this chapter. "The Gothic imagination is, therefore, not only a projection of anxiety striving to reinforce cultural boundaries," Skott and colleagues (2021: 388) underscore, "but is also used to actively disrupt these boundaries, 'exposing their cultural fragility' (Sothcott 2016: 436)."

Sothcott (2016: 431, 436) makes a similar point to Skott and colleagues (2021), suggesting that "the Gothic flourishes in Late Modern Society" and that this "Late Modern Gothic imagination" can be read as "a projection of contemporary anxieties concerning cultural miscegenation, employment insecurities, globalised conflict and a host of other Later Modern troubles onto new Gothicised objects such as the 'neo-medieval' terrorist, depraved paedophile and mindless zombie killer." The difference, Sothcott (2016: 436) emphasizes—and this is consistent with Skott and her coauthors (2021)—is that "such [contemporary] projections now have a far greater impact upon criminal justice interventions than was ever previously apparent."

31. Again, one can draw a comparison to the zombie. As Berreby (2011: 19) writes, "Consider . . . the zombie. Once, he was a person, just like you and me, but then he changed. Now, despite his outward resemblance to a human being, he is a different thing altogether. He cannot disguise himself. He cannot *change back*" (emphasis added). "Another minus," Berreby (2011: 19) continues, is that "he yearns to sink his zombie-plague-spreading teeth into your brain."

32. Albeit reflecting limitations of the period, Washburn Hopkins (1905: 2) provides a fascinating comparative study of the "myths of rejuvenation . . . of varied sorts" that can be "found in many parts of the world."

33. Indeed, we are witnessing a return, of sorts, to "magical thinking," when, during the early stages of the COVID-19 pandemic, President Donald J. Trump wondered aloud to the world whether various charms and spells might make the coronavirus "magically" disappear (see, e.g., Burke 2020; Gusterson 2020).

34. For Bould (2021: 27), "the fantastic expresses our fears and anxieties, our desires and sometimes even our hopes. Frankenstein's monster embodies terrors of reproduction, foreshadows proletarian and anti-colonial revolution. King Kong rampaging through Manhattan enacts white fears of black masculinity and colonial comeuppance. Bodysnatching aliens are avatars of consumerist conformism. Robots are our dehumanised selves. Godzilla is the bomb." This leads him to advise us to ask what monsters represent. In an endnote to that question, Bould (2021: 145n4) adds:

> Though only fools and knaves would then attempt to reduce the monster to a single, fixed meaning. Monsters are polysemic and disorderly: multiple contradictory connotations swirl about them, constantly recontextualising. They always escape our control; if they do not, then—as every episode of *Scooby-Doo* shows us—they are not really monsters at all.

35. Of course, this is not all that the vampire represents. As Murray and Heumann (2016: 42) demonstrate, while "vampires have typically been associated with sexuality, power, evil and the Antichrist, the fluid boundaries between humanity and the monstrous, and intimacy as conquest" are evident in *The Pack* (*La meute*, 2010) and *Strigoi* (2009), where "vampirism most readily compares with consumption, a greed for resources, land, and blood that separates humans from the natural world that provides their home." Indeed, as they contend, "*The Pack* highlights the sometimes horrific and blood-sucking consequences of mistreating the Earth in relation to exploitative mining techniques, which destroy both the land and its human laborers" (Murray and Heumann 2016: 47). For a similar perspective on how zombie narratives allegorize the way humans consume the Earth's resources, see Doyle (2020: 113), discussed in Chapter 5.

36. An extreme version of natural mimicry occurs in *The Ruins* (2008), mentioned earlier, where the two American couples and a German tourist hear a phone ringing from somewhere inside a remote Mayan ruin in the jungle. They later realize that the ringing sound has been made by the flowers of carnivorous vines that inhabit the ruins (see Scherer 2016: 45).

37. This fear, Foltyn (2020: xi) contends, helps explain "why mythic monsters of the ancient world, the Brothers Grimm, and vampire lore feast on human flesh and blood." See Doyle (2020: 105) for a discussion of how "the tendency to refer to zombies as animalistic unveils an anthropocentric anxiety about being consumed by predators literally and figuratively." As Doyle (2020: 106) contends, "The greatest horror is not death, but the total and absolute dissolution of the self and the subject that comes from becoming food object."

Ford (2022), mourning the death of Freya, the young female walrus who was euthanized by the Norwegian Directorate of Fisheries in August 2022, allegedly because "she posed a danger to people" in the Oslofjord, clarifies that "humans have the inherent right to defend themselves when they are in danger." But "so does any other animal," he continues, and "when a person approaches wildlife in a setting where humans do not ordinarily belong, they should not be surprised if an animal attacks them out of self-preservation or territorial defense." Ford (2022) explains that while he "do[es] not want anyone to be injured or killed by a wild animal . . . people should respect and maybe *even fear* wildlife—and they *should fear* the natural consequences of getting too close and too comfortable with wild animals" (emphasis added). Ford (2022) advises that "humans should stay as far away from wildlife as they possibly can—especially when that wildlife weighs as much as some cars"—a reference to bison-goring incidents that have taken place at Yellowstone National Park, after people have ventured too close to these large bovines (see Oladipp 2022).

38. In support of the figure of twenty unprovoked shark attacks in New York City since 1837, Fadulu (2023) cites the Florida Museum of Natural History's International Shark Attack File (ISAF) (see Liang 2024). In support of the statement that the shark bite in early August 2023 was the first confirmed shark attack in New York City since the 1950s (which was a provoked attack), Fadulu (2023) cites the Global Shark Attack File, available at https://sharkattackfile.net/. Later in her article, Fadulu (2023) writes, "Shark bites have become more common on Long Island lately. There were eight in 2022, and there have been at least five this year." This might seem confusing: if Rockaway Beach is on Long Island and if it is a neighborhood in Queens (one of the five boroughs that comprise New York City), how can shark bites have become more common on Long Island if "the biting on Monday [August 7, 2023] was the first confirmed shark attack in New York City since the 1950s"? The answer is that Long Island is divided among four counties: Kings County (coextensive with Brooklyn, another borough of New York City), Queens County (coextensive with the borough of Queens), Nassau County, and Suffolk County. Kings County (Brooklyn) and Queens County (Queens) are both part of Long Island and part of New York City; Nassau County and Suffolk County are part of Long Island, but they are not part of New York City. As Walsh (2019) explains, "when people talk about 'Long Island,' they almost always mean not Brooklyn or Queens, but Nassau and Suffolk counties." Thus, the apparent frequency with which shark bites have been occurring in Long Island means that they have transpired in either Suffolk County (the easternmost county in New York State) or Nassau County (which is sandwiched between Queens County to the east and Suffolk County to the west).

For a recent announcement of a nonfatal shark bite in nearby New Jersey, see Wehner (2023).

39. Citing data from the ISAF (see Liang 2024), Thornton (2023) reports that the thirty-two provoked shark bites "occurred when people [we]re bitten after 'harassing' [sharks], trying to touch [them], trying to feed [them] or removing a fishing hook from a shark." Of the fifty-seven unprovoked shark bites, forty-one happened in the United States (and within the United States, Florida had the most, with sixteen bites)—meaning that "the U.S. leads among all countries for the most unprovoked shark bites."

40. For a further discussion of *Jaws* in relationship to the actual number of shark bites and the film's "demonization of fish," see Alaimo (2001), whose analysis may help explain why human interactions with sharks that do *not* result in bites might still generate news stories (see, e.g., Alund 2023). (Indeed, incidents involving nonhuman animals

behaving "bizarrely"—in ways to which we are unaccustomed—often generate media attention, such as when an "aggressive otter" began stealing surfboards from surfers off the coast of Santa Cruz, California, in July 2023 [Clayton 2023; Jones 2023]—a contrast to its image as a "playful creature[]" [Best 2018].)

For a discussion of "encounters" between orcas and boats in the Atlantic Ocean off the coast of Spain and Portugal, which began in 2020 but which have not resulted in any fatalities, see Chapter 3. As we explain, some experts expressed concern that "framing the encounters as 'attacks' could lead to misunderstandings about killer whales, not dissimilar to the fear of great white sharks inspired by a certain Hollywood movie that changed many people's impressions of the ocean forever" (Vlamis 2023, citing Andrew Trites, director of the Marine Mammal Research Unit of the Institute for the Oceans and Fisheries at the University of British Columbia).

41. According to Dr. Toby S. Daly-Engel, an Assistant Professor in the Department of Ocean Engineering and Marine Sciences at Florida Institute of Technology, "Worldwide, between zero and five people are killed by sharks every year . . . you're more likely to be bitten by a New Yorker" (quoted in Levin 2022: 32).

42. Foltyn (2020: xii) notes that "lions, tigers, bears, sharks, and even the occasional pig will eat each other and us," and that while "[b]illions of pounds of pork are eaten by human beings annually, . . . people are appalled when they hear about a human-eating hog." Similarly, Pihlström (2020: 36) reminds us that, "there are *wild animals* such as lions or sharks—more or less ordinary natural creatures existing in the world described and explained by the natural sciences—occasionally eating humans. Even giant snakes have been observed to have eaten a human being . . . whole" (emphasis in original). On pythons swallowing humans, which is "extremely rare" (Associated Press 2018b), see, e.g., Bowerman and Rossman (2017); CBS/AP (2017); CBS/AFP (2024); Pandolfo (2024); Rossman (2017); Roy (2024); see also Crowley (2023). For a recent report of a death caused by a crocodile attack, see Lyons (2023). For a recent account of an alligator attacking a man near a pond outside a bar in Florida, resulting in the amputation of the man's arm and the euthanizing of the alligator, see Sorace (2023). The point, Pihlström (2020: 36) encourages us to remember, is that while "such cases may be terrible and deeply frightening . . . they are hardly *metaphysically* frightening or disturbing in any ethical or existential sense; moreover, usually we humans are a much more serious threat to this kind of potentially human-eating animals than those animals are to us" (emphasis in original).

43. Giroux (2006: 173) offers some interesting insights into how Hurricane Katrina "first appeared to be a natural catastrophe" and "soon degenerated into a social debacle." As Giroux (2006: 192n1) contends,

> It is worth noting how the media coverage of the war in Iraq and Hurricane Katrina differ when viewed from the contrasting perspectives of a "natural catastrophe" and the ensuing man-made "social debacle." Labeled as a natural disaster, Katrina initially seemed removed from the political realm and social criticism until it had become clear in the aftermath of the tragedy that matters of race and class had to be addressed. The "natural" aspect of the disaster opened the door for media coverage of a domestic tragedy that could articulate dissent in a way that the state-manufactured war coverage could not. In other words, natural catastrophes are not supposed to be politicized in themselves; it was only in the aftermath that racial and class politics emerged that enabled

the media and the public to criticize the negligence and incompetence of the government, and, because the event occurred on domestic soil, the government had less control over the way the media constructed the event, particularly in invoking issues related to poverty, race, and inequality.

More recently—and more generally—Andrews (2019a) reminds us that

> human activities *are* directly responsible for many horrific crimes against nature. Endangered species aren't choosing to engage in mass suicide, trees don't burst into flames because they want to, and waterways don't poison themselves. You can point to any ecosystem that's fallen apart and tie it back to something that humans have done. Climate change is, of course, the big one: Industrial production of more or less everything depends on the burning of fossil fuels, which in turn ends up warming the atmosphere.

Writing about the 2019–2020 Australian bushfires, Chester (2020: 253) asserts that "the case of a 'natural disaster' was prosecuted, by the Prime Minister and other conservatives, throughout the long duration of the bushfires. The use of the word 'natural' connotes no human involvement in causing the drought and promotes an image of the uncontrollable forces of 'mother nature.' This serves to reinforce the climate change scepticism and denial generally held by the Prime Minister's conservative political base. The use of the word 'disaster' was deployed to appeal to Australian patriotism."

44. This has been the case, in particular, with respect to polar bears (see, e.g., Dickie 2018). For an in-depth study of attacks on humans by grizzly and black bears, including an entire chapter devoted to "The Predaceous Black Bear," see Herrero (2002). Levin (2018: 8), who devotes six pages to what to do when humans encounter a bear (black, grizzly, or brown), observes,

> It's an increasingly wild world out there. Wildlife and humans have long been at odds, in ways both big and small. But as we continue to build 4,000-square-foot homes where forests once stood and pile into cities (predator-free, all-you-can-eat buffets for the animals that follow), our lives are intersecting more and more. It turns out, animals appreciate the ease of urban and suburban life as much as we do. They're thriving. We're cowering. And it's getting a little out of hand for everyone involved.

Levin's observations echo those of Ford (2022), who reminds us that "the world is not so cleanly cut between human spaces and wild spaces" and that encounters between humans and wildlife are becoming more common in recent years:

> Climate change has . . . played a role as animals migrate into unfamiliar territory in search of the means of survival. In the [Sierra Nevada mountains], persistent droughts and fires have displaced bears from more remote habitats and brought them in closer contact with human communities around and near the lake [Lake Tahoe]. Thanks to tourists and new residents who feed bears directly or indirectly through improper garbage disposal, some bears have become more acclimated to human garbage than their normal diets. A bear

named Hank the Tank allegedly broke into at least 28 homes in search of meals in recent years. . . . Some media outlets [have] cast the bears as the aggressors in these circumstances, but it can't be stressed enough that the bears are not truly intruding into human spaces. Humans are consciously and often haphazardly intruding into theirs.

On "Hank the Tank," see Lukpat (2022).

Bears are also the victims and "monsters" in the 1979 film *Prophecy* (directed by John Frankenheimer), in which they mutate to become violent killers as a result of mercury pollution in the local water and woodland caused by the operations of a paper mill. Other related environmental damage is also signaled in the film such as overgrown salmon and tadpoles.

45. We agree. Later in this book (Chapter 4 and Chapter 5), we take up the question of whether such texts and tropes can actually *stimulate* ecological awareness or whether *representations* of environmental disruption are haunting (adversely influencing) humanity's relationship to the nonhuman world—whether they serve to *reinforce* attitudes toward nature as "monstrous" and treatment *of nature* in horrifying ways.

46. Stevenson's description of a "disanthropic" ethos or mode in Swinburne's poetry derives from Garrard (2012: 41), who conceptualizes "disanthropic" as "inspired, in part, by ordinary misanthropic hatred of 'the crowd,' but [as] distinguished by [man's] *absence* from the future he envisages" (emphasis in original).

47. In support of her proposition, Keetley (2021: 36n1) cites Gambin's (2012: 18) contention that the "natural horror film" began in the 1950s and Wood's (1986: 83) discussion of "the revenge of Nature motif" in horror since the 1960s. On whether the *Oil Wells of Baku: Close View* (1896), directed by Auguste Lumière and Louis Lumière, constitutes the first "eco-disaster" film, see Murray and Heumann (2006; 2016: 192–94).

CHAPTER 3

1. This is a recurring theme in film. For example, in *Suicide Squad* (2016), based on the antihero/supervillain team of the same name appearing in DC Comics, Amanda Waller (Viola Davis) describes Waylon Jones/Killer Croc (Adewale Akinnuoye-Agbaje), who was born with a rare form of atavism that gave him reptilian traits (resembling epidermolytic hyperkeratosis) and whose condition was enhanced by the presence of a "metagene," in the following way: "He looked like a monster. So they treated him like a monster. Then he became a monster."

Skott and colleagues (2021: 397) contend that because it is "representative of our social traumas, the monster illuminates boundaries, serving as a warning and becoming the focal point of the story of gender-based violence. . . . As a personification of both the uncanny and the abject, the monster, which breaches the boundaries it illuminates, must be terminated if identity and order are to be protected. Because if these boundaries are dissolved—if the monstrous creeps into the mundane—the Self and the Other become unstable categories and we, ourselves, become monsters." Similarly, Pihlström (2020: 35) puts forth that "in aesthetic theories of horror and the gothic . . . the role played by undead monsters as abnormal and impure being breaching conceptual and metaphysical categories is crucial." "As such," Pihlström (2020: 35, 41) continues, "'in between' creatures," such as vampires, which we discussed in the previous chapter, "typically challenge our conceptual categorization of reality in general, and this contributes to the epistemological and metaphysical as well as ethical and aesthetic significance of the genre of gothic. . . . Breaching categories at a fundamental modal and metaphysical level could be regarded as even more horrific than merely breaching our natural or scientific categories of thought."

In a different vein, Linnemann (2022: 16) asserts that "the power to identify and name the monster, as well as to conceal one's own monstrosity, is a potent—perhaps the ultimate—political act." While Linnemann's larger argument is that the police are not the self-pronounced "monster-fighters" that they claim to be, but monsters *themselves*, the overall point remains the same: *we* (humans) produce our monsters for a variety of reasons. This may help explain why, in Pihlström's (2020: 45) terms, "the conceptual boundary between the human and the inhuman is one of the categorizations violated by horror and the figure of the monster; this violation may be even more striking when a human being breaches this boundary, sliding to inhumanity." On "the monster-killer/evil-hunter rhetoric of policing" and how those in positions of power use their authority to define who or what should be considered "the monster," see Damm (2023). On whether monsters need names, see Coupland (2010: 133).

2. On Plumwood (1991), see Parker (2016: 215).

3. Similarly, Butler (1993: 186n2) notes that "abjection (in latin, *ab-jicere*) literally means to cast off, away, or out and, hence, presupposes and produces a domain of agency from which it is differentiated."

4. Hook actually mis-cites Butler here. "Operation of repulsion" appears in Butler (1990: 170); "operation of exclusion" can be found in Butler (1993: xx). Varghese (2020: 5) provides the correct attribution and source for the quotation from Butler: "To borrow Judith Butler's phrase, th[e] self-constituting 'operation of repulsion' (Butler 1990: 170) induces hatred, disgust and horror of the other, the abject. . . . Abjection . . . is a border anxiety. It is the process by which the borders between self and other are created." On abjection as a "border anxiety" and a "border-making process," see Varghese (2020: 10, 14, 76).

5. To be fair, Hook's (2012) interest is not so much in abjection, per se, as it is in racism, apartheid (specifically, post-apartheid South Africa), psychology, psychoanalysis, and postcolonial thought. As Hook (2012: 65) writes, "The concept of abjection as applied here is not intended as providing a 'total theory' of racism. There is, importantly, no direct one-to-one-correspondence between racism and abjection; the notion of abjection to cast light upon certain (and primarily 'extra-discursive') features of racism." "More specifically," Hook (2012: 65) continues, "the notion of abjection provides a means of understanding the sociality (indeed, 'the psychology') of dehumanization; as such it is helpful in elucidating the societal functioning of racism at its most brutal, denigrating and objectifyng." To this, Hook (2012: 65) adds that abjection is "a theory that attempts to avoid the pitfalls of those historical applications of psychoanalysis that prioritize individual complexes over the consideration of history, cultural and social forces." Hook's (2012: 66) stated goal is "to offer a critical exposition of the notion of abjection that goes beyond the descriptive [a limiting feature, Hook claims, in the work of Young (1990a, 1990b) and McClintock (1995)], that opens up new possibilities for the critical social psychological analyses of racism."

6. As Lotringer (2020: 33) explains, although Bataille introduced the idea of "abjection" in the 1920s in the French Surrealist art magazine *Documents*, "Most of what circulated about the abject . . . in English-speaking countries derived from Kristeva's essay *Powers of Horror: An Essay on Abjection*, and [that] the notion eventually gained currency in the United States with *Abject Art: Repulsion and Desire in American Art*"—an exhibition at the Whitney Museum of American Art from June 23 to August 29, 1993. Lotringer (2020: 33) hypothesizes that "few people have paid attention to Bataille's original concept" because "his seminal essay, 'Abjection and Miserable Forms,' was not translated at the time [of the exhibition at the Whitney]," although it bears mention that Kristeva does make reference to and quotes Bataille in *Powers of Horror: An Essay on Abjection* (1982: 56, 64, 138, 207, 208). For a review of *Abject Art: Repulsion and Desire in American Art*, see Cotter (1993). For a discussion of *Documents* and Bataille's involvement with the journal, see Ades and Bradley (2006).

7. Varghese (2020: 4–5) notes that "Fanon's writing offers both a diagnostic of abjection and also a methodology for resisting abjectionality"—that Fanon's analysis in *Black Skin, White Masks* ([1952] 2008) of "the psychological effects on the colonial abject rests upon his central argument that processes of racialization have played a fundamental role in the dialectical relationship between colonizer and colonized." While Varghese (2020: 5) acknowledges that Fanon's "account of racism shares some commonalities with . . . Kristeva's discussion of abjection," he urges caution "when applying the term abjection to Fanon because it is not one he used."

8. As Hennefeld and Sammond (2020: 3; see also 2020: 16) add, this "Other"—this "cultural Other"—included, during the first term of Donald J. Trump's presidency, "women, people of color, immigrants, gays, trans folk"—essentially, "the usual scapegoats of misogynistic white bigotry and structural racism." Appealing to (mostly) xenophobic White men, Trump asserted that in order to prohibit contact with "the Other"—to exclude the abject—it was necessary to build a wall (between the United States and Mexico).

In an insightful piece on "the present left-to-right acceleration," Joyce and Sharlet (2023) describe how the American politician and attorney Robert F. Kennedy, Jr., has come to advocate for sealing the southern border (the border between the United States and Mexico) because "the tsunami of migrants walking across farm fields and defecating in irrigation canals threatens the safety of [our] food supply" (https://twitter.com/RobertKennedyJr/status/1666261036264222720?lang=en, posted at 9:49 p.m. on June 6, 2023).

9. As Sammond (2020: 229) clarifies, "For Bataille, social abjection requires a larger sovereign body, and the abjectly poor, sick, or despised represent that which is cast off to secure the integrity and well-being of the sovereign body. The miserable, he argues, once evoked pity and a sense of care. Now, that pity has given way to disgust, and to be miserable, to be immiserated, is to be abject, worthy of being cast out from sovereign society." As an example, we might look to Hurricane Katrina, where Rhode and Abelson (2005: A1) reported that "of the dead collected so far in the New Orleans area, more than a quarter of them, or at least 154, were patients, mostly elderly, who died in hospitals or nursing homes," observing that "the breadth of the collapse of one of society's most basic covenants—to care for the helpless—suggests that the elderly and critically ill plummeted to the bottom of priority lists as calamity engulfed New Orleans" (on this last point, see Giroux 2006: 173). Under Bataille's formulation, the elderly and critically ill in New Orleans evoked not pity but disgust: they had to be rendered abject.

10. In Bataille's ([1934] 1993: 10–11) words, "Filth, snot, and vermin are enough to render an infant vile; his personal nature is not responsible for it, only the negligence and helplessness of those raising it. General abjection is of the same nature as the child; wreaked by impotence under given social conditions: it is formally distinct from sexual perversions in which abject things are cultivated and which derives from subversion."

11. Our use of the phrase "in comparison" at the beginning of the sentence is intentional. Hennefeld and Sammond (2020: 2) describe Bataille's approach to abjection "*in contrast*" to Kristeva's concept (emphasis added). Arya and Chare (2016: 1–2) also point to dissimilarities, stating that "Bataille's treatment of abjection is different from Kristeva's. . . . where it is clear that his focus is rooted in the socio-political (rather than the psychoanalytic, which is where Kristeva's predominant focus lies) and accounts for the dynamic of rejection and exclusion in relation to the socially disenfranchised." Skott and colleagues (2021: 389, 397) suggest, however, that Kristeva (1982) promulgated the idea of abjection as the othering of *female* identities and as an expression of gendered power hierarchies—which sounds an awful lot like a concern for "the politics of the social"/"the socio-political." Skott and colleagues' (2021) reading of Kristeva, then, appears rather *Bataillean*. Although they do not cite Bataille, it appears that for them, Bataille's and Kristeva's theories are (or could be) *complementary*. We prefer this perspective.

12. Nations, Baker, and Krszjzaniek (2017: 405) expound on this in their study of how the grief process, abjection, and ritual transform the social meanings of a loved one's lifeless human body:

> In some cultures, including the United States, the identity of a human being is defined by living and is disassociated from that which is non-living (dead). We recognize the life in others, and when that life ceases and all that is left is the material body absent of life, it jars us into a confrontation with that which we must actively deny through living—that we will one day die. Even though we might deny and avoid it, death eventually infects our lives and forces us to confront it. When we live our life denying that something exists, confrontation with the thing we avoid is ambiguous and unfamiliar; it is abject.

13. For a discussion of this often-quoted passage from Kristeva, see, e.g., Doyle (2020: 108); Linnemann (2016: 64–65); Nations, Baker, and Krszjzaniek (2017: 419); Skott et al. (2021: 389); Valier (2002: 332).

14. As Skott and colleagues (2021: 397) explain, "In the same way that Kristeva (1982) defined abjection as the othering of feminine identities, where it functions as an expression of white or urban power orders. Since the abject also threatens our identity, national as well as personal, and must be ejected in order for both borders and identities to be protected (Kristeva 1982), narratives such as the ones evident by [professionals working on preventing gender-based violence] also risk further alienation and possible discrimination of already othered groups."

15. O'Connell (2020) explores "massive underground shelters where high-net-worth individuals could weather the end of the world in the style and comfort to which they had been accustomed," but he does not explain what makes one a "high-net-worth individual." Similarly, Osnos (2017) describes a group known as "high-net-worth individuals" (or "H.N.W.I."), but he, too, does not specify a financial threshold one would have to surpass to be characterized as an "H.N.W.I." The "Mint Press News Desk" (2013)

defines a "high net worth individual" as "someone with 'investible assets of $1 million or more, excluding primary residence, collectibles, consumables, and consumer durables.'" Kenton (2024) describes "ultra-high-net-worth individuals (UHNWI)" as "people with a net worth of at least $30 million." As he explains, "This category is composed of the wealthiest people in the world, who control a tremendous amount of global wealth." Although "this group of people is small in terms of total population" (Kenton 2024)—just over 600,000 individuals globally at the end of 2023—the exact number of individuals is difficult to pinpoint given fluctuations in net wealth (see Harley 2023). *Forbes*, for example, publishes "The World's Real-Time Billionaires," which ranks the daily worth of UHNWIs on its "wealth-tracking platform." The platform "tracks the daily ups and downs of the world's richest people" and

> provides ongoing updates on the net worth and ranking of each individual confirmed by *Forbes* to be a billionaire. The value of individuals' public holdings are [*sic*] updated every 5 minutes when respective stock markets are open (there will be a 15-minute delay for stock prices). Individuals whose fortunes are significantly tied to private companies will have their net worths [*sic*] updated once a day. (Forbes 2025)

According to the webpage's "Methodology" (at the bottom of the page), "[a] rotating cast [as if it were a cinematic or theatrical production] of the five biggest winners and losers throughout the day is featured at the top of the page, followed by the complete list of billionaires ranked in order of net worth." Thus, visitors to the page will immediately see "Today's Winners and Losers" (reflecting "changes since 5pm EST of prior trading day").

16. Guidi (2022: 34) adds that "as ecological breakdown becomes more acute, people of color and immigrants around the world"—the "national abjects," to borrow from Tyler (2013: 9)—will "face an additional burden—more of them will be *blamed* for anthropogenic climate change" (Guidi 2022: 34, emphasis added). Guidi (2022: 32, 33) continues: "Blaming immigrants for widespread environmental challenges is bogus. . . . All the available evidence suggests that it's not working-class immigrants but large-scale industry and [the] affluent . . . that are driving consumerism, climate change, and the loss of wildlife habitat." Thus, the UHNWIs despoil the Earth and then reject that which they destroy—the environment and the people who live in these environments (while, in the process, often attributing the degradation *to those disadvantaged groups*)—and then use such conditions as a reason, rationale or excuse for creating their bunkers and fortresses and rocket ships (discussed elsewhere in this chapter).

It should be clear that our notion of "double abjection" differs significantly from that described by Valier (2002). Drawing on Kristevan theory, Valier (2002: 332) claims that "crime against children [i]s particularly abject" and that, in turn, "a crime committed by one child against another is doubly abject."

17. On this point, see Senf (2020), who argues that the vampire in Bram Stoker's *Dracula* ([1897] 1920) reflected—or gave expression to—pervasive fears of foreign invasion in Britain in the late nineteenth century. Looking at the film, *Dracula* (1979), directed by John Badham and starring Frank Langella (as Dracula) and Laurence Olivier (as Professor Abraham Van Helsing), Senf (2020: 68) contends that Jonathan Harker (played by Trevor Eve) "suspects that Dracula plans to conquer England by draining its citizens and remaking them in his image"—much the same way that Britons were anxious about and feared foreign incursion, dominance, and power (see also Khapaeva 2020: 10).

18. Similarly, Arya and Chare (2016: 10) observe that "abjection threatens identity and there is a danger that to counteract it individuals or groups will project their fears on to an Other," while Hennefeld and Sammond (2020: 16) explain that "the abject has always concerned the fragility of boundaries between pleasure and disgust." Likewise, Skott and colleagues (2021: 389) note that "the abject" is "'that which breaches borders'" (Valier 2002: 321) and involves the unsettling of borders and perceived boundaries between self and other, subject and object." Drawing a distinction between the concepts of "the uncanny" and "the abject," Skott and her coauthors (2021: 389) contend that "while the uncanny disrupts, disturbs, or unsettles boundaries, that which is abject needs to be removed in order to maintain these boundaries."

19. Also known as *Battle: LA* and, internationally, as *World Invasion: Battle Los Angeles* (see Brisman 2015).

20. See, e.g., Little Green Men Transcripts (2024).

21. The closing narration to the episode: "The cycle of going from dust to dessert. The metamorphosis from being the ruler of a planet to an ingredient in someone's soup" (quoted in Foltyn 2020: xiii). Thus, the "resources" the Kanamits seek on Earth are *humans*, not the planet's metals, minerals, or water.

In *War of the Worlds* (2005), Steven Spielberg's adaptation of H. G. Wells's novel *The War of the Worlds* (1898), the alien invaders bring "red weed"—a vine-like organism—to Earth as a food source, which is fertilized using human blood and tissue. In Spielberg's version, it is not clear whether this is the purpose of the invasion—i.e., they need humans to fertilize their crops—or because they seek Earth's resources more generally, due to the fact that the resources on their home planet are dwindling, making it inhospitable. For a broad discussion of why aliens might invade Earth, see Anders (2013). For a discussion of why they might not bother—there is plenty of water and mineral resources on other planets and space bodies, and the idea of humans as food makes assumptions about alien physiology and digestion!—see the thoughts of astrobiologist Dr. Lewis Dartnell (2017). For different interpretations of H. G. Wells's novel as a whole, see Cokinos (2023).

22. In *Battleship* (2012), it is not entirely clear why aliens from Planet G (a loose reference, perhaps, to the "extra-solar planet candidate," Gliese 581g, announced in 2010, but whose existence has been called into question; see Howell 2016) attack Earth. Shostak (2012) muses that "Hollywood usually guesses that extraterrestrials would only be interested in one of three things: (1) They want to breed with us, because their own reproductive machinery is on the blink; (2) They want Earth's resources; or (3) They want the Earth. All of it" (for a discussion, see Brisman 2015).

23. Biello's (2013) interview with Dr. Charles Higgins, a professor of neuroscience and electrical engineering, explores whether, "given that crude exoskeleton suits as well as thought-controlled drones and prosthetic limbs already exist[,] . . . the kind of machine-enhanced human abilities in *Elysium* are likely anytime soon."

24. Blomkamp's full statement in Smith (2013: 39–40) on this point is as follows: "'Everybody wants to ask me lately about my predictions for the future, whether I think this is what will happen in 140 years'. . . . 'No, no no. This isn't science fiction. This is today. This is now.'" Evidently, Blomkamp has been fairly committed to this perspective, for similar comments have appeared elsewhere: "The entire film is an allegory. I tend to think a lot about wealth discrepancy. . . . People have asked me if I think this is what will happen in 140 years, but this isn't science fiction. This is today. This

is now" (Hiscock 2013; see also Mirrlees and Pedersen 2016: 305). We might note that Blomkamp's assessment is rather ironic given that the interview occurred "in the comfort of a Beverly Hills hotel," according to Hiscock (2013).

25. As Giuliani (2021: 36) explains, "The term 'we' . . . is meant to indicate a historical community that encompasses Europe and the West and benefits today from the outcome (material *and* symbolic) of epistemic and physical violence. It also connotes an imagined community that consolidates itself and mobilises in response to fears and perceived threats, as in the case of anticolonial wars in the past and acts of terror in the present" (emphasis in original).

26. For examples of how "the abject" functions to define the boundary between "civilization and barbarism," see Varghese (2020: 6, 12, 13). This opposition of "civilization" and "barbarism" is a popular and powerful discursive frame. For example, in the aftermath of Hurricane Katrina, Žižek (2005) observed,

> Even if *all* the reports on violence and rapes had proven to be factually true, the stories circulating about them would still be "pathological" and racist, since what motivated these stories were not facts, but racist prejudices, the satisfaction felt by those who would be able to say: "You see, Blacks really are like that, violent barbarians under the thin layer of civilization!" (emphasis in original)

For a discussion, see Giroux (2006: 176).

27. In this way, Giuliani's argument resonates with that of Dederer (2017), who asks, "Who is this 'we' that's always turning up in critical writing . . . ?" and then responds, "*We* is an escape hatch. *We* is cheap. *We* is a way of simultaneously sloughing off personal responsibility and taking on the mantle of easy authority. . . . *We* is corrupt. *We* is make-believe" (emphasis in original).

28. Giuliani's (2021: 11) point—about how "it is those who would be sacrificed first in the event of an apocalypse that is being presented as nothing more than a crisis, a period of transition to a post-apocalyptic world in which logics and ontologies of the Anthropocene will once again prevail"—resonates with Brooks's (2023) recent claim that "members of our [educated] class are always publicly speaking out for the marginalized, but somehow we always end up building systems [such as the modern meritocracy] that serve ourselves."

29. Darian-Smith (2021: 66) draws on Gillespie and Lopez (2015a) to argue that "*all of us, individually and collectively*, are implicated in the practices of capitalism that dehumanize some people and then allow them to die for the benefit of certain others" (emphasis added). While Darian-Smith's assertion runs the risk of—and veers close to—the "blanket blaming" that Giuliani cautions against, we (Brisman and South) reiterate our acknowledgment earlier that we are advantaged scholars, residing in Global Northern countries, that have enjoyed the benefits of capitalism and its rapacious and dehumanizing forces.

30. See, e.g., Chang (2024, 2025a, 2025b); Chow (2018, 2019); Dunn (2021); Lynes (2023); Marikar (2018); McFall-Johnsen and Mosher (2020); McNamee, Intagliata, and Shapiro (2023); Powell (2019); Rushkoff (2022a, 2022b, 2023); Savage (2021); Seemangal (2016); Slezak and Solon (2017); Solon (2018); Vdovychenko (2022); Weinersmith and Weinersmith (2023a, 2023b); Weise (2024); Woolf (2016); Yuhas (2017); see generally Lagatta (2024); Walrath-Holdridge and Lagatta (2024); cf. Clark (2023); Kern (2021).

31. Gittlitz (2017) chides "Peter Thiel, Elon Musk and Mark Zuckerberg [for] feel[ing] empowered to propose science fiction premises, like space colonization and post-scarcity economics, as solutions to actual social problems," contending that "while rapid changes in the social order that are the dream of Silicon Valley's disruptors are acquiring an aura of inevitability, a world absent of intense poverty and bigoted hostility feels unimaginable." Indeed, Gittlitz (2017) adds, "the eliminationist suggestions of the far right . . . argue, in effect, for a walling-off of the world along lines of class, nationality and race, even if this might condemn millions to death." In a similar fashion, Lynes (2023: 306–7) laments that Bezos's space flights "demonstrate the pinnacle of being 'released from the normal restrictions of everyday life' while simultaneously leaving humanity behind, including the approximately 197 million people who buy from Amazon (Dayton 2021) and the 1.3 million workers (Soper 2021) who have all invested money and labour into fulfilling his ultimate dream." For Bezos, Lynes (2023: 313) contends, it is "clear that the humans who work for his company are almost indistinguishable from the machinery that will be working to propel him to the stars." Lynes (2023: 313–14) continues: "When Bezos finally reaches his goal and looks back at the pale blue dot we call Earth (Sagan 1994), he will likely gaze at its beauty and reflect upon how he built such a powerful and profitable business. He will likely give little thought to the thousands of people that continually face a myriad of harms on a daily basis in order to fuel his lifestyle and next grand adventure beyond the limits most of us can only dream of." Lynes (2023: 314) concludes that "as the global capitalist system is approaching an apocalyptic zero point (Žižek [2011]), with humanity facing a number of existential threats to our very way of life, it is rather fitting that Bezos and other members of the economic elite are seeking to abandon the very dystopia that they have helped to accelerate in their own pursuit of pleasure."

Naomi Alderman, in an interview with Ari Shapiro on *National Public Radio* regarding her new novel, *The Future* (2023), warns such "tech billionaires" that "there is no ark that you can get on and you can escape, and everybody else will die and you'll be fine because, fundamentally, the living through that and deciding to do that—instead of using your billions and billions of dollars to help people—is what will ultimately destroy you" (quoted in McNamee, Intagliata, and Shapiro 2023).

On whether space travel, including missions to Mars, might *cause harm* to Earth upon return—such as with microbial or organic contamination—see, e.g., Bianciardi (2022); Chan et al. (2020); Van Houdt et al. (2012).

32. The reality, the Anti-Creep Climate Initiative (2022: 16) explains, is as follows:

> When we assign "cancerous" behavior to all humans, we limit our vision to a very recent economic system of resource exploitation. This ignores most of human history, where the majority of human beings have not caused global environmental destruction and climate collapse. The humans-are-a-cancer metaphor was popularized in the mid-20th century by James Lovelock's Gaia Hypothesis in work funded by Royal Dutch Shell. Lovelock's metaphor mimics fossil fuel companies' climate change disinformation campaigns: covering up the causes, shoring up profits, and continuing to harm those least responsible. The metaphor suggests climate change is nature's revenge, offering a simple cause-and-effect logic that suggests those who suffer deserve it. As such, the humans-as-cancer metaphor avoids explicit racism, while it perpetuates harm by naturalizing the vastly unequal impacts of climate change. When we universalize humans as

cancerous or a disease, we propagate a nihilism that prevents us from joining
the movements fighting for more just and regenerative environmental futures.

33. Hunt (2023) likens the "'orca rising' meme," discussed later in this chapter, to
the "'nature is healing' meme from early in the [COVID-19] pandemic, when signs of
wildlife returning to city streets emptied by lockdowns were hailed—first earnestly, then
ironically—as evidence that 'we are the virus' harming the world." On the "nature is
healing" meme (also known as the "nature is healing, we are the virus" meme) during
the pandemic, see Anson (2020: 70); Bosworth (2022); Felton (2020a, 2020b); McNeil
(2021); Manavis (2020); Yoder (2020); on the differences between the orca memes and
the "We Are the Virus" memes, see Guasco (2023).
In early 2021, Smith and Brisman (2021: 303) noted, with caution, that "the planet
appeared to breathe a sigh of relief as flights were grounded, industry slowed and cars
remained parked on driveways during the COVID-19 lockdown of 2020 (see, e.g.,
Biswas 2020; Bond et al. 2020; Cooper 2020; Crist 2020; Gardiner 2020; Le Quéré
et al. 2020; Mohm 2020; Plumer and Popovich 2020; Schwartz 2020; Simpkins 2020;
Stone 2020; Zarnett 2020)." Lam, South, and Brisman (2023: 335), in their examination of bunkerization as an individualistic reaction to the converging crises of climate
change and COVID-19, mentioned that "as a result of government orders to bunker at
home and shelter-in-place, much of the cruise industry was ground to a halt, which, in
turn, enabled some positive impacts on the environment . . . such as a temporary decline
in greenhouse gas emissions and associated forms of pollution (Jaggard 2020; Koren
2020; Meredith 2020; see generally Cohen 2020)." They also pointed out that "with the
suspension of cruise ship operations during the global pandemic, wildlife could return
to some ecosystems. With reduced air and boat traffic, people worldwide reported seeing clearer skies and cleaner waterways (see, e.g., Daly 2020). The clarity of the Venice
lagoon, for instance, improved dramatically in the absence of cruise liners and tourist
boats (Brunton 2020)" (Lam, South, and Brisman 2023: 336). But Lam, South, and
Brisman (2023: 339n7, 339n8) made clear that "while the slowdown of human activity, including reduced travel, was associated with some positive environmental effects
during the pandemic's 'anthropause,' some species actually struggled during the same
period because of the lack of human protection or resources (Anthes 2022)," and that
"while many cities recorded a lower number of 'fine particulate matter' (PM2.5)—
the world's deadliest air pollutant—over a 3-week period of coronavirus lockdown in
2020, especially when compared with 2019 levels," some did not; for example, Rome
"recorded a 30% increase in particulate pollution during the measured time period due
to greater reliance on residential heating systems" (citing Meredith 2020).
It is a small step from acknowledging, noting, reporting on and studying how
worldwide lockdowns to control the spread of COVID-19 impacted—and, in some
instances, may have had a temporary positive effect on—wildlife and the environment, more generally (such as with Smith and Brisman 2021 and Lam, South, and
Brisman 2023, already mentioned; see also Bosworth 2020; Ellis-Petersen et al. 2020;
Felton 2020a, 2020b; Sandra E. Garcia 2020; Rutz et al. 2020; Watts and Kommenda
2020; cf. Edmond 2020; Joshi 2020; Sierra Garcia 2020; Le Quéré et al. 2021; Osaka
2020a, 2020b; Teirstein 2020; Wright 2020), while remaining "sensitive to the immense
human suffering caused by COVID-19" (Rutz et al. 2020: 1157), to claims that "nature
healed" (during the COVID-19 pandemic), to assertions that "humans are . . . parasites"
(Watson 2015: 271), to "the idea that humanity *should be removed* for the benefit of

other living creatures" (Khapaeva 2020: 28, emphasis added). This idea that "humanity should be removed," Khapaeva (2020: 28–29) explains, "evokes the guiding principles of . . . deep ecology" as well as "those of the Voluntary Human Extinction Movement, which proclaims that 'phasing out the human [species] by voluntarily ceasing to breed will allow Earth's biosphere to return to good health'" (quoting Voluntary Human Extinction Movement n.d.).

34. For lyrics to the song "World Starvation," see Fifteen (1994).

35. The American television series *Fallout*, which premiered in April 2024 and which is based on the role-playing video game of the same name, makes a nice reference to the era of fallout shelter sales advertising and "traditional post-nuclear apocalypse tropes," combing "semi-ironic takes on 50s motifs, B-movie conventions and horror-level blood and gore" (Mangan 2024).

36. For further discussion on these points, see Lam et al. (2025).

37. On orca-human interactions, see, e.g., *Andalucia Today* (2021a); Carmichael and Triggs (2023); Carty (2023); Cavanagh (2020); Kwai (2023); Jones (2020a, 2020c); White (2022d, 2022e, 2022f, 2023); see generally *Al Jazeera* (2023a); Peltier (2020); cf. Munroe (2022).

38. In further support of this proposition, see, e.g., Beddington (2023); Dacosta (2023); Hardach (2023); Kachar et al. (2018); Neuman (2022); Norsworthy (2023); Pag (2021); Vlamis (2023); Watercutter (2023); White (2022a).

39. Media attention has been extensive (see, e.g., Cohen and Orwig 2023; Esteban et al. 2022; Fine 2023; Hamilton 2023; Hoare 2023b; Hunt 2023; Pare 2023; Roeloffs 2023; Syed 2023; Watercutter 2023; White 2022a, 2022b, 2022c, 2022f, 2023; see also Aitken 2023; Alicante Today 2021a; Andalucia Today 2021a, 2021c; Blackwell 2022; Cohen 2023; Donn 2022a; ESPN News Services 2023; Kwai 2023; McFall-Johnsen and Zitser 2023; Neuman 2023; Norsworthy 2023; Osborne 2020c, 2021; Pag 2021; Propper 2024; Thomson 2023).

40. For instances, examples, and reports, see, e.g., Beddington (2023); Bradford and Pester (2022); Carmichael and Triggs (2023); Cavanagh (2020); Ciccarelli (2020, 2022a, 2022b, 2023); Hoare (2023a, 2023b); Jones (2020a, 2020b, 2020c, 2020d); Pag (2021); Pappas (2022); Pare (2023); Propper (2024); *Spanish News Today* (2022); see also Froelich (2020); Skinner (2023); White (2022c, 2022g).

41. For additional descriptions, see, e.g., Aitken (2023); *Al Jazeera* (2023a, 2023b); *Alicante Today* (2020, 2021a, 2021b); *Andalucia Today* (2021b, 2021c); Autoridade Marítima Nacional (2020); Beddington (2023); Blackwell (2022); Bradford and Pester (2022); Carty (2023); Ciccarelli (2020, 2022b, 2023); Cohen and Orwig (2023); Cole (2023); Dewan (2023); Dunn (2022b); ESPN News Services (2023); Fine (2023); Froelich (2020); Gill (2023); Gill and Stephens (2023); Hamilton (2023); Hardach (2023); Hoare (2023a, 2023b); Jones (2020a, 2020b, 2020c, 2020d); Kwai (2023); McFall-Johnsen and Zitser (2023); *Murcia Today* (2021); Neuman (2023); Norsworthy (2023); Osborne (2020a, 2020b, 2020c); Ogao (2023); Pag (2021); Pappas (2022); Peltier (2020); Robledo (2023); Roeloffs (2023); Salvoni (2023); Smillie (2020a, 2020b); *Spanish News Today* (2022); Syed (2023); Thomson (2023); Vlamis (2023); Watercutter (2023); White (2022a, 2022b, 2022c, 2022f, 2022g, 2023); Winsor (2023).

42. As most criminologists recognize, criminal behavior is often learned in interaction with others, although the *mechanisms* by which such behavior is learned may be distinct—and there is a difference between "attempts to teach or convey the attitudes,

values, norms and beliefs appropriate for a particular social role" and *imitation*, which "refers to engagement in behaviour after the observation of similar behaviour in others" (Jensen 2017: 116). On whether the orcas' behavior was spread because orcas were *teaching* their young or because some orcas were *imitating* others, see Norsworthy (2023); Guasco (2023).

There was some disagreement as to whether the behavior had been transmitted vertically (from [the] matriarch[s] to the young) and later horizontally within the/one pod *or* from community/pod to community/pod, although experts seemed to feel that "because the behavior ha[d] been observed only in this particular subpopulation of orcas . . . it was unlikely to pass onto distinct orca groups that populate waters around the world" (Kwai 2023 [citing Dr. Alfredo López Ferndandez of the University of Aveiro in Portugal]). For differing perspectives, see, e.g., Ciccarelli (2023); Cohen and Orwig (2023); Donn (2021); ESPN News Services (2023); Gill and Stephens (2023); Hamilton (2023); Neuman (2023); Norsworthy (2023); Pag (2021); Pare (2023); see generally Carty (2023); Cohen (2023); Cole (2023); Dacosta (2023); Dewan (2023); Fine (2023); Gill (2020); Guasco (2023); McFall-Johnsen and Zitser (2023); Ogao (2023); Robledo (2023); Thomson (2023); Vlamis (2023); White (2022c, 2022g).

43. On this point, see also *Al Jazeera* (2023a); *Alicante Today* (2020); *Andalucia Today* (2021a); Beddington (2023); Carty (2023); Cohen (2023); Cohen and Orwig (2023); Cole (2023); Dacosta (2023); Dewan (2023); Donn (2021, 2022a); Fine (2023); Gill (2020); Gill and Stephens (2023); Hamilton (2023); Jones (2020b, 2020c); Kwai (2023); *Murcia Today* (2021); Neuman (2022, 2023); Norsworthy (2023); Osborne (2020a, 2020b, 2021); Peltier (2020); Robledo (2023); Syed (2023); Vlamis (2023); White (2022a, 2022c, 2022f, 2022g).

On the importance of play for predators, see Kwai (2023); on the importance of play for marine mammal learning, see Peltier (2020).

44. For similar interpretations, see, e.g., Cohen and Orwig (2023); Cole (2023); Guasco (2023); Hamilton (2023); Hardach (2023); Neuman (2022, 2023); Roeloffs (2023); White (2022f, 2022g); Winsor (2023).

45. Cole (2023) reports that "the theory that's making the most headlines after this . . . spate of encounters . . . [is] that the orcas could be responding to a traumatizing event involving a boat in the region," but notes that for Dr. Deborah Giles, Science and Research Director at Wild Orca, "the trauma response theory doesn't make a lot of sense" because "if that was the case, then they would be 'attacking' fishing boats. And they're not.'" For different takes on trauma as a possible motivation, see, e.g., Cohen (2023); Cohen and Orwig (2023); Dacosta (2023); Guasco (2023); Hamilton (2023); Hardach (2023); McFall-Johnsen and Zitser (2023); Neuman (2023); Norsworthy (2023); Ogao (2023); Pare (2023); Salvoni (2023); Thomson (2023); Watercutter (2023); see generally *Al Jazeera* (2023a); Cavanagh (2020); Fine (2023); Robledo (2023); cf. Syed (2023).

46. Initially, Dr. López opined that the conduct did not appear premeditated (Cicarelli 2020) but later stated that "the orcas [we]re doing this on purpose" (quoted in Pare 2023; see also Cole 2023, McFall-Johnsen and Zitser 2023, Neuman 2023, Salvoni 2023, and Thomson 2023 for similar statements by López). While López explained that "orcas are not resentful" (quoted in Hardach 2023), he did acknowledge that "human activities, even in an indirect way, are at the origin" (quoted in Hoare 2023a; Hunt 2023; see also Hardach 2023 for a similar statement by López) with "increased marine

traffic, dwindling food sources, warming seas and noise pollution . . . all [potentially] play[ing] a part" (quoted in Hoare 2023a).

47. Cole (2023) did admit that "at first glance, nature sure does seem to be fighting back, defending itself after decades of abuse by the shipping, fishing, and military industries. Killer whales have a lot to be bitter about, and few humans would fault them for plotting revenge."

48. Indeed, despite Cole's (2023) contention that "their name is a bit of a misnomer," as quoted earlier, because "the killer whale name was originally 'whale killer,' as ancient sailors saw them hunting in groups to *take down* large whales" (Bradford and Pester 2022, emphasis added), Froelich (2020) exclaimed that "killer whales off the coast of Spain are *living up to their name*, but instead of targeting great white sharks, pods of fish or seals as they have done in the past—they're now after *people and boats*" (emphasis added).

49. One reader, "Sheilamarie23," from "Contrapasso, United States," helpfully pointed out in the comments at the bottom of the page that "those are not DEADLY attacks." As the reader continued, "If they wanted us dead, they would attack humans swimming. They never do (except at Seaworld). Orcas are extremely intelligent. Orcas and other dolphins possess an area of the brain that humans dont [*sic*]. Its [*sic*] an extension of the emotional brain that is believed to guide them to act in the interests of the group rather than just themselves. These orcas are taking care of their families. Humans could learn a lesson from them."

50. Hoare was not alone in this regard, with Hardach (2023) relating that "scientists prefer to call these clashes 'interactions,' since the orcas' intention may be playful rather than hostile," Pag (2021) pointing out that using the term "interaction" rather than "attack" might help reduce fear of and hatred towards orcas, and Donn (2021) using terminology such as "disruptive behavior," "incident," and "interaction" because "the word 'attack' is too strong: it could be the whales are just 'having fun.'" Similarly, for Dr. López (quoted in White 2022e), "They are *not attacks*, they are *interactions*, that is, killer whales detect a foreign object that enters their lives and respond to its presence, but not in an aggressive way, they do not show aggressiveness in their behavior, but by touching and manipulating it. That is what we define as *interactions*" (emphasis added). Vlamis (2023) admitted that while "'Killer Whale Attacks!' sure makes for a great headline, . . . it may not be quite accurate when used to describe the encounters between orcas and boats that have been taking place near the Iberian Peninsula in recent years." Rather than "using the word attack," he stated, "which implies aggressive and violent action, it might be more accurate to simply describe the literal behavior that the orcas are engaging in: such as striking, ramming, targeting, or hitting boats." Carty (2023), however, reported that for Dr. Deborah Giles, mentioned in n.45 of this chapter, the term "interacting" is preferable to "ramming" because "the latter implies aggression"—a sentiment shared by Dr. Ruth Esteban of the Madeira Whale Museum in Caniçal (in the municipality of Machico on the Portuguese island of Madeira), who acknowledged that while incidents between orcas and boats might be "really scary" for sailors, "we don't want to call it an attack. We call it an interaction."

51. Dr. Justin Gregg of the Dolphin Communication Project pontificated that "we always want to sort of see [orcas'] behavior as humanlike, which is why people think of it as revenge, because that's a very humanlike thing to do" (quoted in Carty 2023; Watercutter 2023). In a similar vein, Dr. David Lusseau, Professor of

marine sustainability at the Technical University of Denmark (Dansmarks Tekniske Universitet), mused, "In short, we really don't know; and that's the interesting point for me: we have a species interacting with us in a way we don't understand. We project on these interactions all the human emotions we can find, but at the end of the day, they are not humans; they are another species with a very large brain, complex social lives, and [they are] a master problem solver. They have their reason for these attacks, I like to keep an open option that they have their own, alien, reason or motivation which humans can't understand" (quoted in White 2022a). For Cole (2023), "Orcas are intelligent and complicated creatures, much like humans, so their actions can be difficult to interpret with definitive answers." Nevertheless, "*because* [orcas] are so relatably clever," Cole (2023) continues, "they make an easy canvas to project our deepest fears about the future onto, and our most joyful, chaotic fantasies for how we'd like to take control of it. And because humans are storytelling creatures, we look for analogs in the natural world to project our anxieties about things like wealth inequality or the very real destruction of the planet. Lately, we happen to find it in these animals. But the orcas can't save us—or themselves—from any of that" (emphasis added). Cole (2023) concludes that "if we're dreaming of killer whale revenge, we can also imagine that the orcas, with their sophisticated communication skills, are telling each other stories about what the people freaking out about their rudder games are doing up there—and waiting anxiously for the next chapter of the human uprising, too."

52. Gill (2020) related that "on social media, amid gifs and jokes about the ocean fighting back, there were comments suggesting people on their yachts should 'stay in their mansions' and that the orcas had been enlisted in a 'fight against yacht owners.'" Similarly, Guasco (2023), writing in May 2023, reported that "the internet [has] found a new hero: anti-capitalist, direct-action-taking killer whales," noting that "tweets picked up on the suggestion that whales targeted yachts and other luxury vessels, hoping the rogue whales might seek out billionaire Amazon owner Jeff Bezos next. Users [made reference to] 'direct action,' 'solidarity with orca saboteurs,' and 'grassroots organizing.'" Later, in the same piece, Guasco (2023) explained that "part of what makes these boat-sinking whales into anti-capitalist allies is their choice of targets. Much of the coverage and response focuses on the whales' attacking yachts in a popular European vacationing location. These yachts symbolize excesses of wealth under capitalism. This story simply wouldn't have the same appeal or political resonance if the whales weren't targeting symbols of wealth, waste, and opulence."

53. Similarly, Watercutter (2023) reported that "thinking that orcas are out for vengeance [becomes] just an act of projection. . . . Supporting an orca revolt . . . then becomes a kind of catharsis."

54. Likewise, Gabriela Cowperthwaite, who directed *Blackfish* (2013), the documentary film about captive orcas (and centering on Tilikum, the orca held by SeaWorld), mused, "Even though we can't know why they [the orcas] are doing this, one good thing [in] just entertaining the idea that they're defending themselves or retaliating means we have to look at ourselves. . . . It means we have to reflect on what a brutally invasive species we are in general" (quoted in Watercutter 2023).

55. When we do so—when we try to place orcas' behaviors into elementary groupings—"We make them [orcas] into caricatures," asserts Dr. Lori Marino, a neuroscientist and founder and president of the Whale Sanctuary Project (quoted in Gill 2020).

56. Looking "across a wide range of time periods and geographies," Guasco (2023) reveals how "various whale species have altered their behaviors in relation to changing human activities." As she explains, "whales are not *static objects* affected by human history, but rather *active participants* who change alongside shifts in political, social, and cultural conditions" (emphasis added). What happens, then, is that "whales change their behaviors in relationship with humans' social changes, and alongside these shifts come shifts in human *perception* and *interpretation* of those behaviors and changes" (emphasis in original).

57. Watson (2015: 275) writes that "the birth of the subject [in our case, humanity] renders the mother [in our case, the Earth] abject. Mother [Earth], a discarded waste product . . . is . . . banished . . . like excrement or pollution." Elsewhere, Watson (2015: 277) cautions that because "interplanetary migration is not yet feasible, humans must begin to attend to the well-being of the earth, their only viable host. We must quit abjecting Mother Earth."

58. To be sure, this is but one way to formulate the relationship. Consider, for example, the following from Mazzilli-Daechsel (2019: 243):

> If a technological mentality were to become more mainstream and inform our relationship to technology, Simondon (2009, 2014) argues that it could spark a shift from "closed" to "open" technical objects, both in terms of design and consumer preference. As is the case with the vast majority of commercial products, a closed object is "completely new and valid when it first comes out of the factory, and then, it enters a kind of ageing period, it loses status, it degrades . . . because it has lost contact with contemporary reality" (Simondon 2014: 401). The closed object starts to degrade as soon as it is finished because it was not designed to evolve in step with new technological developments. Its parts cannot be replaced without compromising its integrity and it quickly falls into disrepair.
>
> In contrast, an open object is designed to be maintained and altered in such a way that its ageing is slowed to a minimum; it continues to "progress with technological developments" (Simondon 2014: 402) because its parts can be replaced and updated. It should be modular, alterable, repairable and designed to prevent obsolescence (Simondon 2009).

The argument, then, would be that we—or, at least, *some* of us—have treated Earth as if we think of it as a "closed" object. Instead, we should have treated the Earth as if we wanted to maintain it and repair it, rather than treat it as something that would eventually become obsolete.

59. The description of the Earth in years 2153 and 2174 bears a frightening similarity to the fourth and fifth "Shared Socio-Economic Pathways" (or "SSPs") which, according to the Intergovernmental Panel on Climate Change (IPCC), "were designed to span a range of challenges to climate change mitigation and adaptation" (IPCC 2023: 63). "For the assessment of climate impacts, risk and adaptation," the IPCC (2023: 63) explains, "the SSPs are used for future exposure, vulnerability and challenges to adaptation. Depending on levels of GHG mitigation, modelled emissions scenarios based on the SSPs can be consistent with low or high warming levels." Mason (2021) summarizes the SSPs as follows: "(SSP$_1$) the world goes smoothly, collaboratively and enthusiastically green and more socially just; (SSP$_2$) the same but too slowly; (SSP$_3$) the world system breaks up into competing regional powers, with each country prioritising its own growth and energy security; (SSP$_4$) global inequality dominates, with high social unrest and poor

progress on decarbonisation in the developing world; (SSP_5) hyper-neoliberalism, where we just burn carbon and rely on the market, and economic development, to curb population growth and (eventually) find a geo-engineering solution for the burning planet." While the IPCC (2023: 63) takes steps to emphasize that these "modelled scenarios and pathways are used to explore future emissions, climate change, related impacts and risks, and adaptation strategies," that they are "based on a range of assumptions, including socio-economic variables and mitigation options," and, importantly, that "[t]hese are quantitative *projections . . .* [not] *predictions* [or] *forecasts*" (emphasis added), Mason (2021) is far less measured or restrained. Without sugarcoating matters, Mason (2021) asserts that "the bad news under even the most benign scenario, we still hit 1.5 degrees by 2040" and that "the worse news is that all these models now look *unrealistic*" (emphasis added). "What we are going to get," Mason (2021) rues—"unless something changes radically," he adds—"is a mixture of the bad bits of SSP_3, SSP_4 and SSP_5: a fragmented global system, with high inequality, regional rivalry and social unrest—with transnational institutions powerless and the financial elite still dreaming that technology will save us"—or that technology will whisk us away (or some of us, as discussed earlier in this chapter) to another planet. On the SSPs, see, e.g., O'Neill et al. (2014).

60. See also O'Connell (2020), who notes that "apocalypse . . . means only this: a revelation, an uncovering of the truth."

61. Given the role that "Mother Earth" may play in apocalyptic imaginaries, readers may find it interesting to contemplate that in Greek, *apokálypsis* is feminine. We thank Cary Tsamas for pointing this out to us.

Anson (2020: 61) explains that "from the Greek word *apokalypsis*, meaning 'something revealed or uncovered,' the apocalyptic mode of storytelling is often associated with Judeo-Christian tradition that narrates revelation and judgment day, the promise of the end of the world and a new beginning for a *particular* people" (emphasis added). Foster (2014: 48) notes that "from the Greek word, '*apokálypsis*,' apocalypse is most often defined as the *end* of *human* civilization," but that "'apocalypse' is also connected to a *lifting of a veil*, a *revealing* of prophesies of the end of the world, and an unveiling of previously unknown 'truths.'"

In her examination of environmentalism's "dark side" and the problems with celebrating COVID-19's "silver lining" (discussed earlier), Sierra Garcia (2020) quotes the following tweet (from March 17, 2020):

> Citizens of Wuhan can finally hear birds chirping after years, Venice's water canals are clear and full of fish, and you can even see the Tatra mountains from Kraków because the smog has lifted.
> This isn't an apocalypse. It's an awakening.

Almost certainly, the author of the tweet did not realize that etymologically (and eschatologically), an "apocalypse" *is* an "awakening."

CHAPTER 4

1. Embryonic versions of this chapter were presented as conference papers/presentations, invited lectures, and seminar talks (Brisman 2012b, 2013a, 2013b, 2013c; South and Brisman 2013b). The authors thank attendees for their helpful comments and questions.

2. Drezner (2014: 829) observes that "a welter of private sector, civil society, and public sector actors has appropriated the zombie metaphor to advance their own ideas, interests, and products" and that "because the living dead resonate so strongly in the cultural zeitgeist, it should not be surprising that various provocateurs and policy entrepreneurs use the living dead as a hook for their ideas." Indeed, Drezner (2014: 829) quips that "it seems difficult for the *New York Times* op-ed page to go a week without a contributor bringing up zombies (Collins 2012a, 2012b, 2013; Wilenz 2012; Krugman 2013)" with "most of these commentators . . . using the term 'zombie' to refer to the stagnant set of ideas propagated by their ideological doppelgängers."

On "zombie cases," meaning lawsuits that "have been kicking around for years," see Eliason (2024); on "zombie debt" and "zombie mortgages," see Zilber (2024); on "zombie offices"—offices/commercial real estate properties that are "still officially occupied even with few workers in them . . . thanks to yearslong lease terms"—see Smialek (2024); on "zombie votes"—"[b]allots cast for candidates who have suspended their campaigns"—see Lemonides and Zhang (2024); see also Kessler (2013).

3. That the zombie is—or has become—more pervasive in popular culture does not mean that it has not "changed" or "evolved" over time. In their introduction, Lauro and Christie (2011: 2) identify "the three most recognizable stages of twentieth- and twenty-first century zombie configurations: the classic mindless corpse, the relentless instinct-driven newly dead, and the millennial voracious and fast-moving predator," which they use to structure their book and explore "zombie evolution." In the afterword to the book, Lauro (2011: 232) asserts that "the zombie has changed so much over the course of twentieth-century cinema as to become nearly unrecognizable from its earliest filmic instantiation."

4. St. John (2006) reports that in the early years of the 2000s, "in films, books and video games, the undead are once again on the march, elbowing past werewolves, vampires, swamp things and mummies to become the post-millennial ghoul of the moment" (for a discussion, see Bishop 2009: 19). Saunders (2012: 80) points to Grossman's (2009) article in *Time* as evidence that "the subject has moved well beyond the horror genre and into the media mainstream." For a related argument about mainstream attention to and coverage of "the zombie renaissance," see Bishop (2009: 19).

5. Drezner (2014: 825, 826) states that "by any observable metric, the living dead have become the hottest paranormal pop cultural phenomenon of this century"—at least, *so far*, the author might have added—and that "even prior to the Great Recession, flesh-eating ghouls—as opposed to the more historically accurate definition of zombies as slaves (Wilentz 2012)—had become one of the most important sources of post-apocalyptic cinema (Phelan 2009)." This "strong growth in movie production," Drezner (2014: 826) continues, "is merely the most obvious data point. The number of zombie books published annually has quadrupled over the past decade (Drezner 2011). A series of 1990s zombie video games, including the *Resident Evil* and *Left 4 Dead* franchises, served as a precursor for the renaissance of zombie cinema. These have been followed up by even more video games, including *Plants vs. Zombies* and *The Last of Us*. The undead have also spread to television in recent years, led by AMC's *The Walking Dead*. In 2013, the television ratings for *The Walking Dead* beat all other shows in its time slot—including Sunday Night Football. In the decade after 2004, the annual mentions of 'zombie' in the *New York Times* increased more than eightfold."

6. Harris (2009) begins his article by asserting that "suddenly the Apocalypse is in fashion," explaining that "from arthouse films to animation to popcorn blockbusters,

destroying the world has never been more in vogue. Directors and movie studios are clambering over one another to see who can create the most dystopian and destructive vision of the near-future. Nor is it just Hollywood movies. Apocalyptic themes have spread to American television and books, too." This contention would seem to contradict his later claim that "a fixation on the apocalypse is . . . nothing new." In support of this latter proposition, Harris (2009) quotes Christopher Sharrett, now Professor Emeritus of Visual and Sound Media in the College of Human Development, Culture, and Media, at Seton Hall University, who opines that "the apocalyptic tendency is very deeply cemented in the American psyche.'"

Twenty-five years earlier, Sharrett (1984: 255) wrote that "it would be a fallacy to assert that the apocalypse of the contemporary horror film is the product simply of a particular set of crises occurring in America over the past several years. While it is true that many of the themes of the horror film are responses to recent American experience, this apocalypticism must be viewed against the backdrop of a long history of millennialism in American art." "In this sense," Sharrett (1984: 255) continued, "American cinema has functioned as a repository for various ideas, including systems of apocalyptic belief, and how a strain of pessimistic (or 'counter-revelatory') apocalyptic thinking has found a culmination in the horror genre."

Rather than read Harris's "suddenly . . . in fashion" declaration as controverting his later "nothing new" statement, we choose to reconcile the two by proposing that the fixation with the apocalypse has a long history, but that *heightened* interest comes in waves. The apocalypse has been "suddenly . . . in fashion [again]" many times before and the *more recent*—and seemingly *amplified*—preoccupation may stem from new art forms and media and more (avenues for) commercialization of the cultural groundswell of doom and disaster literature and movies (see also Denby 2014: 94), including the zombie films mentioned in note 8.

7. Buell (1995: 296) identifies "two largely unrelated developments during the seventeenth century [that permanently affected apocalyptic thinking in America]." The first, Buell (1995: 296) describes, "was the impact of the Copernican and Newtonian revolutions on Christian cosmology, threatening the belief that the world must end in a divinely ordained catastrophe. Scientific developments precipitated in the short run a panicky series of revisionary sacred histories." The second, Buell (1995: 296–97) claims, "specific to Puritan America, was the late seventeenth-century apotheosis of the first generation as what Theodore Dwight Bozeman calls a *primordium*, an image of the state of primitive Christianity [that] Puritanism had for more than a century sought to recover" (emphasis added). As Buell (1995: 297) explains, "The first development began to convert eschatological thinking from a game of deductive logic into a form of speculative free play; the second set the precedent for visualizing the American state in millennial terms and for regulating the imagery of ultimate hope or destruction, as the case may be, as a function of the relationship between the state of contemporary secular society and an idealized historical antecedent."

8. Bishop (2009: 18) argues that zombie movies "seem to have played themselves out by the mid-1980s, especially after the arrival of Michael Jackson's 'Thriller' video in 1983," explaining that "this campy short film tried to be uncanny and frightening, but once the walking dead started to dance and jive with the King of Pop, zombies became nothing more than a joke." Bishop (2009: 18) continues: "Although [George A.] Romero tried to revitalize zombie films in 1985 with *Day of the Dead* (the metaphor this time

addressing Cold War fears and paranoia), the genre was in its death throes," which Maddrey (2004: 129, quoted in Bishop 2009: 18) speculates may have occurred because "audiences in the carefree, consumer-friendly 1980s apparently did not feel the need for such a serious examination of personal and societal values." Bishop (2009: 18) contends that in the mid-1980s and 1990s, "consumers wanted comedic movies"—which he later refers to as "zombedies" (2009: 25n8, n9). "Even though zombies were no longer a source of terror on the silver screen," Bishop (2009: 18) states that in the 1990s, "young people found renewed interest in zombies through violent video games"—a position shared by Dendle (2011: 178), who also charts this decrease in/of zombie movies, but makes clear that "zombie cult following continued to thrive throughout the '90s . . . thanks to video games such as the *Resident Evil* series and to the growth of fansites and online communities."

9. For a discussion of this particular passage from Bishop (2009), see Bloodsworth-Lugo and Lugo-Lugo (2013: 245). Dendle (2011: 266n17) contrasts zombie movies of the "Millennial Generation" with "*Invaders from Mars* or *Invasion of the Body Snatchers*-style 1950s movies that represented Cold War parables of communist infiltration." As Dendle (2011: 266n17) describes, "Cold War movies in which a seemingly normal person has been taken over by an alien personality portray not the threat of immediate bodily violence, but of long-term social assimilation as part of the program of cultural sabotage."

10. As Giddens (1991: 28), citing Beck (1986), contends, "It is quite accurate to characterize modernity, as Ulrich Beck does, as a 'risk society,' a phrase which refers to more than just the fact that modern social life introduces new forms of danger which humanity has to face." "Living in the 'risk society,'" as Giddens (1991: 28) explains, "means living with a calculative attitude to the open possibilities of action, positive and negative, with which, as individuals and globally, we are confronted in a continuous way in our contemporary social existence."

11. Bishop (2009: 22) adds that "the post-9/11 zombie film remains remarkably true to the genre's original protocols." Bishop (2009: 22) admits that while "the zombies are not always literally dead [in the post-9/11 zombie movies], as in Romero's films," he notes that "the apparent apocalypse and collapse of societal infrastructures remain central features." Furthermore, Bishop (2009: 22) continues, "the genre tends to emphasize certain causes for the end of the world, including infectious disease, biological warfare, euthanasia, terrorism, and even immigration. Although the genre is forty years old, these concepts resonate more strongly with present-day Americans than ever before, where events like the September 11 attacks, the war in Iraq, and Hurricane Katrina provide comparable forms of shocking ideas and imagery." For related points about Iraq and Hurricane Katrina, see Beale (2004) and Onstad (2008), respectively; for a discussion of changes that Romero made to *Land of the Dead* "to accommodate post-9/11 fears about terrorism," see Beale (2004). On George W. Bush's "zombielike reading of 'The Pet Goat' [by Siegfried Engelmann] to elementary-school children *while* the towers burned" on September 11, 2001—which might have augured the return of zombie media—see Swartz (2018, emphasis added).

12. Note that "radicalisation" is not the same as "brainwashing." In a helpful article, Baggini (2014) describes "brainwashing" as "changing someone's beliefs against their will." According to Baggini (2014), "brainwashing" is "a well-worn trope of dystopian fiction, from Nineteen Eighty-Four to A Clockwork Orange, but it is arguable whether

or not such a feat is actually possible in the real world" because "even if it were, it would require a great deal of time and effort." "Radicalisation," however, is not "brainwashing," Baggini (2014) explains: "what we currently call radicalisation is not some sinister manipulation, but a process by which people come to freely choose a dangerously and wickedly misguided path that they nonetheless perceive to be a virtuous calling. . . . Like religious conversions, these experiences are ones that transform a person's worldview, in such a way that it appears to provide newfound moral clarity and certainty."

13. St. John 2006 (quoting Brian Keene, author of *The Rising* series). (*The Rising* series consists of *The Rising* [(2003) 2013b], *City of the Dead* [(2005) 2013a], *The Rising: Selected Scenes from the End of the World* [(2008) 2013c], and *The Rising: Deliverance* [2015].) Elsewhere, in the same article, St. John (2006) reiterates this point: "Zombies . . . are the perfect goblin for such times, in part because they suggest broad social collapse, when anyone—a policeman, a nurse, a friend—can turn into a force of evil. With a werewolf or vampire, all the evil is concentrated on a single creature; with zombies, the evil is everywhere" (citing Max Brooks, author of *The Zombie Survival Guide: Complete Protection from the Living Dead* [2003] and *World War Z: A Oral History of the Zombie War* [2006]).

14. It is worth remembering that "certain monsters go in and out of fashion, depending on the cultural winds . . . werewolves were popular in the 1980's and vampires in the 1990's, before zombies lurched back on the scene" (St. John 2006, citing Monica S. Kuebler, an editor at *Rue Morgue* magazine, which covers the horror genre).

The actor, author, and humorist John Hodgman (2017) jests that "all middle-aged dads dream about the end of the world as we know it" because "it is a comfort to them. For some, the fantasy is blunt, vengeful and aspirational. The zombie epidemic is a very popular apocalypse scenario among middle-aged men for a very simple reason: When chaos consumes civilization, you can start over. You get to be young again." While Hodgman (2017) claims that "dreaming about societal collapse and global apocalypse" is one of a number of "classic weird dad hobbies," to our disappointment, he does not expound on whether or why other apocalyptic scenarios—ones that do not involve zombies—could result in "chaos consum[ing] civilization" and the promise of starting over (by being young again).

15. For a discussion of this passage, see Brisman (2015: 288).

16. We would be remiss not to acknowledge that we have quoted this very passage on three previous occasions (see Brisman 2015: 288; Brisman and South 2013a: 1; South 2012: 97).

17. As Bishop (2009: 24) explains, "Romero's *Land of the Dead* [2005] depicts a post-zombied society, a world where the enemy is literally at the gates. Pittsburgh has been converted into an island stronghold, with rivers and electric fencing keeping the zombies out (and the residents safely in). Class division is more critical than in other zombie films: the upper class lives an opulent lifestyle in Fiddler's Green, a luxurious high-rise, while ignoring the problem; the commoners, however, must face reality while living in the slums below" (see Beale 2004 for a comparable description of Fiddler's Green). Bishop (2009: 24) points out that "the wealthy elite in Fiddler's Green are literally isolated from the grim facts that make their lifestyle possible." In order to maintain the status quo, Kaufman, "the self-appointed leader of Pittsburgh," played by Dennis Hopper, "constructs the world's most extreme border security," where "blown up and barricaded bridges make the rivers impassable; in an extreme example of xenophobia, soldiers shoot on sight." For Bishop (2009: 24), these forms of immigration control—which, we would

add, also bring to mind the dynamics in *Elysium* (2013), discussed in Chapter 3—"have become even more jarringly familiar with recent debates about erecting a fence between the United States and Mexico and the redeployment of National Guard troops to guard the United States' southern bordering during George W. Bush's presidency."

On some of the meanings of Romero's other films, see, e.g., Onstad (2008), who writes: "Over five films and four decades . . . Romero's slack-jawed undead have been tour guides through a brainless, barbaric America that seems barely hospitable to the living. They lurch across a bigoted civil-rights-era countryside ('Night of the Living Dead,' 1968), claw at a suburban shopping mall ('Dawn of the Dead,' 1978) and wander dazed in an anxious post-9/11 world ('Land of the Dead,' 2005)."

18. For Vint (2013: 134, quoting Žižek 2011: 334), because it is "'easier to imagine a total catastrophe which ends all life on earth than it is to imagine a real change in capitalist relations' . . . we revel in the imagination of apocalyptic disaster." "This fascination is so pronounced," Vint (2013: 134) continues, "that the zombie became "'the official monster of the recession'" (which began in late 2007 and lasted until mid-2009; quoting Grossman 2009). Thus, if the events of September 11, 2001, reinaugurated the ascendancy of the zombie genre—or, at least, revitalized it—the Great Recession, as Vint (2013) and Grossman (2009) suggest, helped perpetuate it.

19. In an endnote, Lauro (2011: 275n8) offers two examples: (1) *I Am Legend* (2007), the third cinematic version of Richard Matheson's novel *I Am Legend* (1954), after *The Last Man on Earth* (1964) and *The Omega Man* (1971), where (in the 2007 version of the film) the "Krippin Virus" develops from the measles virus that had been genetically engineered to cure cancer; and (2) *28 Days Later* (2002), where the "rage virus"—a bioengineered aggression-inducing virus—spreads rapidly from an infected chimpanzee freed from its cage in a Cambridge laboratory by animal rights activists. Interestingly, in *I Am Legend* (2007), Dr. Alice Krippin (Emma Thompson), who has created the virus, articulates how "the measles virus . . . has been engineered at a genetic level to be helpful rather than harmful. . . . I find the best way to describe it is . . . if you can imagine your body as a highway . . . and you picture the virus as a very fast car being driven by a very bad man . . . imagine the damage that that car could cause. But then if you replace that man with a cop . . . the picture changes. And that's essentially what we've done"—an explanation that (unintentionally) illustrates beautifully many of the points in Linnemann's *The Horror of Police* (2022), mentioned elsewhere in this book. In *28 Days Later* (2002), the release of the chimpanzees by environmental activists not only offers a commentary on animal liberation but also exemplifies the problems with the nature "bites back" refrain, discussed in Chapter 2 and Chapter 3.

20. In support of the proposition that some zombie stories or apocalyptic narratives depict a "human-less" Earth "reclaiming its space" (or *place*), Lauro (2011: 234) points to scenes from *28 Days Later*, as well as *The Omega Man* (1971) and *I Am Legend* (2007), "in which deer begin to repopulate what were once human habitats . . . and grass begins to grow where formerly there were busy intersections." Again, we would refer readers back to Chapter 3's discussion of the "nature is healing" meme during the COVID-19 pandemic. Note also that, today, this statement from Lauro (2011) is interesting for further reasons. For example, because we have changed the countryside and made it harder for wildlife to find food there, they may be migrating to cities—although this may not be as recent a development as often assumed (on urban foxes, see, e.g., Irwin 2017). In many places facing a crisis in public finances, infrastructure is surrounded by

overgrown grass and wildflowers—mainly because the public sector cannot afford the maintenance. This, too, attracts wildlife, as does a commitment to "rewilding," which entails leaving some spaces wild to encourage birds and insects, such as butterflies, to return (see, e.g., National Highways 2022; Wyatt 2024).

21. A similar narrative—one that weaves together the "revenge of nature" trope (discussed in Chapter 2) with the zombie apocalypse motif—can be found in the 2016 film *The Girl with all the Gifts* and the television series *The Last of Us*, which premiered in January 2023. The cause of both "events" here has been a pandemic fungus infection, *Ophiocordyceps unilateralis* (commonly known as "zombie-ant fungus"). Lu (2019) explains:

> They walk among us: insects hijacked by parasitic fungi that control their every move.
>
> The *Ophiocordyceps unilateralis* fungus has just one goal: self-propagation and dispersal. Researchers think the fungus, found in tropical forests, infects a foraging ant through spores that attach and penetrate the exoskeleton and slowly takes over its behavior.
>
> As the infection advances, the enthralled ant is compelled to leave its nest for a more humid microclimate that's favorable to the fungus's growth. The ant is compelled to descend to a vantage point about 10 inches off the ground, sink its jaws into a leaf vein on the north side of a plant, and wait for death.
>
> Meanwhile, the fungus feeds on its victim's innards until it's ready for the final stage. Several days after the ant has died, the fungus sends a fruiting body out through the base of the ant's head, turning its shriveled corpse into a launchpad from which it can jettison its spores and infect new ants.

On "zombie viruses," see Cleveland Clinic (2023); for a review of "zombie biology," "zombie epidemiology," and "zombie infections," see Smith (2015).

22. More than thirty-five years earlier, Sharrett (1984: 265) made a similar observation:

> Cannibalism has always been *implied* as a theme in horror, especially in the werewolf and vampire films; analysts have referred to oral attacks on the victim as emblematic of regression to the infantile stage, where attempts to satisfy libidinal impulses overlap with the instinct for nourishment and survival. George Romero's *Night of the Living Dead* was the first work to literalize the theme of cannibalism, to . . . illustrate the image of society "feeding on itself." (emphasis in original)

23. Levina and Bui (2013: 1–2) argue that "monstrous narratives of the past decade have become omnipresent specifically because they represent collective social anxieties over resisting and embracing change in the twenty-first century. They can be read as a response to a rapidly changing cultural, social, political, economic, and moral landscape."

24. In his description of *2012* (2009), directed by Roland Emmerich, Harris (2009) explains that the trailer for the film, whose title is "tied to the date on which, according to a popular interpretation of an ancient Mayan calendar, the world might end," depicts—"in two and a half minutes"—"a tidal wave sweeping over the Himalayas, Los

Angeles destroyed by an earthquake and slipping into the sea, a meteor shower hitting the Earth, the Vatican collapsing and its dome rolling down the street and crushing worshippers, the statue of Christ in Rio de Janeiro falling down and an aircraft being dumped on top of an exploding White House by a tsunami." The trailer, Harris (2009) charges, is "so over the top when it comes to destruction that it might justifiably be dubbed 'Apocalypse porn.'"

25. "Geoengineering" refers to "'the deliberate, large-scale intervention in the climate system to counter global warming or offset some of its effects' (Hamilton 2013: A17; see also Davies 2012; Dickel 2013: 248–50; Maas et al. 2013: 213–14; Mooney 2010: 5; Scheffran and Cannaday 2013)" (Brisman 2015: 299). Hulme (2014: 5) acknowledges that "'geoengineering' is a rather eclectic catch-all expression," but then employs the Royal Society's (2009) definition—"'the deliberate, large-scale manipulation of the planetary environment in order to counteract anthropogenic climate change.'" According to Hulme (2014: 2–3), geoengineering "technologies are united in their ambition to deliberately manipulate the atmosphere's mediating role in the planetary heat budget. They aim to do one of two things: either to accelerate the removal of carbon dioxide [CO_2] from the global atmosphere; or else to reflect more sunlight away from the Earth's surface and so to compensate for the heating of the planet caused by rising concentrations of greenhouse gases." This is consistent with the Royal Society's approach, which divides geoengineering technologies into two types: carbon dioxide removal (CDR) and solar radiation management (SRM). As the names suggest, the former type of technologies endeavor to remove CO_2 and isolate and sequester the carbon in a variety of "long-term reservoirs," while the latter—sometimes referred to as sunlight reflection methods (also abbreviated as SRM)—attempt to "offset global warming by reducing incoming solar radiation . . . by reflecting more sunlight back into space" (Hulme 2014: 6). Whereas CDR tries to "revers[e] the process of fossil-fuel combustion" by removing the CO_2 and storing the carbon, SRM "leave[s] atmospheric concentrations of CO_2 unaffected." For a description of four SRM technologies (stratospheric aerosol injection, marine cloud brightening, orbital mirrors, and urban whitewashing) and four CDR methods (biochar [charcoal], ocean fertilization, carbon capture and storage [also known as "post-combustion capture"], and enhanced weathering), see Hulme (2014: 7–10); for a brief overview of geoengineering, see Dickel (2013: 248–50); Hulme (2009: 25, 315–17, 333, 335, 349, 350, 352, 259); McNall (2011: 38, 65–66); Scheffran and Cannaday (2013: 270–88); for a discussion of historical attempts at weather modification ("weather mod") and the international treaties pertaining thereto, see Hulme (2014: 71–3); Lee (2009: 156–60); see also Zilinskas (1995); on "cloud seeding," see Prud'homme (2011); for a discussion of geoengineering for military purposes, see Hulme (2014: 72–73); Zilinskas (1995: 236, 244, 248, 251–52).

26. Also known as *The Fast and the Furious* media franchise, consisting of ten (10) films to date: *The Fast and the Furious* (2001); *2 Fast 2 Furious* (2003); *The Fast and the Furious: Tokyo Drift* (2006); *Fast and Furious* (2009); *Fast Five* (2011); *Fast and Furious 6* (2013); *Furious 7* (2015); *The Fate of the Furious* (2017); *F9* (2021); and *Fast X* (2023). (The franchise also includes the spin-off film, *Fast and Furious Presents: Hobbs & Shaw* [2019], as well as the animated television series, *Fast & Furious Spy Racers* [2019–2021].)

27. As we mentioned at the end of Chapter 3, this notion of "apocalypse" as "end times" differs from the original Greek meaning of the word.

28. The *Mad Max* media franchise, created by George Miller and Byron Kennedy, consists of *Mad Max* (1979), *Mad Max 2* (1981) (released in the United States as *The*

Road Warrior and thus sometimes referred to as *Mad Max 2: The Road Warrior*), *Mad Max Beyond Thunderdome* (1985) (also known as *Mad Max 3*), *Mad Max: Fury Road* (2015), and *Furiosa: A Mad Max Saga* (2024). Arguably, the second, third, fourth, and fifth films could be considered *post-apocalyptic* in that they take place after global war and the collapse of civilization, wherein Max Rockatansky is now a *former* police officer.

29. For analyses of the impact of *The Day After Tomorrow* on moviegoers' perceptions of climate change risk, see, e.g., Leiserowitz (2004), Lowe et al. (2006), and Reusswig and Leiserowitz (2005).

30. In *The Drowned World* (1962), global warming has been brought about by increased solar radiation. The cause of this increased solar radiation and subsequent warming is not made clear, however.

31. Nevil Shute's novel *On the Beach* (1957), later adapted as a film (in 1959, with Gregory Peck, Ava Gardner, Fred Astaire, and Anthony Perkins, and as a television film, in 2000, with Armand Assante, Bryan Brown, and Rachel Ward) combines both psychological and survival elements. Set mostly in and around Melbourne, Australia, with World War III having destroyed most of the Northern Hemisphere, killing all human and nonhuman animal life, and having polluted the atmosphere with nuclear fallout, the book and film(s) describe how various characters navigate the realization that global air currents slowly carrying the lethal nuclear fallout to the Southern Hemisphere will mean eventual death from radiation poisoning. Some live out their remaining days in denial, others drink and party, others hope and search for possible remaining humans in the Northern Hemisphere.

32. A third possibility is that she possesses the callousness that Alex Garland, who wrote the screenplay for the zombie film *28 Days Later* (2002), feels is necessary to become a hardened war correspondent or photojournalist, such as those depicted in his recent film, *Civil War* (2024) (see Brisman 2024), and that she is a budding shutterbug.

33. At the time of writing, various regional conflicts and events may yield many realistic plotlines for apocalyptic fiction and alternative history scenarios.

34. At one juncture in the book, when the characters are discussing flying to the South Pole, Scott makes reference to *On the Beach*, noted earlier: "more than 95 percent of the bombs used were aimed at targets in the Northern Hemisphere. And that's where the bulk of the fallout is concentrated. There is only one way to go to avoid it: south. Some of you may remember a novel years ago by Nevil Shute—*On the Beach*—where people in an Australian town waited for the fallout to come down from the north. Well, we have a similar situation—but a thousand times worse than Shute could have ever imagined" (Graham [1979] 1981: 189).

35. "Peak oil" refers to the hypothetical or theoretical point in time when the maximum rate of petroleum extraction is reached, after which the rate of production is expected to enter gradual, irreversible and terminal decline (see Brisman 2015: 287n3). As Mooallem (2009: 31) explains, "The theory of peak oil concludes that the productivity of the earth's oil wells will soon peak—if it hasn't already—and, once production falls short of demand, the market for our fundamental resource will rapidly spiral into chaos, potentially pulling much of society down with it." For an in-depth discussion of "peak oil," see Aleklett 2012; on the relationship of climate change to "peak oil," see Urry (2010: 193–98); for Kunstler's nonfiction writing on "peak oil," see Kunstler (2005, 2007).

36. By "pseudo-feudalism," we mean a system in which people live and work on land that they do not own and give the lord/nobleman a share of the fruits of the labor

in return for protection. In so doing, we draw a distinction with contemporary notions of "neo-feudalism" and "new medievalism." Schmidt (2014) describes how "our neo-Feudalist age of student loan and mortgage indebtedness" have replaced "pre-colonial economics of land tenancy." Kaufman (2013: 11) employs the term "new medievalism" to refer to "a corporate-government hybrid to which the whole world is doomed to be enslaved." As Kaufman (2013: 11) explicates, "Companies like Google created 'villages' for their employees"—somewhat akin to the "amenities" and housing in The Circle, a powerful internet company depicted in Dave Eggers's (2013) dystopian novel by the same name. Meanwhile, "banks indenture us," Kaufman (2013: 11) continues, "through escalating interest rates on credit cards, mortgages, and loans. Monsanto's iron-fisted control of land, water, and seed echoes injunctions against hunting on the king's land. As corporations consolidated power at an alarming rate, the onset of a new Middle Ages seems all but inevitable." For criminological engagement with "neo-feudalism," see, e.g., Shearing (2001); Shearing and Stenning (1983); see also Braithwaite (2000); Zedner (2006).

37. "TEOTWAWKI" is often used synonymously with "ABAO" ("All Bets Are Off") as well as with "WSHTF" ("When Shit Hits the Fan") (see, e.g., Gold 2023). Rawles, who edits SurvivalBlog, discussed elsewhere in this chapter, prefers "WTSHTF," which he defines as:

> When the Schumer Hits the Fan. (I formerly said "Stuff" hits the fan, but I think that the implied smell of Congressman Chuck Schumer's voting record is more descriptive. BTW, I also synonymously use the terms TEOTWAWKI, The Crunch, worst case, and the old military saying "when the balloon goes up.") (SurvivalBlog n.d.)

For Rawles, "Schumer" is "the stuff that the septic tank pumper truck hauls away. (Full offense intended to Senator Charles Schumer, a scum-sucking ultra-liberal hoplophobe)" (SurvivalBlog n.d.).

38. For a discussion of some of the commonalities and key differences between Douglas Coupland's *Player One: What Is to Become of Us* (2010), David Graham's *Down to a Sunless Sea* [1979] 1981), and James Howard Kunstler's *World Made by Hand* (2008), in their portrayals of the relationship between environment and conflict, see Brisman (2015: 286–89).

39. Denby (2014: 94) claims that "the current designers of awe, in Hollywood and elsewhere . . . [have] created what might be called the Seven Horsemen of the Multiplex: aliens, pandemics, floods, ice, comets and other interplanetary flotsam, nuclear war, and zombies," although he makes clear that "the traumatic inspiration now is less the world going up in a mushroom cloud than the threats of climate change and SARS and Ebola."

40. Thus, for Rawles, "There is Value in Redundancy. A common saying of SurvivalBlog readers is: 'Two is one, and one is none.' You must be prepared to provide for your family in a protracted period of societal disruption. That means storing up all of the essential 'beans, bullets, and Band-Aids' in *quantity*" (emphasis in original) (SurvivalBlog n.d.).

41. See, for example, LoJack, "The Surprising Role of the Car in the Creation of the Cell Phone," April 19, 2022, https://www.lojack.com/blog/2022/04/surprising-role-of-car-in-creation-of-cell-phone/.

42. Young (2022: 16) adds that "the advice given in the West, with its focus on the individual and the family, has been interpreted as a way of keeping ordinary citizens distracted while ensuring the continuity of the state." While we would concur with the first part of the statement, we might amend the end of Young's sentence to read "the continuity of a particular (neoliberal) state-corporate arrangement."

43. Schmidt's (2014) next point is that these movies "ultimately suggest a conservative return to patriarchal structures, a 'return to the land' and its moral values." This "return"—or "turn"—certainly resonates with other visualizations of "what will come after" or "what preparation is needed before" the apocalyptic "event" (as discussed earlier in this chapter and in Chapter 3). For example, *The Handmaid's Tale* (Atwood 1985) received critical acclaim when it was published in the mid-1980s, but in 2017, it became a globally successful television series with a plotline beginning with a fertility and population crisis caused by forms of "pollution" (the immorality of sexually transmitted diseases and lack of care for the environment). The echoes of other contemporary ideologies and philosophies cannot be explored in full here but might be found in the goals, motivations, and mindsets of both "prepper" and "survivalist" groups (see, e.g., Kelly 2016; see also Chapter 3), in the increase in articulations of positions described as "ecofascist" (see, e.g., Anson and Banerjee 2023; see also Chapter 1 and Chapter 3), and in elements of the appeal of the MAGA movement and the presidential campaigns of Donald J. Trump (see, e.g., Brooks 2017; Cardona 2019; Gage 2019; Lifshutz 2019; Nally 2017; Robertson 2016; but see Douthat 2017).

44. Spitznagel (2010) seems rather contemptuous of the notion of zombies and zombie films as metaphors, complaining that "zombies, as any cultural critic who's ever written about zombies will tell you, are metaphors. They represent our societal and generational fears, or something." "Take George A. Romero's Night of the Living Dead," Spitznagel (2010) continues, "that seminal zombie masterpiece from 1968." The zombies in that film "aren't just reanimated corpses who can't resist bum-rushing a Pennsylvania farmhouse," Spitznagel (2010) explains. "They symbolize Cold War paranoia and homosexual repression and mainstream tensions about the counterculture and Vietnam War anxiety and bunch of other stuff too, depending on who you ask." Indeed, Spitznagel (2010) seems so eager to dismiss the metaphorical power, potential, and possibility of zombies that, in an interview with Romero, asks the director: "To paraphrase Freud, sometimes things have symbolism and sometimes a cigar is just a cigar. Are the zombies in your movies always a metaphor, or are they sometimes just bloodthirsty walking corpses?" Romero's initial response would appear to suggest the latter: "To me, the zombies have always been zombies. They've always been a cigar. When I first made Night of the Living Dead, it got analyzed and overanalyzed way out of proportion. The zombies were written about as if they represented Nixon's Silent Majority or whatever. But I never thought about it that way" (quoted in Spitznagel 2010). Romero's next sentence, however, implies otherwise: "My stories are about humans and how they react, or fail to react, or react stupidly. I'm pointing the finger at us." Elsewhere, in disparaging the "horror market dominated by all-gore-all-the-time franchises like 'Saw' and 'Hostel,'" Romero asserts: "'I don't get the torture porn films. They're lacking metaphor'" (quoted in Onstad 2008: AR13).

45. Elsewhere, Cheuse (2008a) reiterates this perspective on Kunstler's book: "Things in Union Grove always seem to get worse before they improve, and society never returns to the heyday of yesterday. But in the end, Kunstler's brilliant cautionary fiction

convinces us that this brave new world, a world made by hand, just might prove as pleasing and unpredictable as our own. And that, that is no small feat of reassurance."

46. As Leone (2008) notes in his review of *World Made by Hand*, Kunstler's futuristic tale post-dates fifteen years' worth of predictions about the consequences of peak oil: for Kunstler, Leone (2008) explains, "an economic and cultural conflagration is all but inevitable . . . and the only way to cope with such a debacle is for Americans to live simple, more localized lives." In *World Made by Hand*, Leone (2008) continues, Kunstler "lends imagination to that theory and creates a story that seems . . . acutely realistic."

47. That Young seems to be incorrect about one of these portrayals also raises a point about how much of "the real thing" filmmakers think "the public" really wants to see. Unless there is a Hollywood version for which we cannot find a reference, *Threads* was not a Hollywood movie but a 1984 British-Australian television film, produced by the BBC and Nine Network. It is notable for the bleak realism of the aftermath of a nuclear strike and can be contrasted with *The Day After*—the 1983 American television film that aired on the ABC television network. As this commentary from "Java_Joe" on May 27, 2019, IMDb.com suggests, "The 80's were a different time. Everybody was making money, everybody was having a great time, things never looked better. Except there was always the threat of nuclear war hanging above our heads. This was more than just an idea. We felt it. It was always there just at the edges of your awareness and you could never really ignore it. Enter 'The Day After' which was an American made for TV movie showing what would happen. It was scary and it was effective but it showed an undercurrent of hope. That even in such a tragedy we could survive, pull together and win. Threads has no such message. It shows that even in a limited strike we are well and truly boned. No hope. No chance of a better world. The lucky ones would be the ones that died in the initial blast or that died shortly afterwards. The unlucky ones are the ones that would go on living and slowly get sick before dying" (https://www.imdb.com/title/tt0090163/reviews).

48. Drezner (2014: 832) cautions that "the horror genre . . . allows people to talk about present-day problems without addressing them directly," explaining that, for example, "instead of droning on about climate change, one can highlight the problem by changing the threat to the living dead." That being said—and in light of Vlahos's (2013) argument—Drezner (2014: 832) admits that "both informing and enabling effects highlight the positive ways that the living dead can be expropriated as a metaphor to spark interest in new ideas. The moment zombies are added into the mix, a dry public policy problem suddenly becomes a rollicking argument accessible to ordinary citizens."

49. That survival on the screen might lead people to miscalibrate risk and the odds of defying death in the real world might cause some to chuckle. As American film critic Roger Ebert (2004) wrote in his review of *The Day After Tomorrow*, "[The] plot gives itself away. When cataclysmic events shred uncounted lives but the movie zeroes in on only a few people, of *course* they survive, although some supporting characters may have to be sacrificed. What's amusing in movies like 'The Day After Tomorrow' is the way the screenplay veers from the annihilation of subcontinents to whether Sam [Jake Gyllenhaal] should tell Laura [Emmy Rossum] he loves her" (emphasis added).

50. Stephens (2022) explains that he "had other doubts, too." For him, "it seemed hubristic, or worse, to make multitrillion-dollar policy bets based on computer models trying to forecast climate patterns decades into the future. Climate activists kept promoting policies based on technologies that were either far from mature (solar energy) or sometimes actively harmful (biofuels)."

51. Moser and Dilling (2004: 43–44) make a similar assertion: "Critically important . . . for communicating the magnitude of the challenge before us are not measures of doom but yet-to-be-developed imaginative, compelling indicators that allow us to assess our progress toward that 'better world.' For, as futurist Robert Olsen [*sic*] says (paraphrasing historian Frederik Polak [1973]), 'the future may well be decided by the images of the future with the greatest power to capture our imaginations and draw us to them, becoming self-fulfilling prophecies'" (quoting Olson 1995: 34). More recently, Wallace-Wells (2024) speaks of the "vocal 'doomers' about A.I. and climate change, long Covid and Covid vaccines, fertility levels and the 'woke mind virus,' among other sources of panic." He continues: "there is now another emerging archetype: doomers about doomerism, who believe that pessimism is a kind of social poison, and that bleak visions of the future have probably already curdled our culture and its prospects, and may consign future generations to worse outcomes still."

52. Correspondingly, Micah L. Sifry, author of *Spoiling for a Fight: Third-Party Politics in America* (2003), affirms that "fear of a dark future isn't the best motivator; hope for a better one is" (quoted in Friedman 2006: A27).

53. Itzkoff (2020) reports that Graeme Manson, the showrunner of *Snowpiercer* (the television series), noted earlier in the chapter, "did not want the series to be seen solely as a bleak fiction, but neither did he want it to forsake its moral mission." "'I do think it has a duty to warn but also a duty to entertain, too,' Manson said. 'I'm an optimistic person, but how do you balance optimism and activism?'" Soloski (2024) suggests that it may be a fine balance, indeed, describing how "scientist[s] . . . who had once needed to push back against the public's climate skepticism [are] now facing people who believe[] in a coming global catastrophe perhaps too much."

54. For Nixon (2011: 2), "slow violence" is "a violence that occurs gradually and out of sight, a violence of delayed destruction that is dispersed across time and space, an attritional violence that is typically not viewed as violence at all." For a discussion of Nixon's idea of "slow violence," see, e.g., Davies (2018, 2022); de Froideville and Gibbs (2023).

55. Indeed, LaFrance (2024) issued this declaration on April 8, 2024—the date of the "Great North American Eclipse" (Carter 2024; Chow et al. 2024; Klesman 2024)—accompanied by the observation that "the human tradition of treating an eclipse as an occasion for apocalyptic doomsaying is ancient" and that it was "expected" that "the solar eclipse would generate some degree of collective foreboding."

56. O'Connell (2020) reports that Vicino "had some strange beliefs"—"beliefs that were supplementary to his basic apocalyptic vision." As O'Connell explains:

> He [Vicino] believed that the Earth had a tendency to shift abruptly on its axis, causing massive earthquakes and tidal waves. He believed in the existence of a rogue planet the size of Jupiter called Niburu, which was out there just roaming around untethered to any particular solar system, and that it was on a collision course with our own world, and that the government knew about this, too, and was hiding it from us. He believed that everything that happened, from North Korea to Brexit, was orchestrated with the intention of bring us closer to one world government.
>
> He wasn't particularly evangelical about these beliefs. He was mostly just putting them out there, it seemed . . . .

Essentially, for Vicino, one can choose one's own version of cataclysms:

> We have all heard the prophecies of the "End Times". The Bible warns of it. Nostradamus foresaw it. Edgar Cayce predicted it. The Hopi Indians, the Third Secret of Fatima, Saint Malachy and prophets throughout the ages all warn of the same epic global catastrophes that will befall upon the Earth. We have been warned of Armageddon, Nibiru/Planet X, a sudden pole shift, future plagues, an EMP blast, a solar kill shot, a super volcanic eruption, major earth changes, killer asteroids and comets, a mega tsunami, an economic meltdown and even the anarchy that will certainly follow any one of these events. (Vivos 2024)

But those who do not buy—into his business model, into his vision(s)—or who do not purchase his shelters—risk having limited choices for their short futures after whatever worst case scenario befalls us.

CHAPTER 5

1. While an exhaustive account of all books and media with "Goodbye Earth" in the title is outside the scope of this chapter, we note Sam Sidawi's *Goodbye Earth: Air, Land, Water, Ozone . . . It's All Connected* (2011) and Ernie Schmidt's *Good-Bye Earth?* (2008), as well as the new Netflix K-drama, *Goodbye Earth*, based on a novel by Kotaro Isaka (see ComingSoon.Net n.d.).

2. For Greta Thunberg's speech, "Our House Is on Fire," at the World Economic Forum in Davos in January 2019, see https://www.theguardian.com/environment/2019 /jan/25/our-house-is-on-fire-greta-thunberg16-urges-leaders-to-act-on-climate. For her speech, "Our House Is Still on Fire," at the World Economic Forum in Davos in January 2020, see, e.g., Thunberg (2020a, 2020b). For a review of *Our House Is on Fire: Scenes of a Family and a Planet in Crisis* (Thunberg et al. 2020), see Mitchell (2020). For a children's book that tells the story of Greta Thunberg, see Winter (2019); for a related title, see Tucker (2019).

3. Veldman (2012: 5, 7) acknowledges that while "apocalyptic rhetoric [can] induce[] feelings of hopelessness and fatalism," there is evidence to suggest that "apocalypticism . . . often goes hand in hand with activism," and that "apocalyptic beliefs . . . *motivate* practices such as 'monkeywrenching,' or ecological sabotage, civil disobedience, and the more conventional 'paper monkeywrenching' (lobbying, engaging in public information campaigns to shift legislative priorities, or using lawsuits when these tactics fail) . . . for most radical environmentalists, apocalypticism and activism are bound closely together" (emphasis added). In contrast, Bettini (2013: 68) observes that "[a] 'standard' critique to narratives that mobilize fear (and to the securitization of an issue) is that they can pave the way for exceptional measures. As pointed out by Gregory White, when environmental narratives formulate C-M [climate-induced migration] as a threat, they risk finding 'unlikely bedfellows' (White 2011) in conservative standpoints that call for restrictive approaches towards migration." In other words, for Bettini (2013)—and White (2011)—fear *motivates* and *mobilizes* in *counterproductive* and *oppressive* ways. This is consistent with Andrews (2019b), who quotes Dr. Lise Van Susteren, a forensic psychologist with expertise on the physical and psychological effects of climate change, for the proposition that "we regress when we're fearful," and

who implies that fear can lead people to seek scapegoats rather than solutions. This position would seem to resonate with that of Tidwell (2018: 117), who asserts that ecohorror—the subject of Chapter 2—"reflects our fears about non-human nature in a variety of ways." "Perhaps animals will attack us," she continues, "perhaps we will lose our place at the top of the animacy hierarchy, or perhaps we will have to acknowledge our interconnectedness with other beings. In doing so, ecohorror risks reinforcing those fears and categories they are built upon. . ." (Tidwell 2018: 117). That being said, Tidwell (2018: 117) maintains that "ecohorror also asks us to reconsider some of those fears and to imagine what might happen if we were not to insist so vehemently upon such divisions" (see also Tidwell and Soles 2021: 14). We return to this point when we make the case for needing to help ensure that those fears are *not* reinforced.

4. As we acknowledge in Chapter 3 and describe further in this chapter, however, some of us are more "monstrous" than others.

5. Pihlström (2020: 44–45) goes on to suggest that "human beings (real or imagined) reduced to the state of monstrosity due to their consumption of other human beings' flesh may be the most abnormal and therefore the most horrific—even more abnormal, impure, and horrific than the typical supernatural monsters—precisely because they have lost their full humanity while maintaining, at least in some limited sense, the capacity of recognizing the humanity of their victims."

6. Jayatissa (2024) asks: "Who is the real monster? Fifty years later, we've come to understand that it's not Carrie but the world that made her." (The plot of American author Stephen King's first horror novel, *Carrie*, revolves around a high school girl named Carrie White, who is friendless and bullied but who possesses tremendous telekinetic powers.)

7. Elsewhere, Kniss (2021: 73) makes the interesting point that "the grave, like the wilderness, has the power to transform the human into the monstrous. . . . To enter the grave is to enter the alien world of the wilderness and come into contact with nature as Other—the inhuman, frightening not-me. The grave is where humanity not only comes into contact with this form of monstrous nature but also *becomes* monstrous and othered through the process of decomposition" (emphasis in original).

For a discussion of Kniss's argument that "a theological soul/body split . . . drives a wedge between humanity and the natural world," see Stevenson (2021: 99).

8. Skott (2024) notes that "prison is an insatiable threat continuously making new monsters." To this we would add that we make monsters through our prisons; these monsters are (thus) expendable (because they are in prison). On how "monsters are frightening because they are the abject" and how "the abject" is "something that must be cast away in order for life to continue," see Levina and Bui (2013: 3, citing Dika 1996). On "abject posthumanism," including the relationship of zombies, labor, and neoliberalism, see Vint (2013).

9. For Skott and colleagues (2021: 390), "the monster is thus a paradox: on the one hand, representative of the behaviors that threaten society and, on the other, that which makes such incivilities possible, even justifying such behavior in the name of the common good." "Monsters are agents of moralized fear," they continue, "to which social cruelty is normalized in the name of 'the civil' (Ingebretsen 2001: 3)" and "because the monster must also be destroyed, it cannot be allowed to live if society is to purge itself of whatever social ill it represents" (Skott et al. 2021: 390). What is particularly worrisome about Trump's rhetoric and the passions that it excites is that, as Skott and colleagues

(2021: 390) contend, "what makes the monster different from other forms of othering is . . . that it needs to be annihilated"—*and* "that such annihilation is *legitimized* and *condoned*" (emphasis added).

Skott and colleagues (2021: 390) proceed to illuminate how "the construction of the monstrous offender, building on the Gothic idea of the predatory criminal, whereby offenders are portrayed as 'animalistic, incorrigible and innately evil' (Surette 2007: 205), has been popularized recently through the portrayals of offenders in the media landscape"—something that we are certainly witnessing today. Skott and colleagues (2021: 390) contend that "Gothic narratives of violence can, therefore, be seen as politically useful tools to legitimize the intensification of social control mechanisms and to increase state control"—something that Trump promised he would do during his campaign to return to office.

For Skott and colleagues (2021: 390), "the Gothicity of violence, specifically the construction of monstrosity, has been . . . an important feature of the exercise of colonial power (Higgins and Swartz 2018). The state or colonizers, then, themselves, engage in monstrous responses, which are justified and made invisible by the threat entailed by the constructed monster."

10. See Foltyn (2020: xiii), who states that because "popular culture reflects events, trends, and attitudes in mass culture, perhaps we have redefined ourselves as food for monsters as penance for our collective guilt for being the ultimate monsters: consumers of other creatures and despoilers of their and our own habitats."

11. This resonates with Friedman's (2016) point that "our planet is now 'under attack'—*by us*" (quoting actress Alison Sudol, an IUCN [International Union for Conservation of Nature] goodwill ambassador, emphasis in original). See Staples (2017), who explains that for George Romero, one of his "great warning[s] was that evil often resides in the utterly familiar." Staples (2017) then quotes Romero for the proposition that "What I'm trying to show . . . is how the monster, the evil, is not something lurking in the distance, but something actually inside all of us."

Not only is humanity's behavior toward nature monstrous, but when governmental entities actually try to deal with environmental issues, they are often treated *monstrously*. As Monbiot (2023) writes, "Several grisly bloodsports, legal or otherwise, are enjoyed in the English countryside. But none is as popular as shooting the messenger. Rather than attend to our environmental crisis, politicians, lobbyists and the media"—as well as property developers and business interests—"prefer to hunt the people seeking to address the problem."

On the relationship of art and monstrousness and whether artists need to be monsters to complete their work, see Dederer (2017).

12. In criticizing the term, *Anthropocene*, Anson (2020: 71) argues that "in its assertion of 'the human,' the Anthropocene fossilizes an epistemological and systemic position that cannot imagine solving a problem any other way than cataclysmic redemption of a settled (settler) future, in yet another acquittal of white violence. Fetishizing a golden spike event, it cashes in on a catastrophic mode that renders all, so none, guilty." Her note at the end of the sentence is particularly germane to our discussion here: "[The] Anthropocene thus updates what Hannah Arendt warned in the context of Nazi Germany, that to accuse everyone equally is 'a highly effective whitewash of all those who had actually done something, for where all are guilty no one is,' in Responsibility and Judgment . . ." (Anson 2020: 79n56).

13. Compare Dixon (2008) with Khapaeva (2020: 20), who writes that "popular culture does not exist in an intellectual void: penetrated by political ideas and indirectly informed by philosophical trends, it responds to them in its own way: it commercializes their meanings."

14. The augural purpose of monsters is a recurring theme in Skott and colleagues' (2021) article: for example, "monsters serve to redefine frayed boundaries, as well as to warn the public—in a process that helps society reinterpret itself" (2021: 388), and "the monster illuminates boundaries, serving as a warning" (2021: 397).

15. Elsewhere in the same chapter, Alaimo (2001: 283) avows that "monster movies work to reassert solid differences between humans and nature" (for a discussion, see Parker 2016: 216).

16. Compare Parker's (2016) statement with Lauro and Christie (2011: 2), who "question whether the zombie resembles our prehistoric past, acts as a mirror reflecting our present anxieties, or suggest whether the future will house a more evolved post-humanity or merely the graves of a failed civilization."

In a different vein, it is worth noting that some contend that the study of ecohorror does not *just* provide us with insight into human-nature/human-environment relationships. As Tidwell (2021: 43) asserts, "ecohorror is more central to horror as a genre than has previously been acknowledged—it cannot fully be separated from body horror or cosmic horror, and it appears in many other kinds of horror too. . . . Incorporating the concerns of other horror subgenres into ecohorror analyses strengthens ecohorror by acknowledging the ways in which environmental concerns are not isolated from concerns such as health and disability or from existential crises." Elsewhere, Tidwell (2021: 60) stresses that "ecohorror is—and must be—concerned not only with the environment, narrowly defined, but also with human bodies (always implicated in and impacted by ecological issues) as well as with large-scale threats, such as climate change, that are not easily grasped by the single human mind or experience."

17. It bears mention that sometimes the feelings we embrace can still have harmful environmental impacts. For example, Nijman and Nekaris (2017: 85), reporting on "the rise of popularity of wild-caught owls as pets in Indonesia, both in absolute numbers and relative to the number of other birds offered for sale, following the release of the Harry Potter series," examined "whether or not the Harry Potter novels and films, and in particular the normalization of keeping owls as companions, has led to an increase in owls offered for sale as pets, both in absolute terms and relative to other species of birds in trade." Nijman and Nekaris (2017: 91) stop short of identifying "a causal link between the Harry Potter novels and films and the rise of popularity of owls as pets in Indonesia, i.e. a Harry Potter effect." As they contend, "The increase in the number of owls offered for sale since 2010 not only in Jakarta but throughout Java and Bali, coincided with an increase in the number and level of organisation of the pet owl communities, online and offline, and this, as much as the Harry Potter films and novels, might explain the popularity of owls as pets in Indonesia. A similar increase in popularity has been documented for civets in Indonesia (Nijman et al. 2014) without having been championed by a fictional character." Nevertheless, they argue that "it is clear that in recent years the impact of trade in owls for various reasons has increased dramatically" and that because "the current ban on wild-caught birds is failing to limit the commercial trade in owls . . . this necessitates a rethink of how best to regulate trade as part of an overall management strategy of owls in Indonesia" (Nijman and Nekaris 2017: 93).

Nijman and Nekaris (2021: 85) note that "an increase in popularity of certain animals following their appearance on the big screen or in television series is a well-known phenomenon," although they acknowledge that "it is rarely quantified and, as ever, correlation does not indicate causation." Moreover, they add, "an increase in popularity seldom is immediate and discernable increases can be delayed for several years" (Nijman and Nekaris 2021: 85). On the popularity of purebred dogs in the United States after the release of *101 Dalmatians* in 1985, see Herzog et al. (2004). On the increase in the global trade in green iguanas (*Iguana iguana*) after the first *Jurassic Park* film in 1993, see Christy (2008) and Nijman and Shepherd (2011). On the impact of sales and imports of clown fish after the release of *Finding Nemo* in 2003, see Militz and Foale (2017), Prosek (2010), and Rhyne et al. (2012).

18. On the issue of "entertainment," see Giuliani (2021: 14), who reminds us that "key differences in the way film, television and the news media frame *moral panic* owe much to the fact that the primary purpose of popular culture is entertainment" (emphasis in original).

19. Carnes and Goren (2023: 11) call attention to the criticism that "superhero stories *encourage a sort of political compliance* by depicting worlds in which the major problems can only be solved by impossibly exceptional individuals; they leave readers hoping that a 'hero will save us' and in the process discourage people from thinking in terms of the sustained, collective, often unglamorous community and political action that is usually necessary to solve problems in the real world" (emphasis in original), while Goren (2023: 96) contends that "from political officials who are seen to have some superpower to policy solutions that depend on not-yet-invented mechanisms and capacities, citizens are looking for superheroic solutions to mounting and extreme problems that we face, such as COVID-19, global climate change, and systemic racism." Elsewhere in the same volume, Hirschmann (2023: 176–77) laments how one of the messages of the MCU is that "global warming is so overwhelming that *only* a superhero can fix it" (emphasis in original).

20. Indeed, Hirschmann (2023: 179) suggests that "perhaps superheroes are not suited to deal with environmental threats, which require collective action; maybe Thanos's mistake was a failure to consult and collaborate." On Earth, Hirschmann (2023: 179) continues, "On our (real) earth," that is, "the Swedish teenager Greta Thunberg has shown us that children can be inspiring and fearless leaders and crusaders for the environment. She reveals that young people have the imaginations that have been cramped by a culture of overuse, exploitation, and disposability. She also challenges the idea that superheroes are only good at protecting us from external enemies through physical violence; what has come to define 'superhero' fits the neoliberal model of the individual working alone, but Thunberg's superpower is the ability to bring people together to urge governments to collective action."

21. While Hirschmann (2023: 177) acknowledges the value of the message, "we must be our own environmental heroes," she worries about the way in which this has been done, "with self-righteous condemnation of plastic grocery bags, plastic straws, and even asthma inhalers, [which] focuses attention on . . . relatively helpless humans rather than the corporations that have been built on the exploitation of natural resources and human vulnerability."

22. Jordan (2017) suggests that "when we enter a theatre, we all carry our own experiences with us." Nevertheless, he argues, "no matter how divisive life in this country may

become, the movie theatre has always been a place where we can rediscover what unites us." We would edit Jordan's statement to read that "the movie theatre *might* be a place where we can discover what unites us"—and this will largely depend on whether messages about unity in *Infinity War* and *Endgame* are overshadowed by the ecofascism of Thanos. Thus, when Jordan (2017) comments that "when we see injustice from another perspective on the screen, it makes us more aware of real-life injustices around us," we would respond, "It depends. It is incumbent on us to ensure that awareness, rather than succumb to blindness and denial, which will simply perpetuate such injustices."

.

Bibliography

Abberley, Will. 2011. Virginia Richter, Literature after Darwin. *The British Society for Literature and Science*. Available at: http://www.bsls.ac.uk/reviews/romantic-and -victorian/virginia-richter-literature-after-darwin/.

Abolish Golf Courses (@abolishgolfcourses). 2023. "The orcas have done more for the working class than our elected officials ever have." June 18. Available at: https:// www.instagram.com/p/CtpFR4TR1xX/.

Achanbach, Joel. 2008. Iowa Flooding Could Be an Act of Man, Experts Say. *Washington Post*, June 19: A01. Available at: https://www.nbcnews.com/id/wbna25254541.

Adams, Tim. 2023. End Times by Peter Turchin Review—Can We Predict the Collapse of Societies? *The Guardian*, May 28. Available at: https://www.theguardian .com/books/2023/may/28/end-times-by-peter-turchin-review-elites-counter-elites -and-path-of-political-disintegration-can-we-identify-cyclical-trends-in-narrative -of-human-hope-and-failure.

AFP. 2015. World's Richest 10% Produce Half of Global Carbon Emissions, Says Oxfam. *The Guardian*, December 2. Available at: https://www.theguardian .com/environment/2015/dec/02/worlds-richest-10-produce-half-of-global-carbon -emissions-says-oxfam.

Aguilar, Carlos. 2019. Chart: Everything That Disney Owns. *Cartoon Brew*, April 2. Available at: https://www.cartoonbrew.com/disney/chart-every-company-that -disney-owns-172130.html.

Aistrope, Tim, and Stefanie Fishel. 2020. Horror, Apocalypse, and World Politics. *International Affairs* 96(3): 631–48.

Aitken, Peter. 2023. Killer Whales May Be Attacking Boats as Revenge for Injured Matriarch: Scientists. *Fox News*, May 27. Available at: https://www.foxnews .com/world/killer-whales-may-be-attacking-boats-revenge-injured-matriarch -scientists. [Also published as: Killer Whales Attacking Boats to Avenge Injured Matriarch: Scientists. *New York Post*, May 27. Available at: https://nypost.com/2023 /05/27/killer-whales-attacking-boats-to-avenge-injured-matriarch/.]

Alaimo, Stacy. 2001. Discomforting Creatures: Monstrous Natures in Recent Films. In *Beyond Nature Writing: Expanding the Boundaries of Ecocriticism*, ed. Karla Armbruster and Kathleen R. Wallace, 279–96. Charlottesville and London: University Press of Virginia.

Alderman, Naomi. 2023. *The Future: a novel*. New York: Simon & Schuster.

Aleklett, Kjell. 2012. *Peeking at Peak Oil*. New York: Springer.

Alexander, Kwame. 2016. My Frogs Are Green. *The New York Times* (Sunday Book Review), August 28: 33. Published online as "Kwame Alexander on Children's Books and the Color of Characters," on August 26, 2016, at: https://www.nytimes.com/2016/08/28/books/review/kwame-alexander-on-childrens-books-and-the-color-of-characters.html.

Alicante Today. 2020. Orcas Continue to Attack Boats on the Galician Coastline. September 16. Available at: https://alicantetoday.com/archived-_-orcas-continue-to-attack-boats-on-the-galician-coastline_1505539-a.html.

Alicante Today. 2021a. British Sail Boat Attacked by Killer Whales in A Guarda, Spain. October 1. Available at: https://alicantetoday.com/archived-_-british-sail-boat-attacked-by-killer-whales-in-a-guarda-spain_1656582-a.html.

Alicante Today. 2021b. Cadiz Restricts Navigation Area for Small Boats after Killer Whale Attacks. August 6. Available at: https://alicantetoday.com/archived-_-cadiz-restricts-navigation-area-for-small-boats-after-killer-whale-attacks_1627906-a.html.

Al Jazeera. 2023a. Killer Whales Damage Boat in Latest Orca Incident off Spain Coast. May 26. Available at: https://www.aljazeera.com/news/2023/5/26/killer-whales-damage-boat-in-latest-orca-incident-off-spain-coast.

Al Jazeera. 2023b. "Orca Uprising": Why Are Orca Whales Targeting Boats? June 28. Available at: https://www.aljazeera.com/podcasts/2023/6/28/orca-uprising-why-are-orca-whales-targeting-boats.

Althor, Glenn, James E. M. Watson, and Richard A. Fuller. 2016. Global Mismatch between Greenhouse Gas Emissions and the Burden of Climate Change. *Scientific Reports* 6, article number: 20281. Available at: https://doi.org/10.1038/srep20281.

Alund, Natalie Neysa. 2023. A School of 12-Inch Sharks Were Able to Sink an Inflatable 29-Foot Catamaran in the Coral Sea. *USA Today*, September 7. Accessed at: https://www.usatoday.com/story/news/nation/2023/09/07/cookiecutter-shark-attacks-catamaran-coral-sea/70784653007/.

Amend, Alex. 2019. First as Tragedy, Then as Fascism. *The Baffler*, September 26. Available at: https://thebaffler.com/latest/first-as-tragedy-then-as-fascism-amend.

Amster, Randall. 2003. Patterns of Exclusion: Sanitizing Space, Criminalizing Homelessness. *Social Justice* 30(1): 195–221.

Andalucia Today. 2021a. Investigation Launched into Killer Whale Attacks in Spain. October 25. Available at: https://andaluciatoday.com/archived-_-investigation-launched-into-killer-whale-attacks-in-spain_1671362-a.html.

Andalucia Today. 2021b. Killer Whales Attack Another Sailing Boat in the Strait of Gibraltar. July 16. Available at: https://andaluciatoday.com/archived-_-killer-whales-attack-another-sailing-boat-in-the-strait-of-gibraltar_1617071-a.html.

Andalucia Today. 2021c. Three Boats Rescued in Cádiz after Killer Whale Encounters. August 5. Available at: https://andaluciatoday.com/three-boats-rescued-in-c%C3%A1diz-after-killer-whale-encounters_1627365-a.html.

Anders, Charlie Jane. 2013. Why Would Aliens Come All This Way Just to Invade Earth? *Gizmodo*, May 2. Available at: https://gizmodo.com/why-would-aliens-come-all-this-way-just-to-invade-earth-487437089.

Andersen, Inger. 2019. *Curbing Negative Environmental Impacts of War and Armed Conflict.* News Stories and Speeches (Statements), United Nations Environment Programme, November 5. Available at: https://www.unep.org/news-and-stories/statements/curbing-negative-environmental-impacts-war-and-armed-conflict.

Anderson, Benedict. [1983] 2006. *Imagined Communities: Reflections on the Origin and Spread of Nationalism.* New York: Verso.

Andrews, Eve. 2019a. Humans Cause Climate Change. Do We Just Need Fewer Humans? *Grist*, February 28. Available at: https://grist.org/ask-umbra-series/humans-cause-climate-change-do-we-just-need-fewer-humans/.

Andrews, Eve. 2019b. Why Does Environmentalism Have a Dark Side? *Grist*, August 29. Available at: https://grist.org/article/why-does-environmentalism-have-a-dark-side/.

Anson, April. 2020. "Master Metaphor": Environmental Apocalypse and the Settler States of Emergency. *Resilience: A Journal of Environmental Humanities* 8(1) [Winter]: 60–81. Available at: https://muse.jhu.edu/article/784317.

Anson, April, and Anindita Banerjee. 2023. Green Walls: Everyday Ecofascism and the Politics of Proximity. *boundary 2* 50(1): 137–64. https://doi.org/10.1215/01903659-10192145.

Anson, April, Cassie Galentine, Shane Hall, Alex Menrisky, and Bruno Seraphin. 2022. Anti-Creep Climate Initiative Utilizes Marvel Characters to Educate Public about the Dangerous Fallacies behind Fascistic Thinking on Global Environmental Challenges. *Deceleration*, May 19. Available at: https://deceleration.news/2022/05/19/against-the-ecofascist-creep/.

Anthes, Emily. 2022. "Anthropause" during Pandemic Healed Nature, but Hurt It, Too. *The New York Times*, July 17: A1. Published online as "Did Nature Heal During the Pandemic 'Anthropause'?" on July 16, 2023 (updated June 22, 2023), at: https://www.nytimes.com/2022/07/16/science/pandemic-nature-anthropause.html.

Anti-Creep Climate Initiative [April Anson, Cassie M. Galentine, Shane Hall, Alexander Menrisky, and Bruno Seraphin]. 2022. *Against the Ecofascist Creep: Debunking Ecofascist Myths.* Available at: https://www.asle.org/wp-content/uploads/Against-the-Ecofascist-Creep.pdf.

Appel, Markus. 2008. Fictional Narratives Cultivate Just-World Beliefs. *Journal of Communication* 58(1) [March]: 62–83. https://doi.org/10.1111/j.1460-2466.2007.00374.x.

Appel, Markus, and Tobias Richter. 2007. Persuasive Effects of Fictional Narratives Increase Over Time. *Media Psychology*, 10(1): 113–34. https://doi.org/10.1080/15213260701301194.

Arablouei, Ramtin, and Rund Abdelfatah. 2019. Zombies. *Throughline, National Public Radio*, October 31. Available at: https://www.npr.org/2019/10/30/774809210/zombies.

Arango, Tim, Nicholas Bogel-Burroughs, and Katie Benner. 2019. "Hispanic Invasion": Manifesto of Hate Minutes before Attack. *The New York Times*, August 4: A1.

Published online as "Minutes Before El Paso Killing, Hate-Filled Manifesto Appears Online," on August 3, 2019, at: https://www.nytimes.com/2019/08/03/us/patrick -crusius-el-paso-shooter-manifesto.html.

Arata, Stephen D. 1990. The Occidental Tourist: Dracula and the Anxiety of Reverse Colonization. *Victorian Studies: A Journal of the Humanities, Arts and Sciences*, 33(4) [Summer]: 621–45. Available at: http://www.jstor.org/stable/3827794.

Armitt, Lucie. 2014. *The Gothic and Magical Realism*. In *The Cambridge Companion to the Modern Gothic*, ed. Jerrold E. Hogle, 224–39. Cambridge, U.K.: Cambridge University Press.

Arya, Rina. 2014. *Abjection and Representation: An Exploration of Abjection in the Visual Arts, Film and Literature*. London: Palgrave Macmillan.

Arya, Rina, and Nicholas Chare. 2016. Introduction: Approaching Abjection. In *Abject Visions: Powers of Horror in Art and Culture*, ed. Rina Arya and Nicholas Chare, 1–13. Manchester, U.K.: Manchester University Press.

Associated Press. 2018a. Fans in Africa react to Black Panther. *CBS News*, February 19. Available at: https://www.cbsnews.com/news/fans-in-africa-react-to-black-panther/.

Associated Press. 2018b. Huge Python Eats Woman Checking Her Vegetable Garden. *CBS News*, June 16. Available at: https://www.cbsnews.com/news/python-eats -woman-indonesia-sulawesi-province-muna-island-swallowed-whole/.

Atwood, Margaret. 1985. *The Handmaid's Tale*. Toronto: McClelland and Stewart.

Auerbach, Nina. 1995. *Our Vampires, Ourselves*. Chicago: University of Chicago Press.

Augustine of Hippo. 1063. *The City of God Against the Pagans*.

Autoridade Marítima Nacional. 2020. Autoridade Marítima Nacional alerta para os cuidados a ter em caso de interação ou avistamento de orcas. Autoridade Marítima Nacional (National Maritime Authority, Portugal), November 13. Available at: https://www.amn.pt/Media/Paginas/DetalheNoticia.aspx?nid=3200.

Azarian, Bobby. 2016. How the Fear of Death Makes People More Right-Wing. *Aeon*, November 17. Available at: https://aeon.co/ideas/how-the-fear-of-death-makes -people-more-right-wing.

Baggini, Julian. 2014. Radicalisation Is Not Brainwashing. We Need to Rethink How We Tackle It. *The Guardian*, July 13. Available at: https://www.theguardian.com /commentisfree/2014/jul/13/radicalisation-brainwashing-british-men-syria-julian -baggini.

Bailey, Ronald. 1993. *Eco-Scam: The False Prophets of Ecological Apocalypse*. New York: St. Martin's Press.

Bakhtin, Mikhail. 1984. *Problems of Dostoevsky's Poetics*. Edited and translated by Caryl Emerson. Minneapolis, MN, and London: University of Minnesota Press.

Ballard, J. G. [1962] 2013. *The Drowned World*. New York: Liverlight Publishing Corporation/W.W. Norton.

Barba, Vassia. 2024. Zuckerberg's "Doomsday Bunker" and Billionaires' Hidden Dens "Fulfil Biblical Prophesy." *The Mirror (The Daily Mirror)*, February 19. Available at: https://www.mirror.co.uk/news/us-news/zuckerbergs-doomsday-bunker -billionaires-hidden-32117408.

Barrett, Judi. 1978. *Cloudy with a Chance of Meatballs*. Illustrated by Ron Barrett. New York: Antheneum.

Bataille, Georges. [1934] 1993. Abjection and Miserable Forms. In *More and Less*, ed. Sylvère Lotringer, trans. Yvonne Shafir, 9–13. Cambridge, MA: The MIT Press.

Bauman, Zygmunt. 1989. *Modernity and the Holocaust*. Ithaca, NY: Cornell University Press.

Beale, Lewis. 2004. The Zombies Brought Him: George Romero Is Back. *The New York Times*, November 3: E1, E4. Published online as "The Zombies Brought Him: George Romero Is Back," on November 3, 2004, at: https://www.nytimes .com/2004/11/03/movies/the-zombies-brought-him-george-romero-is-back.html.

Beck, Ulrich. 1986. *Risikogesellschaft: Auf dem Weg in eine andere Moderne*. Frankfurt: Suhrkamp.

Beck, Ulrich. 1992. *Risk Society: Towards a New Modernity*. London: Sage.

Beddington, Emma. 2023. The Orca Uprising: Whales Are Ramming Boats—But Are They Inspired by Revenge, Grief, or Memory? *The Guardian*, July 11. Available at: https://www.theguardian.com/environment/2023/jul/11/the-orca-uprising -whales-are-ramming-boats-but-are-they-inspired-by-revenge-grief-or-memory.

Beirne, Piers. 2017. Classical Criminology. In *The Routledge Companion to Criminological Theory and Concepts,* ed. Avi Brisman, Eamonn Carrabine, and Nigel South, 15–18. Abingdon, Oxon, U.K., and New York: Routledge.

Belew, Kathleen. 2019. Understanding White Nationalism. *The New York Times*, August 5: A19. Published online as "The Right Way to Understand White Nationalist Terrorism," on August 4, 2019, at: https://www.nytimes.com/2019/08 /04/opinion/el-paso-terrorism.html.

Berets, Ralph. 1996. Changing Images of Justice in American Films. *Legal Studies Forum* 20(4): 473–80.

Berg, Julie, and Clifford Shearing. 2018. Governing-Through-Harm and Public Goods Policing. *The ANNALS of the American Academy of Political and Social Science* 679(1): 72–85. https://doi.org/10.1177/0002716218778540.

Berreby, David. 2011. Names Will Hurt You. *The New York Times*, March 6: 19. Published online as "A Philosophy of Genocide's Roots," on March 4, 2011, at: https://www.nytimes.com/2011/03/06/books/review/Berreby-t.html.

Best, Joel. 2018. Constructing Animal Species as Social Problems. *Sociology Compass* 12(11): e12630. https://doi.org/10.1111/soc4.12630.

Bettini, Giovanni. 2013. Climate Barbarians at the Gate? A Critique of Apocalyptic Narratives on "Climate Refugees." *Geoforum* 45(March): 63–72.

Bianciardi, Giorgio. 2022. Is Life on Mars a Danger to Life on Earth? NASA's Mars Sample Return. *Journal of Astrobiology* 11: 14–20. Available at: http:// journalofastrobiology.com/LifeonMarsDangertoLifeonEarthBianciardi.pdf.

Biello, David. 2013. How Long until We Have the Superhuman Exoskeletons from *Elysium*? *Scientific American*, August 7. Available at: https://www.scientificamerican .com/article/how-real-is-elysium-exoskeleton/.

Bishop, Kyle. 2008. The Sub-Subaltern Monster: Imperialist Hegemony and the Cinematic Voodoo Zombie. *Journal of American Culture* 31(2) [June]: 141–52. https://doi.org/10.1111/j.1542-734X.2008.00668.x.

Bishop, Kyle. 2009. Dead Man Still Walking. *Journal of Popular Film and Television* 37(1): 16–25. https://doi.org/10.3200/JPFT.37.1.16-25.

Bishop, Kyle William. 2010. *American Zombie Gothic: The Rise and Fall (and Rise) of the Walking Dead in Popular Culture*. Jefferson, NC: McFarland.

Biskind, Peter. 2018. *The Sky Is Falling: How Vampires, Androids, and Superheroes Made America Great for Extremism*. New York: The New Press.

Biswas, Soutik. 2020. India Coronavirus: Can the Covid-19 Lockdown Spark a Clean Air Movement? *BBC News*, April 21. Available at: https://www.bbc.com/news/world -asia-india-52313972.

Blackwell, Daria. 2022. Scientists Appeal for Reports of Interactions with Orcas. *Sail World*, August 3. Available at: https://www.sail-world.com/news/252267/Scientists -appeal-for-reports-of-orca-interactions.

Blanck, Nili. 2022. The Mesoamerican Influences Behind Namor from "Black Panther: Wakanda Forever." *Smithsonian Magazine*, November 10. Available at: https://www.smithsonianmag.com/history/the-mesoamerican-influences-behind -namor-from-black-panther-wakanda-forever-180981106/.

Bloodsworth-Lugo, Mary K., and Carmen R. Lugo-Lugo. 2013. The Monster Within: Post-9/11 Narratives of Threat and the U.S. Shifting Terrain of Terror. In *Monster Culture in the 21st Century: A Reader*, ed. Marina Levina and Diem-My T. Bui, 243–55. New York and London: Bloomsbury Academic.

Blow, Charles M. 2018. White Extinction Anxiety. *The New York Times*, June 25: A23. Published online as "White Extinction Anxiety," on June 24, 2018, at: https://www .nytimes.com/2018/06/24/opinion/america-white-extinction.html.

Boluk, Stephanie, and Wylie Lenz, eds. 2011. *Generation Zombie: Essays on the Living Dead in Modern Culture*. Jefferson, NC: McFarland.

Bond, Alan James, Angus Morrison-Saunders, Francois Pieter Retief, and Meinhard Doelle. 2020. Environmental Regulations Likely to Be First Casualties in Post-Pandemic Recovery. *The Conversation*, May 15. Available at: https://theconversation .com/environmental-regulations-likely-to-be-first-casualties-in-post-pandemic -recovery-137941.

Bosworth, Kai. 2022. The Bad Environmentalism of "Nature Is Healing" Memes. *Cultural Geographies* 29(3): 353–74.

Botting, Fred. 1996. *Gothic*. London and New York: Routledge.

Bouie, Jamelle. 2024. The Truth of Trump Is Very Far from the Myth. *The New York Times*, June 5, at: https://www.nytimes.com/2024/06/05/opinion/trump-verdict -felon-campaign.html.

Bould, Mark. 2021. *The Anthropocene Unconscious: Climate Catastrophe Culture*. London and New York: Verso.

Bowden, Mark. 2018. Hollywood's Booming Comic Book Age. *The New York Times*, July 8: SR5. Published online as "Why Are We Obsessed with Superhero Movies?" on July 6, 2018, at: https://www.nytimes.com/2018/07/06/opinion/sunday/ant-man -wasp-movies-superheroes.html.

Bowerman, Mary, and Sean Rossman. 2017. Indonesia Farmer Swallowed Whole by 23-Foot-Long Python. *USA Today*, March 29 (updated March 30). Available at: https://www.usatoday.com/story/news/nation-now/2017/03/29/missing-indonesian -man-swallowed-whole-reticulated-python/99771300/.

Bradford, Alina, and Patrick Pester. 2022. Orcas: Facts about Killer Whales. *Live Science*, October 28. Available at: https://www.livescience.com/27431-orcas-killer -whales.html.

Bradshaw, Corey J. A., and Barry W. Brook. 2014. Human Population Reduction Is Not a Quick Fix for Environmental Problems. *Proceedings of the National Academy of Sciences* 111(46) [November 18]: 16610–16615. https://doi.org/10.1073/pnas .1410465111.

Braithwaite, John. 2000. The New Regulatory State and the Transformation of Criminology. *The British Journal of Criminology* 40(2) [March]: 222–38. https://doi.org/10.1093/bjc/40.2.222.

Brioni, S. 2013. Costruire la razza come monstruosità in Italia. In La sottile linea bianca, ed. G. Giuliani. Special issue. *Studi Culturali* 10(1): 293–303.

Brisman, Avi. 2009. Film Review: Untraceable (2008). *Contemporary Justice Review* 12(3): 371–74. https://doi.org/10.1080/10282580903105939

Brisman, Avi. 2010. Movie Reviews: Felon (2008); The Escapist (2001); The Escapist (2008). *Contemporary Justice Review* 13(3): 347–50. https://doi.org/10.1080/10282580.2010.498254

Brisman, Avi. 2012a. Gamer, Written and Directed by Mark Neveldine and Brian Taylor Lionsgate, Lakeshore Entertainment (production companies); Lionsgate (distributor), 2009, 95 minutes, in English, rated R Hunger, Directed by Steve McQueen Film4, Channel 4, Northern Ireland Screen, the Broadcasting Commission of Ireland, the Wales Creative IP Fund, Blast! Films, Sound & Vision Broadcasting Funding Scheme (production companies), IFC Films (distributor), 2008, 96 minutes, in English, rated R. *Contemporary Justice Review* 15(2): 223–27. https://doi.org/10.1080/10282580.2012.681166.

Brisman, Avi. 2012b. *Green Cultural Criminology and Apocalyptic Environmental Harm*. Paper presented at the 68th Annual Meeting of the American Society of Criminology, Chicago, Illinois, November 15, 2012.

Brisman, Avi. 2012c. The Stoning of Soraya M. (2009). *Contemporary Justice Review* 15(3): 361–64. https://doi.org/10.1080/10282580.2012.707472

Brisman, Avi. 2013a. *Apocalypse Soon? A Green-Cultural Criminological Examination and Analysis of Environmental Catastrophe and the End of the World (As We Know It)*. Paper presented at 2013 American Society of Criminology Annual Meeting, Atlanta, Georgia, November 20, 2013.

Brisman, Avi. 2013b. *Apocalypse Soon? Ecocidal Tendencies, Misericordia, and the End of the World (As We Know It)*. Invited seminar talk, EKU Biological Sciences Seminar Series 2013, Department of Biological Sciences, Eastern Kentucky University, Richmond, Kentucky, November 15, 2013.

Brisman, Avi. 2013c. *Apocalypse Soon? From Ecocide to Misericordia to the End of the World*. Invited seminar talk, Essex Sustainability Institute, University of Essex (Colchester Campus), Colchester, U.K., May 21, 2013.

Brisman, Avi. 2015. Environment and Conflict: A Typology of Representations. In *Environmental Crime and Social Conflict: Contemporary and Emerging Issues,* ed. Avi Brisman, Nigel South and Rob White, 285–311. Surrey, U.K.: Ashgate.

Brisman, Avi. 2016. *Geometries of Crime: How Young People Perceive Crime and Justice*. London: Palgrave Macmillan.

Brisman, Avi. 2017a. An Epilogue to the Book, not an Elegy for the Earth. In *Environmental Crime in Latin America: The Theft of Nature and the Poisoning of the Land*, ed. David Rodríguez Goyes, Hanneke Mol, Avi Brisman and Nigel South, 297–301. London: Palgrave Macmillan.

Brisman, Avi. 2017b. On Narrative and Green Cultural Criminology. *International Journal for Crime, Justice and Social Democracy* 6(2): 64–77. https://doi.org/10.5204/ijcjsd.v6i2.347.

Brisman, Avi. 2017c. Representations of Environmental Crime and Harm: A Green-Cultural Criminological Perspective on *Human-Altered Landscapes*. In *The Routledge*

International Handbook of Visual Criminology, ed. Michelle Brown and Eamonn Carrabine, 523–39. London and New York: Routledge.

Brisman, Avi. 2018. Representing the "Invisible Crime" of Climate Change in an Age of Post-Truth. *Theoretical Criminology* 22(3): 468–91. https://doi.org/10.1177/1362480618787168.

Brisman, Avi. 2019a. The Fable of *The Three Little Pigs*, Climate Change and Green Cultural Criminology. *International Journal for Crime, Justice and Social Democracy*, 8(1): 46–69. https://doi.org/10.5204/ijcjsd.v8i1.470.

Brisman, Avi. 2019b. Stories of Environmental Crime, Harm and Protection: Narrative Criminology and Green Cultural Criminology. In *The Emerald Handbook of Research in Narrative Criminology*, ed. Jennifer Fleetwood, Lois Presser, Sveinung Sandberg and Thomas Ugelvik, 153–72. Bingley, West Yorkshire, U.K.: Emerald Publishing Limited.

Brisman, Avi. 2020. Cultural criminology and narrative criminology's shared interests. More than just criminological Verstehen. *Tijdschrift over Cultuur & Criminaliteit*, 10(3): 14–34. https://doi.org/10.5553/TCC/221195072020010003002.

Brisman, Avi. 2022. *Fieldnotes on a Study of Young People's Perceptions of Crime and Justice: Scaffolding as Structure*. Abingdon, Oxon, U.K., and New York: Routledge.

Brisman, Avi. 2024. *Civil War*: A Film Review. *Crime, Media, Culture*, August 9.

Brisman, Avi, and Alison Rau. 2009. From Fear of Crime to Fear of Nature: The Problem with Permitting Loaded, Concealed Firearms in National Parks. *Golden Gate University Environmental Law Journal* 2(2): 255–72.

Brisman, Avi, and Nigel South. 2013a. Introduction: Horizons, Issues, and Relationships in Green Criminology. In *Routledge International Handbook of Green Criminology*, ed. Nigel South and Avi Brisman, 1–23. Abingdon, Oxon, U.K., and New York: Routledge.

Brisman, Avi, and Nigel South. 2013b. Resource Wealth, Power, Crime, and Conflict. In *Emerging Issues in Green Criminology: Exploring Power, Justice and Harm*, ed. Reece Walters, Diane Solomon Westerhuis and Tanya Wyatt, 57–71. Basingstoke, Hampshire, U.K.: Palgrave Macmillan.

Brisman, Avi, and Nigel South. 2014. *Green Cultural Criminology: Constructions of Environmental Harm, Consumerism, and Resistance to Ecocide*. Abingdon, Oxon, U.K., and New York: Routledge.

Brisman, Avi, and Nigel South. 2017a. Consumer technologies, crime and environmental implications. In *The Routledge Handbook of Technology, Crime and Justice*, ed. M.R. McGuire and Thomas J. Holt, 310–24. London and New York: Routledge.

Brisman, Avi, and Nigel South. 2017b. Criminología verde cultural [Green cultural criminology]. In *Introducción a la criminología verde. Conceptos para nuevos horizontes y diálogos socioambientales [Introduction to Green Criminology: Concepts for New Horizons and Socio-Environmental Dialogues]*, ed. Hanneke Mol, David Rodríguez Goyes, Nigel South, and Avi Brisman, 97–127. Bogotá, Colombia: Editorial Temis S.A. and Universidad Antonio Nariño, Fondo Editorial.

Brisman, Avi, and Nigel South. 2017c. Green Cultural Criminology, Intergenerational (In)equity and "Life Stage Dissolution." In *Greening Criminology in the 21st Century: Contemporary Debates and Future Directions in the Study of Environmental Harm*, ed. Matthew Hall, Jennifer Maher, Angus Nurse, Gary Potter, Nigel South and Tanya Wyatt, 219–32. Abingdon, Oxon, U.K., and New York: Routledge.

Brisman, Avi, and Nigel South. 2018. Green Cultural Criminology. In *Routledge Handbook of Critical Criminology*, 2nd ed., ed. Walter S. DeKeseredy and Molly Dragiewicz, 132–42. London and New York: Routledge.

Brisman, Avi, and Nigel South. 2020. Toward a Green Cultural Criminology of the South. In *Routledge International Handbook of Green Criminology*, 2nd ed., ed. Avi Brisman and Nigel South, 624–37. Abingdon, Oxon, U.K., and New York: Routledge.

Brisman, Avi, and Nigel South. 2022. Criminologia verde cultural: Explorando a literature e narrativas culturais indígenas da América Latina [Green cultural criminology: Exploring literary and Indigenous cultural narratives from Latin America]. In *Introdução à criminologia verde: Perspectivas críticas, decoloniais e do Sul* [Introduction to Green Criminology: Southern, decolonial and critical perspectives], ed. Marília de Nardin Budó, David Rodríguez Goyes, Lorenzo Natali, Ragnhild Sollund and Avi Brisman, 103–15. São Paulo: Tirant lo Blanch.

Brisman, Avi, and Nigel South. 2023. Green Criminology. In *The Oxford Handbook of Criminology*, 7th ed., Alison Liebling, Shadd Maruna, and Lesley McAra, 519–39. Oxford, U.K.: Oxford University Press.

Brisman, Avi, Nigel South, and Reece Walters. 2018a. Climate Apartheid and Environmental Refugees. In *The Palgrave Handbook on Criminology and the Global South*, ed. Kerry Carrington, Russell Hogg, John Scott and Máximo Sozzo, 301–21. London: Palgrave Macmillan.

Brisman, Avi, Nigel South, and Reece Walters. 2018b. Southernizing Green Criminology: Human Dislocation, Environmental Injustice, and Climate Apartheid. *Justice, Power and Resistance* 2(1): 1–21.

Brisman, Avi, Nigel South, and Reece Walters. 2020. Global Environmental Divides and Dislocations: Climate Apartheid, Atmospheric Injustice, and the Blighting of the Planet. In *Routledge International Handbook of Green Criminology*, 2nd ed., ed. Avi Brisman and Nigel South, 187–204. Abingdon, Oxon, U.K., and New York: Routledge.

Brisman, Avi, Nigel South, and Rob White. 2015. Toward a Criminology of Environment-Conflict Relationships. In *Environmental Crime and Social Conflict: Contemporary and Emerging Issues,* ed. Avi Brisman, Nigel South and Rob White, 1–38. Surrey, U.K.: Ashgate.

Broderick, Mick. 1993. Surviving Armageddon: Beyond the Imagination of Disaster. *Science Fiction Studies* 20(3) [November]. Available at: https://www.depauw.edu /sfs/backissues/61/broderick61art.htm.

Brody, Richard. 2018. "Avengers: Infinity War," Reviewed: The Latest Marvel Movie Is a Two-and-a-Half-Hour Ad for All the Previous Marvel Movies. *The New Yorker,* April 27. Available at: https://www.newyorker.com/culture/richard-brody/avengers -infinity-war-reviewed-the-latest-marvel-movie-is-a-two-and-a-half-hour-ad-for-all -the-previous-marvel-movies.

Brody, Richard. 2019. Martin Scorsese's Radical Attack on Marvel Movies. *The New Yorker*, November 6. Available at: https://www.newyorker.com/culture /cultural-comment/martin-scorsese-avenges-the-auteur.

Brooks, David. 2023. What If We're the Bad Guys Here? *The New York Times*, August 4: A18. Published online as "What If We're the Bad Guys Here?" on August

2, 2023, at: https://www.nytimes.com/2023/08/02/opinion/trump-meritocracy
-educated.html.

Brooks, Katherine. 2017. How "The Handmaid's Tale" Villains Were Inspired by Trump. *HuffPost*, May 24. Available at: https://www.huffpost.com/entry/-handmaids-tale-villains-inspired-by-trump_n_5925bf4ce4b0ec129d31a7b3.

Brooks, Max. 2003. *The Zombie Survival Guide: Complete Protection from the Living Dead*. New York: Broadway Books/Random House, Inc.

Brooks, Max. 2006. *World War Z: An Oral History of the Zombie War*. New York: Broadway Books/Random House, Inc.

Brown, Jennifer. 2013. *Cannibalism in Literature and Film*. Basingstoke, Hampshire, U.K.: Palgrave Macmillan.

Browne, S. G. 2009. *Breathers: A Zombie's Lament*. New York: Broadway Books/The DoubleDay Publishing Group/Random House.

Bruney, Gabrielle. 2019. Francis Ford Coppola Thinks Marvel Movies Are "Despicable." *Esquire*, October 20. Available at: https://www.esquire.com/news-politics/a29526467/francis-ford-coppola-marvel-martin-scorsese-despicable/.

Brunton, John. 2020. "Nature Is Taking Back Venice": Wildlife Returns to Tourist-Free City. *The Guardian*, March 20. Available at: https://www.theguardian.com/environment/2020/mar/20/nature-is-taking-back-venice-wildlife-returns-to-tourist-free-city.

Buell, Lawrence. 1995. *The Environmental Imagination: Thoreau, Nature Writing, and the Formation of American Culture*. Cambridge, MA, and London: Belknap Press of Harvard University Press.

Buell, Lawrence, Ursula K. Heise, and Karen Thornber. 2011. Literature and Environment. *Annual Review of Environment and Resources* 36: 417–40. https://doi.org/10.1146/annurev-environ-111109-144855.

Burke, Daniel. 2020. The Religious Roots of Trump's Magical Thinking on Coronavirus. *CNN*, May 21. Available at: https://www.cnn.com/2020/05/21/politics/trump-magical-thinking-peale-coronavirus/index.html.

Butler, Erik. 2010. *Metamorphoses of the Vampire in Literature and Film: Cultural Transformations in Europe, 1732–1933*. Rochester, NY: Boydell & Brewer/Camden House.

Butler, Judith. 1990. *Gender Trouble: Feminism and the Subversion of Identity*. New York and London: Routledge.

Butler, Judith. 1993. *Bodies That Matter: On the Discursive Limits of "Sex."* Abingdon, Oxon, U.K., and New York: Routledge.

Byron, Glennis. 2012. Global Gothic. In *A New Companion to the Gothic*, ed. David Punter, 367–78. West Sussex, U.K.: Wiley-Blackwell.

Calderone, Michael, and Nick Baumann. 2017. Hiring Another Anti-Trump Voice Expands Opinions Represented in Paper, New York Times Says. *HuffPost*, April 14. Available at: https://www.huffpost.com/entry/bret-stephens-new-york-times_n_58f12c80e4b0b9e9848bed3e.

Callicott, J. Baird, and Michael P. Nelson, eds. 1998. *The Great New Wilderness Debate: An Expansive Collection of Writings Defining Wilderness from John Muir to Gary Snyder*. Athens, GA, and London: University of Georgia Press.

Caputi, Mary. 2013. *Feminism and Power: The Need for Critical Theory*. Lanham, MD: Lexington Books.

Cardona, Maria. 2019. We Cannot Allow "The Handmaid's Tale" to Become Reality TV. *The Hill*, May 17. Available at: https://thehill.com/opinion/civil-rights/444054 -we-cannot-allow-the-handmaids-tale-to-become-reality-tv/.

Carlson, Kit. 2022. *The Book of Killer Plants: A Field Guide to Nature's Deadliest Creations.* Illustrated by Emily Sullivan. Kennebunkport, ME: Cider Mill Press.

Carmichael, Callie, and Ariana Triggs. 2023. British Couple Sailing through "Orca Alley" Gets Attacked by Hungry Killer Whales. *USA Today/AP Press*, May 26. Available at: https://www.usatoday.com/videos/news/2023/05/26/terrifying -moment-killer-whales-attack-boat-sailing-orca-alley/11971375002/.

Carnes, Nicholas, and Lilly J. Goren. 2023. An Introduction to the Politics of the Marvel Cinematic Universe. In *The Politics of the Marvel Cinematic Universe*, ed. Nicholas Carnes and Lilly J. Goren, 1–15. Lawrence: University Press of Kansas.

Carpentier, Megan. 2011. Dick Cheney: Organ Grinder to George Bush's Monkey. *The Guardian*, August 30. Available at: https://www.theguardian.com/commentisfree /cifamerica/2011/aug/30/dick-cheney-memoir-george-bush.

Carrier, Nicolas. 2023. Monstrosity, Correctional Healing, and the Limits of Penal Abolitionism. *Crime Media Culture* 19(1): 95–113.

Carroll, Chloe. 2021. What Monsters Tell Us about the Modern World. RTÉ News and Current Affairs (*RTÉ News/Nuacht RTÉ*), May 25. Available at: https://www .rte.ie/brainstorm/2021/0525/1223784-monster-theory-monsters-society-culture -othering/.

Carroll, Noël. 1987. The Nature of Horror. *The Journal of Aesthetics and Art Criticism* 46(1) [Autumn]: 51–59.

Carroll, Noël. 1990. *The Philosophy of Horror; or, Paradoxes of the Heart.* New York: Routledge.

Carter, Jamie. 2024. Annular Solar Eclipse 2024: Everything You Need to Know about the Next Solar Eclipse. *Space.com*, April 9. Available at: https://www.space.com /annular-solar-eclipse-oct-2-2024-guide.

Carty, Magan. 2023. Orcas Are Ramming into Boats, But Experts Warn against Calling It Revenge on Humans. *CBC Radio*, July 3. Available at: https://www.cbc .ca/radio/thecurrent/orca-boat-incidents-social-media-reaction-1.6895465.

Casanova-Vizcaíno, Sandra, and Inés Ordiz, eds. 2017. *Latin American Gothic in Literature and Culture.* New York and Abingdon, Oxon, U.K.: Routledge.

Cassino, Dan. 2023. Men and Supermen: Gender and (Over)Compensation in the Marvel Cinematic Universe. In *The Politics of the Marvel Cinematic Universe*, ed. Nicholas Carnes and Lilly J. Goren, 249–65. Lawrence: University Press of Kansas.

Cavanagh, Niamh. 2020. Out for Blood: Rogue Pod of Orcas Attacking Boats in Revenge for Harpoon Slaughter by Poachers, Expert Warns. *The Sun*, October 1. Available at: https://www.the-sun.com/news/1563875/orca-attacks-boats-expert -revenge/.

Cavin, Tony. 2022. Why NPR Isn't Using the Word "Manifesto." *National Public Radio*, May 15. Available at: https://www.npr.org/2022/05/15/1099014432/why -npr-isnt-using-the-word-manifesto.

CBS/AFP. 2024. Missing Mother Found Dead inside 16-Foot-Long Python after It Swallowed Her Whole in Indonesia. *CBS News*, June 8. Available at: https://www .cbsnews.com/news/python-swallows-woman-whole-indonesia/.

CBS/AP. 2017. Villagers "Shocked" to Find Man Swallowed Whole by Python. *CBS News*, March 30. Available at: https://www.cbsnews.com/news/man-eaten-python -snake-indonesia-attacked-from-behind-sulawesi/.

Chait, Jonathan. 2017. Social Darwinism Is What Truly Guides Trump. *Intelligencer/New York Magazine*, June 25. Available at: https://nymag.com/intelligencer/2017/06/social -darwinism-is-what-truly-guides-trump.html.

Chamanara, Sanaz, S. Arman Ghaffarizadeh, and Kaveh Madani. 2023. The Environ-mental Footprint of Bitcoin Mining Across the Globe: Call for Urgent Action. *Earth's Future* 11 [October 24]: e2023EF003871. https://doi.org/10.1029/2023EF003871.

Chamary, JV. 2018. Is Thanos Right about Overpopulation In "Avengers: Infinity War"? *Forbes*, April 30. Available at: https://www.forbes.com/sites/jvchamary/2018 /04/30/avengers-infinity-war-overpopulation/#.

Chan, Queenie Hoi Shan, Rhonda Stroud, Zita Martins, and Hikaru Yabuta. 2020. Concerns of Organic Contamination for Sample Return Space Missions. *Space Science Reviews* 216(4): 1–40. https://doi.org/10.1007/s11214-020-00678-7.

Chang, Kenneth. 2024. SpaceX's 3rd Starship Launch Outdoes First 2. *The New York Times*, March 15: A20. Published online as "SpaceX Blazes Forward with Latest Starship Launch," on March 14, 2024, at: https://www.nytimes.com/2024/03/14 /science/spacex-starship-rocket-launch.html.

Chang, Kenneth. 2025a. Blue Origin Scrubs New Glenn Rocket's Debut Launch. *The New York Times*, January 12 (updated January 13), at: https://www.nytimes.com /live/2025/01/12/science/blue-origin-launch-new-glenn.

Chang, Kenneth. 2025b. Wait May Be Over for the Launch of Bezos' Big New Glenn Rocket. *The New York Times*, January 11: A21. Published online as "The Very Long Wait for Jeff Bezos' Big Rocket Is Coming to an End," on January 11, 2025, at: https:// www.nytimes.com/2025/01/11/science/blue-origin-jeff-bezos-new-glenn-launch.html.

Chenowith, Robin. 2019. Rudine Sims Bishop: "Mother" of Multicultural Children's Literature. College of Education and Human Ecology, *Education and Human Ecology News*, The Ohio State University, September 5. Available at: https://ehe.osu .edu/news/listing/rudine-sims-bishop-diverse-childrens-books.

Chester, Lynne. 2020. The 2019–2020 Australian Bushfires: A Potent Mix of Climate Change, Problematisation, Indigenous Disregard, a Fractured Federation, Volunteerism, Social Media, and More. *Review of Evolutionary Political Economy* 1(2): 245–64. https://doi.org/10.1007/s43253-020-00019-y.

Cheuse, Alan. 2008a. In a "World Made by Hand," Kunstler Reassures. *All Things Considered, National Public Radio*, March 24. Available at: https://www.npr.org /templates/story/story.php?storyId=88984792.

Cheuse, Alan. 2008b. Starting Over: A Small Town Tries to Move On in Postapocalyptic America. *Chicago Tribune*, March 8. Available at: https://www.chicagotribune.com /2008/03/08/starting-over-32/.

Chomsky, Noam. 2014. Why Americans Are Paranoid About Everything (Including Zombies). *AlterNet*, February 14. Available at: http://www.alternet.org/noam -chomsky-why-americans-are-paranoid-about-everything-including-zombies.

Chow, Denise. 2018. Sorry, Elon Musk. New Study Says Terraforming Mars Is Simply Impossible. *NBC News*, August 9. Available at: https://www.nbcnews.com/mach /science/sorry-elon-musk-new-study-says-terraforming-mars-simply-impossible -ncna899021.

Chow, Denise. 2019. Jeff Bezos' Blue Moon: Here's What We Know So Far about Blue Origin's New Lunar Lander. *NBC News*, May 10. Available at: https://www.nbcnews.com/mach/science/jeff-bezos-blue-moon-here-s-what-we-know-so-ncna1004326.

Chow, Denise, Al Roker, Jesse Kirsch, Kate Snow, and Maura Barrett. 2024. Highlights from the Total Solar Eclipse: Live Videos, Photos and Updates. *NBC News*, April 8. Available at: https://www.nbcnews.com/science/space/live-blog/solar-eclipse-2024-live-updates-rcna145900.

Christie, Lauren. 2020. The Evolution of Monsters in Children's Literature. *Palgrave Communications* 6(41): [1–7]. https://doi.org/10.1057/s41599-020-0414-7.

Christy, Bryan. 2008. *The Lizard King: The True Crimes and Passions of the World's Greatest Reptile Smugglers*. New York: Twelve/Hatchette Book Group.

Ciccarelli, Raffaella. 2020. Scientists Think They Know Why Orcas Are Ramming Boasts off Spanish Coast. *9 News*, October 1. Available at: https://www.9news.com.au/world/orca-attacks-scientists-think-they-know-why-killer-whales-are-ramming-vessels-off-spanish-coast/004f5287-37d1-4dbd-86a6-8bb6aaff1d70.

Ciccarelli, Raffaella. 2022a. Five Rescued after Orcas Attack and Sink Boat off Portuguese Coast. *9 News*, August 4. Available at: https://www.9news.com.au/world/orca-attack-five-rescued-after-killer-whales-attack-and-sink-boat-off-portuguese-coast/d7739372-f0a6-4d33-b09a-ade075700c2e.

Ciccarelli, Raffaella. 2022b. Large Pod of Orcas Sink Sailboat off Portugal as "Scary" Encounters Continue. *9 News*, November 9. Available at: https://www.9news.com.au/world/orcas-portugal-large-pod-sink-sailboat-off--viana-do-castle-as-scary-encounters-continue/1c09a9d7-9351-4261-80b3-fbbf3325a483.

Ciccarelli, Raffaella. 2023. "There's Something Down There": Moment Sailor Realised Boat Was Being "Attacked" by Apex Predator. *9 News*, May 9. Available at: https://www.9news.com.au/world/orca-attack-moment-british-sailor-greg-blackburn-realised-boat-being-attacked-tangier-strait-of-gibraltar/05fe4dec-6442-4b07-a7fc-a78ab3bcc507.

Clark, Richard D. 2013. The Control of Conflict Minerals in Africa and a Preliminary Assessment of the Dodd-Frank Wall Street Reform and Consumer Act. In *Routledge International Handbook of Green Criminology*, ed. Nigel South and Avi Brisman, 214–29. Abingdon, Oxon, U.K., and New York: Routledge.

Clark, Stuart. 2023. Space Race 2.0: Why Europe Is Joining the New Dash to the Moon. *The Guardian*, November 26. Available at: https://www.theguardian.com/science/2023/nov/26/europe-moon-space-race-esa-india-russia-china-japan.

Clark, Zoila. 2014. The Myth of La Llorona in the Film Mama. *Studies in Gothic Fiction* 3(2): 64–80.

Clasen, Mathias. 2017. *Why Horror Seduces*. New York: Oxford University Press.

Clayton, Abené. 2023. An "Aggressive" Sea Otter Is Snatching Surfers' Boards. Experts Are Puzzled. *The Guardian*, July 12. Available at: https://www.theguardian.com/us-news/2023/jul/12/sea-otter-surfing-santa-cruz-california.

Cleveland Clinic. 2023. The Science Behind Zombie Viruses and Infections. *Cleveland Clinic: healthessentials: Health Conditions: Infectious Disease*, March 29. Available at: https://health.clevelandclinic.org/zombie-virus.

Cohen, Jeffrey Jerome. 1996. Monster Culture (Seven Theses). In *Monster Theory: Reading Culture*, ed. Jeffrey Jerome Cohen, 3–25. Minneapolis: University of Minnesota Press.

Cohen, Rebecca. 2023. A Man Who Started a Website That Tracks Orca Incidents with Boats Near Spain and Portugal Said That Encounters Happen at Least Every Day Now. *Business Insider*, June 15. Available at: https://www.businessinsider.com /orca-encounters-happening-every-day-near-spain-and-portugal-2023-6.

Cohen, Rebecca, and Jessica Orwig. 2023. White Gladis, the Killer Whale Who Could Be behind Orcas Attacking Boats, May Have Been Pregnant When She Started the "Uprising." *Business Insider*, June 29. Available at: https://www.businessinsider.com /white-gladis-orca-attacking-boats-pregnant-killer-whale-uprising-2023-6.

Cohen, Roger. 2020. A Silent Spring Is Saying Something. *The New York Times*, March 28: A23. Published online as "A Silent Spring Is Saying Something," on March 27, 2020, at: https://www.nytimes.com/2020/03/27/opinion/coronavirus-pandemic .html.

Cokinos, Christopher. 2023. H. G. Wells' Alien-Invasion Novel Is Night-Before-Halloween Scary. But It's a Lot More Too. *Los Angeles Times*, October 30. Available at: https://www.latimes.com/opinion/story/2023-10-30/halloween-h-g-wells-war-of -the-worlds-science-fiction-space-invaders.

Cole, Samantha. 2023. There's Something Sad About Our Obsession with the "Orca Uprising." *Vice*, June 16. Available at: https://www.vice.com/en/article/m7bbnn /orca-uprising-attacking-boats.

Collard, Andrée, with Joyce Contrucci. 1989. *Rape of the Wild: Man's Violence against Animals and the Earth*. Bloomington and Indianapolis: Indiana University Press.

Collier, Peter. 1970. Ecological Destruction Is a Condition of American Life: An Interview with Ecologist Paul Ehrlich. *Mademoiselle* (April): 188–89, 291–94, 296, 298.

Collins, John Jay. 2014. What Is Apocalyptic Literature? In *The Oxford Handbook of Apocalyptic Literature*, ed. John Jay Collins, 1–18. Oxford, U.K.: Oxford University Press.

Collins, Gail. 2012a. Another Boom Year. *The New York Times*, December 13: A35. Published online as "Another Boom Year," on December 12, 2012, at: https://www .nytimes.com/2012/12/13/opinion/collins-another-boom-year.html.

Collins, Gail. 2012b. Of Hooters, Zombies, and Senators. *The New York Times*, October 6: A21. Published online as "Of Hooters, Zombies, and Senators," on October 5, 2012, at: https://www.nytimes.com/2012/10/06/opinion/collins-of -hooters-zombies-and-senators.html.

Collins, Gail. 2013. Senators Bearing Arms. *The New York Times*, March 9: A17. Published online as "Senators Bearing Arms," on March 8, 2013, at: https://www .nytimes.com/2013/03/09/opinion/collins-senators-bearing-arms.html.

Collins, Margo, and Elson Bond. 2011. "Off the Page and into Your Brains!": New Millennium Zombies and the Scourge of Hopeful Apocalypses. In *Better Off Dead: The Evolution of the Zombie as Post-Human*, ed. Deborah Christie and Sarah Juliet Lauro, 187–204. New York: Fordham University Press.

ComingSoon.Net. n.d. "Goodbye Earth: Everything to Know about Ahn Eun-Jin New Netflix K-Drama." Available at: https://www.comingsoon.net/k-drama /news/1679163-goodbye-earth-everything-to-know-about-ahn-eun-jin-new-netflix -k-drama.

Conrad, Joseph. 1899[2010]. *Heart of Darkness*. New York: Tribeca Books.

Cooper, Dave. 2020. Nature Is Still in Charge. *The Cumberland* 54(6) [May/June]: 11.

Cooper, Dave. 2023. Thinking about Road Kill. *The Cumberland* 57(6) [July–August]: 5.

Corcione, Adryan. 2020. Eco-fascism: What It Is, Why It's Wrong, and How to Fight It. *Teen Vogue*, April 30. Available at: https://www.teenvogue.com/story/what-is-ecofascism-explainer.

Corrigan, Sophie. 2020. *The Not Bad Animals*. Minneapolis, MN: Francis Lincoln Children's Books/The Quarto Group.

Cotter, Holland. 1993. At the Whitney, Provocation and Theory Meet Head-On. *The New York Times*, August 13: C23. Available online as "Review Art; At the Whitney, Provocation and Theory Meet Head-On," at: https://www.nytimes.com/1993/08/13/arts/review-art-at-the-whitney-provocation-and-theory-meet-head-on.html.

Coupland, Douglas. 2010. *Player One: What Is to Become of Us?* Toronto: House of Anansi Press.

Cowie, Zayne (with help from Pamela Drukerman, Leah Varjacques, and Julie Lunde). 2019. *Goodbye, Earth*. Illustrated by Joey Abisso. *The New York Times*, https://www.nytimes.com/2019/03/14/opinion/climate-change-march-goodbye-earth.html and https://int.nyt.com/data/documenthelper/671-goodbye-earth-story-for-adults/fc6ebe2bb70412ecc352/optimized/full.pdf.

Crandall, Bryan Ripley. 2022. "As In" An Award-Winning Writer: Kwame Alexander. In *More Mirrors, Windows, and Sliding Doors: A Period of Growth in African-American Young Adult Literature (2001–2021)*, ed. Steven T. Bickmore and Shanetia P. Clark, 33–44. Lanham, MD: Rowman and Littlefield.

Creamer, Colleen. 2022. In Congested National Parks, Roads Less Traveled. *The New York Times*, August 1: B6. Published online as "In 5 National Parks, Hidden Gems and Roads Less Traveled," on July 30, 2022, at: https://www.nytimes.com/2022/07/20/travel/national-parks-hidden-gems.html.

Crist, Meehan. 2020. What the Pandemic Means for Climate Change. *The New York Times*, March 29: SR4. Published online as "What the Coronavirus Means for Climate Change," on March 27, 2020, at: https://www.nytimes.com/2020/03/27/opinion/sunday/coronavirus-climate-change.html.

Cronon, William. 1995. The Trouble with Wilderness; or, Getting Back to the Wrong Nature. In *Uncommon Ground: Toward Reinventing Nature*, ed. William Cronon, 69–90. New York and London: W.W. Norton.

Cronon, William. 1996. The Trouble with Wilderness: Or, Getting Back to the Wrong Nature. *Environmental History* 1(1) [January]: 7–28.

Crosby, Sara L. 2014. Beyond Ecophilia: Edgar Allan Poe and the American Tradition of Ecohorror. *ISLE: Interdisciplinary Studies in Literature and Environment* 21(3) [Summer]: 513–25.

Crossette, Barbara. 1999. Korean Famine Toll: More Than Two Million. *The New York Times*, August 20: A6, at: https://www.nytimes.com/1999/08/20/world/korean-famine-toll-more-than-2-million.html.

Crowley, Kinsey. 2023. Florida Woman Captures Everglades Alligator Eating Python. Wildlife Enthusiasts Rejoice. *USA Today*, December 22. Available at: https://www.usatoday.com/story/news/nation/2023/12/22/burmese-python-eating-alligator/72010210007/.

Dacosta, Shaun. 2023. Killer Whale Boat Attack Videos Might Not Be What They Seem. *BBC News*, June 2023. Available at: https://www.bbc.com/news/newsbeat-65949040.

D'Alessandro, Anthony. 2018. "Black Panther" Poised to Pounce on B.O.: Advance Ticket Sales Beating "Captain America: Civil War." *Deadline*, January 10. Available at: https://deadline.com/2018/01/black-panther-box-office-projection-fandango -advance-ticket-sales-marvel-1202239707/.

Daly, Mary. 1978. *Gyn/ecology: The Metaethics of Radical Feminism*. Boston, MA: Beacon Press.

Daly, Natasha. 2020. Fake Animal News Abounds on Social Media as Coronavirus Upends Life. *National Geographic*, March 20. Available at: https://www .nationalgeographic.com/animals/article/coronavirus-pandemic-fakeanimal-viral -social-media-posts, March 22, at https://www.nationalgeographic.co.uk/animals /2020/03/fake-animal-news-abounds-on-social-media-as-coronavirus-upends-life.

Damm, Johnny. 2023. Monsters Are Real. *Crime Media Culture* 19(2): 325–26. https:// doi.org/10.1177/17416590231173833.

Danner, Mark. 2014. How Dick Cheney Became the Most Powerful Vice President in History. *The Nation*, February 11. Available at: https://www.thenation.com/article /archive/how-dick-cheney-became-most-powerful-vice-president-history/.

Dargis, Manohla. 2008. Something Lethal Lurks in the Rustling Trees. *The New York Times*, June 13, at: https://www.nytimes.com/2008/06/13/movies/13happ.html.

Darian-Smith, Eve. 2021. Dying for the Economy: Disposable People and Economies of Death in the Global North. *State Crime Journal* 10(1): 61–79.

Dartnell, Lewis. 2017. Why Would Aliens Even Bother with Earth? *Literary Hub*, May 8. Available at: https://lithub.com/why-would-aliens-even-bother-with-earth/.

Darwin, Charles. 1859. *The Origin of Species by Means of Natural Selection*. London: John Murray.

Davey, Graham C. L. 1994. The "Disgusting" Spider: The Role of Disease and Illness in the Perpetuation of Fear of Spiders. *Society and Animals* 2(1): 17–25. Available at: https://doi.org/10.1163/156853094X00045.

Davies, Dave. 2011. The High Probability of Finding "Life Beyond Earth." *Fresh Air, National Public Radio*, April 1. Transcript available at: http://www.npr.org /templates/transcript/transcript.php?storyId=135040012.

Davies, Dave. 2012. Climate "Weirdness" Throws Ecosystems "Out of Kilter." *Fresh Air, National Public Radio*, August 14. Available at: http://www.npr.org/templates /transcript/transcript.php?storyId=158756024; transcript available at: http://www .npr.org/templates/transcript/transcript.php?storyId=158756024.

Davies, Thom. 2018. Toxic Space and Time: Slow Violence, Necropolitics, and Petrochemical Pollution. *Annals of the American Association of Geographers* 108(6): 1537–1553. https://doi.org/10.1080/24694452.2018.1470924.

Davies, Thom. 2022. Slow Violence and Toxic Geographies: "Out of Sight" to Whom? *EPC: Politics and Space* 40(2): 409–27. https://doi.org/10.1177/2399654419841063.

Davis, Janae, Alex A. Moulton, Levi Van Sant, and Brian Williams. 2019. Anthropocene, Capitalocene, . . . Plantationocene? A Manifesto for Ecological Justice in an Age of Global Crises. *Geography Compass* 13(5): e12438. https://doi.org/10.1111/gec3 .12438.

Davis, Julie Hirschfeld, Sheryl Gay Stolberg, and Thomas Kaplan. 2018. In Vulgar Terms, Trump Disparages Some Immigrants. *The New York Times*, January 12: A1. Published online as "Trump Alarms Lawmakers with Disparaging Words for Haiti and Africa," on January 11, 2018, at: https://www.nytimes.com/2018/01/11/us /politics/trump-shithole-countries.html.

Davis, Mike. 2010. Who Will Build the Ark? *New Left Review* 61(January–February): 29–46.

Dayton, Emily. 2021. Amazon Statistics You Should Know: Opportunities to Make the Most of America's Top Online Marketplace. *Big Commerce.* Available at: https:// www.bigcommerce.co.uk/blog/amazon-statistics/.

Deckard, Sharae. 2013. "Uncanny States": Global Eco-Gothic and the World-Ecology in Rana Dasgupta's *Tokyo Cancelled.* In *EcoGothic,* ed. Andrew Smith and William Hughes, 177–94. Manchester, U.K.: Manchester University Press.

Dederer, Claire. 2017. What Do We Do with the Art of Monstrous Men? *The Paris Review,* November 20. Available at: https://www.theparisreview.org/blog/2017/11 /20/art-monstrous-men/.

de Froideville, Sarah Monod, and Andrew Gibbs. 2023. Silencing Paritutu. *Crime, Law and Social Change* 80(3) [October]: 287–306. https://doi.org/10.1007/s10611 -023-10083-0.

DeGregori, Thomas R. 1982. Apocalypse Yesterday. In *The Apocalyptic Vision in America: Interdisciplinary Essays on Myth and Culture,* ed. Lois Parkinson Zamora, 206–21. Bowling Green, OH: Bowling Green University Popular Press.

Deibler, Emily. 2015. The Sublime's Effects in Gothic Fiction. *The Artifice,* December 29. Available at: https://the-artifice.com/the-sublimes-effects-in-gothic-fiction/.

DeLuca, Ashleigh. 2022. Breaking Down the Hidden Messages in "Black Panther: Wakanda Forever." *Temple Now,* November 11. Available at: https://news.temple.edu /news/2022-11-11/breaking-down-hidden-messages-black-panther-wakanda-forever.

Denby, David. 2014. Endgames. *The New Yorker,* July 7 and 14: 94–95. Available at: https://www.newyorker.com/magazine/2014/07/07/endgames.

Dendle, Peter. 2001. *The Zombie Movie Encyclopedia.* Jefferson, NC: McFarland.

Dendle, Peter. 2011. Zombie Movies and the "Millennial Generation." In *Better Off Dead: The Evolution of the Zombie as Post-Human,* ed. Deborah Christie and Sarah Juliet Lauro, 175–86. New York: Fordham University Press.

De Semlyen, Nick. 2019. The Irishman Week: Empire's Martin Scorsese Interview. *Empire,* November 7. Available at: https://www.empireonline.com/movies/features /irishman-week-martin-scorsese-interview/.

Desta, Yohana. 2018. *Black Panther*'s Four-Day Total: $427 Million Worldwide and a Slew of Shattered Records. *Vanity Fair,* February 20. Available at: https://www .vanityfair.com/hollywood/2018/02/black-panther-box-office-domestic-worldwide.

Dewan, Pandora. 2023. Ship Captain Attacked by Killer Whales Says People Gearing Up to Shoot Them. *Newsweek,* June 1. Available at: https://www.newsweek.com /ship-captain-attacked-killer-whale-orca-revenge-shoot-1803911.

Dickel, Sascha. 2013. Beyond Cynicism: Climate Engineering Technologies and Vegan Diets as Alternative Solutions for Climate Change. In *Global Environmental Change: New Drivers for Resistance, Crime, and Terrorism?* ed. Achim Maas, Balázs Bodó, Clementine Burnley, Irina Comardicea, and Roger Roffey, 243–59. Baden-Baden, Germany: Nomos.

Dickie, Gloria. 2018. As Polar Bear Attacks Increase in Warming Arctic, a Search for Solutions. *YaleEnvironment360,* Yale School of the Environment, December

19. Available at: https://e360.yale.edu/features/as-polar-bear-attacks-increase-in -warming-arctic-a-search-for-solutions.

Dika, Vera. 1996. From Dracula—with Love. In *The Dread of Difference: Gender and the Horror Film*, ed. Barry Keith Grant. Austin: University of Texas Press.

Dimaline, Cherie. 2023. *An Anthology of Monsters: How Story Saves Us from Anxiety.* Edmonton, Canada: University of Alberta Press and Canadian Literature Centre/ Centre de littérature canadienne.

Dixon, Deborah P. 2008. The Blade and the Claw: Science, Art, and the Creation of the Lab-Borne Monster. *Social &Cultural Geography* 9(6): 671–92. https://doi.org /10.1080/14649360802292488.

Donn, Natasha. 2021. Scientists at Loss to Explain Killer Whales "Apparent Aggressive Behaviour." *Portugal Resident*, September 9. Available at: https:// www.portugalresident.com/scientists-at-loss-to-explain-killer-whales-apparent -aggressive-behaviour/.

Donn, Natasha. 2022a. Five Flee Sinking Sailboat after Orca "Intervention" off Sines. *Portugal Resident*, July 31. Available at: https://www.portugalresident.com/five-flee -sinking-sailboat-after-orca-intervention-off-sines-coast/.

Donn, Natasha. 2022b. Second Orca "Attack" on Day Sailing Boat Sunk near Sines. *Portugal Resident*, August 9. Available at: https://www.portugalresident.com/second -orca-attack-on-day-sailing-boat-sunk-near-sines/.

Douglas, Mary. 1966[2002]. *Purity and Danger: An Analysis of Concept of Pollution and Taboo.* Abingdon, Oxon, U.K., and New York: Routledge and Kegan Paul/ Routledge Classics.

Douthat, Ross. 2017. "The Handmaid's Tale," and Ours. *The New York Times*, May 24, at: https://www.nytimes.com/2017/05/24/opinion/handmaids-tale-and-ours.html.

Doyle, Kelly. 2020. Edible Humans: Undermining the Human in *The Walking Dead* and Other Zombie Television. In *Man-Eating Monsters: Anthropocentrism and Popular Culture*, ed. Dina Khapaeva, 97–114. Bingley, U.K.: Emerald Publishing Limited.

Drezner, Daniel W. 2011. *Theories of International Politics and Zombies.* Princeton, NJ: Princeton University Press.

Drezner, Daniel W. 2014. Metaphor of the Living Dead: Or, the Effect of the Zombie Apocalypse on Public Policy Discourse. *Social Research: An International Quarterly* 81(4) [Winter]: 825–49. Available at: https://www.jstor.org/stable/26549655.

Duclos, Denis. 1998. *The Werewolf Complex: America's Fascination with Violence.* New York: Berg Publishers/Bloomsbury Publishing.

Dumont, Katana. 2022. Did You Know the NRA Supported Gun Control When the Black Panther Party Was Armed. *Yahoo!News*, June 17. Available at: https://news .yahoo.com/did-know-nra-supported-gun-130553292.html.

Dunn, Marcia. 2022. Jeff Bezos Blasts into Space on Own Rocket: "Best Day Ever!" *AP News*, July 21. Available at: https://apnews.com/article/jeff-bezos-space -e0afeaa813ff0bdf23c37fe16fd34265.

Dunne, Tim. 2009. How Do We Secure the Environment? [Review of *Security and Environmental Change* by Simon Dalby, Polity, 2009]. *Times Higher Education* 1917 (October 8): 46.

Du Rées, Helena. 2001. Can Criminal Law Protect the Environment? *Journal of Scandinavian Studies in Criminology and Crime Prevention* 2(2): 109–26.

Ebert, Roger. 2004. The Day After Tomorrow. *RogerEbert.com*, May 28. Available at: https://www.rogerebert.com/reviews/the-day-after-tomorrow-2004.

Economist, The. 2015. The Force Is Strong in This Firm. December 19. Available at: https://www.economist.com/briefing/2015/12/19/the-force-is-strong-in-this-firm.

Eden Gallery. 2021. *What Is Fine Art?* July 11. Available at: https://www.eden-gallery .com/news/fine-art-definition.

Edmond, Charlotte. 2020. China's Air Pollution Has Overshot Pre-Pandemic Levels as Life Begins to Return. *World Economic Forum*, July 7. Available at: https://www .weforum.org/agenda/2020/07/pollution-co2-economy-china/.

Edmundson, Mark. 1997. *Nightmare on Main Street: Angels, Sadomasochism, and the Culture of Gothic*. Cambridge, MA: Harvard University Press.

Eggers, Dave. 2013. *The Circle*. New York: Alfred A. Knopf.

Eisner, Manuel Peter. 2012. Author Meets Critics: The Better Angels of Our Nature: Why Violence Has Decline (Critic). 68th Annual Meeting of the American Society of Criminology, Chicago, Illinois, November 15, 2012.

Eliason, Randall D. 2024. I Was Skeptical of the "Zombie" Trump Case. I Stand Corrected. *The New York Times*, May 31, at: https://www.nytimes.com/2024/05 /31/opinion/trump-trial-defense.html.

Ellison, Aaron M., and Lubonír Adamec. 2018. Preface. In *Carnivorous Plants: Physiology, Ecology, and Evolution*, ed. Aaron M. Ellison and Lubomír Adamec, xxiii–xxiv. Oxford, U.K.: Oxford University Press.

Ellis-Petersen, Hannah, Rebecca Ratcliffe, Sam Cowie, Joe Parkin Daniels, and Lily Kuo. 2020. "It's Positively Alpine!" Disbelief in Big Cities as Air Pollution Falls. *The Guardian*, April 11. Available at: https://www.theguardian.com/environment /2020/apr/11/positively-alpine-disbelief-air-pollution-falls-lockdown-coronavirus.

Emsley, Michael. 1982. The Evolution and Imminent Extinction of an Avaricious Species. In *The Apocalyptic Vision in America: Interdisciplinary Essays on Myth and Culture*, ed. Lois Parkinson Zamora, 183–205. Bowling Green, OH: Bowling Green University Popular Press.

Encarnación, Omar G. 2023. Spain Is Going to Be Fine. *The New York Times*, July 20, at: https://www.nytimes.com/2023/07/20/opinion/spain-election-sanchez-vox .html.

ESPN News Services. 2023. Orcas Attack Boat during Around-the-World Ocean Race. *ESPN*, June 23. Available at: https://www.espn.com/olympics/story/_/id/37903994 /orcas-attack-boat-world-ocean-race.

"Esquire Editors." 2019. Watchmen Writer Alan Moore's Take on Modern Superhero Movies Is Much Harsher Than Scorsese's. *Esquire Middle East*. November 19. Available at: https://www.esquireme.com/culture/film-and-tv/41153-watchmen -writer-alan-moores-take-on-modern-superhero-movies-is-much-harsher-than -scorseses.

Esteban, Ruth, Alfredo López, Álvaro Garcia de los Rios, Marisa Ferreira, Francisco Martinho, Paula Méndez-Fernandeza, Ezequiel Andréu, José C. García-Gómez, Liliana Olaya-Ponzone, Rocío Espada-Ruiz, Francisco J. Gil-Vera, Cristina Martín Bernal, Elvira Garcia-Bellido Capdevila, Marina Sequeira, and José A. Martínez-Cedeira. 2022. Killer Whales of the Strait of Gibraltar, an Endangered Subpopulation Showing a Disruptive Behavior. *Marine Mammal Science* 38(4) [October]: 1699–1709.

Estok, Simon C. 2009. Theorizing in a Space of Ambivalent Openness: Ecocriticism and Ecophobia. *ISLE: Interdisciplinary Studies in Literature and Environment*, 16(2) [Spring]: 203–25.

Fadulu, Lola. 2023. Shark Bites Swimmer in Queens in the City's First Known Attack Since the 1950s. *The New York Times*, August 9: A15. Published online as "Woman Is Bitten by Shark in First New York City Attack in Years," on August 8, 2023, at: https://www.nytimes.com/2023/08/08/nyregion/rockaway-beach-closed-shark -attack.html.

Fanon, Frantz. [1952] 2008. *Peau noire, masques blancs [Black Skin, White Masks.]* Translated by Richard Philcox. Paris: Éditions du Seuil/New York: Grove Press.

FashionTribes.com. 2007. "Zombies Plague the Silver Screen & the Zeitgeist. From 'Shaun of the Dead' to 'Dawn of the Dead,' Directors Like George Romero Help Us Deal With Our Paranoia & Fear of an Unseen Enemy + Top 10 Zombie Movies." May 25. Available at: https://fashiontribes.typepad.com/fashion/2007/05/zombies -plague-.html.

Faust, Kelly L., and David Kauzlarich. 2008. Hurricane Katrina: Victimization as a State Crime of Omission. *Critical Criminology: An International Journal* 16(2): 85–103.

Felton, Emmanuel. 2020a. The Coronavirus Meme About "Nature Is Healing" Is So Damn Funny. *BuzzFeed News*, April 7. Available at: https://www.buzzfeednews .com/article/emmanuelfelton/coronavirus-meme-nature-is-healing-we-are-the-virus.

Felton, Emmanuel. 2020b. The Townspeople Went Inside to Shelter. Then the Goats Arrived. *BuzzFeed News*, March 31. Available at: https://www.buzzfeednews.com /article/emmanuelfelton/coronavirus-town-empty-goats-wales.

Fernández, Alexia. 2019. Martin Scorsese Says Marvel Films Are "Not Cinema" as Josh Whedon and James Gunn Respond. *People*, October 4. Available at: https:// people.com/movies/martin-scorsese-slams-marvel-films-not-cinema/.

Ferrell, Jeff. 1999. Cultural Criminology. *Annual Review of Sociology* 25: 395–418.

Ferrell, Jeff, Keith Hayward, and Jock Young. 2015. *Cultural Criminology: An Invitation*, 2nd ed. London: SAGE.

Fiddler, Michael. 2013. Playing *Funny Games* in *The Last House on the Left*: The Uncanny and the "Home Invasion" Genre. *Crime Media Culture* 9(3): 281–99. https://doi.org/10.1177/1741659013511833.

Fiddler, Michael. 2019. Ghosts of Other Stories: A Synthesis of Hauntology, Crime, and Space. *Crime Media Culture* 15(3): 463–77. https://doi.org/10.1177 /1741659018788399.

Fifteen. 1994. World Starvation. Lyrics available at: https://genius.com/Fifteen-world -starvation-lyrics.

Fine, Camille. 2023. Boats off Spain's Coast Are Seeing More Killer Whales Touch, Push, and Even Turn Vessels. *USA Today*, June 13 (updated June 15). Available at: https://www.usatoday.com/story/news/world/2023/06/13/orcas-attacking-boats /70317257007/.

Fineman, Nicole. 2017. Beyond the Scream: What I Learned from Horror Movies. *The New York Times*, October 13. Available at: https://www.nytimes.com/2017/10/13 /us/horror-race-women-society.html.

Fisher, John A. 2013. High Art Versus Low Art. In *The Routledge Companion to Aesthetics,* 3rd ed., ed. Berys Gaut and Dominic McIver Lopes, 473–84. Abingdon,

Oxon, U.K., and New York: Routledge. Available at: https://spot.colorado.edu/~jafisher/OnLine%20papers/High%20Low%20Art%20Ch%2046.pdf.

Foltyn, Jacque Lynn. 2020. Foreword. In *Man-Eating Monsters: Anthropocentrism and Popular Culture*, ed. Dina Khapaeva, xi–xvi. Bingley, U.K.: Emerald Publishing Limited.

Fontana, Margherita. 2023. A Proposal for a Bunker Aesthetics from Paul Virilio's Archaeology to Virtual Architecture. In IMG23: Atti del IV Convegno Internazionale e Interdisciplinare su Immagini e Immaginazione [IMG23: Proceedings of 4th International and Interdisciplinary Conference on Images and Imagination], ed. Stefano Bruscaporci, Pamela Maiezza, Adriana Marra, Ilaria Trizio, Francesca Savini, and Alessandra Tata, 162–69. Alghero, Italy: Publica. Available at: https://www.publicapress.it/wp-content/uploads/2023/07/IMG2023-Proceedings.pdf.

Forbes. 2025. The World's Real-Time Billionaires. Available at: https://www.forbes.com/real-time-billionaires/#6fef93333d78.

Ford, Matt. 2022. Wildlife Shouldn't Suffer Because of Human Stupidity. *The New Republic*, August 17. Available at: https://newrepublic.com/article/167442/freya-walrus-killed-human-stupidity.

Foster, Gwendolyn Audrey. 2014. *Hoarders, Doomsday Preppers, and the Culture of Apocalypse*. New York: Palgrave Macmillan.

Foucault, Michel. [1961] 2006. [*Folie et Déraison: Histoire de la folie à l'âge Classique Madness and Civilization: A History of Insanity in the Age of Reason*]. Edited by Jean Khalfa. Translated by Jonathan Murphy. London and New York: Routledge.

Foucault, Michel. [1976] 2003. *"Society Must Be Defended": Lectures at the Collège de France, 1975–76*. Edited by Mauro Bertani and Alessandro Fontana. Translated by David Macey. New York: Picador.

Fox, Killian. 2021. Paul Mason: "Modern Fascism's Interests Are Being Represented in Government by Rightwing Populists." *The Guardian*, August 14. Available at: https://www.theguardian.com/books/2021/aug/14/paul-mason-how-to-stop-fascism.

Foy, Joseph J. 2010a. Introduction. Tuning in to Democratic Dissent: Oppositional Messaging in Popular Culture. In *Homer Simpson Marches on Washington: Dissent Through American Popular Culture*, ed. Timothy M. Dale and Joseph J. Foy, 1–17. Lexington: University Press of Kentucky.

Foy, Joseph J. 2010b. It Came from Planet Earth: Eco-Horror and the Politics of Postenvironmentalism in the Happening. In *Homer Simpson Marches on Washington: Dissent Through American Popular Culture*, ed. Timothy M. Dale and Joseph J. Foy, 167–88. Lexington: The University Press of Kentucky.

Francis, Beryl. 2012. Before and After Jaws: Changing Representations of Shark Attacks. *The Great Circle* 34(2): 44–64. Available at: http://www.jstor.org/stable/23622226.

Fraser, Steve. 2024. The End of the Future. *Jacobin*, March 2. Available at: https://jacobin.com/2024/03/left-politics-future-history-capitalism-progress.

Fredriksson, Tea. 2019. Abject (M)Othering: A Narratological Study of the Prison as an Abject and Uncanny Institution. *Critical Criminology: An International Journal* 27(2): 261–74. https://doi.org10.1007s10612-018-9412-0.

Friedman, Thomas L. 2006. Seeds for a Geo-Green Party. *The New York Times*, June 16: A6. Published online as "Seeds for a Geo-Green Party," on June 16, 2006, at: https://www.nytimes.com/2006/06/16/opinion/16friedman.html.

Friedman, Thomas L. 2016. We Are All Noah Now. *The New York Times*, September 7: A23. Published online as "We Are All Noah Now," on September 7, 2016, at: https://www.nytimes.com/2016/09/07/opinion/we-are-all-noah-now.html.

Friedman, Thomas L. 2020a. How We Broke the World. *The New York Times*, May 30, at: https://www.nytimes.com/2020/05/30/opinion/sunday/coronavirus-globalization.html.

Friedman, Thomas L. 2020b. We Need Herd Immunity from Trump and the Coronavirus. *The New York Times*, April 25, at: https://www.nytimes.com/2020/04/25/opinion/coronavirus-immunity-trump.html.

Froelich, Paula. 2020. Killer Whales Orchestrating Revenge Attacks on Boats off Spain. *New York Post*, October 10 (updated October 12). Available at: https://nypost.com/2020/10/10/killer-whales-orchestrating-revenge-attacks-on-boats-off-spain/.

Frosh, Stephen. 2013. *Hauntings: Psychoanalysis and Ghostly Transmissions*. London: Palgrave.

Fullerton, Huw. 2019. Did Avengers: Endgame Ruin Thanos? *Radiotimes.com*, May 12. Available at: https://www.radiotimes.com/tv/sci-fi/did-avengers-endgame-ruin-thanos/.

Gage, John. 2019. "This Is Happening": Producer and Actress with "The Handmaid's Tale" Think the Show Is Turning into Real Life. *Washington Examiner*, June 2. Available at: https://www.washingtonexaminer.com/news/this-is-happening-producer-and-actress-with-the-handmaids-tale-crew-think-the-show-is-turning-into-real-life.

Gambin, Lee. 2012. *Massacred by Mother Nature: Exploring the Natural Horror Film*. Baltimore, MD: Midnight Marquee.

Gammon, Katharine. 2021. How the Billionaire Space Race Could Be One Giant Leap for Pollution. *The Guardian*, July 19. Available at: https://www.theguardian.com/science/2021/jul/19/billionaires-space-tourism-environment-emissions.

Garcia, Sandra E. 2020. It's Getting Wild Outside. *The New York Times*, April 7: D4. Published online as "When Humans Are Sheltered in Place, Wild Animals Will Play," on April 1, 2020, at: https://www.nytimes.com/2020/04/01/science/coronavirus-animals-wildlife-goats.html.

Garcia, Sierra. 2020. "We're the Virus": The Pandemic Is Bringing Out Environmentalism's Dark Side. *Grist*, March 30. Available at: https://grist.org/climate/were-the-virus-the-pandemic-is-bringing-out-environmentalisms-dark-side/.

Gardiner, Beth. 2020. Pollution Made COVID-19 Worse. Now Lockdowns Are Clearing the Air. *National Geographic*, April 8. Available at: https://www.nationalgeographic.com/science/2020/04/pollution-made-the-pandemic-worse-but-lockdowns-clean-the-sky/.

Garland, David. 1996. The Limits of the Sovereign State: Strategies of Crime Control in Contemporary Society. *The British Journal of Criminology* 36(4): 445–71.

Garrard, Greg. 2012. Worlds Without Us: Some Types of Disanthropy. *SubStance* 41(1) [Issue 127]: 40–60.

Garrett, Bradley L. 2022. "Our Top Search Term Is Nuclear": US Bunker Sales Soar as Anxiety over Russia Rises. *The Guardian*, March 29. Available at: https://www.theguardian.com/us-news/2022/mar/29/bunker-sales-soar-anxiety-over-russia-rises-ukraine.

Ghosh, Amitav. 2016. *The Great Derangement: Climate Change and the Unthinkable.* Chicago and London: University of Chicago Press.

Giddens, Anthony. 1991. *Modernity and Self-Identity: Self and Society in the Late Modern Age.* Stanford, CA: Stanford University Press.

Gill, Victoria. 2020. Have Rogue Orcas Really Been Attacking Boats in the Atlantic? *BBC News*, November. Available at: https://www.bbc.co.uk/news/extra/buqvasp1rr /orcas-spain-portugal.

Gill, Victoria, and Kate Stephens. 2023. Atlantic Orcas "Learning from Adults" to Target Boats. *BBC News*, August 2. Available at: https://www.bbc.com/news/science -environment-66384045.

Gillani, Noor. 2021. Is Space Infinite? We Asked 5 Experts. *The Conversation*, August 10. Available at: https://theconversation.com/is-space-infinite-we-asked-5-experts -165742.

Gillespie, Kathryn A., and Patricia J. Lopez. 2015a. Economies of Death: An Ethical Framework and Future Directions. In *Economies of Death: Economic Logics of Killable Life and Grievable Death*, ed. Patricia J. Lopez and Kathryn A. Gillespie, 179–90. Abingdon, Oxon, U.K., and New York: Routledge.

Gillespie, Kathryn A., and Patricia J. Lopez. 2015b. Introducing Economies of Death. In *Economies of Death: Economic Logics of Killable Life and Grievable Death*, ed. Patricia J. Lopez and Kathryn A. Gillespie, 1–13. Abingdon, Oxon, U.K., and New York: Routledge.

Gillespie, Stuart. 2014. Oxford Researcher Is a Broadcast Star of the Future. *Oxford Arts Blog*, June 2. Available at: http://www.ox.ac.uk/news/arts-blog/oxford-researcher -broadcast-star-future.

Gilmore, David D. 2003. *Monsters: Evil Beings, Mythical Beasts, and All Manner of Imaginary Terrors.* Philadelphia: University of Pennsylvania Press.

Giroux, Henry A. 2006. Reading Hurricane Katrina: Race, Class, and the Biopolitics of Disposability. *College Literature* 33(3) [Summer]: 171–96.

Gittlitz, A. M. 2017. "Make It So": "Star Trek" and Its Debt to Revolutionary Socialism. *The New York Times*, July 24, at: https://www.nytimes.com/2017/07/24 /opinion/make-it-so-star-trek-and-its-debt-to-revolutionary-socialism.html.

Giuliani, Gaia. 2021. *Monsters, Catastrophes and the Anthropocene: A Postcolonial Critique.* Abingdon, Oxon, U.K., and New York: Routledge.

Giuliani, Gaia, Júlia Garraio, and Sofia José Santos. 2020. Online Social Media and the Construction of Sexual and Moral Panic around Migrants in Europe. *Socioscapes* 1(1): 161–80. Available at: http://www.socioscapes.org/index.php/sc/article/view/9 /13.

Gleiberman, Owen. 2017. George A. Romero: A Maestro of Zombie Terror Who Created the Ultimate Horror-Movie Metaphor. *Variety*, July 16. Available at: https://variety .com/2017/film/columns/george-a-romero-was-a-maestro-of-fear-1202497182/.

Gloyne, Howard F. 1950. Tarantism: Mass Hysterical Reaction to Spider Bite in the Middle Ages. *American Imago* 7(1) [March]: 29–42. Available at: http://www.jstor .org/stable/26301236.

Gold, Michael. 2024a. Trump Blasts Biden's Speech and Mocks Stutter. *The New York Times*, March 11: A20. Published online as "Trump Vilifies Migrants and Mocks Biden's Stutter in Georgia Speech," on March 10, 2024, at: https://www.nytimes .com/2024/03/10/us/politics/trump-biden-georgia-rally.html.

Gold, Michael. 2024b. Trump Vows Deportations and Hedges on Violence. *The New York Times*, May 1: A14. Published online as "Trump Again Vows Mass Deportations and Won't Rule Out Political Violence," on April 30, 2024, at: https://www.nytimes.com/2024/04/30/us/politics/trump-time-migrants-election.html.

Gold, Sean. 2023. WSHTF | When Shit Hits the Fan. *Trueprepper.com*, June 6. Available at: https://trueprepper.com/wshtf-when-shit-hits-the-fan/.

Goldberg, Michelle. 2023. The Danger of Jumping to Conclusions. *The New York Times*, October 22: SR2. Published online as "It Is Impossible to Know What to Believe in This Hideous War," on October 20, 2023, at: https://www.nytimes.com/2023/10/20/opinion/israel-war-gaza-hospital-danger.html.

Goren, Lilly J. 2023. Nostalgia, Nationalism, and Marvel Superheroics. In *The Politics of the Marvel Cinematic Universe*, ed. Nicholas Carnes and Lilly J. Goren, 95–108. Lawrence: University Press of Kansas.

Goyes, David Rodríguez, and Nigel South. 2019. Between "Conservation" and "Development": The Construction of "Protected Nature" and the Environmental Disenfranchisement of Indigenous Communities. *International Journal for Crime, Justice and Social Democracy* 8(3): 89–104. https://doi.org/10.5204/ijcjsd.v8i3.1247.

Graham, David. [1979] 1981. *Down to a Sunless Sea*. New York: Fawcrest/Ballantine Books.

Green, Penny. 2005. Disaster By Design: Corruption, Construction and Catastrophe. *The British Journal of Criminology* 45(4): 528–46.

Green, Penny, and Tony Ward. 2004. *State Crime: Governments, Violence, and Corruption*. London and Sterling, VA: Pluto Press.

Green, Stephanie. 2011. Dexter Morgan's Monstrous Origins. *Critical Studies in Television* 6(1): 22–35. https://doi.org/10.7227/CST.6.1.4.

Greenberg, David. 2003. Fallout Can Be Fun: How the Cold War Civil-Defense Programs Became Farce. *Slate*, February 20. Available at: http://www.slate.com/articles/news_and_politics/history_lesson/2003/02/fallout_can_be_fun.html.

Gregersdotter, Katarina, Johan Höglund, and Nicklas Hållén, eds. 2015. *Animal Horror Cinema: Genre, History, and Criticism*. New York: Palgrave Macmillan.

Greshko, Michael. 2019. The Universe Seems to Be Expanding Faster Than All Expectations. *National Geographic*, April 25. Available at: https://www.nationalgeographic.com/science/article/hubble-constant-universe-expanding-faster-than-all-expectations.

Greshko, Michael. 2021. The Universe Is Expanding Faster Than It Should Be. *National Geographic*, December 17. Available at: https://www.nationalgeographic.com/science/article/the-universe-is-expanding-faster-than-it-should-be.

Gribbin, Sean. 2021. Venom Drops the Mic at a Rave in a New Teaser. *CBR*, September 26. Available at: https://www.cbr.com/venom-let-there-be-carnage-rave-teaser-drops-the-microphone/.

Grønstad, Asbørn. 2008. *Transfigurations: Violence, Death, and Masculinity in American Cinema*. Amsterdam: Amsterdam University Press.

Grossman, Lev. 2009. Zombies Are the New Vampires. *Time*, April 9. Available at: https://content.time.com/time/subscriber/article/0,33009,1890384,00.html.

"Guardian staff and agency." 2021. Fatal Attraction: Rare Corpse Flower Draws Hundreds of Onlookers. *The Guardian*, May 19. Accessed at: https://www.theguardian.com/environment/2021/may/19/corpse-flower-san-francisco-bay-area.

Guasco, Anna. 2023. Whales Have Attacked Plenty of Boats Before. This Time Is Different. *Slate*, May 24. Available at: https://slate.com/culture/2023/05/orcas -whales-attack-boats-yachts-white-gladis.html.

Guerrero, Jean. 2022. Column: In "Wakanda Forever," Black Filmmakers Did Right by Indigenous Peoples. *Los Angeles Times*, December 26. Available at: https://www.latimes .com/opinion/story/2022-12-26/wakanda-forever-namor-tenoch-huerta-indigenous.

Guidi, Ruxandra. 2022. Two Tales of a City. *Sierra* 107(4) [Winter]: 30–37. Available at: https://digital.sierramagazine.org/publication/?i=770798&article_id=4400381.

Gusterson, Hugh. 2020. COVID-19 and the Turn to Magical Thinking. *Sapiens*, May 12. Available at: https://www.sapiens.org/column/conflicted/covid-19-magic/.

Gustines, George Gene. 2017. On Creating Black Superheroes. *The New York Times*, March 3: D8. Published online as "Ta-Nehisi Coates on Creating Black Superheroes," on March 2, 2017, at: https://www.nytimes.com/2017/03/02/fashion /mens-style/ta-nehisi-coates-marvel-comics-black-panther-between-the-world-and -me.html.

Haberman, Maggie, and Michael Gold. 2024. At Fund-Raiser, Trump Says He Wants More Immigrants From "Nice" Countries. *The New York Times*, April 8: A16. Published online as "Trump, at Fund-Raiser, Says He Wants Immigrants From 'Nice' Countries," on April 7, 2024, at: https://www.nytimes.com/2024/04/07/us /politics/trump-immigrants-nice-countries.html.

Hale, Kori. 2022. African American and Hispanic Audiences Spur "Black Panther: Wakanda Forever" to $180 Million Opening Weekend. *Forbes*, November 14. Available at: https://www.forbes.com/sites/korihale/2022/11/14/african-american -and-hispanic-audiences-spur-black-panther-wakanda-forever-to-180-million -opening-weekend/?sh=4cdbf43ce6c5.

Hale, Mike. 2020. Working on the Dystopian Railroad. *The New York Times*, May 15: C1. Published online as "Review: 'Snowpiercer' on a New Track," on May 14, 2020, at: https://www.nytimes.com/2020/05/14/arts/television/review-snowpiercer .html.

Hall, Matthew. 2016. The Sense of the Monster Plant Pages. In *Plant Horror: Approaches to the Monstrous Vegetal in Fiction and Film*, ed. Dawn Keetley and Angela Tenga, 243–55. London: Palgrave Macmillan.

Hall, Stuart. 1981. Notes on Deconstructing "The Popular." In *People's History and Socialist Theory*, ed. Raphael Samuel, 227–41. London and Boston: Routledge and Kegan Paul.

Halttunen, Karen. 1998. *Murder Most Foul: The Killer and the American Gothic Imagination*. Cambridge, MA: Harvard University Press.

Hamilton, Clive. 2013. Geoengineering: Our Last Hope, or a False Promise? *The New York Times*, May 27: A17. Published online as "Geoengineering: Our Last Hope, or a False Promise?" on May 26, 2013, at: https://www.nytimes.com/2013/05/27 /opinion/geoengineering-our-last-hope-or-a-false-promise.html.

Hamilton, Jessica. 2023. Killer Whale Named White Gladis Who "Started the Trend" of Animals Ramming Boats off the Coast of Spain and Portugal "Was Pregnant When She Began the Orca Uprising." *Daily Mail*, June 29 (updated August 28). Available at: https://www.dailymail.co.uk/news/article-12246987/Killer-whale -named-White-Gladis-started-trend-animals-ramming-boats-pregnant.html.

Hancock, Elaina. 2022. A Darker Shade of Green: Understanding Ecofascism. *UConn Today*, September 7. Available at: https://today.uconn.edu/2022/09/a-darker-shade -of-green/#.

Haraway, Donna. 1988. Situated Knowledges: The Science Question in Feminism and the Privilege of Partial Perspective. *Feminist Studies* 14(3) [Autumn]: 575–99. Available at: https://www.jstor.org/stable/3178066?origin=JSTOR-pdf.

Hardach, Sophie. 2023. Why Are Orcas Suddenly Ramming Boats? *BBC*, June 27. Available at: https://www.bbc.com/future/article/20230626-why-are-orcas -suddenly-ramming-boats.

Harley, Flora. 2023. *The Wealth Report Series: Wealth Populations*. Knight Frank LLP. Available at: https://content.knightfrank.com/research/83/documents/en/the -wealth-report-wealth-populations-10198.pdf.

Harris, Paul. 2009. Hollywood Searches for Escapism after the Apocalypse. *The Guardian*, August 8. Available at: https://www.theguardian.com/film/2009/aug/09 /hollywood-apocalypse-movies-anxiety.

Harris, Violet J. 2007. In Praise of a Scholarly Force: Rudine Sims Bishop. *Language Arts* 85(2): 153–59.

Haug, Sebastian, Jacqueline Braveboy-Wagner, and Günther Maihold. 2021. The "Global South" in the Study of World Politics: Examining a Meta Category. *Third World Quarterly* 42(9): 1923–1944. https://doi.org/10.1080/01436597.2021 .1948831.

Hayward, Keith J. 2016. Cultural criminology: Script rewrites. *Theoretical Criminology*, 20(3): 297–321. https://doi.org/10.1177/1362480615619668.

Hediger, Ryan. 2018. Uncanny Homesickness and War: Loss of Affect, Loss of Place, and Reworlding in *Redeployment*. In *Affective Ecocriticism: Emotion, Embodiment, Environment*, ed. Kyle Bladow and Jennifer Ladino, 155–74. Lincoln: University of Nebraska Press.

Heholt, Ruth 2016. Introduction: Unstable Landscapes: Affect, Representation, and a Multiplicity of Hauntings. In *Haunted Landscapes: Super-Nature and the Environment*, ed. Ruth Heholt and Niamh Downing, 1–20. New York: Rowman and Littlefield International.

Hennefeld, Maggie, and Nicholas Sammond. 2020. Introduction: Not It, or, The Abject Objection. In *Abjection Incorporated: Mediating the Politics of Pleasure and Violence*, ed. Maggie Hennefeld and Nicholas Sammond, 1–31. Durham, NC, and London: Duke University Press.

Herbst, Michael. 1999. Goya's Grotesque: Abjection in *Los Capriochos, De Sastres de la Guerra*, and *Lost Disparatas*. Unpublished Ph.D. dissertation, submitted to the Faculty of Arts, University of the Witwatersrand, Johannesburg, South Africa, November 24. Available at: https://core.ac.uk/download/pdf/188776039.pdf.

Herrero, Stephen. 2002. *Bear Attacks: Their Causes and Avoidance*. Guilford, CT: The Lyons Press/The Globe Pequot Press.

Hertz, Robert. 1960. A Contribution to the Study of the Collective Representation of Death. In *Death and the Right Hand*. Translated by Rodney and Claudia Needham, 19–33. New York: Free Press.

Herzog, Harold A., R. Alexander Bentley, and Matthew W. Hahn. 2004. Random Drift and Large Shifts in Popularity of Dog Breeds. August 7. *Proceedings of the Royal Society B* 271(Suppl 5): S353–S356. https://doi.org/10.1098/rsbl.2004.0185.

Higgins, Ethan M., and Kristin Swartz. 2018. The Knowing of Monstrosities: Necro-power, Spectacular Punishment and Denial. *Critical Criminology: An International Journal* 26(1): 91–106. https://doi.org/10.1007/s10612-017-9382-7.

Higgins, Polly. 2010. *Eradicating Ecocide: Laws and Governance to Prevent the Destruction of Our Planet*. London: Shepheard-Walwyn.

Higgins, Polly, Damien Short, and Nigel South. 2013. Protecting the Planet: A Proposal for a Law of Ecocide. *Crime, Law and Social Change* 59(3): 251–66. https://doi.org/10.1007/s10611-013-9413-6.

Hill, Jonquilyn. 2019. What Gave Life to the Idea of the Zombie? *1A, WAMU, National Public Radio*, October 31. Available at: https://the1a.org/segments/2019-10-31-what-gave-life-to-the-idea-of-the-zombie/.

Hillard, Tom J. 2009. "Deep into That Darkness Peering": An Essay on Gothic Nature. *ISLE: Interdisciplinary Studies in Literature and Environment* 16(4) [Autumn]: 685–95.

Hirschmann, Nancy J. 2023. Environmentalism and the Marvel Cinematic Universe: *Spider-Man: Far From Home* as a Cautionary Tale. In *The Politics of the Marvel Cinematic Universe*, ed. Nicholas Carnes and Lilly J. Goren, 166–81. Lawrence: University Press of Kansas.

Hiscock, John. 2013. Neill Blomkamp interview: "Elysium Isn't Science Fiction. It's Now." *The Telegraph*, August 19. Available at: https://www.telegraph.co.uk/culture/film/10244979/Neill-Blomkamp-interview-Elysium-isnt-science-fiction.-Its-now.html.

Hoare, Philip. 2008. *Leviathan, Or, The Whale*. London: Fourth Estate/HarperCollins.

Hoare, Philip. 2021. *Albert and the Whale: Albrecht Dürer and How Art Imagines Our World*. New York: Pegasus Books.

Hoare, Philip. 2023a. Orca Rams into Yacht off Shetland in First Such Incident in Northern Waters. *The Guardian*, June 21. Available at: https://www.theguardian.com/environment/2023/jun/21/orca-rams-yacht-off-shetland-first-such-incident-northern-waters.

Hoare, Philip. 2023b. Orcas Are Ramming Yachts off the Spanish Coast—Is the Whale World Rising Up? *The Guardian*, May 25. Available at: https://www.theguardian.com/commentisfree/2023/may/25/orcas-ramming-yachts-spanish-whale-behaviour-trauma-humans.

Hodgman, John. 2017. I Am Sorry for This Mess. *The New York Times*, October 22: SR8. Published online as "I Am Sorry for This Straggly Mess on My Face," on October 21, 2017, at: https://www.nytimes.com/2017/10/21/opinion/sunday/john-hodgman-beard.html.

Hoffman, Andrew J. 2015. *How Culture Shapes the Climate Change Debate*. Stanford, CA: Stanford University Press.

Hook, Derek. 2012. *A Critical Psychology of the Postcolony: The Mind of Apartheid*. Abingdon, Oxon, U.K., and New York: Routledge.

Horkheimer, Max, and Theodor W. Adorno. [1947] 2002. *Gesammelte Schriften Band 5: Dialektik der Aufklärung und Schriften 1940–1950* [*The Dialectic of the Enlightenment Volume 5: Philosophical Fragments*. Edited by Gunzelin Schmid Noerr and translated by Edmund Jephcott.]. Stanford, CA: Stanford University Press.

Howell, Elizabeth. 2016. Gliese 581g: Potentially Habitable Planet—If It Exists. *Space.com*, May 4. Available at: https://www.space.com/23821-gliese-581g.html.

Howell, Peter. 2013. The Colony Recycles Old Sci-Fi Ideas: Review. *Toronto Star*, April 25. Available at: https://www.thestar.com/entertainment/movies /the-colony-recycles-old-sci-fi-ideas-review/article_bbaaec15-ecb3-5aae-81c6 -5f5207415957.html.

Hubbard, L. Ron. 1982. *Battlefield Earth: A Saga of the Year 3000*. New York: St. Martin's Press.

Hulme, Mike. 2009. *Why We Disagree About Climate Change: Understanding Controversy, Inaction and Opportunity*. Cambridge, U.K.: Cambridge University Press.

Hulme, Mike. 2014. *Can Science Fix Climate Change? A Case against Climate Engineering*. Cambridge, U.K., and Malden, MA: Polity Press.

Hunt, Elle. 2023. Orcas Are Attacking Boats. But to Say They're "Fighting Back" Is All Too Human. *The Guardian*, July 19. Available at: https://www.theguardian.com /commentisfree/2023/jul/19/orcas-boats-human-killer-whales-animal-life.

Hurley, Jessica, and Dan Sinykin. 2018. Apocalypse: Introduction. *ASAP/Journal* 3(3) [September]: 451–66. https://doi.org/10.1353/asa.2018.0034.

Hurley, Kelly. 2002. British Gothic Fiction 1885–1930. In *The Cambridge Companion to Gothic Fiction*, ed. Jerrold E. Hogle, 189–208. Cambridge, U.K.: Cambridge University Press.

Hutchinson, Alex. 2022. Getting to This Resort Is the Only Hard Part. *The New York Times*, May 2: B8. Published online as "At Wilderness Resort in Canada, Getting There Is the Only Hard Part," on April 27, 2022, at: https://www.nytimes.com /2022/04/27/travel/shadow-lake-lodge-canada-backcountry.html.

Hwang, Haewon. 2013. *London's Underground Spaces: Representing the Victorian City, 1840–1915*. Edinburgh: Edinburgh University Press.

IMDb. 2018. Michael B. Jordan: Erik Killmonger. Available at: https://www.imdb .com/title/tt1825683/characters/nm0430107.

IMDb. 2019. Threads: User Reviews: No Punches Pulled. Available at: https://www .imdb.com/title/tt0090163/reviews/.

Ingebretsen, Edward. J. 2001. *At Stake: Monsters and the Rhetoric of Fear in Public Culture*. Chicago and London: University of Chicago Press.

IPCC. 2023. Sections. In *Climate Change 2023: Synthesis Report. Contribution of Working Groups I, II and III to the Sixth Assessment Report of the Intergovernmental Panel on Climate Change*, ed. H. Lee and J. Romero, 35–115. IPCC, Geneva, Switzerland. Available at: https://www.ipcc.ch/report/ar6/syr/downloads/report /IPCC_AR6_SYR_LongerReport.pdf.

Irwin, Aisling. 2017. There Are Five Times More Urban Foxes in England Than We Thought. *New Scientist*, January 4. Available at: https://www.newscientist .com/article/2116583-there-are-five-times-more-urban-foxes-in-england-than-we -thought/.

Itzkoff, Dave. 2020. All Aboard for the Apocalypse. *The New York Times*, May 17: AR13, AR18. Published online as "On Track for the Apocalypse, 'Snowpiercer' Comes to Television," on May 14, 2020, at: https://www.nytimes.com/2020/05/14 /arts/television/snowpiercer-tnt.html.

Ivakhiv, Adrian J. 2022. Readings on Ecofascism and Far-Right Ecologism. *Immanence*, July 29. Available at: https://blog.uvm.edu/aivakhiv/2022/07/29/readings-on -ecofascism-and-far-right-ecologism/.

Jacob, Mary K. 2022. Billionaire Peter Thiel's $13.5M Dream Home in New Zealand Is Doomed. *New York Post*, August 19. Available at: https://nypost.com/2022/08/19/peter-thiels-plans-for-dream-home-in-new-zealand-are-gone/.

Jaggard, Victoria. 2020. What Kind of Future Will This Planet Have in Store? *National Geographic*, March 25. Available at: https://www.nationalgeographic.com/newsletters/science/article/what-future-planet-havestore-march-25.

James, Simon P. 2015. *Environmental Philosophy: An Introduction*. Cambridge, U.K., and Malden, MA: Polity Press.

Jayatissa, Amanda. 2024. The Rage in "Carrie" Feels More Relevant Than Ever. *The New York Times*, April 7: SR9. Published online as "The Rage in 'Carrie' Feels More Relevant Than Ever," on April 5, 2024, at: https://www.nytimes.com/2024/04/05/opinion/stephen-king-carrie-anniversary.html.

Jefferies, Richard. 1885[1980]. *After London; Or Wild England*. New York: Oxford University Press.

Jensen, Gary. 2017. Social Learning Theory. In *The Routledge Companion to Criminological Theory and Concepts*, ed. Avi Brisman, Eamonn Carrabine, and Nigel South, 115–19. Abingdon, Oxon, U.K., and New York: Routledge.

Jerolmack, Colin. 2008. How Pigeons Became Rats: The Cultural-Spatial Logic of Problem Animals. *Social Problems* 55(1): 72–94.

Jewkes, Yvonne. 2015. *Media and Crime*. 3rd ed. Thousand Oaks, CA: Sage Publications.

Jewkes, Yvonne, and Travis Linnemann. 2018. *Media and Crime in the U.S.* Thousand Oaks, CA: Sage Publications.

Johnston, Dais. 2021. Fascinating "Avenger: Endgame" Theory Reveals Thanos' True Philosophy. *Inverse*, July 13. Available at: https://www.inverse.com/entertainment/avengers-endgame-theory-thanos-philosophy.

Jones, Dustin. 2023. An Otter in Santa Cruz Is Hassling Surfers—and Stealing Their Boards. *National Public Radio*, July 13. Available at: https://www.npr.org/2023/07/13/1187295769/otter-santa-cruz-surfboard-surfers-california.

Jones, Nancy Caye. 2017. *Goodbye Earth: A Children's Book for Grownups Who Persist*. Illustrated by Andy Rubin. n.p.: Common Earth Press and Bubbie Publishing.

Jones, Sam. 2020a. Boats off Spain Damaged in Orca Encounters. *The Guardian*, September 1. Available at: https://www.theguardian.com/environment/2020/sep/01/boats-off-spain-damaged-in-orca-encounters.

Jones, Sam. 2020b. Previous Incident May Have Led Orcas to Target Boats, Say Experts. *The Guardian*, October 6. Available at: https://www.theguardian.com/environment/2020/oct/06/previous-incident-may-have-led-orcas-to-target-boats-say-experts-spain-portugal.

Jones, Sam. 2020c. Spain Bans Yachts from Stretch of Sea after Orcas Damage Boats. *The Guardian*, September 23. Available at: https://www.theguardian.com/world/2020/sep/23/spain-bans-yachts-from-stretch-of-sea-after-orcas-damage-boats.

Jones, Sam. 2020d. "They Were Having a Real Go": Man Tells of Orca Encounter off Spain. *The Guardian*, September 24. Available at: https://www.theguardian.com/environment/2020/sep/24/they-were-having-a-real-go-scottish-man-recounts-orca-attack.

Jordan, Jr., Vernon E. 2017. Movies That Unite Us. *The New York Times*, February 19: SR3. Published online as "The Power of Movies to Change Our Hearts," on

February 18, 2017, at: https://www.nytimes.com/2017/02/18/opinion/sunday/the
-power-of-movies-to-change-our-hearts.html.

Joshi, Kentan. 2020. Watch Out for This Symptom of Corona Virus: Lazy Ecofascism. *Kentanjoshi.co*, March 20. Available at: https://ketanjoshi.co/2020/03/20/watch-out
-for-this-symptom-of-corona-virus-lazy-ecofascism/.

Joyce, Kathryn, and Jeff Sharlet. 2023. Losing the Plot: The "Leftists" Who Turn Right. *In These Times*, December 12. Available at: https://inthesetimes.com/article
/former-left-right-fascism-capitalism-horseshoe-theory.

Kachar, Marina, Ewa Sawosz, and Andre Chwalibog. 2018. Orcas Are Social Mammals. *International Journal of Avian & and Wildlife Biology* 3(4): 291–95. Special issue. https://doi.org/10.15406/ijawb.2018.03.00101; https://core.ac.uk/download/pdf/269306405.pdf.

Kamel, Zachary, Mack Lamoureaux, and Ben Makuch. 2020. "Eco-Fascist" Arm of Neo-Nazi Terror Group, The Base, Linked to Swedish Arson. *Vice*, January 29. Available at: https://www.vice.com/en/article/qjdvzx/eco-fascist-arm-of-neo-nazi
-terror-group-the-base-linked-to-swedish-arson.

Kāmîr, Ôrît. 2012. What Makes Stalking Monsters So Monstrous, and How to Survive Them? In *Speaking of Monsters: A Teratological Anthology*, ed. Caroline Joan S. Picart and John Edgar Browning, 161–71. Basingstoke, Hampshire, U.K.: Palgrave Macmillan.

Kanthak, Kristin. 2023. From "Grrrl Power" to "She's Got Help": Captain Marvel as the Superhero of Second-Wave Feminism. In *The Politics of the Marvel Cinematic Universe*, ed. Nicholas Carnes and Lilly J. Goren, 211–23. Lawrence: University Press of Kansas.

Kaplan-Levenson, Laine, and Rund Abdelfatah. 2019. A History of Zombies in America. *Morning Edition, National Public Radio*, October 31. Available at: https://www.npr.org/2019/10/31/774985441/a-history-of-zombies-in-america.

Kaufman, Amy S. 2013. Our Future Is Our Past: Corporate Medievalism in Dystopian Fiction. In *Studies in Medievalism XXII: Corporate Medievalism II*, Volume 22, ed. Karl Fugelso, 11–19. Rochester, NY: Boydell and Brewer/D. S. Brewer. Available at: https://www.jstor.org/stable/10.7722/j.ctt2tt1q7.6.

Kaufman, Marc. 2011. *First Contact: Scientific Breakthroughs in the Hunt for Life Beyond Earth*. New York: Simon and Schuster.

Keene, Brian. 2003. *The Rising*. New York: Leisure Books/Dorchester Publishing.

Keene, Brian. 2005. *City of the Dead*. New York: Leisure Books/Dorchester Publishing.

Keene, Brian. 2008. *The Rising: Selected Scenes from the End of the World*. North Webster, IN: Delirium Books.

Keene, Brian. 2013a. *City of the Dead*. Author's preferred edition. Portland, OR: Deadite Press.

Keene, Brian. 2013b. *The Rising*. Author's preferred edition. Portland, OR: Deadite Press.

Keene, Brian. 2013c. *The Rising: Selected Scenes from the End of the World*. Author's preferred edition. Portland, OR: Deadite Press.

Keene, Brian. 2015. *The Rising: Deliverance*. Portland, OR: Deadite Press.

Keetley, Dawn, ed. 2014. *"We're All Infected": Essays on AMC's* The Walking Dead *and the Fate of the Human*. Jefferson, NC: McFarland.

Keetley, Dawn. 2016. Introduction: Six Theses on Plant Horror; or, Why Are Plants Horrifying? In *Plant Horror: Approaches to the Monstrous Vegetal in Fiction and Film*, ed. Dawn Keetley and Angela Tenga, 1–30. London: Palgrave Macmillan.

Keetley, Dawn. 2021. Tentacular Ecohorror and the Agency of Trees in Algernon Blackwood's "The Man Whom the Trees Loved" and Lorcan Finnegan's *Without Name*. In *Fear and Nature: Ecohorror Studies in the Anthropocene*, ed. Christy Tidwell and Carter Soles, 23–41. University Park: Pennsylvania State University Press.

Keetley, Dawn, and Angela Tenga, eds. 2016. *Plant Horror: Approaches to the Monstrous Vegetal in Fiction and Film*. London: Palgrave Macmillan.

Kelly, Casey Ryan. 2016. The Man-Pocalypse: *Doomsday Preppers* and the Rituals of Apocalyptic Manhood. *Text and Performance Quarterly* 36(2–3): 95–114. https://doi.org/10.1080/10462937.2016.1158415.

Kennedy, Margaret S. 2017. A Breath of Fresh Air: Eco-Consciousness in *Mary Barton* and *Jane Eyre*. *Victorian Literature and Culture* 45(3) [September]: 509–26. https://doi.org/10.1017/S1060150317000031.

Kenny, Glenn. 2016. A Mutant Superhero Sequel 5,000 Years in the Making. *The New York Times*, C11. Published online as "Review: 'X-Men: Apocalypse,' a Sequel 5,000 Years in the Making," on May 26, 2016, at: https://www.nytimes.com/2016/05/27/movies/x-men-apocalypse-review.html.

Kenton, Will. 2024. Ultra-High-Net-Worth Individual (UHNWI): Definition and Criteria. *Investopedia*, October 7. Available at: https://www.investopedia.com/terms/u/ultra-high-net-worth-individuals-uhnwi.asp#citation-9.

Kern, Sim. 2021. No, Billionaires Won't "Escape" to Space While the World Burns. *Salon*, July 7. Available at: https://salon.com/2021/07/07/no-billionaires-wont-escape-to-space-while-the-worldburns/.

Kessler, Glenn. 2013. The Case of "Zombie" Voters in South Carolina. *Washington Post*, July 25. Available at: https://www.washingtonpost.com/blogs/fact-checker/post/the-case-of-zombie-voters-in-south-carolina/2013/07/24/86de3c64-f403-11e2-aa2e-4088616498b4_blog.html.

Khapaeva, Dina. 2020a. Eaten in Jurassic World: Antihumanism and Popular Culture. In *Man-Eating Monsters: Anthropocentrism and Popular Culture*, ed. Dina Khapaeva, 15–34. Bingley, U.K.: Emerald Publishing Limited.

Khapaeva, Dina. 2020b. Introduction: Food for Monsters: Popular Culture and Our Basic Food Taboo. In *Man-Eating Monsters: Anthropocentrism and Popular Culture*, ed. Dina Khapaeva, 1–13. Bingley, U.K.: Emerald Publishing Limited.

Killingsworth, M. Jimmie, and Jacqueline S. Palmer. 1996. Millennial Ecology: The Apocalyptic Narrative from *Silent Spring* to *Global Warming*. In *Green Culture: Environmental Rhetoric in Contemporary America*, ed. Carl G. Herndl and Stuart C. Brown, 21–45. Madison, WI, and London: The University of Wisconsin Press.

Kingsolver, Barbara. 2012. *Flight Behavior: A Novel*. New York: HarperCollins Publishers.

Klarreich, Erica. 2004. Toss Out the Toss-Up: Bias in Heads-or-Tails. *Science News Online*, 165(9) [February 28]: 131. Available at: https://www.sciencenews.org/article/toss-out-toss-bias-heads-or-tails.

Klesman, Alison. 2024. The Sky This Week from April 5 to 12. A Great North American Eclipse. *Astronomy.com*, April 5. Available at: https://www.astronomy.com/observing/the-sky-this-week-from-april-5-to-12-2024/.

Kloß, Sinah Theres. 2017. The Global South as Subversive Practice: Challenges and Potentials of a Heuristic Concept. *The Global South* 11(2) [Fall]: 1–17. https://doi.org/10.2979/globalsouth.11.2.01.

Kneitz, Agnes. 2015. "As If the River Was Not Meat and Drink to You!": Social Novels as a Means of Framing Nineteenth-Century Environmental Justice. *ISLE: Interdisciplinary Studies in Literature and Environment* 22(1) [Winter]: 47–62. https://doi.org/10.1093/isle/isv006.

Kniss, Ashley. 2021. "The Hand of Deadly Decay": The Rotting Corpse, America's Religious Tradition, and the Ethics of Green Burial in Poe's "The Colloquy of Monos and Una." In *Fear and Nature: Ecohorror Studies in the Anthropocene*, ed. Christy Tidwell and Carter Soles, 68–88. University Park: Pennsylvania State University Press.

Koren, Marina. 2020. The Pandemic Is Turning the Natural World Upside Down. *The Atlantic*, April 2. Available at: https://www.theatlantic.com/science/archive/2020/04/coronavirus-pandemic-earth-pollution-noise/609316/#.

Kristeva, Julia. 1982. *Powers of Horror: An Essay on Abjection*. Translated by Leon S. Roudiez. New York: Columbia University Press.

Krotz, Sarah Wylie. 2023. Foreword: The CLC Kreisel Lecture Series. In *An Anthology of Monsters: How Story Saves Us from Anxiety*, ed. Cherie Dimaline, v–vii. Edmonton, Canada: University of Alberta Press and Canadian Literature Centre/Centre de littérature anadienne.

Krugman, Paul. 2012. The Ultimate Zombie Idea. *The New York Times*, November 3, https://archive.nytimes.com/krugman.blogs.nytimes.com/2012/11/03/the-ultimate-zombie-idea/?searchResultPosition=2.

Krugman, Paul. 2013. Rubio and the Zombies. *The New York Times*, February 15: A27. Published online as "Rubio and the Zombies," on February 14, 2013, at: https://www.nytimes.com/2013/02/15/opinion/krugman-rubio-and-the-zombies.html.

Krugman, Paul. 2020. *Arguing with Zombies: Economics, Politics, and the Fight for a Better Future*. New York: W.W. Norton.

Kunstler, James Howard. 1993. *The Geography of Nowhere: The Rise and Decline of America's Man-Made Landscape*. New York: Touchstone/Simon and Schuster.

Kunstler, James Howard. 2005. *The Long Emergency: Surviving the Converging Catastrophes of the Twenty-First Century*. New York: Atlantic Monthly Press.

Kunstler, James Howard. 2007. Making Other Arrangements. *Orion*, January-February. Available at: https://www.orionmagazine.org/article/making-other-arrangements/.

Kunstler, James Howard. 2008. *World Made by Hand*. New York: Grove Press.

Kwai, Isabella. 2023. Orcas Have Been Battering Boats in Southern Europe, Puzzled Scientists Say. *The New York Times*, May 25: A4. Published online as "Orcas Sank 3 Boats in Southern Europe in the Last Year, Scientists Say," on May 24, 2023, at: https://www.nytimes.com/2023/05/24/world/europe/orcas-sink-boats-spain.html.

Kweku, Ezekiel. 2017. To Donald Trump, the American City Will Always Be a Dystopic, "Eighties Movies" New York. *MTV News*, March 27. Available at: https://www.mtv.com/news/bjt9n9/to-donald-trump-the-american-city-will-always-be-a-dystopic-eighties-movies-new-york.

LaFrance, Adrienne. 2024. Humanity's Enduring Obsession with the Apocalypse. *The Atlantic*, April 8. Available at: https://www.theatlantic.com/ideas/archive/2024/04/solar-eclipse-apocalypse/677999/.

Lagatta, Eric. 2024. SpaceX Launch: Starship Reaches New Heights Before Being Lost on Re-Entry Over Indian Ocean. *Austin America-Statesman*, March 14.

Available at: https://www.statesman.com/story/news/nation/2024/03/14/spacex-launch-starship-live/72968478007/.

Lam, Anita, Nigel South, and Avi Brisman. 2023. A Convergence of Crises: COVID-19, Climate Change, and Bunkerization. *Crime Media Culture* 19(3): 327–44. https://doi.org/10.1177/17416590221120581 [First Published September 4, 2022].

Lam, Anita, Nigel South, and Avi Brisman. 2025. "If There Was an Observer on Mars, They Would Probably Be Amazed That We Have Survived This Long": Environmental Decline, Elite Escapes, and Space Colonies. In *Crime, Criminal Justice and Ethics in Outer Space: International Perspectives,* ed. Yarin Eski and Jack Lampkin, 122–36. Abingdon, Oxon, U.K., and New York: Routledge.

Lambie, Ryan. 2011. The 10 Finest Sewers of B-Movie Cinema. *Den of Geek*, October 20. Available at: https://www.denofgeek.com/movies/the-10-finest-sewers-of-b-movie-cinema/.

Lane, Anthony. 2018. Imaginary Kingdoms: "Black Panther" and "Early Man." *The New Yorker* 94(2) [February 26]: 60–62. Available at: https://www.newyorker.com/magazine/2018/02/26/black-panther-and-early-man.

Langmann, Brady. 2019. Martin Scorsese's Debate That Marvel Movies Aren't Art Is Still Going Strong. *Esquire*, October 17. Available at: https://www.esquire.com/entertainment/movies/a29388082/martin-scorcese-marvel-art-controversy-james-gunn-samuel-jackson-explained/.

Langmann, Brady. 2022. *Watchmen* Writer Alan Moore Is Still Bashing Superhero Movies. *Esquire*, October 10. Available at: https://www.esquire.com/entertainment/movies/a29843311/watchmen-alan-moore-marvel-martin-scorsese-debate/.

Lauro, Sarah Juliet. 2011. Afterword: Zombie (R)evolution. In *Better Off Dead: The Evolution of the Zombie as Post-Human*, ed. Deborah Christie and Sarah Juliet Lauro, 231–35. New York: Fordham University Press.

Lauro, Sarah Juliet, ed. 2017. *Zombie Theory: A Reader*. Minneapolis, MN, and London: University of Minnesota Press.

Lauro, Sarah Juliet, and Deborah Christie. 2011. Introduction. In *Better Off Dead: The Evolution of the Zombie as Post-Human*, ed. Deborah Christie and Sarah Juliet Lauro, 1–4. New York: Fordham University Press.

Lawrence, Julian, and Neil Archer. 2019. Martin Scorsese Says Superhero Movies Are "Not Cinema": Two Experts Debate. *The Conversation*, October 24. Available at: https://theconversation.com/martin-scorsese-says-superhero-movies-are-not-cinema-two-experts-debate-125771.

Lee, James R. 2009. *Climate Change and Armed Conflict: Hot and Cold Wars*. London and New York: Routledge.

Leiserowitz, Anthony A. 2004. Before and after The Day After Tomorrow: A U.S. Study of Climate Change Risk Perception. *Environment* 46(9): 24–37. Available at: https://climatecommunication.yale.edu/wp-content/uploads/2016/02/2004_11_Before-and-after-The-Day-After-Tomorrow.pdf.

Lemonides, Alex, and Christine Zhang. 2024. What to Make of the "Zombie Vote" against Donald Trump. *The New York Times*, April 24, https://www.nytimes.com/interactive/2024/04/24/us/elections/nikki-haley-trump-zombie-votes.html.

Lenhardt, Corinna. 2020. *Savage Horrors: The Intrinsic Raciality of the American Gothic*. Bielefeld, Germany: Transcript Verlag.

Lennard, Dominic. 2019. *Brute Force: Animal Horror Movies*. Albany: State University of New York Press.

Leone, Michael. 2008. Fiction Review: Prescient "World Made by Hand." *San Francisco Chronicle*, May 6. Available at: https://www.sfgate.com/books/article/Fiction-review -Prescient-World-Made-by-Hand-3285297.php.

Le Quéré, Corinne, Robert B. Jackson, Matthew W. Jones, Adam J. P. Smith, Sam Abernethy, Robbie M. Andrew, Anthony J. De-Gol, David R. Willis, Yuli Shan, Josep G. Canadell, Pierre Friedlingstein, Felix Creutzig, and Glen P. Peters. 2020. Temporary Reduction in Daily Global CO_2 Emissions during the COVID-19 Forced Confinement. *Nature Climate Change* 10(May 19): 647–53. https://doi.org /10.1038/s41558-020-0797-x.

Le Quéré, Corinne, Robert B. Jackson, Matthew W. Jones, Adam J. P. Smith, Sam Abernethy, Robbie M. Andrew, Anthony J. De-Gol, Yuli Shan, Josep G. Canadell, Pierre Friedlingstein, Felix Creutzig, and Glen P. Peters. 2021. Supplementary Data: Temporary Reduction in Daily Global CO_2 Emissions during the COVID-19 Forced Confinement. *Integrated Carbon Observation System*, Last update: version 1.4, September 22. https://doi.org/10.18160/RQDW-BTJU and https://www.icos -cp.eu/gcp-covid19-v14 (last accessed June 19, 2024).

Levin, David. 2022. Chum. *Oberlin Alumni Magazine*, 117(2) [Summer]: 30–35.

Levin, Rachel. 2018. *Look Big: And Other Tips for Surviving Animal Encounters of All Kinds*. New York: Ten Speed Press/Crown Publishing Group/Penguin Random House LLC.

Levina, Marina, and Diem-My T. Bui. 2013. Introduction: Toward a Comprehensive Monster Theory in the 21st Century. In *Monster Culture in the 21st Century: A Reader*, ed. Marina Levina and Diem-My T. Bui, 1–13. New York and London: Bloomsbury.

Lewis, Dan. 2012. Gamblers Take Note: The Odds in a Coin Flip Aren't Quite 50/50. *Smithsonian Magazine*, November 30. Available at: https://www.smithsonianmag .com/science-nature/gamblers-take-note-the-odds-in-a-coin-flip-arent-quite-5050 -145465423/.

Liang, Jiayu. 2024. Shark Bites Consistent with Recent Trends, with Small Spike in Fatalities. Florida Museum, February 5. Available at: https://www.floridamuseum .ufl.edu/science/shark-bites-consistent-with-recent-trends-with-small-spike-in -fatalities/.

Lifshutz, Hannah. 2019. The "Handmaid's Tale" Season 3 Illustrates Parallels Between Gilead and Trump's America. *Complex*, June 6. Available at: https://www.complex .com/pop-culture/a/hannah-lifshutz/handmaids-tale-season-3-illustrates-parallels -between-gilead-trump-america.

Linnemann, Travis. 2016. *Meth Wars: Police, Media, Power*. New York: New York University Press.

Linnemann, Travis. 2022. *The Horror of Police*. Minneapolis, MN, and London: University of Minnesota Press.

Linnemann, Travis, and Tyler Wall. 2013. "This Is Your Face on Meth": The Punitive Spectacle of "White Trash" in the Rural War on Drugs. *Theoretical Criminology* 17(3): 315–34.

Linnemann, Travis, Tyler Wall, and Edward Green. 2014. The Walking Dead and Killing State: Zombification and the Normalization of Police Violence. *Theoretical Criminology* 18(4): 506–27.

Litonjua, M. D. 2014. The Making of the Third World: Is the Term Still Meaningful and Useful? *Journal of Third World Studies* 31(1): 101–27.

Little Green Men Transcripts. 2024. Battle Los Angeles 2011. Contributed by user "bunniefuu," January 31. Available at: https://transcripts.foreverdreaming.org /viewtopic.php?t=144387.

Lloyd, Anthony. 2023. Disney World: Orlando, Florida, USA. In *50 Dark Destinations: Crime and Contemporary Tourism*, ed. Adam Lynes, Craig Kelly, and James Treadwell, 315–21. Bristol, U.K.: Policy Press.

Lloyd, Nicky. 2018. Haunted Landscapes: Super-Nature and the Environment. Edited by Ruth Heholt and Niamh Downing. *Green Letters* 22(2): 211–13. https://doi.org /10.1080/14688417.2018.1496672.

LoJack. 2022. "The Surprising Role of the Car in the Creation of the Cell Phone." April 19, 2022. Available at: https://www.lojack.com/blog/2022/04/surprising-role -of-car-in-creation-of-cell-phone.

Long, Kathleen. 2012. "Nature Abhors Normality": Theories of the Monstrous from Aristotle to *The X-Files* (1993–2002). In *Speaking of Monsters: A Teratological Anthology*, ed. Caroline Joan S. Picart and John Edgar Browning, 195–208. Basingstoke, Hampshire, U.K.: Palgrave Macmillan.

Loskutoff, Maxim. 2018. The Beast in Me. *The New York Times*, August 19: SR4. Published online as "The Beast in Me," on August 17, 2018, at: https://www.nytimes .com/2018/08/17/opinion/the-beast-in-me.html.

Lotringer, Sylvère. 2020. The Politics of Abjection. In *Abjection Incorporated: Mediating the Politics of Pleasure & Violence*, ed. Maggie Hennefeld and Nicholas Sammond, 33–39. Durham, NC, and London: Duke University Press.

Lowe, Thomas, Katrina Brown, Suraje Dessai, Miguel de França Doria, Kat Haynes, and Katharine Vincent. 2006. Does Tomorrow Ever Come? Disaster Narrative and Public Perceptions of Climate Change. *Public Understanding of Science* 15(4): 435– 57. https://doi.org/10.1177/0963662506063796.

Lowry, T. S. 2021. Things Only Adults Notice in Cloudy with a Chance of Meatballs. *Looper*, March 21. Available at: https://www.looper.com/354427/things-only-adults -notice-in-cloudy-with-a-chance-of-meatballs/.

Lu, Jennifer. 2019. How a Parasitic Fungus Turns Ants into "Zombies." *National Geographic*, April 18. Available at: https://www.nationalgeographic.com/animals /article/cordyceps-zombie-fungus-takes-over-ants.

Lujala, Päivi, and Siri Aas Rustad. 2011. High-Value Natural Resources: A Blessing or a Curse for Peace? *Sustainable Development Law and Policy* 12(1): 19–22, 56–57. Available at: https://digitalcommons.wcl.american.edu/sdlp/vol12/iss1/7/.

Lukpat, Alyssa. 2022. This Marauding Black Bear Has an Appetite for Home. *The New York Times*, February 22: A18. Published online as "Hank the Tank, a 500-Pound Bear, Ransacks a California Community," on February 20, 2022, at: https:// www.nytimes.com/2022/02/20/us/lake-tahoe-bear.html.

Lundberg, Kajsa Olivia. 2023. *Everyday Harms and Extraordinary Crises: Exploring the Edges of the City*. Ph.D. thesis, School of Social and Political Sciences, Faculty of Arts, University of Melbourne, Victoria, Australia.

Lynes, Adam. 2023. Amazon Warehouse Tours: Rugeley, UK or Virtual Tour. In *50 Dark Destinations: Crime and Contemporary Tourism*, ed. Adam Lynes, Craig Kelly, and James Treadwell, 305–14. Bristol, U.K.: Policy Press.

Lyons, Emmet. 2023. Costa Rican Soccer Player Killed in Crocodile Attack after Jumping into River. *CBS News*, August 4. Available at: https://www.cbsnews.com /news/costa-rica-soccer-player-crocodile-river-attack/.

Maas, Achim, Irina Comardicea, and Balázs Bodó. 2013. Environmental Terrorism—a New Security Challenge? In *Global Environmental Change: New Drivers for Resistance, Crime and Terrorism?* ed. Achim Maas, Balázs Bodó, Clementine Burnley, Irina Comardicea, and Roger Roffey, 203–20. Baden-Baden, Germany: Nomos.

Mackay, Neil. 2020. Eco-Fascism: How the Environment Could Be a Green Light for the Far Right. *The Herald*, April 19. Available at: https://www.heraldscotland.com /news/18389683.eco-fascism-environment-green-light-far-right/.

Maddrey, Joseph. 2004. *Nightmares in Red, White and Blue: The Evolution of the American Horror Film*. Jefferson, NC: McFarland.

Mahdawi, Arwa. 2024. The Latest Billionaire Trend? Doomsday Bunkers with a Flammable Moat. *The Guardian,* February 25. Available at: https://www.theguardian .com/commentisfree/2024/feb/25/billionaire-doomsday-bunkers-end-times.

Malabrigo, Pastor, Jr., Adriane B. Tobias, Joko Witono, Sofi Mursidawati, Agus Susatya, Mat Yunoh Siti-Munirah, Adhito Wicaksono, Reza Raihandhany, Sarah Edwards, and Chris J. Thorogood. 2023. Most of the World's Largest Flowers (Genus *Rafflesia*) Are Now on the Brink of Extinction. *Plants, People, Planet*, 1–16. https://doi.org/10.1002/ppp3.10431.

Manavis, Sarah. 2018. Eco-Fascism: The Ideology Marrying Environmentalism and White Supremacy Thriving Online. *The New Statesman*, September 21 (updated April 4, 2022). Available at: https://www.newstatesman.com/science-tech/2018/09 /eco-fascism-ideology-marrying-environmentalism-and-white-supremacy.

Manavis, Sarah. 2020. Is Coronavirus Leading to a Rise in Eco-Fascism? *The New Statesman*, May 11 (updated September 21, 2021). Available at: https://www .newstatesman.com/science-tech/2020/05/coronavirus-leading-rise-eco-fascism.

Mangan, Lucy. 2024. Fallout Review—an Absolute Blast of a TV Show. *The Guardian*, April 11. Available at: https://www.theguardian.com/tv-and-radio/2024/apr/11 /prime-fallout-review-an-absolute-blast-of-a-tv-show.

Mann, Geoff. 2022. Are We Approaching a New Wave of Fascism? *The New Statesman*, February 11. Available at: https://www.newstatesman.com/ideas/2022/12/fascism -new-wave-climate-change.

Marchese, David. 2023. What If People Don't Need to Care about Climate Change to Fix It? *The New York Times Magazine*, December 28, https://www.nytimes.com /interactive/2023/12/31/magazine/hannah-richie-interview.html.

Marcus, Celeste. 2024. When Artists Can't Go Home, All That's Left Is Their Art. *The New York Times*, February 25, at: https://www.nytimes.com/2024/02/25/opinion/ culture/chaim-soutine-art-identity.html.

Marikar, Sheila. 2018. The Rich Are Planning to Leave This Wretched Planet. *The New York Times*, June 9, at: https://www.nytimes.com/2018/06/09/style/axiom -space-travel.html.

Marshall, Emily Zobel. 2022. Black Panther: Wakanda Forever Reclaims the Myth of an African Utopia. *The Conversation*, November 25, 2022. Available at: https:// theconversation.com/black-panther-wakanda-forever-reclaims-the-myth-of-an -african-utopia-195157.

Martí, Mónica. 2020. Ecocritical Archaeologies of Global Ecocide in 21st-Century Post-Apocalyptic Films. In *Avenging Nature: The Role of Nature in Modern and*

Contemporary Art and Literature, ed. Eduardo Valls Oyarzun, Rebeca Gualberto Valverde, Noella Malla Garcia, María Colom Jiménez, and Rebecca Cordero Sánchez, 179–93. Lanham, MD: Lexington Books/Rowman and Littlefield.

Martyn, Monika. 2023. How Many Deer Are Killed Each Year—A Heart-Breaking Situation for These Beautiful Creatures. *World Animal Foundation*, October 19. Available at: https://worldanimalfoundation.org/advocate/deer-accidents-statistics/.

Mason, Paul. 2021. Why Only Radical Social Transformation Can Avert a Climate Catastrophe. *The New Statesman*, August 12. Available at: https://www.newstatesman.com/politics/2021/08/why-only-radical-social-transformation-can-avert-climate-catastrophe.

Matczak, Anna, and Sylvia I. Bergh. 2023. A Review of the (Potential) Implications of Climate Change for Policing Practice Worldwide. *Policing: A Journal of Policy and Practice*, 17 [September 25]: paad062. https://doi.org/10.1093/police/paad062

Matheson, Richard. 1954. *I Am Legend*. Garden City, NY: Nelson Doubleday, Inc.

Mayer, Jed. 2011. A Darker Shade of Green: William Morris, Richard Jefferies, and Posthumanist Ecologies. *The Journal of William Morris Studies* 19(3): 79–92.

Mazzilli-Daechsel, Stefano. 2019. Simondon and the Maker Movement. *Culture, Theory and Critique* 60(3–4): 237–49.

McClanahan, Bill, Avi Brisman, and Nigel South. 2017. Green Criminology, Culture, and Cinema. In *The Oxford Encyclopedia of Crime, Media, and Popular Culture*, ed. Michelle Brown and Eamonn Carbine. New York and Oxford, U.K.: Oxford University Press. Available at: http://criminology.oxfordre.com/view/10.1093/acrefore/9780190264079.001.0001/acrefore-9780190264079-e-151.

McClintock, Anne. 1995. *Imperial Leather: Race, Gender, and Sexuality in the Colonial Contest*. New York and Abingdon, Oxon, U.K.: Routledge.

McClintock, Pamela. 2018. Weekend Box Office: "Avengers: Infinity War" Crosses $1B in Record Time. *The Hollywood Reporter*, May 4. Available at: https://www.hollywoodreporter.com/movies/movie-news/box-office-avengers-infinity-war-crossing-1b-record-time-1108547/.

McClure, Tess. 2022. Billionaire Peter Thiel Refused Consent for Sprawling Lodge in New Zealand. *The Guardian*, August 18. Available at: https://www.theguardian.com/technology/2022/aug/18/peter-thiel-refused-consent-for-sprawling-lodge-in-new-zealand-local-council.

McCright, Aaron M. 2007. Dealing with Climate Change Contrarians. In *Creating a Climate for Change: Communicating Climate Change and Facilitating Social Change*, ed. Susanne C. Moser and Lisa Dilling, 200–212. Cambridge, U.K.: Cambridge University Press.

McFall-Johnsen, Morgan, and Dave Mosher. 2020. Elon Musk Says He Plans to Send 1 Million People to Mars by 2050 by Launching 3 Starship Rockets Every Day and Creating "a Lot of Jobs" on the Red Planet. *Business Insider*, January 17. Available at: https://www.businessinsider.com/elon-musk-plans-1-million-people-to-mars-by-2050-2020-1.

McFall-Johnsen, Morgan, and Joshua Zitser. 2023. Orcas Sank a Third Boat. Scientists Think "Brutal" Attacks May Be Trauma-Driven. *Business Insider*, May 19. Available at: https://www.businessinsider.com/portugal-orcas-sink-a-sailboat-and-ram-another-in-atlantic-2022-8.

McGregor, Rafe. 2022. *Critical Criminology and Literary Criticism*. Bristol, U.K.: Bristol University Press.

McNall, Scott G. 2011. *Rapid Climate Change: Causes, Consequences, and Solutions*. New York and London: Routledge.

McNamee, Kai, Christopher Intagliata, and Ari Shapiro. 2023. "The Future" Asks If Technology Will Save Humanity or Accelerate Its End. *National Public Radio*, November 8. Available at: https://www.npr.org/2024/01/09/1223805499/the-future -asks-if-technology-will-save-humanity-or-accelerate-its-end.

McNeil, Brian. 2021. A New VCU Study Explores the "Nature Is Healing" Memes That Dominated Social Media at the Height of the Pandemic. *VCU News*, May 18. Available at: https://news.vcu.edu/article/a_new_vcu_study_explores_the_nature _is_healing_memes_that_dominated.

Meil, Gabriel, and Emily Rylander. 2008. *Goodbye Earth, Hello Moon*. Portland, ME: Warren Machine Co.

Mena, Rodrigo, Summer Brown, Laura E. R. Peters, Ilan Kelman, and Hyeonggeun Ji. 2022. Connecting Disasters and Climate Change to the Humanitarian-Development-Peace Nexus. *Journal of Peacebuilding & Development* 17(3): 324–40. https://doi.org/10.1177/15423166221129633.

Mendelson, Scott. 2020. "Avengers: Endgame": Why Its Box Office Records May Never Be Broken. *Forbes*, May 19. Available at: https://www.forbes.com/sites /scottmendelson/2020/05/19/box-office-record-avengers-tenet-star-wars-avatar -jurassic/?sh=257e7d3c7140.

Merchant, Brian. 2012. The Evolution of Eco-Horror, from Godzilla to Global Warming. *Vice*, November 14. Available at: https://www.vice.com/en/article/xyy473 /the-evolution-of-eco-horror-from-godzilla-to-global-warming.

Meredith, Sam. 2020. Coronavirus Lockdowns Have Led to an Unprecedented Fall in Air Pollution for These Major Cities. *CNBC*, April 22. Available at: https:// www.cnbc.com/2020/04/22/coronavirus-air-pollution-hasfallen-dramatically-for -these-cities.html.

Metz, Jessie-Lane. 2013. A Future Without Me: Matt Damon is the Great White Hope in "Elysium." *Bitch*, August 21.

Miles, Robert. 2002. The 1790s: The Effulgence of Gothic. In *The Cambridge Companion to Gothic Fiction*, ed. Jerrold E. Hogle, 41–62. Cambridge, U.K.: Cambridge University Press.

Militz, Thane A., and Simon Foale. 2017. The "Nemo Effect": perception and reality of *Finding Nemo*'s impact on marine aquarium fisheries. *Fish and Fisheries*, 18(3): 596–606. First published: 24 January 2017. Available at: http://dx.doi.org /10.1111/faf.12202.

Miller, Ross. 2015. Marvel's Master Plan: The Complete Novice's Guide to Infinity Stones. *The Verge*, May 7. Available at: https://www.inverse.com/article/44383 -avengers-infinity-war-thanos-ethics-philosophy.

Milman, Oliver. 2021. Right Seizes Trump Playbook to Blame Migrants for Environmental Harm. *The Guardian*, May 20. Available at: https://www.theguardian .com/world/2021/may/20/environment-migrants-population-us-right-trump.

"Mint Press News Desk." 2013. Income Inequality Worsens: Ranks of Millionaires Swell as Poor Tread Water. *Mint Press News*, July 23. Available at: https://www .mintpressnews.com/income-inequality-worsens-ranks-of-millionaires-swell-as -poor-tread-water/165802/.

Mirrlees, Tanner, and Isabel Pedersen. 2016. *Elysium* as a Critical Dystopia. *International Journal of Media and Cultural Politics* 12(3): 305–22.

Mitchell, David. 2020. Our House Is on Fire by Greta Thunberg et al Review—A Family and Planet in Crisis. *The Guardian*, March 4. Available at: https://www.theguardian.com/books/2020/mar/04/our-house-is-on-fire-review.

Mohm, Tanya. 2020. The Traffic Trade-Off. *The New York Times*, June 5: A9. Published online as "The Traffic Trade-Off," on June 4, 2020 (updated June 5, 2020), at: https://www.nytimes.com/2020/06/04/climate/coronavirus-traffic-air-quality.html.

Monbiot, George. 2014. Western Australia Shark Cull Is Driven by Irrational Fear. *The Guardian*, February 19. Available at: http://www.theguardian.com/environment/georgemonbiot/2014/feb/19/western-australia-shark-cull-irrational-fear.

Monbiot, George. 2023. To Understand the Right's Climate Backlash, Look No Further Than Its Monstering of Natural England. *The Guardian*, July 20. Available at: https://www.theguardian.com/commentisfree/2023/jul/20/right-climate-backlash-natural-england-conservation.

Montanaro, Domenico. 2022. How the "Replacement" Theory Went Mainstream on the Political Right. *National Public Radio*, May 22. Available at: https://www.npr.org/2022/05/17/1099223012/how-the-replacement-theory-went-mainstream-on-the-political-right.

Mooallem, Jon. 2009. The End Is Near! *The New York Times Magazine*, April 19: 28–32, 34. Published online as "The End Is Near! (Yay!)," on April 16, 2009, at: https://www.nytimes.com/2009/04/19/magazine/19town-t.html.

Mooney, Chris. 2010. Viewpoint: Geoengineering Our Climate Future. *The Westchester Guardian*, September 11: 5, 11. Available at: https://www.mlive.com/opinion/kalamazoo/2010/09/viewpoint_geoengineering_our_c.html.

Moore, Sam, and Alex Roberts. 2022. *The Rise of Ecofascism: Climate Change and the Far Right*. Cambridge, U.K.: Polity Press.

Moran, Sibley Anne Labandeira. 2022. Prosperity and Paranoia. Engineering Atomic Fear with Cold War Images. *Quaderns de filosofia* 9(1): 165–91. https://doi.org/10.7203/qfia.9.1.21849.

Morello-Frosch, Rachel, Manuel Pastor, and James Sadd. 2001. Environmental Justice and Southern California's "Riskscape": The Distribution of Air Toxics Exposures and Health Risks among Diverse Communities. *Urban Affairs Review* 36(4): 551–78. https://doi.org/10.1177/10780870122184993.

Morton, Timothy. 2010. *The Ecological Thought*. Cambridge, MA: Harvard University Press.

Morton, Timothy. 2021. *All Art Is Ecological*. Milton Keynes, U.K.: Penguin Books.

Moser, Susanne C., and Lisa Dilling. 2004. Making Climate Hot: Communicating the Urgency and Challenge of Global Climate Change. *Environment* 46(10): 32–46.

Muffett, Carroll, and Carl Bruch. 2011. Introductory Comments: The Pervasive, Persistent, and Pofound Links Between Conflict and the Environment. *Sustainable Development Law & Policy* 12(1): 4–6. Available at: https://digitalcommons.wcl.american.edu/sdlp/vol12/iss1/4/.

Muni, S. D. 1979. The Third World: Concept and Controversy. *Third World Quarterly* 1(3) [July]: 119–28.

Munroe, Randall. 2022. Shark or Orca: Which to Fear More? *The New York Times*, August 16: D5. Published online as "Shark or Orca: Which Should You Fear More?"

on August 15, 2022, at: https://www.nytimes.com/2022/08/15/science/sharks-killer
-whales-swimming.html.

Muntean, Nick, and Matthew Thomas Payne. 2009. Attack of the Livid Dead: Recalibrating Terror in the Post-September 11 Zombie Film. In *The War on Terror and American Popular Culture: September 11 and Beyond*, ed. Andrew Schopp and Matthew B. Hill, 239–58. Madison and Teaneck, NJ: Farleigh Dickinson University Press.

Murcia Today. 2021. Killer Whales Attack Two Sailing Vessels off the Cadiz Coastline in the Andalusia Region of Spain. July 2. Available at: https://murciatoday.com /killer-whales-attack-two-sailing-vessels-off-the-cadiz-coastline-in-the-andalusia -region-of-spain_1612940-a.html.

Murphy, Bernice M. 2013. *The Rural Gothic in American Popular Culture: Backwoods Horror and Terror in the Wilderness*. New York: Palgrave.

Murphy, Tim. 2013. Barackalypse Now. *Mother Jones* 38(1) [January/February]: 49–51. Published online as "Preppers Are Getting Ready for the Barackalypse," at: https:// www.motherjones.com/politics/2012/12/preppers-survivalist-doomsday-obama/.

Murray, Robin L., and Joseph K. Heumann. 2006. The First Eco-Disaster Film? *Film Quarterly* 59(3) [Spring]: 44–51.

Murray, Robin L., and Joseph K. Heumann. 2016. *Monstrous Nature: Environment and Horror on the Big Screen*. Lincoln, NE, and London: University of Nebraska Press.

Mustafa, Daanish. 2005. The Production of an Urban Hazardscape in Pakistan: Modernity, Vulnerability, and the Range of Choice. *Annals of the Association of American Geographers* 95(3) [September]: 566–86. https://doi.org/10.1111/j.1467 -8306.2005.00475.x

Nally, Claire. 2017. How The Handmaid's Tale Is Being Transformed from Fantasy into Fact. *The Independent*, May 31. Available at: https://www.independent.co.uk/arts -entertainment/tv/features/the-handmaids-tale-elizabeth-moss-channel-4-margaret -atwood-donald-trump-feminism-abortion-a7763646.html.

Nash, Roderick. 1982. *Wilderness and the American Mind*. 3rd ed. New Haven, CT: Yale University Press.

National Highways. 2022. National Highways and The Wildlife Trusts Announce Biodiversity Boost across England. *National Highways*, May 13. Available at: https:// nationalhighways.co.uk/about-us/national-highways-and-the-wildlife-trusts -announce-biodiversity-boost-across-england/.

Nations, Courtney, Stacey Menzel Baker, and Eric Krszjzaniek. 2017. Trying to Keep You: How Grief, Abjection, and Ritual Transform the Social Meanings of a Human Body. *Consumption Markets and Culture* 20(5): 403–22. https://doi.org/10.1080 /10253866.2017.1367678.

Negroni, María. 2009. *Galería fantástica* [Fantastic gallery]. Buenos Aires: Siglo XXI.

Nelson, Michael P., and J. Baird Callicott, eds. 2008. *The Wilderness Debate Rages On*. Athens, GA, and London: University of Georgia Press.

Neocleous, Mark. 2014. The Monster and the Police: Dexter to Hobbes. *Radical Philosophy* 185(May–June): 8–18.

Neocleous, Mark. 2016. *The Universal Adversary: Security, Capital, and "The Enemies of All Mankind."* Abingdon, Oxon, U.K., and New York: GlassHouse/Routledge.

Neuman, Scott. 2022. Killer Whales Are "Attacking" Sailboats near Europe's Coast. Scientists Don't Know Why. *National Public Radio*, August 20. Available at: https://www.npr.org/2022/08/20/1117993583/orcas-attacks-spain-portugal-killer-whales.

Neuman, Scott. 2023. Revenge of the Killer Whales? Recent Boat Attacks Might Be Driven by Trauma. *National Public Radio*, June 13. Available at: https://www.npr.org/2023/06/13/1181693759/orcas-killer-whales-boat-attacks.

Nijman, Vincent, and K. Anne-Isola Nekaris. 2017. The Harry Potter Effect: The Rise in Trade of Owls as Pets in Java and Bali, Indonesia. *Global Ecology and Conservation* 11(July): 84–94.

Nijman, Vincent, and Chris R. Shepherd. 2011. The Role of Thailand in the International Trade in CITES-Listed Live Reptiles and Amphibians. *PloS One* 6(3) [March 25]: e17825. https://doi.org/10.1371/journal.pone.0017825.

Nijman, Vincent, Denise Spaan, E. J. Rode-Margono, Peter D. Roberts, Nekaris KAI Wirdateti, and K. Anne Isola Nekaris. 2014. Trade in Common Palm Civet *Paradoxurus hermaphroditus* in Javan and Balinese Markets, Indonesia. *Small Carnivore Conservation* 51 [December]: 11–17. Available at: https://smallcarnivoreconservation.com/index.php/sccg/issue/view/271/73.

Nixon, Rob. 2011. *Slow Violence and the Environmentalism of the Poor*. Cambridge, MA: Harvard University Press.

Norsworthy, Andrew. 2023. Orcas Out for Revenge? *The Dallas Express*, May 29. Available at: https://dallasexpress.com/health/orcas-out-for-revenge/.

North, Anna. 2014. From Daleks to Zombies: What Monsters Mean to Us. *The New York Times*, October 27. Available at: https://archive.nytimes.com/op-talk.blogs.nytimes.com/2014/10/27/from-daleks-to-zombies-what-monsters-mean-to-us/.

North, Anna. 2015. A "Star Trek" Future Might Be Closer Than We Think. *The New York Times*, July 10. Available at: https://archive.nytimes.com/takingnote.blogs.nytimes.com/2015/07/10/a-star-trek-future-might-be-closer-than-we-think/.

Nugent Connie, Gilbert Berdine, and Kenneth Nugent. 2018. The *Undead* in Culture and Science. *Proceedings of Baylor University Medical Center* 31(2): 244–49. https://doi.org/10.1080/08998280.2018.1441216.

Nurse, Angus. 2015. *Policing Wildlife: Perspectives on the Enforcement of Wildlife Legislation*. Basingstoke, Hampshire, U.K.: Palgrave Macmillan.

Nuzzo, Luciano. 2013. Foucault and the Enigma of the Monster. *International Journal for the Semiotics of Law* 26(1): 55–72.

O'Brien, Keith. 2012. How to Survive Societal Collapse in Suburbia. *The New York Times Magazine*, November 18: 36. Published online as "How to Survive Societal Collapse in Suburbia," on November 16, 2012, at: https://www.nytimes.com/2012/11/18/magazine/how-to-survive-societal-collapse-in-suburbia.html.

O'Connell, Mark. 2020. Real Estate for the Apocalypse: My Journey into a Survival Bunker. *The Guardian*, March 17. Available at: https://www.theguardian.com/news/2020/mar/17/real-estate-for-the-apocalypse-my-journey-into-a-survival-bunker.

O'Connor, Rory. 2018. Ethan Hawke on Dreaming of a Fourth "Before" Film, Why He's Not Having a McConaughey Moment, and the Necessity of Film Festivals. *The Film Stage*, August 23. Available at: https://thefilmstage.com/ethan-hawke-on-dreaming-of-a-fourth-before-film-why-hes-not-having-a-mcconaughey-moment-and-the-necessity-of-film-festivals/.

Ogao, Emma. 2023. Killer Whales Learn "Coordinated" Attacks on Sailboats, Some Observers Say. *ABC News*, May 24. Available at: https://abcnews.go.com /International/killer-whales-learn-coordinated-attacks-sailboats-observers/story ?id=99534426.

Oladipo, Gloria. 2022. Woman Gored by Bison in Yellowstone National Park. *The Guardian*, June 1. Available at: https://www.theguardian.com/environment/2022/ jun/01/woman-gored-bison-yellowstone-national-park.

Olney, Ian. 2017. *Zombie Cinema*. New Brunswick, Camden, and Newark, NJ, and London: Rutgers University Press.

Olorunnisola, Israel. 2023. MCU: Was Thanos Right? *MovieWeb.com*, February 6. Available at: https://movieweb.com/mcu-thanos-was-right-why/.

Olson, Robert L. 1995. Sustainability as a Social Vision. *Journal of Social Issues* 51(4) [Winter]: 15–35. https://doi.org/10.1111/j.1540-4560.1995.tb01346.x.

O'Neill, Brian C., Elmar Kriegler, Keywan Riahi, Kristie L. Ebi, Stephane Hallegate, Timothy R. Carter, Rita Mathur, and Detlef P. van Vuuren. 2014. A New Scenario Framework for Climate Change Research: The Concept of Shared Socioeconomic Pathways. *Climatic Change* 122(3) [February]: 387–400. https://doi.org/10.1007 /s10584-013-0905-2.

Onstad, Katrina. 2008. Horror Auteur Is Unfinished with the Undead. *The New York Times*, February 10: A8. Published online as "Horror Auteur Is Unfinished With the Undead," on February 10, 2008, at: https://www.nytimes.com/2008/02/10 /movies/10onst.html.

Onstad, Katrina. 2017. What World IS This? *The New York Times*, April 23: AR1. Published online as "'The Handmaid's Tale': A Newly Resonant Dystopia Comes to TV," on April 20, 2017, at: https://www.nytimes.com/2017/04/20/arts/television /the-handmaids-tale-elisabeth-moss-samira-wiley-margaret-atwood-hulu.html.

Ordiz, Inés, and Sandra Casanova-Vizcaíno. 2018. Introduction: Latin America, the Caribbean, and the Persistence of the Gothic. In *Latin American Gothic in Literature and Culture*, ed. Sandra Casanova-Vizcaíno and Inés Ordiz, 1–13. New York and Abingdon, Oxon, U.K.: Routledge.

Orr, Christopher. 2004. The Movie Review: "The Day After Tomorrow." *The Atlantic*, October 12. Available at: https://www.theatlantic.com/entertainment/archive/2004 /10/the-movie-review-the-day-after-tomorrow/69511/.

Osaka, Shannon. 2020a. Coronavirus: The Worst Way to Drive Down Emissions. *Grist*, May 3. Available at: https://grist.org/climate/coronavirus-the-worst-way-to -drive-down-emissions/.

Osaka, Shannon. 2020b. What Lockdown? Traffic Returns, and So Do Carbon Emissions. *Grist*, June 15. Available at: https://grist.org/climate/what-lockdown -traffic-returns-and-so-do-carbon-emissions/.

Osaka, Shannon, and Kate Yoder. 2020. Climate Change Is a Catastrophe. But Is It an "Existential Threat"? *Grist*, March 3. Available at: https://grist.org/climate/is-the -climate-crisis-an-existential-threat-scientists-weigh-in/.

Osborne, Hannah. 2020a. Killer Whale Boat Attacks "Getting Worse and Worse," Scientist Says. *Newsweek*, November 13. Available at: https://www.newsweek.com /killer-whale-boat-attack-getting-worse-1547212.

Osborne, Hannah. 2020b. Killer Whales Filmed Attacking Yacht in "Scary" Encounter Lasting Two Hours. *Newsweek*, October 16. Available at: https://www.newsweek.com/killer-whale-attack-yacht-two-hours-1539808.

Osborne, Hannah. 2020c. Scientists Say They Know Why Killer Whales Are Attacking Boats Off the Coast of Spain. *Newsweek*, September 30 (updated October 1). Available at: https://www.newsweek.com/killer-whale-attack-boats-scientists-spain-1535219.

Osborne, Hannah. 2021. Killer Whales Attack Couple's Boat, Leaving Them Adrift Miles from Land. *Newsweek*, November 4. Available at: https://www.newsweek.com/killer-whales-attack-boat-portugal-1645871.

Osnos, Evan. 2017. Doomsday Prep for the Super-Rich. *The New Yorker*, January 22. Available at: https://www.newyorker.com/magazine/2017/01/30/doomsday-prep-for-the-super-rich.

Pag, Andy. 2021. Encounters with Orcas and How to Protect Your Boat. *Yachting Monthly*, November 9. Available at: https://www.yachtingmonthly.com/sailing-skills/encounters-with-orcas-how-to-protect-your-boat-81741.

Pandolfo, Chris. 2024. Python Swallows Woman Whole in Indonesia. *Fox News*, June 8. Available at: https://www.foxnews.com/world/python-swallows-woman-whole-indonesia.

Panofsky, Erwin. 1939[1972]. *Studies in Iconology: Humanistic Themes in the Art of the Renaissance*. Boulder, CO: Icon Editions/Westview Press.

Pappas, Stephanie. 2021. 5 Gruesome Killer Whale Attacks. *Live Science*, August 24. Available at: https://www.livescience.com/gruesome-killer-whale-attacks.html.

Pappas, Stephanie. 2022. Orcas Are Attacking Boats near Europe. It Might Be a Fad. *Live Science*, August 22. Available at: https://www.livescience.com/orcas-attacking-boats-europe.

Pare, Sascha. 2023. Orcas Have Sunk 3 Boats in Europe and Appear to Be Teaching Others to Do the Same. But Why? *Live Science*, May 18. Available at: https://www.livescience.com/animals/orcas/orcas-have-sunk-3-boats-in-europe-and-appear-to-be-teaching-others-to-do-the-same-but-why.

Parker, Elizabeth. 2016. "Just a Piece of Wood": Jan Švankmajer's *Otesánek* and the EcoGothic. In *Plant Horror: Approaches to the Monstrous Vegetal in Fiction and Film*, ed. Dawn Keetley and Angela Tenga, 214–25. London: Palgrave Macmillan.

Parker, Elizabeth, and Michelle Poland. 2019. *Gothic Nature*: An Introduction. *Gothic Nature* 1 [September 14], 1–20. Available at: https://gothicnaturejournal.com/wp-content/uploads/2019/09/Parker-Poland_1-20_Gothic-Nature-1_2019.pdf.

Patrick, Brian Anse. 2014. *Zombology: Zombies and the Decline of the West (and Guns)*. London: Arktos.

Patrick, Stewart, and Alexandra Huggins. 2023. The Term "Global South" Is Surging. It Should Be Retired. *Carnegie Endowment for International Peace*, August 15. Available at: https://carnegieendowment.org/2023/08/15/term-global-south-is-surging.-it-should-be-retired-pub-90376.

Patten, Daniel J. 2016. The Uncatchable Crook: Pursuing Effective State Crime Control. *The Hilltop Review* 9(1) [Fall]: 22–38.

Peltier, Elian. 2020. Orcas Are Ramming Boats Near Spain, and Experts Aren't Sure Why. *The New York Times*, September 20: A10. Published online as "Rough Play or

Bad Intentions? Orca Encounters Off Iberia Baffle Experts," on September 20, 2020, at: https://www.nytimes.com/2020/09/20/world/europe/orca-boat-spain.html.

Pepper, David. 1996. *Modern Environmentalism: An Introduction*. London: Routledge.

Phelan, Chanda. 2009. "Omega-Alpha." Undergraduate thesis, Pomona College, Claremont, CA.

Phillips, Kendall R. 2021. *A Cinema of Hopelessness: The Rhetoric of Rage in 21st Century Popular Culture*. Cham, Switzerland: Palgrave Macmillan.

Phillips, Maya. 2019. The Narrative Experiment That Is the Marvel Cinematic Universe. *The New Yorker*, April 26. Available at: https://www.newyorker.com/culture/culture-desk/the-narrative-experiment-that-is-the-marvel-cinematic-universe.

Phillips, Maya. 2022. "Panther" Has Plenty of Depth. *The New York Times*, November 26, 2022: C1. Published online as "How 'Black Panther' Builds Complex Characters from the Politics of Colonization," on November 25, 2022 (updated June 20, 2023), at: https://www.nytimes.com/2022/11/25/movies/black-panther-wakanda-forever-colonization.html.

Picart, Caroline Joan (Kay) S., and John Edgar Browning. 2012. Introduction: Monstrosity and Multiculturalism. In *Speaking of Monsters: A Teratological Anthology*, ed. Caroline Joan S. Picart and John Edgar Browning, 1–12. Basingstoke, Hampshire, U.K.: Palgrave Macmillan.

Picart, Caroline Joan (Kay), and Cecil E. Greek. 2007. Introduction: Toward a Gothic Criminology. In *Monsters In and Among Us: Toward a Gothic Criminology*, ed. Caroline Joan (Kay) Picart and Cecil E. Greek, 11–44. Madison, NJ: Fairleigh Dickinson University Press.

Pielke, Roger. 2019. The Incredible Story of How Climate Change Became Apocalyptic. *Forbes*, December 6. Available at: https://www.forbes.com/sites/rogerpielke/2019/12/06/the-incredible-story-of-how-climate-change-became-apocalyptic/.

Piepenburg, Erik. 2015. Scary Holiday Movies: See You When You're Sleeping. *The New York Times*, December 23, at: https://www.nytimes.com/2015/12/27/movies/scary-holiday-movies-see-you-when-youre-sleeping.html.

Pihlström, Sami. 2020. Transcendental Guilt and Eating Human Beings, Or Levinas's Meeting with the Zombies. In *Man-Eating Monsters: Anthropocentrism and Popular Culture*, ed. Dina Khapaeva, 35–50. Bingley, U.K.: Emerald Publishing Limited.

Pike, David L. 2005. *Subterranean Cities: The World beneath Paris and London, 1800–1945*. Ithaca, NY, and London: Cornell University Press.

Pitre, Jake. 2023. The Magical Work of Brand Futurity: The Mythmaking of Disney+. *Television & New Media* 24(6): 712–29. https://doi.org/10.1177/15274764221128923.

Plante, Corey. 2018. "Avengers: Infinity War" Fans Think Thanos Did Nothing Wrong. *Inverse*, May 1. Available at: https://www.inverse.com/article/44383-avengers-infinity-war-thanos-ethics-philosophy.

Plumer, Brad, and Nadja Popovich. 2020. Traffic and Pollution Plummet as U.S. Cities Shut Down for Coronavirus. *The New York Times*, March 22, at: https://www.nytimes.com/interactive/2020/03/22/climate/coronavirus-usa-traffic.html.

Plumwood, Val. 1991. Nature, Self, and Gender: Feminism, Environmental Philosophy, and the Critique of Rationalism. *Hypatia* 6(1): 3–27.

Plumwood, Val. 1999. Being Prey. In *The New Earth Reader: The Best of* Terra Nova, ed. David Rothenberg and Marta Ulvaeus, 76–91. Cambridge, MA, and London: The MIT Press.

Polak, Fred. 1973. *The Image of the Future*. San Francisco, CA: Jossey-Bass.

Posick, Chad, and Mackenzie McBride. 2017. Biological Criminology. In *The Routledge Companion to Criminological Theory and Concepts*, ed. Avi Brisman, Eamonn Carrabine, and Nigel South, 28–32. Abingdon, Oxon, U.K., and New York: Routledge.

Powell, Corey S. 2019. Jeff Bezos Foresees a Trillion People Living in Millions of Space Colonies. Here's What He's Doing to Get the Ball Rolling. *NBC News*, May 15. Available at: https://www.nbcnews.com/mach/science/jeff-bezos-foresees-trillion -people-living-millions-space-colonies-here-ncna1006036.

Price, Simon J., Jonathan R. Ford, Anthony H. Cooper, and Catherine Neal. 2011. Humans as Major Geological and Geomorphological Agents in the Anthropocene: The Significance of Artificial Ground in Great Britain. *Philosophical Transactions of the Royal Society A: Mathematical, Physical, and Engineering Sciences*, 369(1938): 1056–84. https://doi.org/10.1098/rsta.2010.0296.

Propper, David. 2024. Killer Whales Bang into 50-Foot Yacht off Morocco, Forcing 2 on Board to Abandon Ship before It Sinks. *New York Post*, May 14. Available at: https://nypost.com/2024/05/14/world-news/pod-of-killer-whales-sink-50-foot -yacht-in-the-strait-of-gibraltar/.

Prosek, James. 2010. Beautiful friendship. *National Geographic*, 217(1) [January]: 120–131.

Prud'homme, Alex. 2011. Drought: A Creeping Disaster. *The New York Times*, July 17: SR3. Published online as "Drought: A Creeping Disaster," on July 17, 2011, at: https://www.nytimes.com/2011/07/17/opinion/sunday/17drought.html.

Puglise, Nicole. 2016. "Worse Than One Thousand Pukes": Fetid Corpse Flower Overwhelms New York. *The Guardian*, July 29. Accessed at: https://www .theguardian.com/environment/2016/jul/29/corpse-flower-new-york-botanical -garden-blooms.

Punter, David, ed. 2000. *A Companion to the Gothic*. Oxford, U.K.: Wiley-Blackwell.

Rafter, Nicole. 2006. *Shots in the Mirror: Crime Films and Society*, 2nd ed. Oxford and New York: Oxford University Press.

Rafter, Nicole, and Per Ystehede. 2010. Here Be Dragons: Lombroso, the Gothic, and Social Control. In *Popular Culture, Crime, and Social Control*, Sociology of Crime, Law and Deviance, Vol. 14, ed. Mathieu Deflem, 263–84. Bingley, U.K.: Emerald Publishing Limited.

Rahner, Mark. 2019. Are You One of the Good People of the Zombie Apocalypse? *Yes!* 89(Spring): 62–63.

Readfearn, Graham. 2017. New York Times Defends Hiring of Climate Science Denier Bret Stephens, Claiming "Intellectual Honesty." *DeSmog*, April 25. Available at: https://www.desmog.com/2017/04/25/new-york-times-defends-hiring-climate -science-denier-bret-stephens-claiming-intellectual-honesty/.

Reich, Robert. 2011. The Rebirth of Social Darwinism. *Robertreich.org*, November 30. Available at: https://robertreich.org/post/13567144944.

Renner, Karen J. 2012. The Appeal of the Apocalypse. *Lit: Literature Interpretation Theory* 23(3): 203–11. https://doi.org/10.1080/10436928.2012.703599.

Reusswig, Fritz, and Anthony A. Leiserowitz. 2005. The International Impact of The Day After Tomorrow (Commentary). *Environment* 47(3): 41–3. Available

at: https://climatecommunication.yale.edu/wp-content/uploads/2016/02/2005_01
_The-International-Impact-of-The-Day-After-Tomorrow.pdf.

Reynolds, Richard. 1992. *Super Heroes: A Modern Mythology*. Jackson: University Press of Mississippi.

Rhode, David, and Reed Abelson. 2005. Storm and Crisis: The Victims; Vulnerable, and Doomed in the Storm. *The New York Times*, September 19: A1. Published online as "154 Patients Died, Many in Intense Heat, as Rescues Lagged," on September 19, 2005, at: https://www.nytimes.com/2005/09/19/us/nationalspecial/154-patients-died-many-inintense-heat-as-rescues-lagged.html.

Rhyne, Andrew L., Michael F. Tlusty, Pamela J. Schofield, Les Kaufman, James A. Morris Jr, and Andrew W. Bruckner. 2012. Revealing the Appetite of the Marine Aquarium Fish Trade: The Volume and Biodiversity of Fish Imported into the United States. *PLOS One* 7(5), e35808. https://doi.org/10.1371/journal.pone.0035808.

Ricard, Marc. 2019. "On the Border Territory between the Animal and the Vegetable Kingdoms": Plant-Animal Hybridity and the Late Victorian Imagination. *Gothic Nature* 1 [September 14]: 127–54. Available at: https://gothicnaturejournal.com/wp-content/uploads/2019/09/Ricard_127-154.pdf.

Rich, Adrienne. 1987. Note toward a Politics of Location. In *Blood, Bread, and Poetry: Selected Prose 1979–1985*, 210–31. London: Virago Press.

Richardson, Kalia. 2023. A Poignant Scene's Special Moments. *The New York Times*, January 8: AR8. Published online as "In 'Black Panther: Wakanda Forever,' One Scene Celebrates and Commemorates," on January 6, 2023 (updated January 11, 2023), at: https://www.nytimes.com/2023/01/06/movies/black-panther-wakanda-forever-funeral-scene.html.

Richter, Virginia. 2011. *Literature after Darwin: Human Beasts in Western Fiction, 1859–1939*. Basingstoke, Hampshire, U.K.: Palgrave Macmillan.

Robbins, Nicholas Walter. 2014. *Civilization of the Living Dead: Canonical Monstrosity, the Romero Zombie, and the Political Subject*. Ph.D. dissertation, Graduate Center, City University of New York (CUNY). Available at: https://academicworks.cuny.edu/cgi/viewcontent.cgi?article=1467&context=gc_etds.

Robertson, Adi. 2016. In Trump's America, The Handmaid's Tale Matters More Than Ever. *The Verge*, November 9. Available at: https://www.theverge.com/2014/12/20/7424951/does-the-handmaids-tale-hold-up-dystopia-feminism-fiction.

Robledo, Anthony. 2023. Orca Attacking Boat near Scotland Marks First in North Sea, following Iberian Coast Incidents. *USA Today*, June 21. Available at: https://www.usatoday.com/story/news/world/2023/06/21/orca-attacks-boat-scotland/70344698007/.

Roeloffs, Mary Whitfill. 2023. Orcas Attack 2 Yachts in Ocean Race: Latest Reports of Killer Whale Antics. *Forbes*, June 23. Available at: https://www.forbes.com/sites/maryroeloffs/2023/06/23/orcas-attack-2-yachts-in-ocean-race-latest-reports-of-killer-whale-antics/.

Rooney, David, and Lovia Gyarkye. 2024. Critics' Conversation: "Civil War" and Civic Anxiety. *Hollywood Reporter*, April 23. Available at: https://www.hollywoodreporter.com/movies/movie-reviews/civil-war-debate-alex-garland-kirsten-dunst-trump-election-critics-1235879241/.

Rosen, Elizabeth K. 2008. *Apocalyptic Transformation: Apocalypse and the Postmodern Imagination*. Lanham, MD: Lexington Books/Rowman and Littlefield.

Rosenthal, Norman. 2000. Apocalypse: Beauty and Horror in Contemporary Art. In *Apocalypse: Beauty and Horror in Contemporary Art*, ed. Norman Rosenthal, Michael Barcher, Michael Bracewell, James Hall, and Nathan Kernan, 12–31. London: Royal Academy of Arts.

Ross, Andrew. 1991. Is Global Culture Warming Up? *Social Text* 28: 3–30. Available at: https://www.jstor.org/stable/466372.

Rossman, Sean. 2017. Pythons Can Kill a Human in Minutes and Swallow Them in an Hour. *USA Today*, March 30. Available at: https://www.usatoday.com/story/news /nation-now/2017/03/30/pythons-can-kill-human-minutes-and-swallow-them-hour /99824246/.

Rothe, Dawn L., and David Kauzlarich. 2022. *Crimes of the Powerful: White-Collar Crime and Beyond*, 2nd ed. Abingdon, Oxon, U.K., and New York: Routledge.

Rothman, Lily. 2014. *Godzilla, Into the Storm,* and More Summer Cli-Fi Thrillers. *Time*, May 8. Available at: https://time.com/92065/godzilla-into-the-storm-and -more-summer-cli-fi-thrillers/.

Rowlands, Ian H. 2001. Transnational Corporations and Global Environmental Politics. In *Non-State Actors and Global Politics*, ed. Daphné Josselin and William Wallace, 133–49. New York: Palgrave Macmillan.

Roy, Cameron. 2024. Horrifying Moment Missing Woman Is Found Eaten Alive by Giant Python—as Locals Cut Her Body out of Snake's Belly in Indonesia. *Daily Mail*, June 8. Available at: https://www.dailymail.co.uk/news/article-13508489 /woman-eaten-alive-giant-python-Indonesia.html.

Royal Society. 2009. *Geoengineering the Climate: Science, Governance and Uncertainty.* September 1, RS Policy document 10/09. London: The Royal Society (Science Policy). Available at: https://royalsociety.org/news-resources/publications/2009 /geoengineering-climate/.

Ruggiero, Vincenzo. 2003. *Crime in Literature: Sociology of Deviance and Fiction.* London and New York: Verso.

Runhovde, Siv Rebekka. 2020. Myths of Causality, Control and Coherence in the "War on Wildlife Crime." In *Routledge International Handbook of Green Criminology,* 2nd ed., ed. Avi Brisman and Nigel South, 543–54. Abingdon, Oxon, U.K., and New York: Routledge.

Rushkoff, Douglas. 2022a. The Super-Rich "Preppers" Planning to Save Themselves from the Apocalypse. *The Guardian*, September 4. Available at: https://www .theguardian.com/news/2022/sep/04/super-rich-prepper-bunkers-apocalypse -survival-richest-rushkoff.

Rushkoff, Douglas. 2022b. *Survival of the Richest: Escape Fantasies of the Tech Billionaires.* New York: W.W. Norton.

Rushkoff, Douglas. 2023. "We Will Coup Whoever We Want!" The Unbearable Hubris of Musk and the Billionaire Tech Bros. *The Guardian,* November 25. Available at: https://www.theguardian.com/books/2023/nov/25/we-will-coup-whoever-we -want-the-unbearable-hubris-of-musk-and-the-billionaire-tech-bros.

Rust, Stephen A., and Carter Soles. 2014. Ecohorror Special Cluster: "Living in Fear, Living in Dread, Pretty Soon We'll All Be Dead." *ISLE: Interdisciplinary Studies in Literature and Environment* 21(3) [Summer]: 509–12.

Rutherford, Jennifer. 2013. *Zombies*. Abingdon, Oxon, U.K., and New York: Routledge.

Rutz, Christian, Matthias-Claudio Loretto, Amanda E. Bates, Sarach C. Davidson, Carlos M. Duarte, Walter Jetz, Mark Johnson, Akiko Kato, Roland Kays, Thomas Mueller, Richard B. Primack, Yan Ropert-Coudert, Marlee A. Tucker, Martin Wikelski, and Francesca Cagnacci. 2020. COVID-19 Lockdown Allows Researchers to Quantify the Effects of Human Activity on Wildlife. *Nature Ecology and Evolution* 4 [June 22], 1156–1159. https://doi.org/10.1038/s41559-020-1237-z.

Ryan, John Charles. 2016. On the Death of Plants: John Kinsella's Radical Pastoralism and the Weight of Botanical Melancholia. *Ecozon@* [*European Journal of Literature, Culture, and Environment/Revista Europea de Literatura, Cultura y Medioambiente*] 7(2): 113–33. https://doi.org/10.37536/ECOZONA.2016.7.2.1004.

Ryzik, Melena. 2017. Climate-Change Film? Is Emma Stone in It? *The New York Times*, October 3: C1. Published online as "Can Hollywood Movies About Climate Change Make a Difference?" on October 2, 2017, at: https://www.nytimes.com/2017/10/02/movies/mother-darren-aronofsky-climate-change.html.

Saadia, Manu. 2016. *Trekonomics*. San Francisco, CA: Pipertext/Inkshares.

Sagan, Carl. 1994. *Pale Blue Dot: A Vision of the Human Future in Space*. New York: Random House.

Salvoni, Elena. 2023. Killer Whales Are Ramming Boats off the Coast of Spain in Spate of Deadly Attacks to Avenge Orca Matriarch Gladis after She Was Injured "by Boat or Fishing Net," Experts Say. *Daily Mail*, May 28. Available at: https://www.dailymail.co.uk/news/article-12133005/Killer-whales-ramming-boats-coast-Spain-avenge-orca-matriarch-Gladis.html.

Sammond, Nicholas. 2020. A Matter of Fluids: EC Comics and the Vernacular Abject. In *Abjection Incorporated: Mediating the Politics of Pleasure and Violence*, ed. Maggie Hennefeld and Nicholas Sammond, 217–42. Durham, NC, and London: Duke University Press.

Sandwell, Ian, and Chris Longridge. 2024. Marvel's "Phases" Explained: What Is Phase 5? What Happened in Phase 3? *Digital Spy*, February 7. Available at: https://www.digitalspy.com/movies/a871567/marvel-phase-4-3-2-1-mcu/.

Santos, Rita, Silvia Roque, and Sofia José Santos. 2018. De-Securitising "the South in the North"? Gendered Narratives on the Refugee Flows in the European Mediascape. *Contexto Internacional* 40(3): 453–77. Available at: https://www.scielo.br/j/cint/a/xJvZXSbTDDRSbwS4KQ5r68p/.

Saunders, Robert A. 2012. Undead Spaces: Fear, Globalisation, and the Popular Geopolitics of Zombiism. *Geopolitics* 17(1): 80–104.

Savage, Luke. 2021. Perhaps We Should Regulate Deranged Billionaires like Elon Musk. *Jacobin*, February 5. Available at: https://jacobinmag.com/2021/02/elon-musk-spacex-satellites-starlink-richest-man.

Scheffran, Jürgen, and Thomas Cannaday. 2013. Resistance to Climate Change Policies: The Conflict Potential of Non-Fossil Energy Paths and Climate Engineering. In *Global Environmental Change: New Drivers for Resistance, Crime and Terrorism?* ed. Achim Maas, Balázs Bodó, Clementine Burnley, Irina Comardicea, and Roger Roffey, 261–92. Baden-Baden, Germany: Nomos.

Scherer, Agnes. 2016. The Pre-Cosmic Squiggle: Tendril Excesses in Early Modern Art and Science Fiction Cinema. In *Plant Horror: Approaches to the Monstrous Vegetal in Fiction and Film*, ed. Dawn Keetley and Angela Tenga, 31–53. London: Palgrave Macmillan.

Schiappa, Edward, Peter B. Gregg, and Dean E. Hewes. 2006. Can One TV Show Make a Difference? *Will & Grace* and the Parasocial Contact Hypothesis. *Journal of Homosexuality* 51(4): 15–37. https://doi.org/10.1300/J082v51n04_02.

Schmeink, Lars. 2016. "Scavenge, Slay, Survive": The Zombie Apocalypse, Exploration, and Lived Experience in *DayZ*. *Science Fiction Studies* 43(1): 67–84. https://doi.org/10.5621/sciefictstud.43.1.0067.

Schmidt, Christopher. 2014. Why are Dystopian Films on the Rise Again? *JSTOR Daily*, November 19. Available at: https://daily.jstor.org/why-are-dystopian-films-on-the-rise-again/.

Schmidt, Ernie. 2008. *Good-Bye Earth?* Baltimore, MD: PublishAmerica.

Schmidt, Ingrid. 2024. Billionaires' Survivalist Bunkers Go Absolutely Bonkers with Fiery Moats and Water Cannons. *Hollywood Reporter*, February 12. Available at: https://www.hollywoodreporter.com/lifestyle/lifestyle-news/bunkers-billionaires-survive-apocalypse-cost-features-1235822762/.

Schoell, William. 2008. *Creature Features: Nature Turned Nasty in the Movies*. Jefferson, NC: McFarland.

Schor, Elana. 2008. Cheney Tried to Alter Climate Change Testimony, Says Official. *The Guardian*, July 9. Available at: https://www.theguardian.com/world/2008/jul/10/dickcheney.climatechange.

Schwartz, John. 2020. Precautions Taken Because of Virus Help to Fight Climate Change, Too. *The New York Times*, March 17: A7. Published online as "Social Distancing? You Might Be Fighting Climate Change, Too," on March 13, 2020, at: https://www.nytimes.com/2020/03/13/climate/coronavirus-habits-carbon-footprint.html.

Scorsese, Martin. 2019. The Dying Art of Filmmaking. *The New York Times*, November 5: A27. Published online as "Martin Scorsese: I Said Marvel Movies Aren't Cinema. Let Me Explain," on November 4, 2019, at: https://www.nytimes.com/2019/11/04/opinion/martin-scorsese-marvel.html.

Scott, Manda. 2023. Thrutopia: The Future of Politics. *Permaculture*, 117(Autumn): 13–17.

Scrimgeour, Guthrie. 2023. Inside Mark Zuckerberg's Top-Secret Hawaii Compound. *Wired*, December 14. Available at: https://www.wired.com/story/mark-zuckerberg-inside-hawaii-compound/.

Seager, Joni. 1993. Creating a Culture of Destruction: Gender, Militarism, and the Environment. In *Toxic Struggles: The Theory and Practice of Environmental Justice*, ed. Richard Hofrichter, 58–66. Philadelphia, PA: New Society Publishers.

Seemangal, Robin. 2016. Elon Musk Charts Path to Colonizing Mars within a Decade. *Observer*, June 6. Available at: https://observer.com/2016/06/elon-musk-charts-path-to-colonizing-mars-within-a-decade/.

Segrin, C., and Robin L. Nabi. 2002. Does Television Viewing Cultivate Unrealistic Expectations about Marriage? *Journal of Communication* 52(2) [June]: 247–63. https://doi.org/10.1111/j.1460-2466.2002.tb02543.x.

Senf, Carol. 2020. Blue Books, Baedekers, Cookbooks, and the Monsters in the Mirror: Bram Stoker's *Dracula*. In *Man-Eating Monsters: Anthropocentrism and Popular Culture*, ed. Dina Khapaeva, 65–81. Bingley, U.K.: Emerald Publishing Limited.

Sepie, Amba J. 2017. More Than Stories, More Than Myths: Animal/Human/Nature(s) in Traditional Ecological Worldviews. *Humanities* 6(4): 78. https://doi.org/10.3390/h6040078.

Serres, Michael. 2010. *Malfeasance: Appropriation through Pollution*. Translated by Anne-Marie Feenberg-Dibon. Stanford, CA: Stanford University Press.

Seymour, Richard. 2023. A World on Fire. *The New Statesman*, July 21–27: 32–36. Published online as "Summer at the End of the World," on July 17, 2023, at: https://www.newstatesman.com/ideas/2023/07/summer-extreme-heat-wave-apocalypse.

Sharf, Zack. 2019. Martin Scorsese Compares Marvel Movies to Theme Parks: "That's Not Cinema." *IndieWire*, October 4. Available at: https://www.indiewire.com/2019/10/martin-scorsese-marvel-movies-not-cinema-theme-parks-1202178747/.

Sharrett, Christopher. 1984. The Idea of Apocalypse in *The Texas Chainsaw Massacre*. In *Planks of Reason: Essays on the Horror Film*, ed. Barry Keith Grant, 255–76. Metuchen, NJ, and London: Scarecrow.

Shead, Sam. 2021. Peter Thiel Files Plans to Build Luxury Lodge, Private Home and Meditation Pod on New Zealand Estate. *CNBC*, September 1. Available at: https://www.cnbc.com/2021/09/01/peter-thiel-files-plans-to-build-luxury-lodge-on-new-zealand-estate.html.

Shearing, Clifford. 2001. Punishment and the Changing Face of the Governance. *Punishment & Society* 3(2) [April]: 203–20. https://doi.org/10.1177/1462474501003002001.

Shearing, Clifford D., and Philip C. Stenning. 1983. Private Security: Implications for Social Control. *Social Problems* 30(5) [June]: 493–506. https://doi.org/10.2307/800267.

Shelley, Mary. 1818[2013]. *Frankenstein: Or, the Modern Prometheus*. Richmond, U.K.: Alma Classics Ltd.

Shoard, Catherine. 2019. Martin Scorsese Says Marvel Movies Are "Not Cinema." *The Guardian*, October 4. Available at: https://www.theguardian.com/film/2019/oct/04/martin-scorsese-says-marvel-movies-are-not-cinema.

Shostak, Seth. 2012. Depth Change: What Do the "Battleship" Aliens Want from Us, Anyway? *Discover*. May 18. Available at: https://www.discovermagazine.com/the-sciences/depth-change-what-do-the-battleship-aliens-want-from-us-anyway.

Shuster, Andrew. 2021. Andy Serkis Calls Let There Be Carnage's Rave Scene Venom's "Coming-Out Party." *CBR*, September 28. Available at: https://www.cbr.com/venom-let-there-be-carnage-rave-scene-coming-out-party/.

Shute, Nevil. 1957. *On the Beach*. New York: William Morrow.

Sidawi, Sam. 2011. *Goodbye Earth: Air, Land, Water, Ozone . . . It's All Connected*. North Charleston, SC: CreateSpace.

Sifry, Micah L. 2003. *Spoiling for a Fight: Third-Party Politics in America*. New York, and Abingdon, Oxon, U.K.: Routledge.

Silver, Marc. 2015. If You Shouldn't Call It the Third World, What Should You Call It? *National Public Radio*, January 4. Available at: https://www.npr.org/sections/goatsandsoda/2015/01/04/372684438/if-you-shouldnt-call-it-the-third-world-what-should-you-call-it.

Silver, Marc. 2021. Memo to People of Earth: "Third World" Is an Offensive Term! *National Public Radio*, January 8. Available at: https://www.npr.org/sections/goatsandsoda/2021/01/08/954820328/memo-to-people-of-earth-third-world-is-an-offensive-term.

Simondon, Gilbert. 2009. Technical Mentality. Translated by Arne De Boever. *Parrhesia: A Journal of Critical Philosophy* 7: 17–27. Available at: https://www .parrhesiajournal.org/parrhesia07/parrhesia07_simondon2.pdf.

Simondon, Gilbert. 2014. *Sur la technique*. Paris: Presses Universitaires de France.

Simons, Paul. 2020. Massive and Malodorous—World's Biggest Flower Found. *The Guardian*, January 14. Accessed at: https://www.theguardian.com/science/2020/jan /14/massive-and-malodorous-worlds-biggest-flower-found.

Simpkins, Graham. 2020. COVID-19 Carbon Cuts. *Nature Reviews Earth & Environment* 1(May 19): 279. https://doi.org/10.1038/s43017-020-0062-x.

Simpson, Catherine. 2010. Australian Eco-Horror and Gaia's Revenge: Animals, Eco-Nationalism and the "New Nature." *Studies in Australasian Cinema* 4(1): 43–54.

Sims Bishop, Rudine. 1990. Mirrors, Windows, and Sliding Glass Doors. *Perspectives* 6(3): ix–xi. Available at: https://scenicregional.org/wp-content/uploads/2017/08 /Mirrors-Windows-and-Sliding-Glass-Doors.pdf.

Skal, David J. 2012. Foreword: What We Talk about When We Talk about Monsters. In *Speaking of Monsters: A Teratological Anthology*, ed. Caroline Joan S. Picart and John Edgar Browning, xi–xiii. Basingstoke, Hampshire, U.K.: Palgrave Macmillan.

Skinner, Anna. 2023. Why Killer Whales Can't Be Responsible for Missing Titanic Sub. *Newsweek*, June 20. Available at: https://www.newsweek.com/killer-whales -responsible-missing-titanic-submersible-titan-1807953.

Skott, Sara. 2024. [Review of] Tea Fredriksson (2023) Haunting Prison: Exploring the Prison as an Abject and Uncanny Institution. Bingley, U.K.: Emerald Publishing Limited. *International Journal for Crime, Justice and Social Democracy*. https://doi .org/10.5204/ijcjsd.3422.

Skott, Sara, Sara Nyhlén, and Katarina Giritli-Nygren. 2021. In the Shadow of the Monster: Gothic Narratives of Violence Prevention. *Critical Criminology: An International Journal* 29(2): 385–400.

Slezak, Michael, and Olivia Solon. 2017. Elon Musk: SpaceX Can Colonise Mars and Build Moon Base. *The Guardian*, September 29. Available at: https://www .theguardian.com/technology/2017/sep/29/elon-musk-spacex-can-colonise-mars -and-build-base-on-oon.

Smialek, Jeanna. 2024. Office Crisis Spells Grief for Lenders. *The New York Times*, February 9: B1. Published online as "'Zombie Offices' Spell Trouble for Some Banks," on February 8, 2024, at: https://www.nytimes.com/2024/02/08/business /economy/commercial-real-estate-banking-industry.html.

Smillie, Susan. 2020a. "I've Never Seen or Heard of Attacks": Scientists Baffled by Orcas Harassing Boats. *The Guardian*, September 13. Available at: https://www .theguardian.com/environment/2020/sep/13/the-tale-of-the-killer-whales.

Smillie, Susan. 2020b. Scientists Baffled by Orcas Ramming Sailing Boats near Spain and Portugal. *The Guardian*, September 13. Available at: https://www.theguardian .com/environment/2020/sep/13/killer-whales-launch-orchestrated-attacks-on -sailing-boats.

Smith, Oliver, and Avi Brisman. 2021. Plastic Waste and the Environmental Crisis Industry. *Critical Criminology: An International Journal* 29(2): 289–309. https:// doi.org/10.1007/s10612-021-09562-4.

Smith, Sean. 2013. "Elysium": Future Shock. *Entertainment Weekly*, August 2: 36–43. Available at: https://ew.com/article/2013/07/26/elysium-future-shock/.

Smith, Tara C. 2015. Zombie Infections: Epidemiology, Treatment, and Prevention. *BJM* [December 14] 351: h6423. Available at: https://www.bmj.com/content/351/bmj.h6423.

Smyth, Richard. 2019. The Green Roots of Fascism. *The New Statesman*, April 3. Available at: https://www.newstatesman.com/culture/2019/04/nature-writings-fascist-roots.

Sollund, Ragnhild. 2017. The Animal Other: Legal and Illegal Theriocide. In *Greening Criminology in the 21st Century: Contemporary Debates and Future Directions in the Study of Environmental Harm*, ed. Matthew Hall, Jennifer Maher, Angus Nurse, Gary Potter, Nigel South, and Tanya Wyatt, 79–99. Abingdon, Oxon, U.K., and New York: Routledge.

Sollund, Ragnhild. 2020. The Victimisation of Women, Children, and Non-Human Species through Trafficking and Trade: Crimes Understood through an Ecofeminist Perspective. In *Routledge International Handbook of Green Criminology*, 2nd ed., ed. Avi Brisman and Nigel South, 512–28. Abingdon, Oxon, U.K., and New York: Routledge.

Solnit, Rebecca. 2023. Billionaires Are Out of Touch and Much Too Powerful. The Planet Is in Trouble. *The Guardian*, November 20. Available at: https://www.theguardian.com/commentisfree/2023/nov/20/billionaires-great-carbon-divide-planet-climate-crisis.

Solon, Olivia. 2018. Elon Musk: We Must Colonise Mars to Preserve Our Species in a Third World War. *The Guardian*, March 11. Available at: https://www.theguardian.com/technology/2018/mar/11/elon-musk-colonise-mars-third-world-war.

Soloski, Alexis. 2024. Climate Catastrophe? Oh, Smile through the Apocalypse. *The New York Times*, April 24: C1. Published online as "Climate Doom Is Out. 'Apocalyptic Optimism' Is In." on April 21, 2024, at: https://www.nytimes.com/2024/04/21/arts/television/climate-change-apocalypse-optimism.html.

Sontag, Susan. 1965. The Imagination of Disaster. *Commentary* 40(4) [October 1]: 42–48. Available at: https://www.commentary.org/articles/susan-sontag/the-imagination-of-disaster/; also available at: https://raley.english.ucsb.edu/wp-content/uploads/Reading/Sontag-disaster.pdf.

Soper, Taylor. 2021. Amazon Now Employs Nearly 1.3 Million People Worldwide after Adding 500,000 Workers in 2020. *GeekWire*, February 2. Available at: https://www.geekwire.com/2021/amazon-now-employs-nearly-1-3-million-people-worldwide-adding-500000-workers-2020/.

Sorace, Stephen. 2023. Florida Man's Arm Amputated after 10-foot Alligator Attacks outside Bar near Pond. *Fox News*, May 23. Available at: https://www.foxnews.com/us/florida-mans-arm-amputated-10-foot-alligator-attacks-outside-bar-pond.

Sothcott, Keir. 2016. Late Modern Ambiguity and Gothic Narratives of Justice. *Critical Criminology: An International Journal* 24(3): 431–44. https://doi.org/10.1007/s10612-015-9287-2.

South, Daniel, and Nigel South. 2021. Bunkerization: Elite Preparedness and Retreat in the Anthropocene. In *City Preparedness for the Climate Crisis: A Multidisciplinary Approach*, ed. Francisco Javier Carillo and Cathy Garner, 234–43. Cheltenham, U.K.: Edward Elgar.

South, Nigel. 2010. The Ecocidal Tendencies of Late Modernity: Trans-National Crime, Social Exclusion, Victims and Rights. In *Global Environmental Harm: Criminological Perspectives*, ed. Rob White, 228–47. Cullompton, Devon, U.K.: Willan.

South, Nigel. 2012. Climate Change, Environmental (In)Security, Conflict, and Crime. In *Criminological and Legal Consequences of Climate Change* (Oñati International Series in Law and Society: A Series Published for the Oñati Institute for the Sociology of Law), ed. Stephen Farrall, Tawhida Ahmed, and Duncan French, 97–111. Oxford and Portland, OR: Hart Publishing.

South, Nigel. 2017. Monstrous Nature: A Meeting of Gothic, Green, and Cultural Criminologies. In *Routledge International Handbook of Visual Criminology*, ed. Michelle Brown and Eamonn Carrabine, 553–66. Abingdon, Oxon, U.K.: Routledge.

South, Nigel, and Avi Brisman. 2013a. Critical Green Criminology, Environmental Rights and Crimes of Exploitation. In *New Directions in Crime and Deviancy*, ed. Simon Winlow and Rowland Atkinson, 99–110. Abingdon, Oxon, U.K., and New York: Routledge.

South, Nigel, and Avi Brisman. 2013b. *Environment, Crime, and Conflict: Typologies of Relationships and Representations*. Invited lecture, Department of Security and Crime Science, University College London, London, U.K., May 21, 2013.

Sow, Mariama, and Amadou Sy. 2018. Lessons from Marvel's Black Panther: Natural Resource Management and Increased Openness in Africa. *Brookings*, February 23. Available at: https://www.brookings.edu/blog/africa-in-focus/2018/02/23/lessons-from-marvels-black-panther-natural-resource-management-and-regional-collaboration-in-africa/.

Spanish News Today. 2022. Two Sailing Boats Towed to Port in 24 Hours after Killer Whale Attacks in the Strait of Gibraltar. May 24. Available at: https://spanishnewstoday.com/two-sailing-boats-towed-to-port-in-24-hours-after-killer-whale-attacks-in-the-strait-of-gibraltar_1780813-a.html.

Spar, Ira. 2009. Flood Stories. *The Metropolitan Museum of Art*, April. Available at: https://www.metmuseum.org/toah/hd/flod/hd_flod.htm.

Spitznagel, Eric. 2010. George A. Romero: "Who Says Zombies Eat Brains?" *Vanity Fair*, May 27. Available at: https://www.vanityfair.com/hollywood/2010/05/george-romero.

Spooner, Catherine. 2007. *Contemporary Gothic*. London: Reaktion Books.

Stack, Tim. 2015. "X-Men: Apocalypse": First Look at the New Generation in EW. *Entertainment Weekly*, July 15. Available at: https://ew.com/article/2015/07/15/x-men-apocalypse-first-look-new-generation-ew/.

Stahl, James E., and William A. Nelson. 2024. Applying the Peter Parker Principle to Healthcare. *Cambridge Quarterly of Healthcare Ethics* 33(2) [April]: 271–74. https://doi.org/10.1017/S0963180122000275. Available at: https://www.cambridge.org/core/journals/cambridge-quarterly-of-healthcare-ethics/article/applying-the-peter-parker-principle-to-healthcare/3F4BE820071ED8B5E1854A722447B785.

Staples, Brent. 2017. All Those Zombies? Blame George Romero. *The New York Times*, July 18: A22. Published online as "George Romero's Zombie Apocalypse," on July 17, 2017, at: https://www.nytimes.com/2017/07/17/opinion/george-romero-zombie-apocalypse-death.html.

Stephens, Bret. 2018. Apocalypse Not. *The New York Times*, February 8, at: https://www.nytimes.com/2018/02/08/opinion/environment-oil-scare.html.

Stephens, Bret. 2022. Climate Change Is Real. Markets, Not Governments, Offer the Cure. *The New York Times*, October 28, at: https://www.nytimes.com/interactive/2022/10/28/opinion/climate-change-bret-stephens.html.

Stevenson, Keri. 2021. The Death of Birdsong, the Birdsong of Death: Algernon Charles Swinburne and the Horror of Erosion. In *Fear and Nature: Ecohorror Studies in the Anthropocene*, ed. Christy Tidwell and Carter Soles, 91–109. University Park: Pennsylvania State University Press.

St. Félix, Doreen. 2018. On Killmonger, The American Villain "Black Panther." *The New Yorker*, February 20. Available at: https://www.newyorker.com/culture/culture -desk/on-killmonger-black-panther-s-american-villain.

St. John, Warren. 2006. Market for Zombies? It's Undead (Aaahhh!). *The New York Times*, March 26: Section 9 (National edition), Page 1. Published online as "Market for Zombies? It's Undead (Aaahhh!)," on March 26, 2006, at: https://www.nytimes .com/2006/03/26/fashion/sundaystyles/market-for-zombies-its-undead-aaahhh.html.

Stoker, Bram. 1897[1920]. *Dracula*. Garden City, NY: Doubleday, Page.

Stone, Madeline. 2015. How Billionaires Will Survive the End of the World. *Business Insider*, October 15. Available at: https://www.businessinsider.com/how-billionaires -survive-the-apocalypse-2015-10.

Stone, Madeline. 2020. Carbon Emissions Are Falling Sharply due to Coronavirus. But Not for Long. *National Geographic*, April 3. Available at: https://www .nationalgeographic.com/science/2020/04/coronavirus-causing-carbon-emissions -to-fall-but-not-for-long/.

Surette, Raymond. 2007. Gothic Criminology and Criminal Justice Policy. In *Monsters in and among Us: Towards a Gothic Criminology*, ed. C. J. Picart and C. Greek, 199–226. Madison, NJ: Fairleigh Dickinson University Press.

SurvivalBlog. n.d. A Glossary of Survival and Preparedness Acronyms/Terms. Available at: https://survivalblog.com/glossary/#WTSHTF.

Swartz, Mimi. 2018. Talking Apocalypse with My Son. *The New York Times*, January 16: A21. Published online as "Talking Apocalypse with My Son," on January 15, 2018, at: https://www.nytimes.com/2018/01/15/opinion/talking-apocalypse-son.html.

Swift, Jonathan. 1729. A Modest Proposal for Preventing the Children of Poor People in Ireland, from Being a Burden on Their Parents or Country, and for Making Them Beneficial to the Publick. Project Gutenberg, ebook 1080. Available at: https://www .gutenberg.org/files/1080/1080-h/1080-h.htm.

Syed, Zayna. 2023. Orcas Are Attacking Boats. But Is It Revenge or Trauma? *Popular Science*, June 15. Available at: https://www.popsci.com/environment/orcas-attacking -boats-why/.

Szasz, Andrew. 2007. *Shopping Our Way to Safety: How We Changed from Protecting the Environment to Protecting Ourselves*. Minneapolis: University of Minnesota Press.

Tassi, Paul. 2018. Thanos' "Avengers: Infinity War" Master Plan Doesn't Make Very Much Sense. *Forbes*, May 1. Available at: https://www.forbes.com/sites/insertcoin /2018/05/01/thanos-avengers-infinity-war-master-plan-doesnt-make-very-much -sense/?sh=639147fe5f8a.

Taylor, Charles. 2007. *A Secular Age*. Cambridge, MA, and London: Harvard University Press.

Taylor, Chris. 2018. We Need to Talk about Thanos' Insane Population Control Scheme in "Infity War." *Mashable*, May 3. Available at: https://mashable.com /article/thanos-half-universe.

Taylor, Gaye. 2022. Webzine Uses Comic Strip Characters to Counter Creeping Ecofascism. *The Energy Mix,* June 5. Available at: https://www.theenergymix.com /2022/06/05/webzine-uses-comic-strip-characters-to-counter-creeping-ecofascism/.

Tcareva, Svetlana. 2020. The Soviet Cannibal: Who Eats Whom in Andrey Platonov's "Rubbish Wind." In *Man-Eating Monsters: Anthropocentrism and Popular Culture*, ed. Dina Khapaeva, 83–95. Bingley, U.K.: Emerald Publishing Limited.

Teirstein, Zoya. 2020. Here's How Coronavirus Affected Carbon Emissions in Every State. *Grist,* May 19. Available at: https://grist.org/climate/heres-how-coronavirus-affected-carbon-emissions-in-every-state/.

Thomson, Jess. 2023. Orca Attacks on Boats May Be Fueled by Revenge. *Newsweek,* May 24. Available at: https://www.newsweek.com/orca-attack-boats-spain-killer-whales-revenge-1802418.

Thornton, Claire. 2023. Shark Bites Leg Off 22-Year-Old US Woman Snorkeling Off Blue Haven Resort in Turks and Caicos. *USA Today,* May 25. Available at: https://www.usatoday.com/story/news/nation/2023/05/25/turks-and-caicos-shark-attack-bites-womans-leg-blue-haven/70256429007/.

Thunberg, Greta. 2020a. Our House Is Still on Fire and You're Fuelling the Flames. *World Economic Forum,* January 21. Available at: https://www.weforum.org/stories/2020/01/greta-speech-our-house-is-still-on-fire-davos-2020/.

Thunberg, Greta. 2020b. "Our House Is Still on Fire": Full Speech by Greta Thunberg at World Economic Forum in Davos. *Democracy Now,* January 21. Available at: https://www.democracynow.org/2020/1/21/our_house_is_still_on_fire.

Thunberg, Greta, Svante Thunberg, Malena Ernman, and Beata Ernman. 2020. *Our House Is on Fire: Scenes of a Family and a Planet in Crisis*. Translated by Paul R. Norlén and Saskia Vogel. New York: Penguin Books.

Tidwell, Christy. 2014. Monstrous Natures Within: Posthuman and New Materialist Ecohorror in Mira Grant's *Parasite*. *ISLE: Interdisciplinary Studies in Literature and Environment* 21(3) [Summer]: 538–49.

Tidwell, Christy. 2018. Ecohorror. In *Posthuman Glossary*, ed. Rosi Braidotti and Maria Hlavajova, 115–17. London and New York: Bloomsbury Academic.

Tidwell, Christy. 2021. Spiraling Inward and Outward: Junji Ito's *Uzumaki* and the Scope of Ecohorror. In *Fear and Nature: Ecohorror Studies in the Anthropocene*, ed. Christy Tidwell and Carter Soles, 42–67. University Park: Pennsylvania State University Press.

Tidwell, Christy, and Carter Soles, eds. 2021a. *Fear and Nature: Ecohorror Studies in the Anthropocene*. University Park: Pennsylvania State University Press.

Tidwell, Christy, and Carter Soles. 2021b. Introduction: Ecorror in the Anthropocene. In *Fear and Nature: Ecohorror Studies in the Anthropocene*, ed. Christy Tidwell and Carter Soles, 1–20. University Park: Pennsylvania State University Press.

Todd, Matthew. 2019. The Climate Emergency and the End of Diversity. In *This Is Not a Drill: An Extinction Rebellion Handbook*, ed. Clare Farrell, Alison Green, Sam Knights and William Skeaping, 69–72. London: Penguin Random House.

Tomlinson, B. R. 2003. What Was the Third World? *Journal of Contemporary History* 38(2) [April]: 307–21.

Townsend, Solitaire. 2018. Why Thanos from "Avengers: Infinity War" Gets Sustainability So Wrong. *Forbes,* May 1. Available at: https://www.forbes.com/sites/solitairetownsend/2018/05/01/why-thanos-sucks-at-sustainability/?sh=7dc97c4c72f5.

Trimble, S. 2019. *Undead Ends: Stories of Apocalypse*. New Brunswick, Camden, and Newark, NJ, and London: Rutgers University Press.

Tucker, Zoë. 2019. *Greta and the Giants: Inspired by Greta Thunberg's Stand to Save the World*. Illustrated by Zoe Persico. Minneapolis, MN: Frances Lincoln Children's Books/The Quarto Group.

Twitchell, James B. 1985. *Dreadful Pleasures: An Anatomy of Modern Horror*. Oxford, U.K.: Oxford University Press.

Tyburski, Susan J. 2013. A Gothic apocalypse: encountering the monstrous in American cinema. In *EcoGothic*, ed. Andrew Smith and William Hughes, 147–159. Manchester, U.K.: Manchester University Press.

Tyler, Imogen. 2013. *Revolting Subjects: Social Abjection and Resistance in Neoliberal Britain*. London and New York: Zed Books.

Ugwu, Reggie. 2018. A Superhero of the Diaspora. *The New York Times*, February 18: AR12. Published online as "The Stars of 'Black Panther' Waited a Lifetime for This Moment," on February 12, 2018, at: https://www.nytimes.com/2018/02/12/movies/black-panther-marvel-chadwick-boseman-ryan-coogler-lupita-nyongo.html.

Ugwu, Reggie. 2022. The Journey To "Wakanda" Took a Turn. *The New York Times*, December 27: C1. Published online as "The 'Black Panther' Sequel That Never Was," on December 23, 2022, at: https://www.nytimes.com/2022/12/23/arts/ryan-coogler-black-panther-wakanda-forever.html.

Ulaby, Neda. 2008. "Eco-Horror": Green Panic on the Silver Screen. *All Things Considered, National Public Radio*, June 14. Available at: https://www.npr.org/templates/story/story.php?storyId=91485965. Transcript available at: https://www.npr.org/transcripts/91485965.

United Nations Peacekeeping. n.d. *Conflict and Natural Resources*. Available at: https://peacekeeping.un.org/en/conflict-and-natural-resources.

United Nations University (UNU). 2023. UN Study Reveals the Hidden Environmental Impacts of Bitcoin: Carbon Is Not the Only Harmful By-Product. Press release, October 24. Available at: https://unu.edu/press-release/un-study-reveals-hidden-environmental-impacts-bitcoin-carbon-not-only-harmful-product.

United States Botanical Garden. 2024. Corpse Flowers. Available at: https://www.usbg.gov/gardens-plants/corpse-flowers.

United States Environmental Protection Agency. 2021. *EPA Report Shows Disproportionate Impacts of Climate Change on Socially Vulnerable Populations in the United States*. EPA Press Office, September 2. Available at: https://www.epa.gov/newsreleases/epa-report-shows-disproportionate-impacts-climate-change-socially-vulnerable.

Urry, John. 2010. Consuming the Planet to Excess. *Theory, Culture and Society* 27(2–3): 191–212. https://doi.org/10.1177/0263276409355999.

Valier, Claire. 2002. Punishment, Border Crossings, and the Powers of Horror. *Theoretical Criminology* 6(3): 319–37.

Van Allsburg, Chris. 1990. *Just a Dream*. Boston: Houghton Mifflin Company.

Van Houdt, Rob, Kristel Mijnendonckx, and Natalie Leys. 2012. Microbial Contamination Monitoring and Control during Human Space Missions. *Planetary and Space Science* 60(1) [January]: 115–20. https://doi.org/10.1016/j.pss.2011.09.001.

Varghese, Gabriel. 2020. *Palestinian Theatre in the West Bank: Our Human Faces*. Cham, Switzerland: Palgrave Macmillan/Springer Nature Switzerland AG.

Vdovychenko, Natalia. 2022. Elon Musk's SpaceX: How the "Space Race" to Mars Adopted the Californian Ideology. *Diggit Magazine*, November 15. Available at: https://www.diggitmagazine.com/articles/elon-musk-spacex.

Veldman, Robin Globus. 2012. Narrating the Environmental Apocalypse: How Imagining the End Facilitates Moral Reasoning among Environmental Activists. *Ethics and the Environment* 17(1): 1–23. Available at: https://muse.jhu.edu/article /478473.

Vint, Sherryl. 2013. Abject Posthumanism: Neoliberalism, Biopolitics, and Zombies. In *Monster Culture in the 21st Century: A Reader*, ed. Marina Levina and Diem-My T. Bui, 133–46. New York and London: Bloomsbury.

Vitali, Ali, Kasie Hunt, and Frank Thorp V. 2018. Trump Referred to Haiti and African Nations as "Shithole" Countries. *NBC News*, January 11. Available at: https://www .nbcnews.com/politics/white-house/trump-referred-haiti-african-countries-shithole -nations-n836946.

Vivos. 2024. Survive the Predictions and Prophecies at Vivos. Available at: https:// www.terravivos.com/prophecy.php.

Vlahos, Michael. 2013. The Civilizational Significance of Zombies. *The Atlantic*, June 18. Available at: https://www.theatlantic.com/entertainment/archive/2013/06/the -civilizational-significance-of-zombies/276948/.

Vlamis, Kelsey. 2023. Stop Calling the Killer Whale Encounters with Boats "Attacks." *Business Insider*, June 27. Available at: https://www.businessinsider.com/stop-calling -killer-whale-encounters-with-boats-attacks-2023-6.

Voluntary Human Extinction Movement. n.d. Available at: https://www.vhemt.org/.

von Mossner, Alexa Weik. 2012. Afraid of the Dark and the Light: Visceralizing Ecocide in *The Road* and *Hell*. *European Journal of Literature, Culture, and Environment/Revista Europea de Literatura, Cultura y Medioambiente* 3(2) [October]: 42–56. https://doi.org/10.37536/ECOZONA.2012.3.2.471.

Wall, Mike. 2016. Elon Musk Plans to Name 1st Mars Colony Ship "Heart of Gold" in Sci-Fi Nod. *Space.com*, September 28. Available at: https://www.space.com/34220 -spacex-first-mars-ship-hitchhikers-guide-galaxy.html.

Wallace, Carvell. 2018. Making a Motherland. *The New York Times Magazine*, February 18: 26. Published online as "Why 'Black Panther' Is a Defining Moment for Black America," on February 12, 2018, at: https://www.nytimes.com/2018 /02/12/magazine/why-black-panther-is-a-defining-moment-for-black-america.html.

Wallace-Wells, David. 2022a. Beyond Catastrophe: *A New Climate Reality Is Coming into View*. *The New York Times*, October 26, at: https://www.nytimes.com/interactive /2022/10/26/magazine/visualization-climate-change-future.html.

Wallace-Wells, David. 2022b. The New World: *Envisioning Life after Climate Change*. *The New York Times*, October 26. Illustrated by Anuj Shrestha, at: https:// www.nytimes.com/interactive/2022/10/26/magazine/visualization-climate-change -future.html.

Wallace-Wells, David. 2024. Why We Gave Up on the Future. *The New York Times*, March 13, at: https://www.nytimes.com/2024/03/13/opinion/politics/politics -nostalgia-economic-growth-pessimism.html.

Walpole, Horace. 1764[2014]. *The Castle of Otranto*. Oxford, U.K.: Oxford University Press.

Walrath-Holdridge, Mary, and Eric Lagatta. 2024. "Splashdown Confirmed!" SpaceX Starship Successful in Fourth Test Launch. *Austin America-Statesman*, June

6. Available at: https://www.statesman.com/story/news/nation/2024/06/06/spacex
-starship-fourth-test-launch/73986115007/.

Walsh, Alistair. 2022. Eco-Fascism: The Greenwashing of the Far Right. *Deutsche Welle*,
May 19. Available at: https://www.dw.com/en/what-is-eco-fascism-the-greenwashing
-of-the-far-right-terrorism-climate-change-buffalo-shooter/a-61867605.

Walsh, Kevin. 2019. Is Brooklyn on Long Island? Is Queens Part of Long Island?
StreetEasy Blog, February 28. Available at: https://streeteasy.com/blog/is-brooklyn
-on-long-island-is-queens-part-of-long-island/.

Wang, Haoyan, and Christina Zhang. 2023. Marvel Cinematic Universe Villains
and Social Anxieties. In *The Politics of the Marvel Cinematic Universe*, ed. Nicholas
Carnes and Lilly J. Goren, 182–91. Lawrence: University Press of Kansas.

Washburn Hopkins, E. 1905. The Fountain of Youth. *Journal of the American Oriental
Society* 26(1905): 1–67. https://doi.org/10.2307/592875.

Watercutter, Angela. 2023. 30 Years After *Free Willy*, White Gladis and Her Killer
Whales Are Getting Revenge. *Wired*, July 7. Available at: https://www.wired.com
/story/orca-uprising-white-gladis-free-willy-blackfish-social-media/.

Watson, Janell. 2015. Mother Earth, Mother City: Abjection and the Anthropocene.
philoSOPHIA 5(2): 269–85.

Watts, Jonathan. 2023. Richest 1% Account for More Carbon Emissions Than
Poorest 66%, Report Says. *The Guardian*, November 19. Available at: https://www
.theguardian.com/environment/2023/nov/20/richest-1-account-for-more-carbon
-emissions-than-poorest-66-report-says.

Watts, Jonathan, and Niko Kommenda. 2020. Coronavirus Pandemic Leading to
Huge Drop in Air Pollution. *The Guardian*, March 23. Available at: https://www
.theguardian.com/environment/2020/mar/23/coronavirus-pandemic-leading-to
-huge-drop-in-air-pollution.

Wehner, Greg. 2023. Pennsylvania Teenager Surfing in New Jersey Suffers Injuries
from Possible Shark Attack: Reports. *Fox News*, May 22. Available at: https://www
.foxnews.com/us/pennsylvania-teenager-surfing-new-jersey-suffers-injuries-possible
-shark-attack-reports.

Weinersmith, Kelly, and Zach Weinersmith. 2023a. *A City on Mars: Can We Settle
Space, Should We Settle Space, and Have We Really Thought This Through?* New York:
Penguin Press.

Weinersmith, Kelly, and Zach Weinersmith. 2023b. Space Billionaires Should Spend
More Time Thinking about Sex. *The New York Times*, November 5, at: https://www
.nytimes.com/2023/11/05/opinion/space-billionaires-sex.html.

Weise, Karen. 2024. Bezos' Blue Origin Ramps Up Space Race. *The New York
Times*, December 17: B1. Published online as "Jeff Bezos Prepares to Close the
Gap in His Space Race With Elon Musk," on December 14, 2024, at: https://
www.nytimes.com/2024/12/17/technology/jeff-bezos-blue-origin-elon-musk.html
?searchResultPosition=3.

Weiss, Joanna. 2024. The New Civil War Movie Is Eerily Right about How the
Country Could Split Apart. *Politico*, April 13. Available at: https://www.politico
.com/news/magazine/2024/04/13/yes-the-new-civil-war-movie-is-terrifying-but
-how-real-is-it-00152064.

Wells, H. G. 1898. *The War of the Worlds*. London: Heinemann.

Welsh, Andrew, Thomas Fleming, and Kenneth Dowler. 2011. Constructing Crime
and Justice on Film: Meaning and Message in Cinema. *Contemporary Justice Review*
14(4): 457–76.

Westervelt, Amy. 2022. Ecofascism: Where the Far Left and Far Right Kiss. *Hot Take*, May 22. Available at: https://www.hottakepod.com/untitled-2/.

Weston, Phoebe. 2023. The World's Largest—and Stinkiest—Flower Is in Danger of Extinction. *Wired*, September 23. Accessed at: https://www.wired.com/story/the-worlds-largest-and-stinkiest-flower-is-in-danger-of-extinction/#. Originally published as "The World's Largest—and Stinkiest—Flower Is in Danger of Extinction, Scientists Say," in *The Guardian*, on September 20, 2023, at: https://www.theguardian.com/environment/2023/sep/20/the-worlds-largest-and-stinkiest-flower-in-danger-of-extinction-rafflesia-aoe.

Whale and Dolphin Conservation. n.d. Fate of Orcas in Captivity. Available at: https://uk.whales.org/end-captivity/orca-captivity/.

White, Gregory. 2011. *Climate Change and Migration: Security and Borders in a Warming World*. Oxford, U.K.: Oxford University Press.

White, Robyn. 2022a. Mystery Orca Attacks Sink Another Boat. *Newsweek*, November 4. Available at: https://www.newsweek.com/mystery-orca-attacks-sink-boat-1756958.

White, Robyn. 2022b. "Oh No": Orca Rams and Lifts Yacht in Latest Portugal Attack. *Newsweek*, October 17. Available at: https://www.newsweek.com/orca-rams-lifts-yacht-latest-portugal-attack-1752460.

White, Robyn. 2022c. Orca Rip Huge Hole in Boat and Swim Away with Rudder in Terrifying Attack. *Newsweek*, November 7. Available at: https://www.newsweek.com/orca-attack-hole-boat-swim-away-rudder-portugal-1757389.

White, Robyn. 2022d. Orcas Attack and Sink Sailboat with Five on Board, Miles from Coast. *Newsweek*, August 3. Available at: https://www.newsweek.com/orca-attack-sink-sailboat-killer-whale-five-board-miles-coast-1730438.

White, Robyn. 2022e. Orcas Attack So Many Boats Sailors Are Being Told to Stay in Port at Night. *Newsweek*, August 9. Available at: https://www.newsweek.com/orca-attack-so-many-boats-sailors-told-stay-port-1732171.

White, Robyn. 2022f. Orca That Sunk Boat with Family on Board Rammed Another Vessel within Hours. *Newsweek*, August 10. Available at: https://www.newsweek.com/orca-that-sunk-sailboat-attacked-another-vessel-within-hours-1732378.

White, Robyn. 2022g. Scientists Edge Closer to Understanding Why and Where Orcas Attack Boats. *Newsweek*, October 14. Available at: https://www.newsweek.com/scientists-closer-understanding-why-where-orca-attack-boats-1751995.

White, Robyn. 2023. Orca "Repeatedly Slammed" Boat in Spate of Attacks. *Newsweek*, May 5. Available at: https://www.newsweek.com/orca-attack-repeatedly-slammed-1798656.

Whyte, David. 2020. *Ecocide: Kill the Corporation Before It Kills Us*. Manchester, U.K.: Manchester University Press.

Wilentz, Amy. 2012. A Zombie Is a Slave Forever. *The New York Times*, October 30, at: https://www.nytimes.com/2012/10/31/opinion/a-zombie-is-a-slave-forever.html.

Williams, Anne. 1995. *Art of Darkness: A Poetics of Gothic*. Chicago: University of Chicago Press.

Williams, Jericho. 2016. An Inscrutable Malice: The Silencing of Humanity in *The Ruins* and *The Happening*. In *Plant Horror: Approaches to the Monstrous Vegetal in Fiction and Film*, ed. Dawn Keetley and Angela Tenga, 227–41. London: Palgrave Macmillan.

Williams, Molly. 2022. *Killer Plants: Growing and Caring for Flytraps, Pitcher Plants, and Other Deadly Flora*. Illustrated by Marisol Ortega. Philadelphia, PA: Running Press.

Willsey, Kristiana. 2014. Hunger Is the Beginning of Every Folktale. *The Toast*, October 9. Available at: https://the-toast.net/2014/10/09/hunger-beginning-every -folktale/.

Wilson, Jason. 2019. Eco-Fascism Is Undergoing a Revival in the Fetid Culture of the Extreme Right. *The Guardian*, March 19. Available at: https://www.theguardian .com/world/commentisfree/2019/mar/20/eco-fascism-is-undergoing-a-revival-in -the-fetid-culture-of-the-extreme-right.

Wing, Nick. 2016. Here's How the Nation Responded When a Black Militia Group Occupied a Government Building. *HuffPost*, January 6 (updated December 21). Available at: https://www.huffpost.com/entry/black-panthers-california-1967_n _568accfce4b014efe0db2f40.

Winsor, Morgan. 2023. Racing Yachts Have Close Encounter with Pod of Orcas near Strait of Gibraltar. *ABC News*, June 23. Available at: https://abcnews.go.com /International/racing-yachts-close-encounter-pod-orcas-strait-gibraltar/story?id= 100329346.

Winter, Jeanette. 2019. *Our House Is on Fire: Greta Thunberg's Call to Save the Planet*. New York: Beach Lane Books/Simon & Schuster.

Wojcik, Daniel. 1997. *The End of the World as We Know It: Faith, Fatalism, and Apocalypse in America*. New York: New York University Press.

Wolf-Phillips, Leslie. 1987. Why "Third World"? Origin, Definition and Usage. *Third World Quarterly* 9(4) [October]: 1311–1327.

Wood, Robin. 1986. *Hollywood from Vietnam to Reagan*. New York: Columbia University Press.

Woolf, Nicky. 2016. SpaceX Founder Elon Musk Plans to Get Humans to Mars in Six Years. *The Guardian*, September 28. Available at: https://www.theguardian.com /technology/2016/sep/27/elon-musk-spacex-mars-colony.

Wright, Rebecca. 2020. There's an Unlikely Beneficiary of Coronavirus: The Planet. *CNN*, March 17. Available at: https://www.cnn.com/2020/03/16/asia/china -pollution-coronavirus-hnk-intl/index.html.

Wyatt, Tanya. 2024. Rewilding in the UK: Harm or Justice? In *Criminal Justice, Wildlife Conservation, and Animal Rights in the Anthropocene*, ed. Ragnhild A. Sollund and Martine S. B. Lie, 168–84. Bristol, U.K.: Bristol University Press.

Wyndham, John. 1951[2008]. *The Day of the Triffids*. London: Penguin.

Yacowar, Maurice. 2003. The Bug in the Rug: Notes on the Disaster Genre. In *Film Genre Reader III*, ed. Barry Keith Grant, 277–95. Austin: University of Texas Press.

Yang, Gene Luen. 2016. Glare of Disdain. *The New York Times*, August 23, at: https:// www.nytimes.com/interactive/2016/04/01/books/review/28sketchbook-yang.html.

Yoder, Kate. 2020. Is Nature All Healed Now? A Look at the Pandemic's Best Meme. *Grist*, July 9. Available at: https://grist.org/climate/is-nature-all-healed-now-a-look -at-the-pandemics-best-meme/.

Young, Iris Marion. 1990a. Abjection and Oppression: Dynamics of Unconscious Racism, Sexism, and Homophobia. In *Crises in Continental Philosophy*, ed. Arleen B. Dallery and Charles E. Scott, 201–14. New York: State University of New York Press.

Young, Iris Marion. 1990b. *Justice and the Politics of Difference*. Princeton, NJ: Princeton University Press.

Young, Jock. 2007. *The Vertigo of Late Modernity*. London: Sage.

Young, Taras. 2022. *Apocalypse Ready: The Manual of Manuals: A Century of Panic Prevention*. London: Thames and Hudson.

Yuhas, Alan. 2017. SpaceX Successfully Launches Falcon 9 Rocket Months after Explosion. *The Guardian*, January 14. Available at: https://www.theguardian.com /science/2017/jan/14/spacex-launch-falcon-9-rocket-elon-musk.

Zakarin, Jordan. 2016. First "X-Men: Apocalypse" Trailer Introduces Oscar Isaac's Immortal Villain and James McAvoy's Bald Head. *Yahoo! Entertainment*, December 11. Available at: https://www.yahoo.com/entertainment/first-x-men-apocalypse -trailer-introduces-oscar-164556062.html.

Zarnett, Brad. 2020. Is Covid-19 the Silver Bullet for a Stable Climate? *CSRwire*, March 13. Available at: https://www.csrwire.com/press_releases/44015-is-covid-19 -the-silver-bullet-for-a-stable-climate-.

Zedner, Lucia. 2006. Policing before and after the Police: The Historical Antecedents of Contemporary Crime Control. *The British Journal of Criminology* 46(1) [January]: 78–96. https://doi.org/10.1093/bjc/azi043.

Zilber, Ariel. 2024a. Elon Musk Nominated for Nobel Peace Prize for Being "Stout Proponent of Free Speech." *New York Post*, https://nypost.com/2024/02/20/business /elon-musk-nominated-for-nobel-peace-prize/.

Zilber, Ariel. 2024b. "Zombie Mortgages" Come Back to Haunt Thousands of Homeowners Now Facing Foreclosure. *New York Post*, June 19. Available at: https:// nypost.com/2024/06/19/business/zombie-mortgages-haunting-homeowners-now -facing-foreclosure/.

Zilinskas, Raymond A. 1995. Preventing State Crimes against the Environment during Military Operations: The 1977 Environmental Modification Treaty. In *Controlling State Crime: An Introduction*, ed. Jeffrey Ian Ross, 235–81. New York and London: Garland Publishing.

Žižek, Slavoj. 2005. The Subject Supposed to Loot and Rape: Reality and Fantasy in New Orleans. *In These Times*, October 20. Available at: https://inthesetimes.com /article/the-subject-supposed-to-loot-and-rape.

Žižek, Slavoj. 2011. *Living in the End Times*. London and New York: Verso.

Index

Beck, Ulrich, 168n10
Beddington, Emma, 69
Beetle Queen Conquers Tokyo (film),
138–139n6
Berreby, David, 146n31
Better Off Dead (Lauro and Christie), 80
Bettini, Giovanni, 178n3
Bezos, Jeff, 60, 64, 65, 66, 118, 158n31,
163n52
Biello, David, 156n23
biological warfare, 168n11
bios (social organization), 119
Bishop, Kyle, 82–84, 108–109, 167–168n8,
168n11, 169n17
Bishop, Rudine Sims, 20, 136n46
Biskind, Peter, 108, 113
"bites back," nature, 33, 67, 70, 71, 170n19
Black female power, 10
Blackfish (film), 163n54
Black History Month, 4
Black Panther (media franchise): *Black
Panther* (film), 4–10, 11, 14, 22, 123,
128n7, 129n11, 129n16, 129n18, 130n22;
Black Panther (Marvel Comics series),
129n13; *Black Panther: Wakanda Forever*
(film), 4–10, 11, 14, 22, 123, 128n7,
129n17, 129n18, 130n22; Mesoamerican
influences and inspiration, 8, 129n17
Black Panther Party, 128–129n10
Black Power movement, 6
Black Skin, White Masks (Fanon), 153n7
blanket blaming, 63, 157n29
"Blip, the," 9, 12, 14, 15, 17, 18. *See also*
"snap, the"
Blomkamp, Neill, 57, 60, 109, 156n24. See
also *Elysium* (film)
boats: "boat-ramming," 67–70, 162n50; boat
traffic, 159n33; fishing boats, 161n45;
orcas "attacking" boats, 67–70, 149n40,
161n45, 162nn49–50, 162–163n51,
163n52; tourist boats, 159n33
bodies and corpses, 35, 46, 48, 146n29,
167n9, 171n21; abject/abjection and, 52,
55; bodysnatching, 147n34; dead bodies,
55, 154n12 (*see also* death); feminist body
horror film, 139n10; gendered bodies, 29;
gross bodies, 54; human body, 61, 154n12,
181n16; "leech-like bodies," 56; mindless
corpse, 166n3; monstrous body/bodies,
29, 34, 89; others' bodies, 87; "privileged bodies," 66; racial-national body,

132n29; reanimated corpse, 85, 174n43;
reanimated zombie, 143n21; reconstructed
bodies, 58; shriveled corpse, 171n21; social
body, 54; soul/body split, 179n7; sovereign body, 153n9; unnatural bodies, 49;
walking corpses, 81, 87, 141n14, 175n44
body horror, 139n10, 181n16
body-modification films, 139n10; *Elysium*,
57–60, 71, 109, 123–124, 139n10,
156n23; *RoboCop*, 139n10
body politic, 55, 120
Bond, Elson, 122
Bong Joon-ho, 90. See also *Snowpiercer* (film)
borders and boundaries, 32, 55; abject and,
49, 55, 56, 154n15, 156n18, 157n26;
"border anxiety," 52, 152n4; borderlands,
32; border-making, 62; border security,
169n17; Croatian-Bosnian Herzegovinian,
56, 121; "dangerous" border crossers, 82,
120, 141n14; digital borders, 3; ecofascist
myths of, 19; Gothic and, 142n15,
146n30, 147n35, 151–152n1; Hungarian-
Serbian, 56, 121; illegal immigration and,
58; monstrosity and, 49, 61, 63, 71, 120,
140n12, 140n14, 181n14; negotiation of,
54; Turkish-Greek, 56, 121; ultra-rich and,
62, 66; U.S.-Mexican, 120, 153n8,
170n17; Western thinking on, 26
Botswana, 5, 128n9
Bould, Mark, 36, 58, 141n14, 147n34
Bowden, Mark, 18
Bozeman, Theodore Dwight, 167n7
Bradshaw, Corey J. A., 17
Braindead (film), 81
brains: brain-computer interfaces, 59;
brain-eating zombies, 80, 85, 146n31;
brainwashing, 84, 123, 168n12; of orcas,
161n49, 163n51
Breathers: A Zombie's Lament (Browne)
bridges, 66, 169n17
Brisman, Avi, 62–64, 66, 157n29, 159n33
Brnovich, Mark, 13
Broderick, Mick, 104
Brody, Richard, 130n24
Brook, Barry W., 17
Brooks, David, 157n28
Brooks, Max, 169n13
Browne, S. G., 143n21
Browning, John Edgar, 23
Bruch, Carl, 130n20
Brummett, Barry, 88

Murray, Robin L., 28–29, 42, 44, 59, 120, 123, 124, 126, 131n26, 138–139n6, 139nn7–10, 147n35
Musk, Elon, 60, 64, 65, 66, 101, 118, 137n48, 158n31
mutants, 42, 121, 131n27
mythmaking, 127n5

Nash, Roderick, 142n16, 142n18
National Rifle Association (NRA), 108, 128n10
Nations, Courtney, 154n12
native species, 15, 133n35
"natural attack film," 42
natural disasters, 39, 61, 62, 83, 107, 110, 149–150n43
natural law, 86, 132n29
natural resources, 5, 8–10, 25, 57, 71, 130n20, 182n21. *See also* resources
Negative Population Growth (anti-immigration organization), 13
Negroni, Maria, 46
Nekaris, K. Anne Isola, 181–182n17
Nelson, Michael P., 154n16
Neocleous, Mark, 72, 142n14
neo-feudalism, 173–174n36
neoliberalism, 48, 58, 60, 61, 63, 165n59, 179n8, 182n20
neurotoxin, 86, 144–145n24
new medievalism, 174n36
news media, 3, 20, 182n18
"New Vampires," zombies as, 80
Night of the Living Dead (film), 105, 141n14, 170n17, 171n22, 175n44
nihilism, 64, 159
Nijman, Vincent, 181–182n17
9/11/2001. *See* September 11, 2001
Nixon, Rob, 113, 177n54
Nixon's Silent Majority, 175n44
Nobel Prize, 66, 79, 80
Nordau, Max, 144n22
normalcy bias, 95, 110
Nostradamus, 178n56
Not Bad Animals, The (Corrigan), 137n1
nuclear weapons and energy: nuclear Armageddon, 104; nuclear attack, 82, 83; nuclear disaster, 40; nuclear energy, 104; nuclear explosion, 100; nuclear fallout, 173n31, 173n34; nuclear holocaust, 25, 84, 96–97, 107; nuclear paranoia narratives, 82

objects, 16, 50, 51, 55, 83, 138n3, 164n56; of abjection, 65; astronomical objects, 89, 93; boundaries and, 156n18; closed and open objects, 164n58; disposable objects, 143n21; food object, 147n37; foreign objects, 162n50; Gothicized objects, 146n30; objectification, 54, 152n5; "racism, phobogenic object of," 140n12
oceans, 8, 38, 68, 69, 94, 117, 119, 144n24, 149nn40–41, 163n52, 172n25; Atlantic Ocean, 93, 149n40; rising levels, 64
O'Connell, Mark, 113, 154n15, 165n60, 177n56
Olorunnisola, Israel, 134nn37–39
Olson, Robert L., 177n51
Omega Man, The (film), 170nn19–20
Onstad, Katrina, 141n14, 168n11, 170n17
On the Beach (film), 172n31
On the Beach (Shute), 94, 173n31, 173n34
On the Beach (television film), 172n31
"operation of exclusion," 152n4
orcas (killer whales), 38, 67–70, 159n33, 159n37, 160n42, 161n45, 161–162n46, 162nn47–48, 163nn53–53; as anti-capitalist, 69, 163n52; as apex predators, 68; attacks, 67–69, 149n40, 161n45, 162nn49–50, 162–163n51, 163n52; brains (neuroanatomy), 162n49, 163n51; cetacean-vessel "interactions," 67; community (pod) of, 161n42; deaths in captivity, 67–69; Iberian orca population, 67; as members of the dolphin family, 67, 68, 162n49; "orca rising," 70, 159n33; playfulness of, 68, 70, 162n50; "ramming boats," 68, 69, 70, 162n50; "rogue killer whales" headline, 68; at SeaWorld Orlando, 162n49, 163n54
Ordiz, Inés, 46
Osaka, Shannon, 15
other, 47, 52–54, 145n28, 152n4, 154n11, 154n14, 156n18, 179n9; "abject Others," 54, 101; alien Other, 34, 146n29; criminology of the, 34, 146n29; cultural Other, 153n8; monstrified personification of Otherness, 119; monstrous Other, 62; nature as, 47, 67, 119–121, 138n2, 179n7; radical enemy Other, 141n14; "white" Other, 54
"Our House Is on Fire" (Thunberg), 177n2
overpopulation. *See* population

Swift, Jonathan, 12, 131n25
Swinburne, Algernon Charles, 44, 151n46
Sy, Amadous, 4–7, 9, 128n9
Syed, Zayna, 70
Szasz, Andrew, 66

Tassi, Paul, 15, 17
Taylor, Chris, 18
Tcareva, Svetlana, 141n14
"tech billionaires," 158n31
"tech elite," 100; Rushkoff, Douglas, 100–101
technology, 59, 60, 64, 65, 83, 87, 88, 89, 105, 144n23, 164n58, 172n25, 176n50; advanced medical technology (in *Elysium*), 58; advanced technology, 5, 6, 7, 57, 58, 125; biotechnologies, 85; "future of technology," 100; Kanamit technology (in *The Twilight Zone*), 57; nontechnological future worlds, 94; replicating technology (in *Star Trek*), 16; technocracy, 64; Wakandan technology, 5, 6, 7
tentacular ecohorror, 33, 49, 145n25
"Teotwawki" ("the end of the world as we know it"), 99, 137n49, 174n37
terror, 28, 31, 43, 45, 61, 84, 89, 93, 105, 118, 147n34, 168n8
terror, war on, 62, 82, 119
terrorism, 87, 88, 97, 120, 145n24, 146n30, 157n25, 168n11; alien, 56, 121; anonymous terrorist attacks, 83, 84; Islamist terrorists, 82, 141n14; terrorist attacks, 82–84, 98; terrorist cells, 119, 119
Thiel, Peter, 157n31
"Third World," 5, 57, 83, 96
Thor: Ragnarok (film), 130n22
Thornton, Claire, 148n39
Threads (film), 107, 176n47
Thunberg, Greta, 118, 178n2, 182n20
Tidwell, Christy, 21, 40, 41–43, 118, 122, 144n24, 178n3, 181n16
Todd, Matthew, 10
tornadoes, 93, 100, 108, 110
torture porn (films), 175n44
Townsend, Solitaire, 17, 125, 130n22, 131n25
"trans-corporeality," 35
transgender people, 10, 153n8
transgression, 1, 26, 34, 49, 139n12, 146n30
transhumanism, 59
Treevenge (film), 33, 44, 144n24
Trekonomics (Saadia), 16
Trimble, S., 101, 104

Trites, Andrew, 149n40
"Trouble with Wilderness, Or, Getting Back to the Wrong Nature, The" (Cronon), 30–31
Trump, Donald J., 4, 98, 116, 120, 141n14, 147n33, 153n8, 179–180n9
Tsamas, Cary, 165n61
28 Days Later (film), 99, 170nn19–20, 173n32
Twilight Saga, The (film series), 145n27
Twilight Zone, The (television program), 57
Twister (film), 107, 110
Twitter, 69, 123, 134n37, 137n48
2012 (film), 171–172n24
Tyler, Imogen, 56, 57, 155n16

Ugwu, Reggie, 129n11
Ulaby, Neda, 28, 33, 40, 140–141n14
"ultra-high-net-worth individuals" (UHNWIs), 55, 66, 69, 94, 100–101, 114, 154–155n15, 155n16
ultra-nationalism, 15
uncanny, the, 36, 151n1, 156n178

Valier, Claire, 146n30, 155n16
vampires, 35, 36, 80, 139n8, 143n21, 144n23, 145n27, 147n35, 147n37, 152n1, 155n17, 169n13, 171n22
Van Allsburg, Chris, 101–103, 106, 115
Van Susteren, Lise, 178–179n3
Varghese, Gabriel, 54, 57, 152n4, 153n7, 156n26
Veldman, Robin Globus, 177–178n3
Venom (film), 146n29
Venom: Let There Be Carnage (film), 145–146n29
Vicino, Robert K., 113, 177n56
Victorian period, 35, 39, 143n20
Vietnam War, 175n44
"vine-horror-film," 33
Vint, Sherryl, 169n18
violence, 6, 14, 19, 34, 58, 60, 61, 88, 99, 128n8, 129n11, 131n27, 132nn28–30, 157n26, 168nn8–9, 180n9, 180n12, 182n20; gender-based, 55, 151n1, 154n14; "Gothicity of," 180n9; "slow," 113, 114, 177n54
virus: humans as a, 19, 64; Krippin Virus" (fictional virus), 170n19; "rage virus," 170n19; "woke mind virus," 177n51; zombie virus, 171n21. *See also* COVID-19

Vivos Group, 113, 177n55
Vlahos, Michael, 108, 178n56
Vlamis, Kelsey, 162n50
Voluntary Human Extinction Movement, 160n33
Von Mossner, Alexa Weik, 113

Wakanda. See *Black Panther* (media franchise)
walking corpses, 81, 87, 141n14, 167n8, 175n44
Walking Dead, The (television drama), 99, 166n5
Wallace, Alfred Russel, 36
Wallace-Wells, David, 177n51
walls, 13, 26, 61, 62, 63, 116, 142n17, 158n31; Berlin Wall, 83; walled compounds, 24
Walpole, Horace, 142n15
Walt Disney Company, 4, 35, 127–128n5
Wang, Haoyan, and Christina Zang, 131n27, 133n34, 134n37, 136n43, 140n13
warfare, 65, 83, 119, 168n11; biological, 168n11; Cold War, 83, 167–168n8, 168n9, 175n44; global, 83; Gulf War, 83; modern, 65; nuclear, 107, 174n39, 176n47; Vietnam War, 175n44; war in Iraq, 149n43, 168n11; war on terror, 62, 82, 119; World War III (in *On the Beach*), 172n31
Warm Bodies (film), 139n9
War of the Worlds (film), 156n21
War of the Worlds, The (Wells), 133n32, 156n21
Waterworld (film), 25, 94, 100
Watson, Janell, 48, 50, 64, 164n57
weapons, 16, 87; atomic, 82; "masculine human-weapon films," 139n10; nuclear, 85, 96; vibranium, 6; Wakandan, 6; weapons of mass destruction, 121
weed, 133n35, 156n21
Wellbeck, Timothy, 8, 9
Wells, H. G., 32, 133n32, 156n21
Welsh, Andrew, 1, 18, 22, 135n41
werewolf, 34–35, 142n15, 143n21, 169n13, 171n22
Werewolf Complex, The (Duclos), 34
West, the: Australian shark cull, 40; colonialism, 8; cultural expressions, 27, 43, 81, 125; democracies, 103; depictions/representations, 21, 67, 141n14; global capitalist history, 57; neo-colonial supremacy,

136n44; political structures, 88; secularism, 61; society, 71; thought, 26, 50
West/Global North, 57, 62, 83
White, Gregory, 178n3
"white extinction," 129n19
white supremacy, 15, 19, 141n14
Why We Disagree About Climate Change (Hulme), 106–107
wild animals, 69, 148n37, 149n42
wildlife, 27, 49, 70, 88, 138n2, 140n12, 148n37, 150n44, 155n16, 159n33, 170–171n20
wild nature, 40
wild places and spaces, 31, 150n44, 171n20
Will & Grace (television sitcom), 135n41
Williams, Anne, 30
Wilson, Jason, 12, 133n34
"window on the world," 20–22
Wojcik, Daniel, 79
worldbuilding, 4, 127–128n5
World Economic Forum, 118, 178n2
World Invasion: Battle Los Angeles (film), 56–57, 156n19
World Made by Hand (Kunstler), 25, 97–99, 105–106, 109, 125, 176n46
"World Starvation" (song), 65, 159n34
wretched, the, 51, 53–54, 101
Wright, Edgar, 87
"WSHTF" ("When Shit Hits the Fan"), 174n37
Wyndham, John, 72

xenophobia, 13, 146n29, 153n8, 169n17
X-Men: Apocalypse (film), 131n37

yachts, 67, 69, 163n52
Yacowar, Maurice, 42–43
Yang, Gene Lueng, 136n46
Young, Jock, 20
Young, Taras, 81, 82–83, 95–96, 103, 107–108, 110, 175n42, 176n47
Ystehede, Per, 30, 32, 34, 144n22

Žižek, Slavoj, 139–140n12, 157n26, 170n18
Zombie Movie Encyclopedia, The (Dendle), 108
zombies: as allegories, 121, 141n14; as avatars, 85; brain-eating zombies, 80, 85, 146n31; classic zombie, 85; eco-zombie, 86; history of, 142n14; human-zombie conflicts, 81, 141n14; as metaphors, 80,

Avi Brisman is Professor in the School of Justice Studies at Eastern Kentucky University, Adjunct Professor in the School of Justice at Queensland University of Technology, Honorary Professor at the Newcastle School of Law and Justice at the University of Newcastle, and University Fellow at the Centre for Law and Social Justice at the University of Newcastle. His most recent monograph is *Fieldnotes on a Study of Young People's Perceptions of Crime and Justice: Scaffolding as Structure*.

Nigel South is Emeritus Professor of Sociology and Criminology at the University of Essex, Honorary Visiting Professor at the Institute for Social Justice and Crime at the University of Suffolk, and Adjunct Professor in the School of Justice at Queensland University of Technology. He received the Outstanding Achievement Award from the British Society of Criminology in 2022 and the Lifetime Achievement Award from the American Society of Criminology, Division on Critical Criminology and Social Justice, in 2013. His work is the focus of the book *Criminological Connections, Directions, Horizons: Essays in Honour of Nigel South*.

www.ingramcontent.com/pod-product-compliance
Lightning Source LLC
Chambersburg PA
CBHW040147270326
41929CB00025B/3417